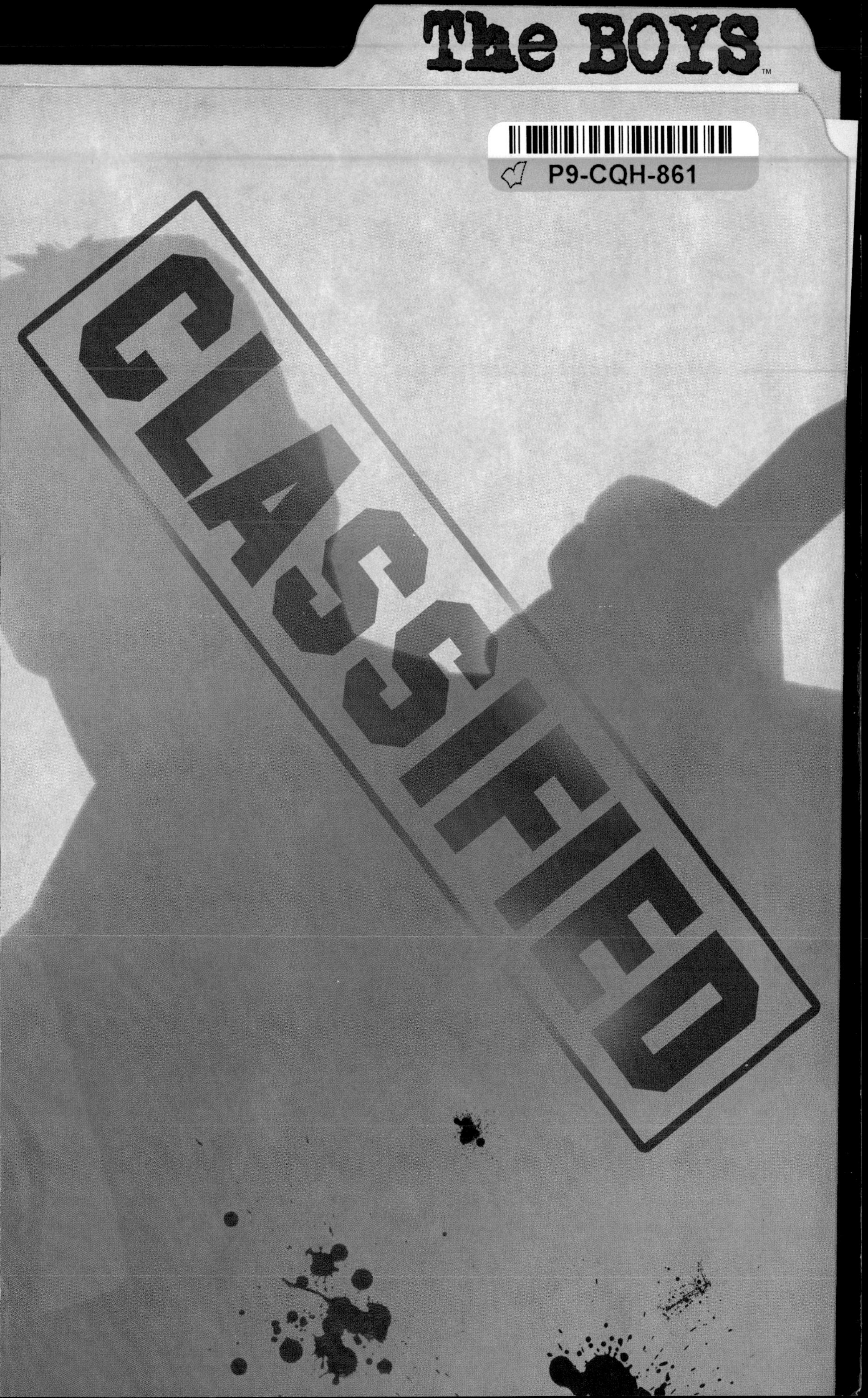
The BOYS™
CLASSIFIED

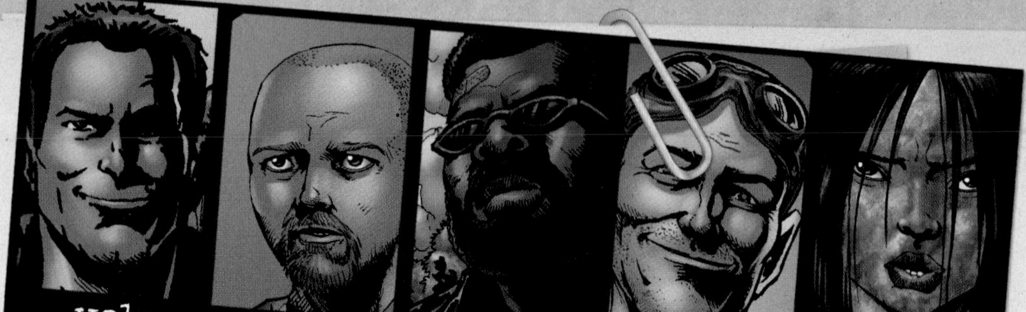

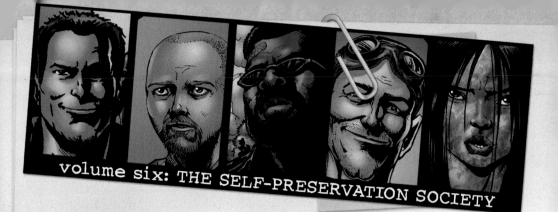

volume six: THE SELF-PRESERVATION SOCIETY

Written by:
GARTH ENNIS

Illustrated by:
DARICK ROBERTSON
CARLOS EZQUERRA
& JOHN McCREA w/
KEITH BURNS

Additional inks by:
HECTOR EZQUERRA
& KEITH BURNS w/
JOHN McCREA

Lettered by:
SIMON BOWLAND

Colored by:
TONY AVIÑA

Covers by:
DARICK ROBERTSON
& TONY AVIÑA

The Boys created by:
GARTH ENNIS &
DARICK ROBERTSON

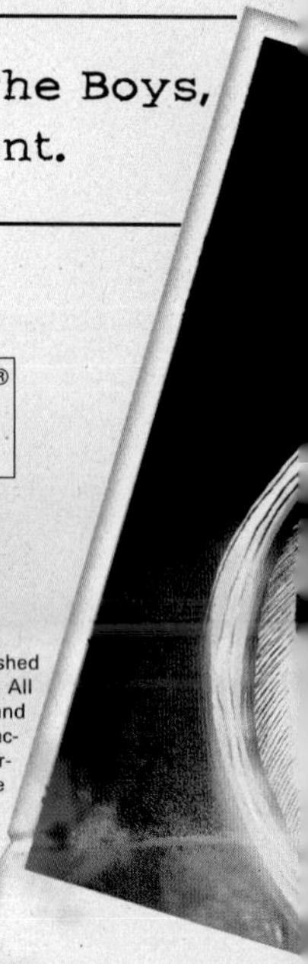

Collects issues thirty-one through thirty-eight of The Boys, originally published by Dynamite Entertainment.

Trade Design By: JASON ULLMEYER

DYNAMITE ENTERTAINMENT
NICK BARRUCCI • PRESIDENT
JUAN COLLADO • CHIEF OPERATING OFFICER
JOSEPH RYBANDT • EDITOR
JOSH JOHNSON • CREATIVE DIRECTOR
JASON ULLMEYER • GRAPHIC DESIGNER

DYNAMITE ENTERTAINMENT
WWW.DYNAMITEENTERTAINMENT.COM

Softcover ISBN-10: 1-60690-125-7 Softcover ISBN-13: 978-1-60690-125-0
Limited Edition Hardcover ISBN-10: 1-60690-141-9 Limited Edition Hardcover ISBN-13: 978-1-60690-141-0
First Printing 10 9 8 7 6 5 4 3 2 1

I fucking love THE BOYS.

That's right, cunts. I said "fucking." And then I said "cunts." Because you can get away with using that particular word under only two conditions:

You are British.

You are writing an introduction for something penned by Garth Ennis.

Unfortunately for me, I am not British.

Which leaves us with Mr. Ennis, who is, in my humble opinion, one of the greatest writers in the history of the medium.

Bold praise, you say? Blatant asskissery, you claim?

Well, blow me, cuntfuck.

Because if you're reading this trade, you are already intimately familiar with the story of Wee Hughie and the rather spectacular group of gentlemen (and lady) he has fallen in with. A group that has a penchant for dressing in black trenchcoats and inflicting horrible pain on their enemies.

Enemies who just happen to be goddamned superheroes.

So what is it, specifically, that I love about THE BOYS? Well… let's start with the gratuitous violence. Ever seen someone bite off someone else's nose? Well, dear reader, you're about to. Oh, sorry. SPOILER ALERT. Go fuck yourself.

Love Reason #2: There are no rules. The Boys don't play by them and neither does Mr. Ennis. And that's just the way I like it. Think you know what's going on? You don't.

Third. The artwork of Darick Robertson. He is a God amongst men. His characters are real… somehow, even in an absurd world, they manage to convey genuine emotion. Fear. Heartbreak. Horniness. His action is exquisite. And man, can he draw boobies.

And finally, what I love about The Boys is how beautifully it integrates the deep and complex mythology of its world with the characters that inhabit it. I feel like I know these people. Care about them. And as much as they sometimes scare me, I understand that they are as close to good as is possible in a world run by Vought-American.

So sit back. Relax. Prepare yourself for some good old-fashioned Nazi-bashing and then wash it down with a cold glass of Mother's Milk…

Because it just gets better from here, folks.

Your Fellow Cunt,

Damon Lindelof
January, 2010

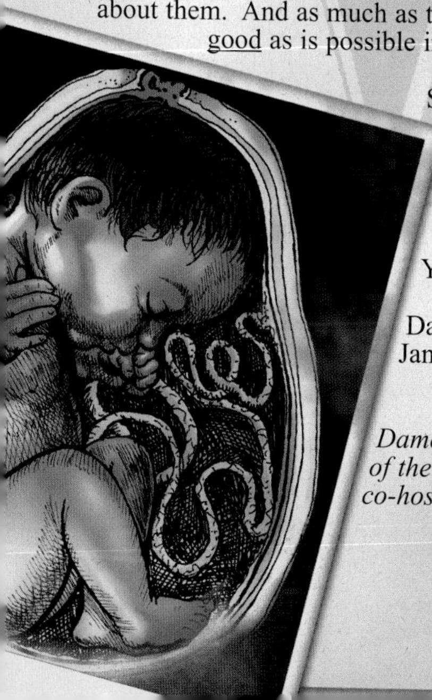

Damon Lindelof is one of the creators and executive producers of the show Lost, and is currently the head writer of the show. He co-hosts the Official Lost Podcast with Carlton Cuse.

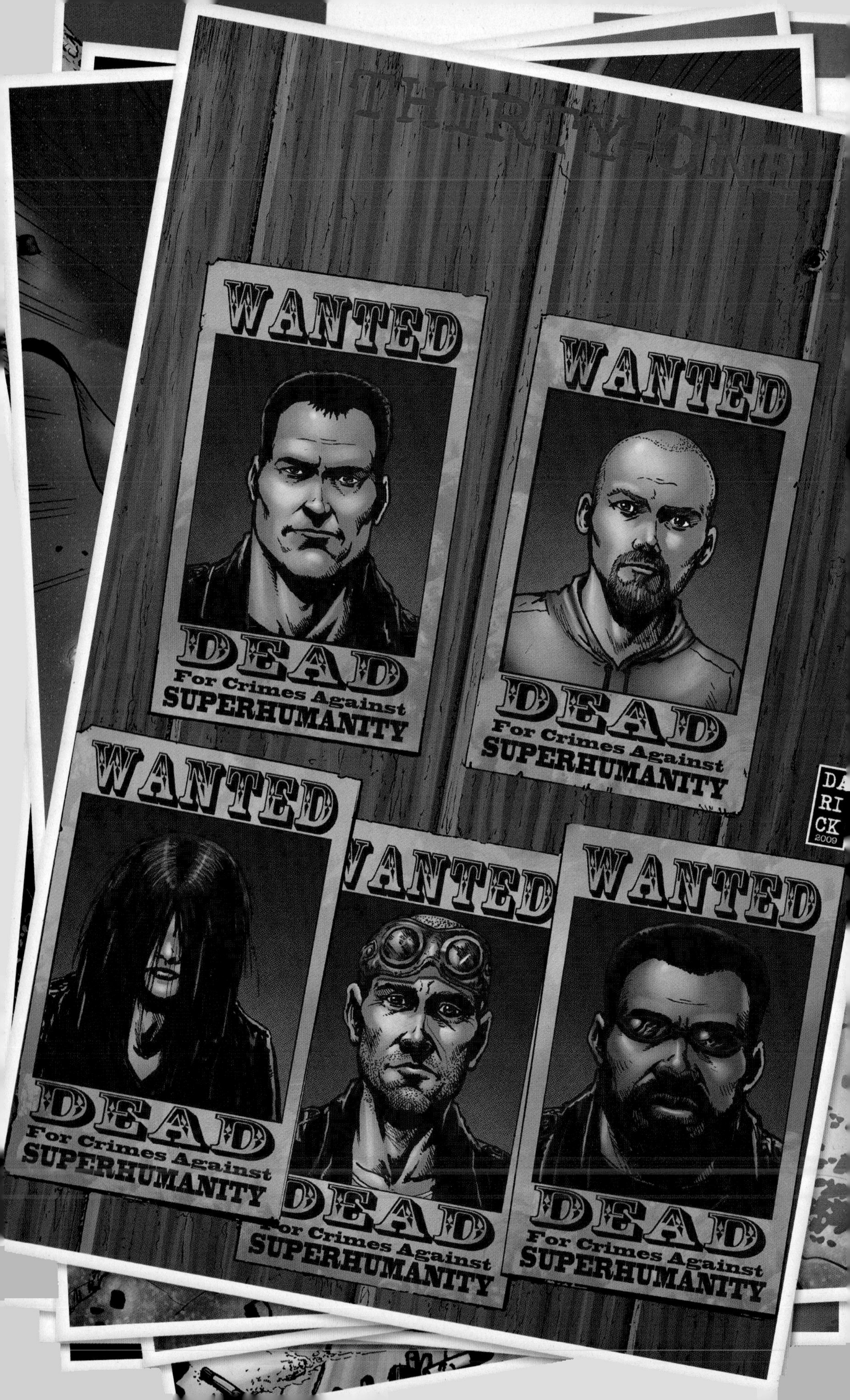
THIRTY-ONE
WANTED
DEAD
For Crimes Against
SUPERHUMANITY
WANTED
DEAD
For Crimes Against
SUPERHUMANITY
WANTED
DEAD
For Crimes Against
SUPERHUMANITY
For Crimes Against
SUPERHUMANITY
WANTED
DEAD
For Crimes Against
SUPERHUMANITY
DARICK 2009

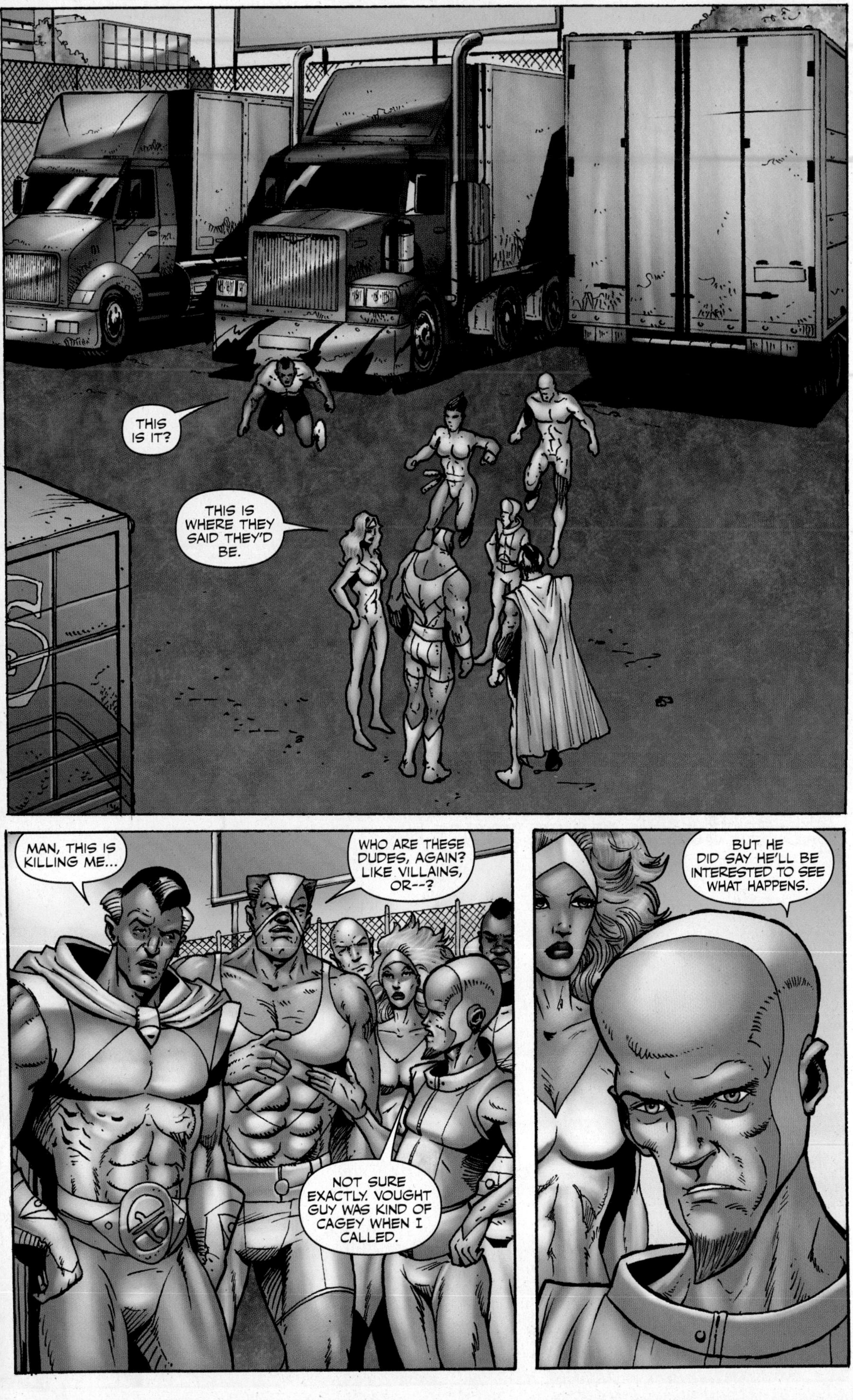

THIS IS IT?
THIS IS WHERE THEY SAID THEY'D BE.
MAN, THIS IS KILLING ME...
WHO ARE THESE DUDES, AGAIN? LIKE VILLAINS, OR--?
NOT SURE EXACTLY. VOUGHT GUY WAS KIND OF CAGEY WHEN I CALLED.
BUT HE DID SAY HE'LL BE INTERESTED TO SEE WHAT HAPPENS.

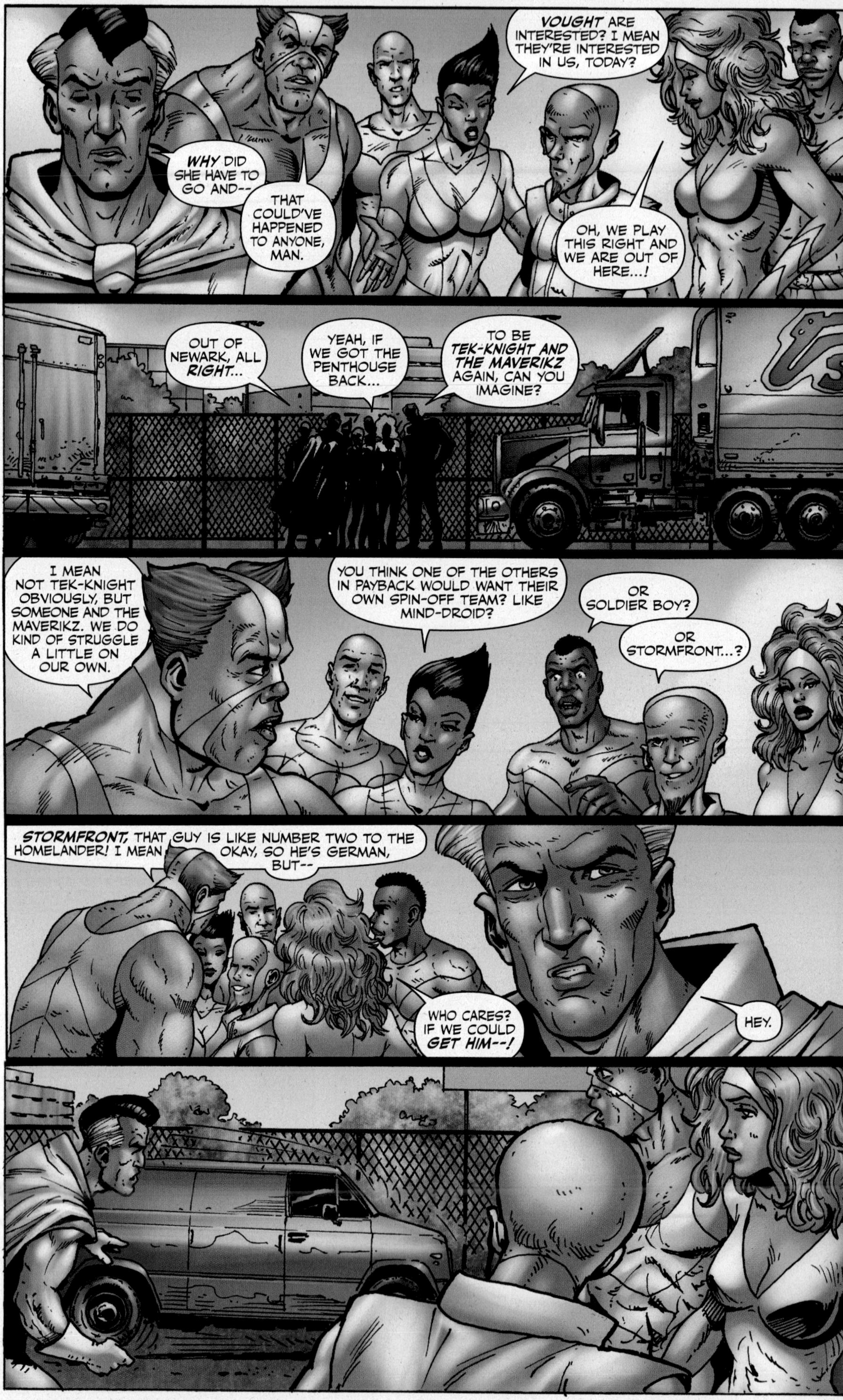
VOUGHT ARE INTERESTED? I MEAN THEY'RE INTERESTED IN US, TODAY?
WHY DID SHE HAVE TO GO AND--
THAT COULD'VE HAPPENED TO ANYONE, MAN.
OH, WE PLAY THIS RIGHT AND WE ARE OUT OF HERE...!
OUT OF NEWARK, ALL RIGHT...
YEAH, IF WE GOT THE PENTHOUSE BACK...
TO BE TEK-KNIGHT AND THE MAVERIKZ AGAIN, CAN YOU IMAGINE?
I MEAN NOT TEK-KNIGHT OBVIOUSLY, BUT SOMEONE AND THE MAVERIKZ. WE DO KIND OF STRUGGLE A LITTLE ON OUR OWN.
YOU THINK ONE OF THE OTHERS IN PAYBACK WOULD WANT THEIR OWN SPIN-OFF TEAM? LIKE MIND-DROID?
OR SOLDIER BOY?
OR STORMFRONT...?
STORMFRONT, THAT GUY IS LIKE NUMBER TWO TO THE HOMELANDER! I MEAN OKAY, SO HE'S GERMAN, BUT--
WHO CARES? IF WE COULD GET HIM--!
HEY.

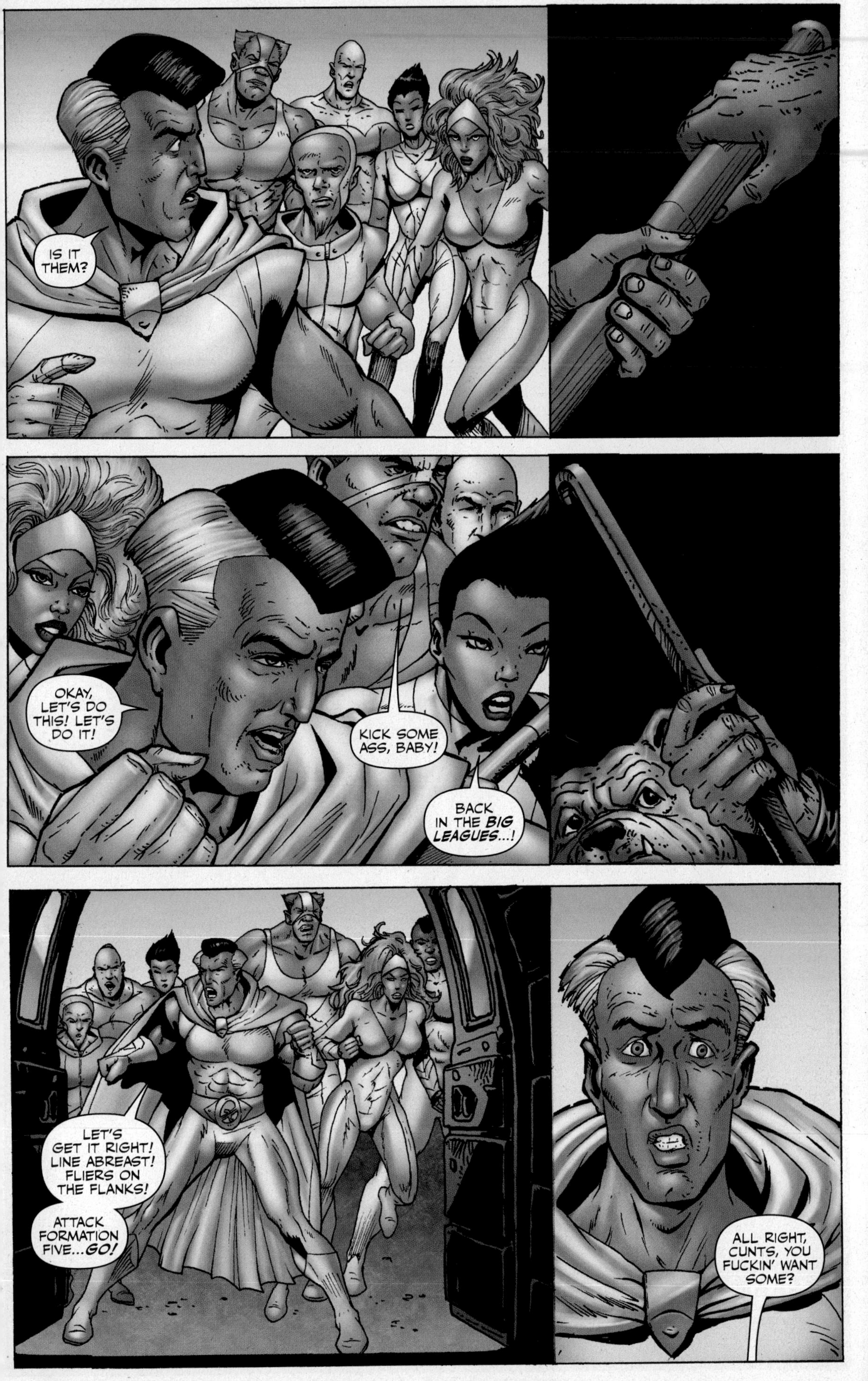
IS IT THEM?
OKAY, LET'S DO THIS! LET'S DO IT!
KICK SOME ASS, BABY!
BACK IN THE *BIG LEAGUES*...!
LET'S GET IT RIGHT! LINE ABREAST! FLIERS ON THE FLANKS!
ATTACK FORMATION FIVE...*GO!*
ALL RIGHT, CUNTS, YOU FUCKIN' WANT SOME?

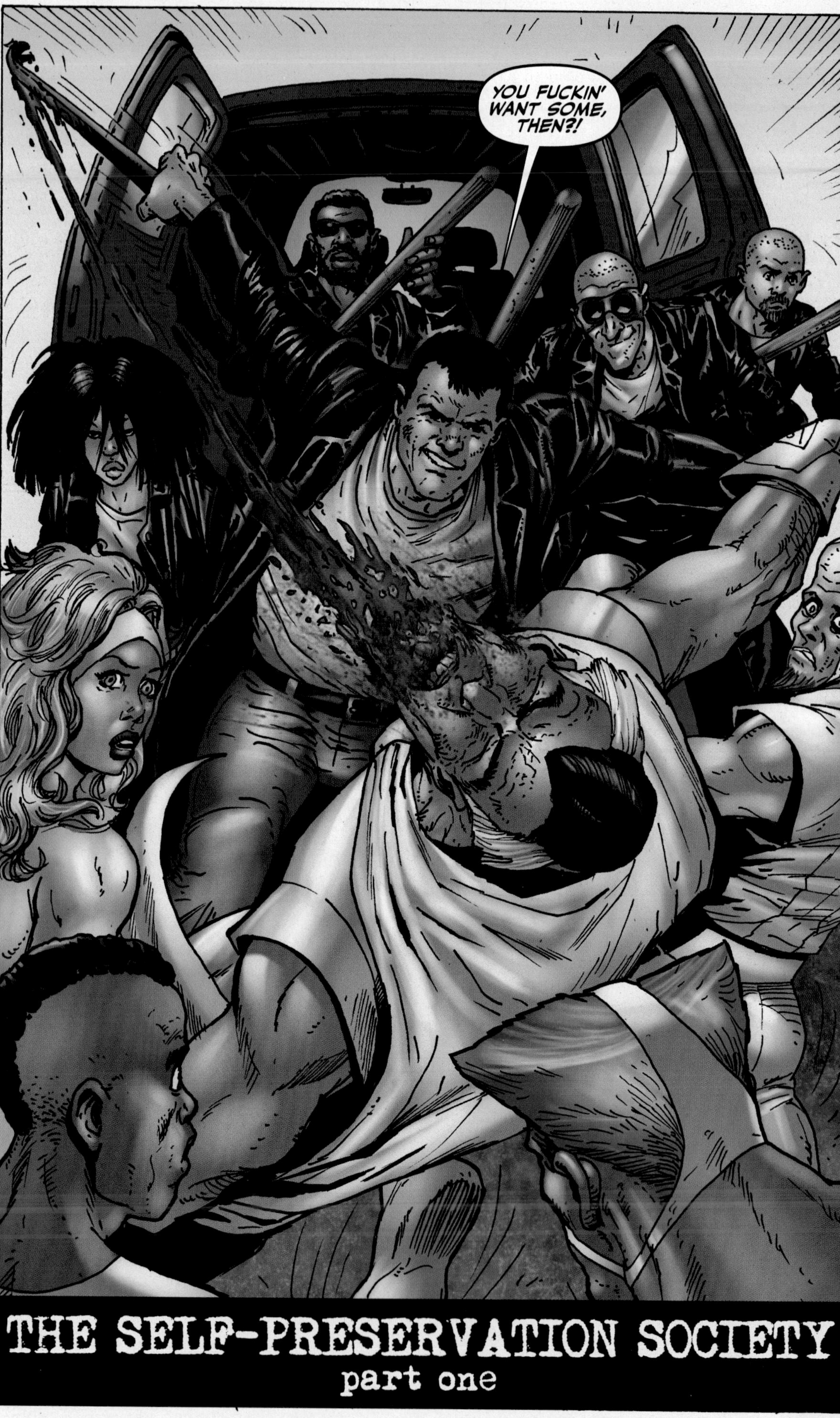
YOU FUCKIN' WANT SOME, THEN?!

THE SELF-PRESERVATION SOCIETY
part one

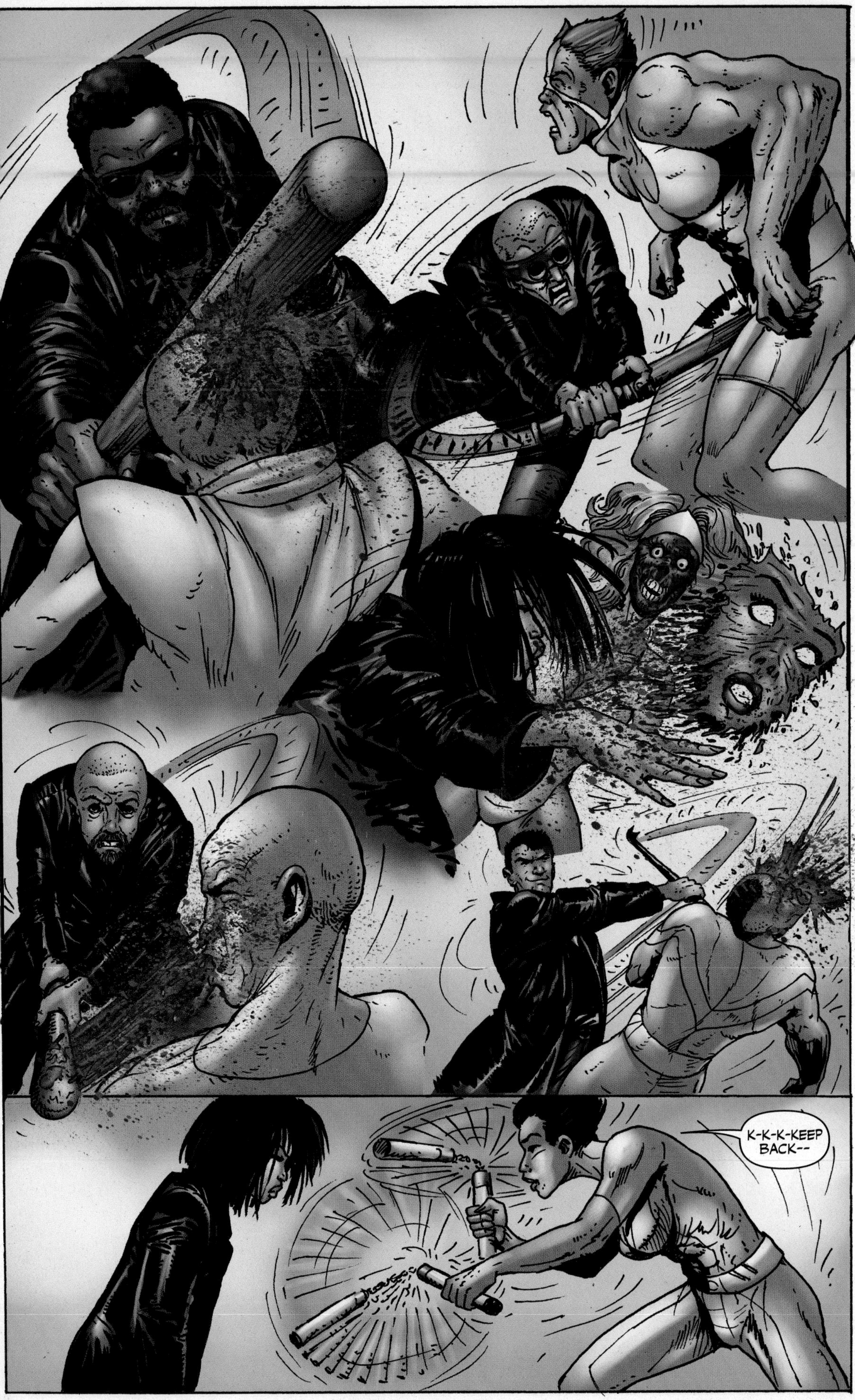
K-K-K-KEEP BACK--

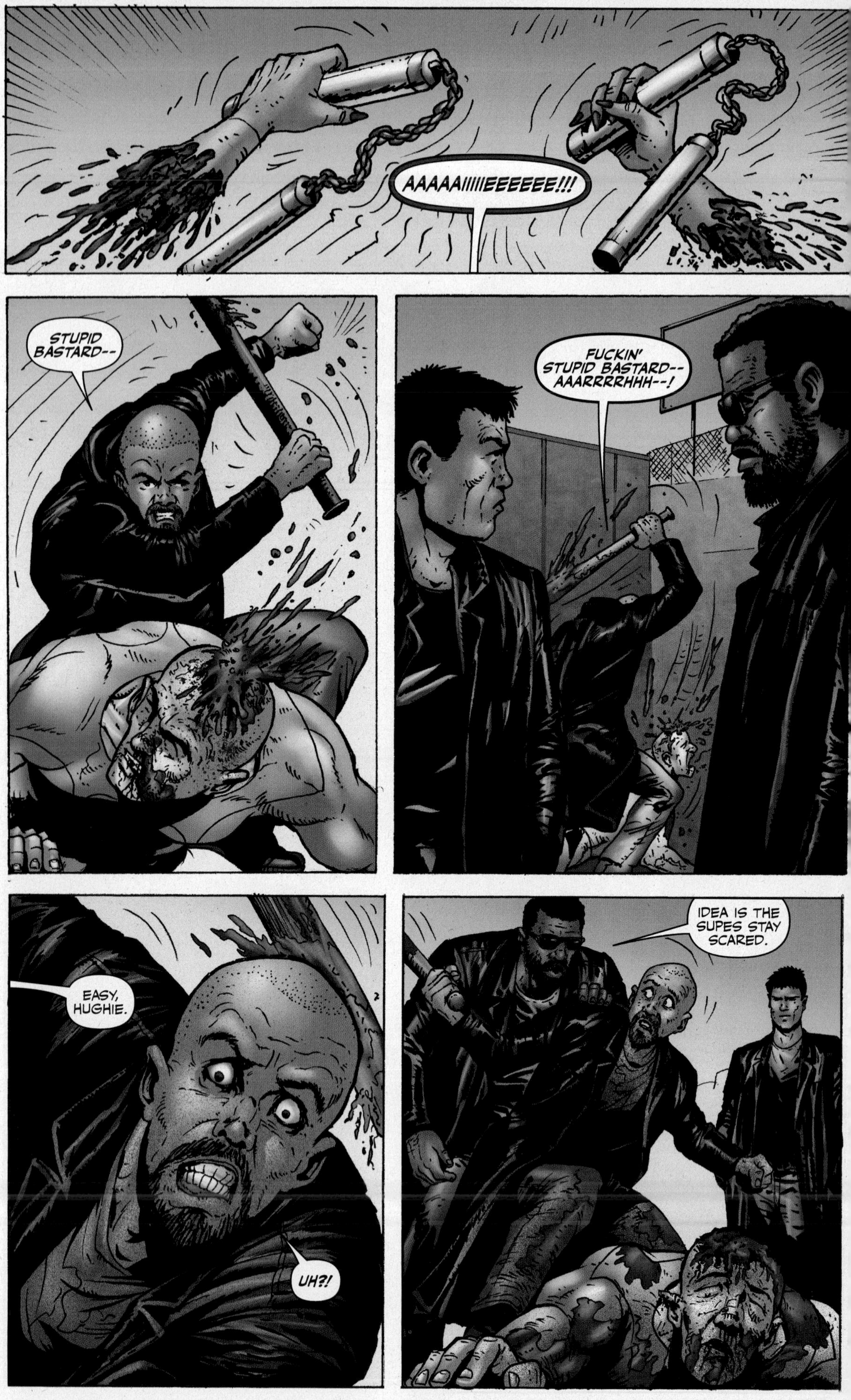
AAAAAIIIIIEEEEEE!!!
STUPID BASTARD--
FUCKIN' STUPID BASTARD-- AAARRRRHHH--!
EASY, HUGHIE.
UH?!
IDEA IS THE SUPES STAY SCARED.

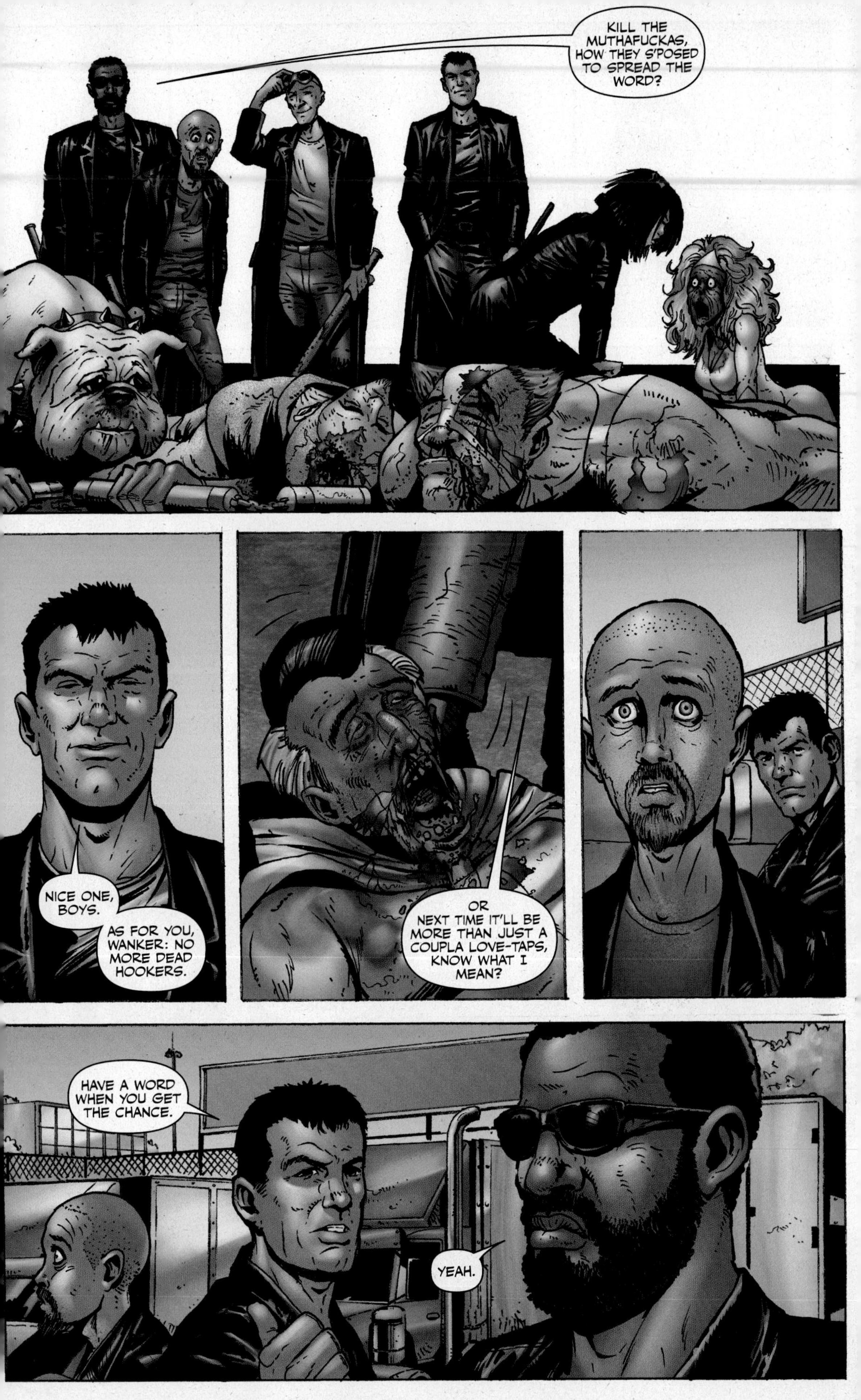
KILL THE MUTHAFUCKAS, HOW THEY S'POSED TO SPREAD THE WORD?
NICE ONE, BOYS.
AS FOR YOU, WANKER: NO MORE DEAD HOOKERS.
OR NEXT TIME IT'LL BE MORE THAN JUST A COUPLA LOVE-TAPS, KNOW WHAT I MEAN?
HAVE A WORD WHEN YOU GET THE CHANCE.
YEAH.

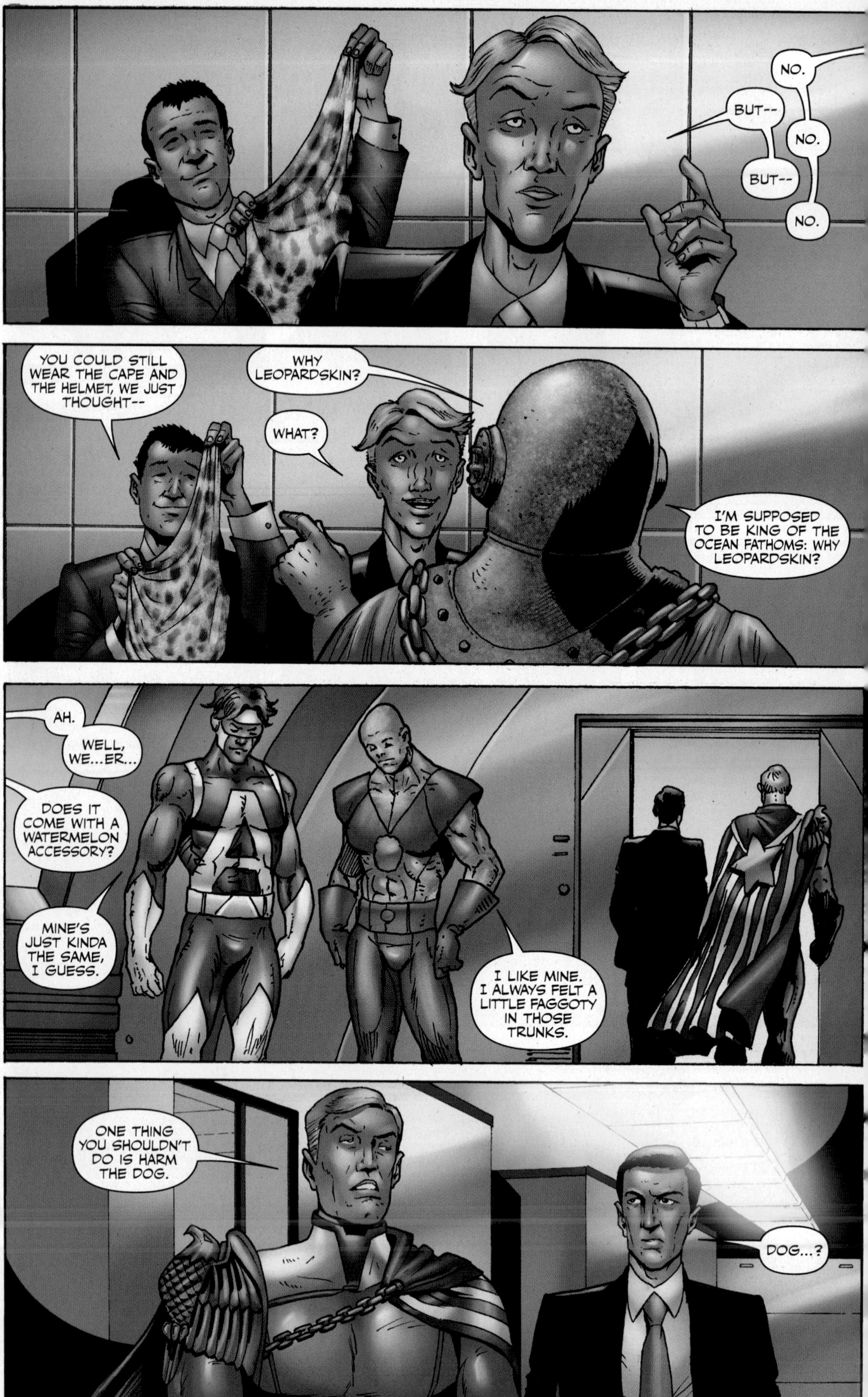
NO.
BUT--
NO.
BUT--
NO.
YOU COULD STILL WEAR THE CAPE AND THE HELMET, WE JUST THOUGHT--
WHY LEOPARDSKIN?
WHAT?
I'M SUPPOSED TO BE KING OF THE OCEAN FATHOMS: WHY LEOPARDSKIN?
AH.
WELL, WE...ER...
DOES IT COME WITH A WATERMELON ACCESSORY?
MINE'S JUST KINDA THE SAME, I GUESS.
I LIKE MINE. I ALWAYS FELT A LITTLE FAGGOTY IN THOSE TRUNKS.
ONE THING YOU SHOULDN'T DO IS HARM THE DOG.
DOG...?

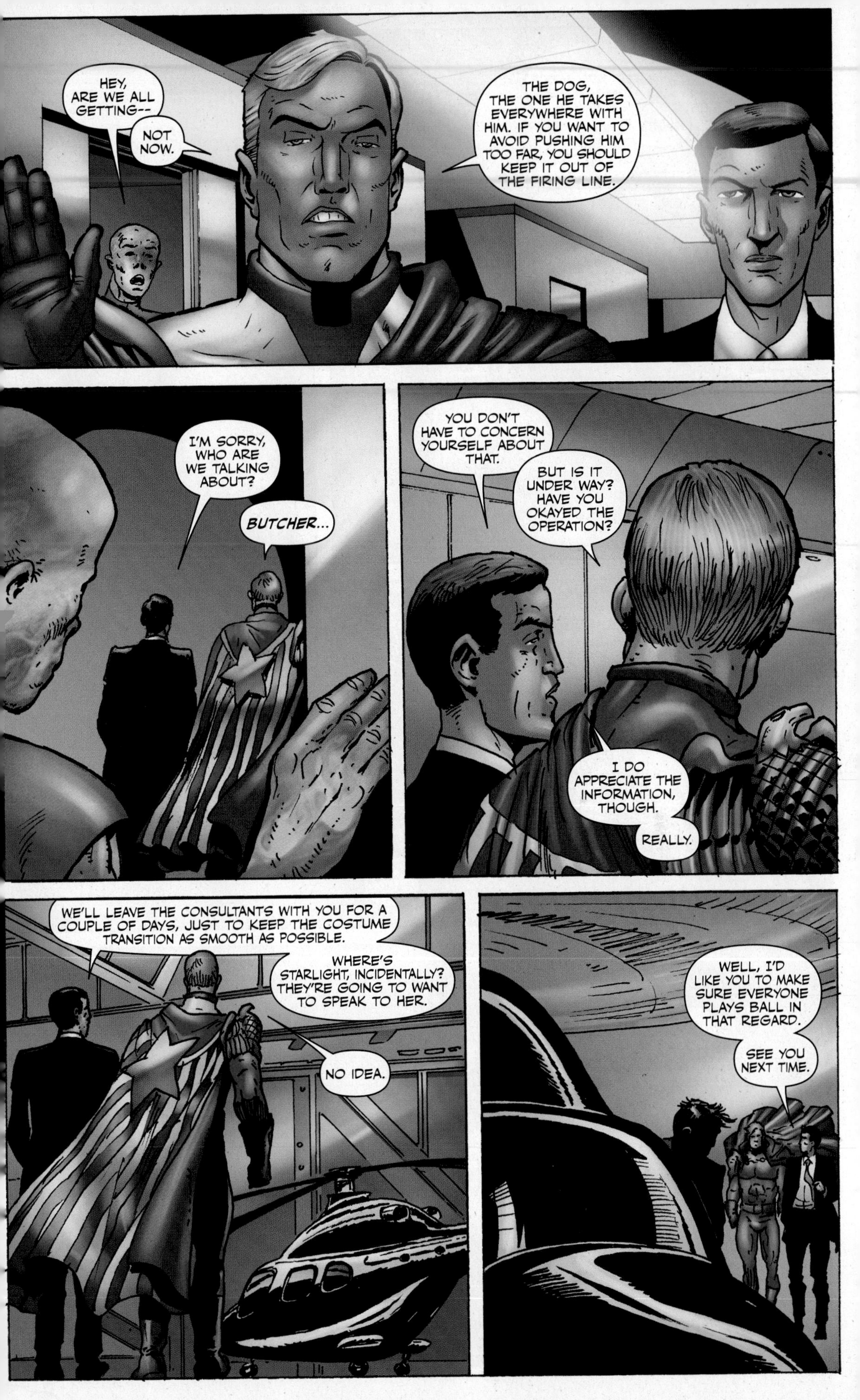
HEY, ARE WE ALL GETTING--
NOT NOW.
THE DOG, THE ONE HE TAKES EVERYWHERE WITH HIM. IF YOU WANT TO AVOID PUSHING HIM TOO FAR, YOU SHOULD KEEP IT OUT OF THE FIRING LINE.
I'M SORRY, WHO ARE WE TALKING ABOUT?
BUTCHER...
YOU DON'T HAVE TO CONCERN YOURSELF ABOUT THAT.
BUT IS IT UNDER WAY? HAVE YOU OKAYED THE OPERATION?
I DO APPRECIATE THE INFORMATION, THOUGH.
REALLY.
WE'LL LEAVE THE CONSULTANTS WITH YOU FOR A COUPLE OF DAYS, JUST TO KEEP THE COSTUME TRANSITION AS SMOOTH AS POSSIBLE.
WHERE'S STARLIGHT, INCIDENTALLY? THEY'RE GOING TO WANT TO SPEAK TO HER.
NO IDEA.
WELL, I'D LIKE YOU TO MAKE SURE EVERYONE PLAYS BALL IN THAT REGARD.
SEE YOU NEXT TIME.

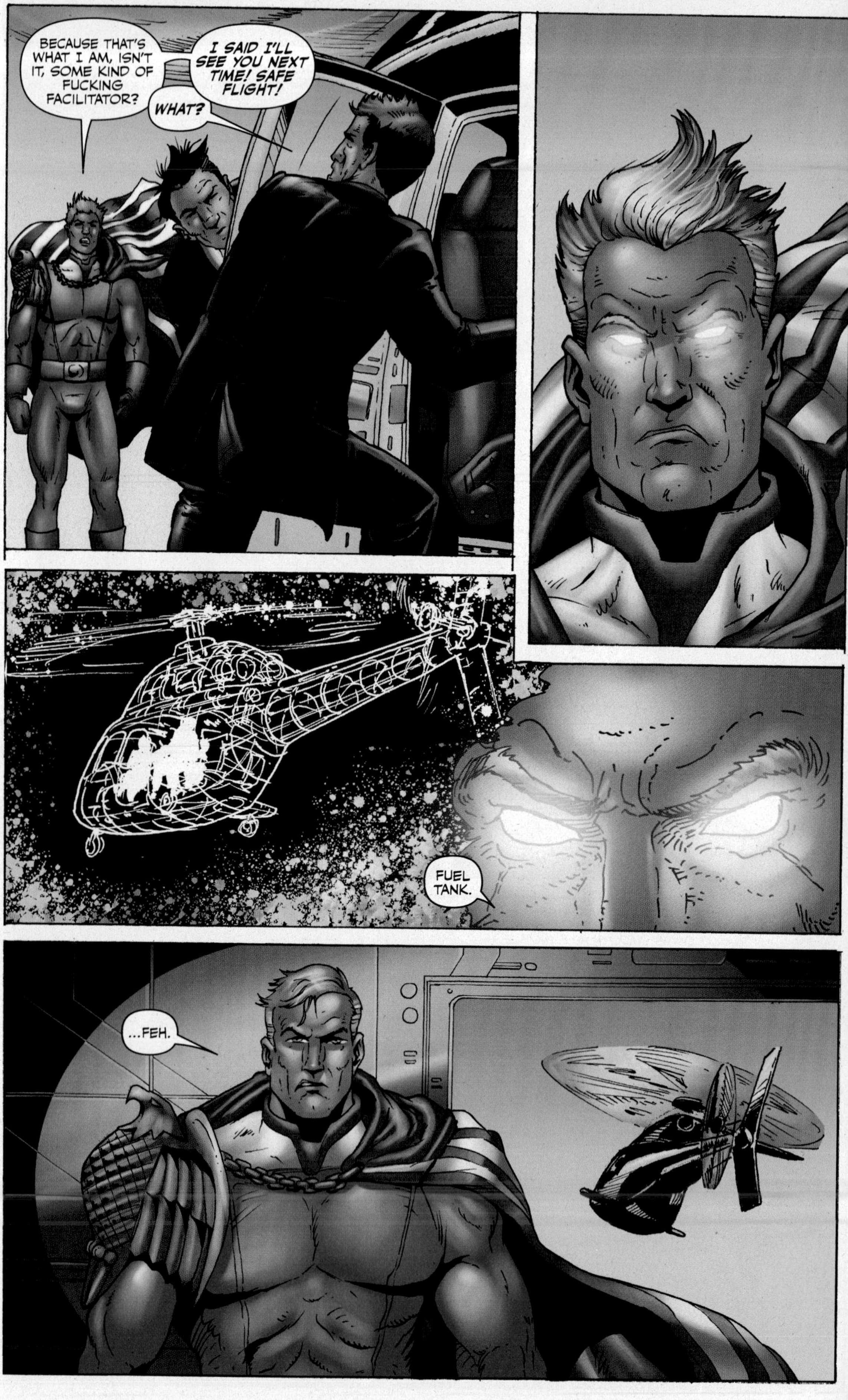
BECAUSE THAT'S WHAT I AM, ISN'T IT, SOME KIND OF FUCKING FACILITATOR?
WHAT?
I SAID I'LL SEE YOU NEXT TIME! SAFE FLIGHT!
FUEL TANK.
...FEH.

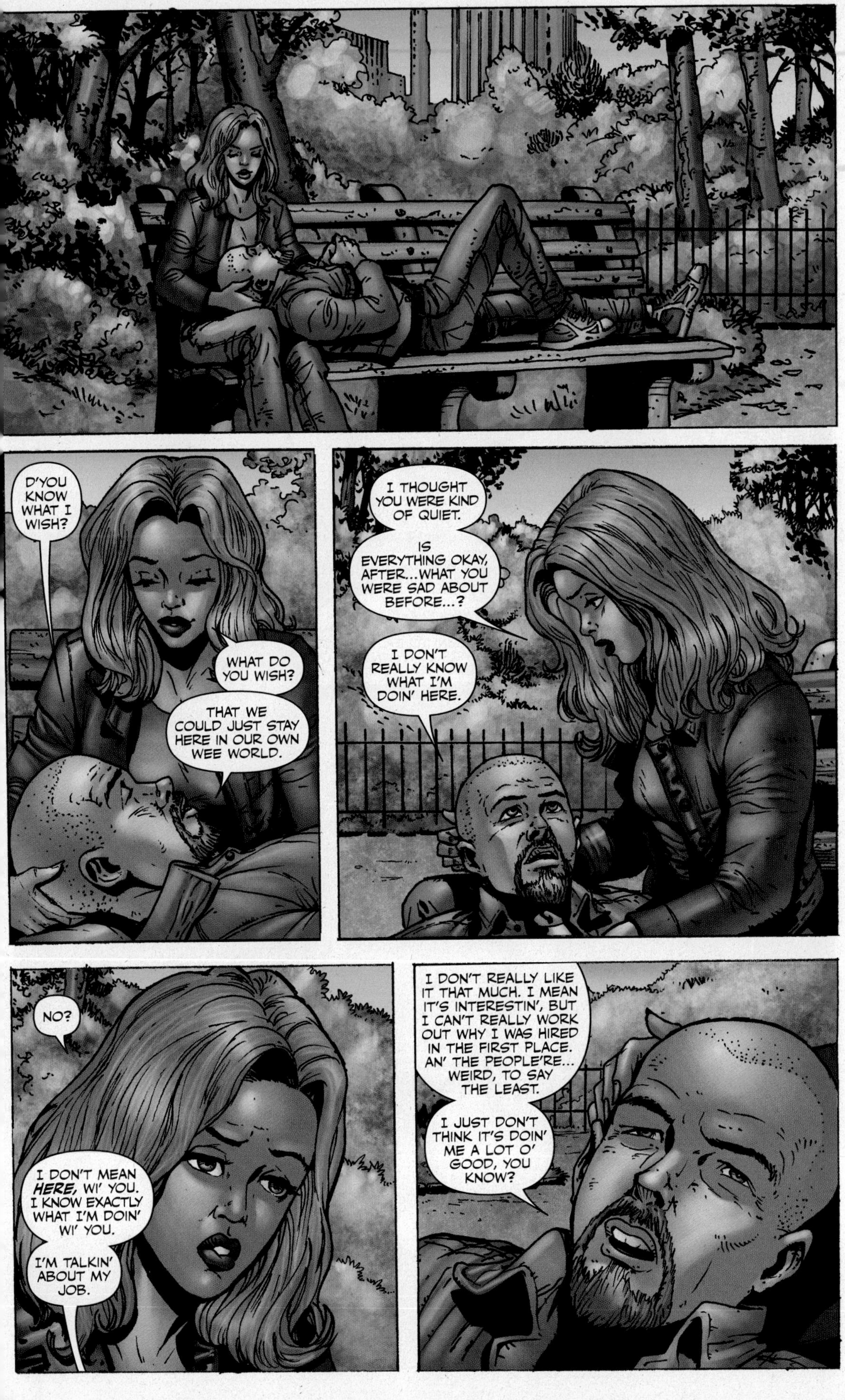
D'YOU KNOW WHAT I WISH?
WHAT DO YOU WISH?
THAT WE COULD JUST STAY HERE IN OUR OWN WEE WORLD.
I THOUGHT YOU WERE KIND OF QUIET.
IS EVERYTHING OKAY, AFTER...WHAT YOU WERE SAD ABOUT BEFORE...?
I DON'T REALLY KNOW WHAT I'M DOIN' HERE.
NO?
I DON'T MEAN HERE, WI' YOU. I KNOW EXACTLY WHAT I'M DOIN' WI' YOU.
I'M TALKIN' ABOUT MY JOB.
I DON'T REALLY LIKE IT THAT MUCH. I MEAN IT'S INTERESTIN', BUT I CAN'T REALLY WORK OUT WHY I WAS HIRED IN THE FIRST PLACE. AN' THE PEOPLE'RE... WEIRD, TO SAY THE LEAST.
I JUST DON'T THINK IT'S DOIN' ME A LOT O' GOOD, YOU KNOW?

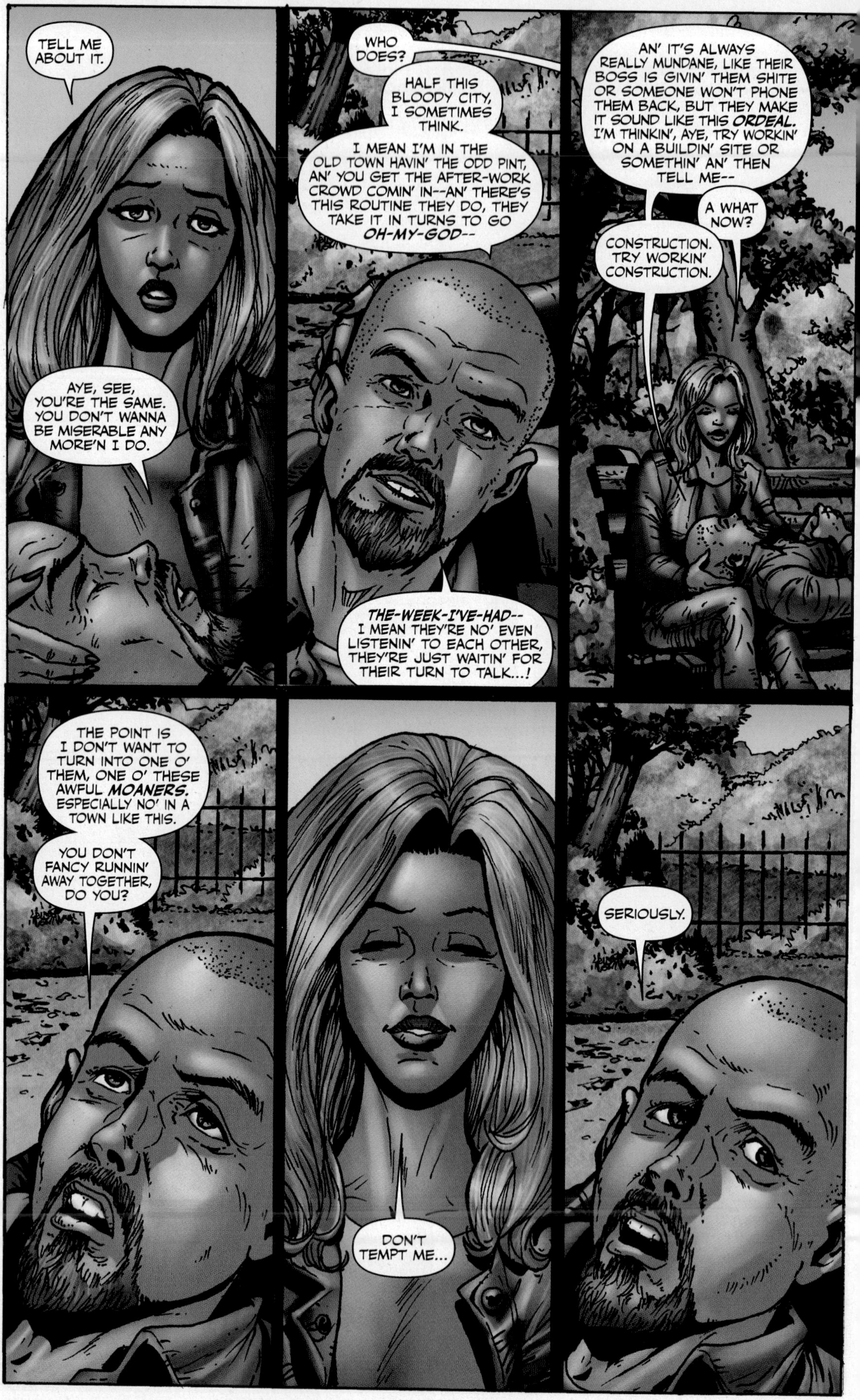
TELL ME ABOUT IT.
AYE, SEE, YOU'RE THE SAME. YOU DON'T WANNA BE MISERABLE ANY MORE'N I DO.
WHO DOES?
HALF THIS BLOODY CITY, I SOMETIMES THINK.
I MEAN I'M IN THE OLD TOWN HAVIN' THE ODD PINT, AN' YOU GET THE AFTER-WORK CROWD COMIN' IN--AN' THERE'S THIS ROUTINE THEY DO, THEY TAKE IT IN TURNS TO GO *OH-MY-GOD--*
THE-WEEK-I'VE-HAD-- I MEAN THEY'RE NO' EVEN LISTENIN' TO EACH OTHER, THEY'RE JUST WAITIN' FOR THEIR TURN TO TALK...!
AN' IT'S ALWAYS REALLY MUNDANE, LIKE THEIR BOSS IS GIVIN' THEM SHITE OR SOMEONE WON'T PHONE THEM BACK, BUT THEY MAKE IT SOUND LIKE THIS *ORDEAL.* I'M THINKIN', AYE, TRY WORKIN' ON A BUILDIN' SITE OR SOMETHIN' AN' THEN TELL ME--
A WHAT NOW?
CONSTRUCTION. TRY WORKIN' CONSTRUCTION.
THE POINT IS I DON'T WANT TO TURN INTO ONE O' THEM, ONE O' THESE AWFUL *MOANERS.* ESPECIALLY NO' IN A TOWN LIKE THIS.
YOU DON'T FANCY RUNNIN' AWAY TOGETHER, DO YOU?
DON'T TEMPT ME...
SERIOUSLY.

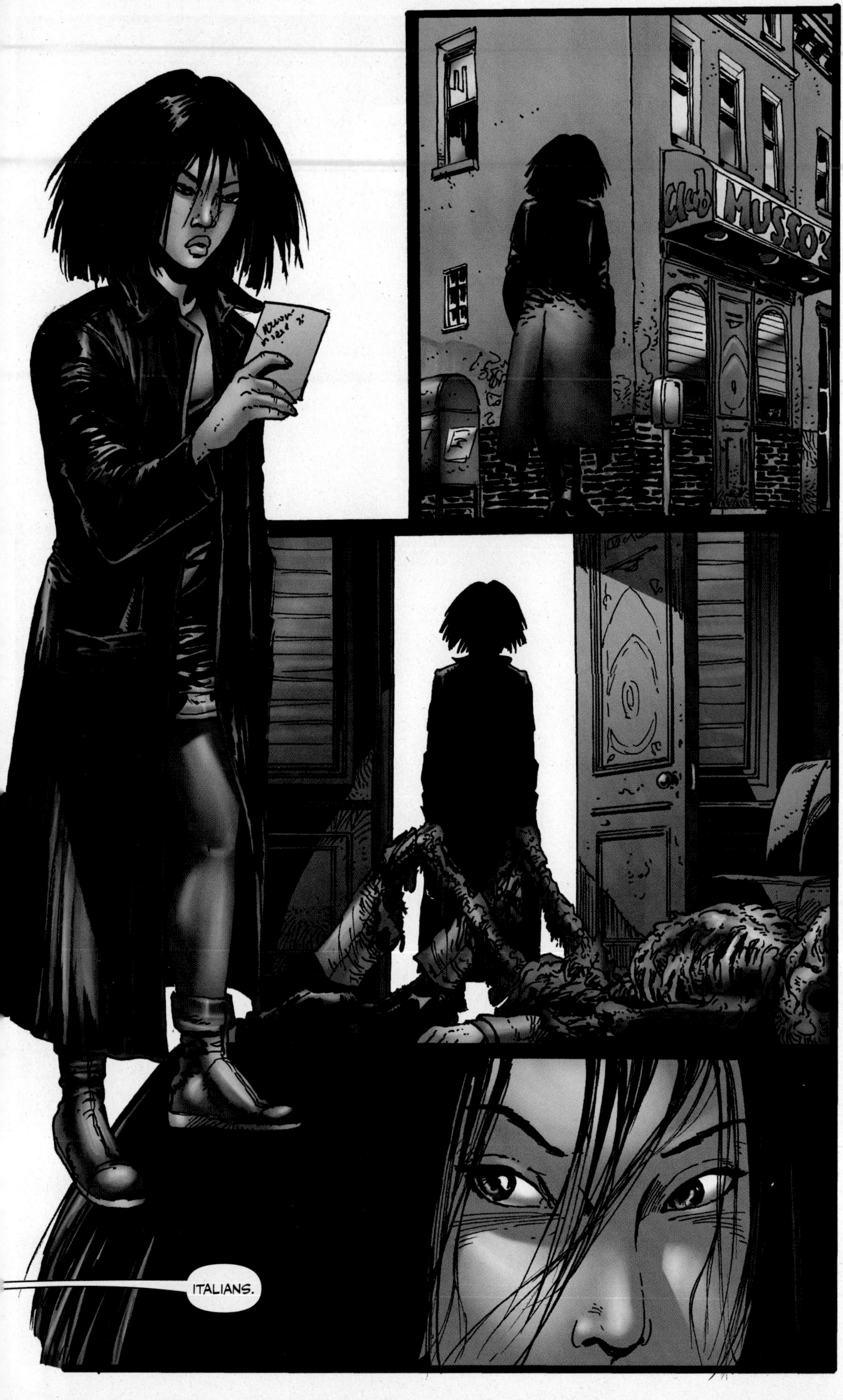
club
ITALIANS.

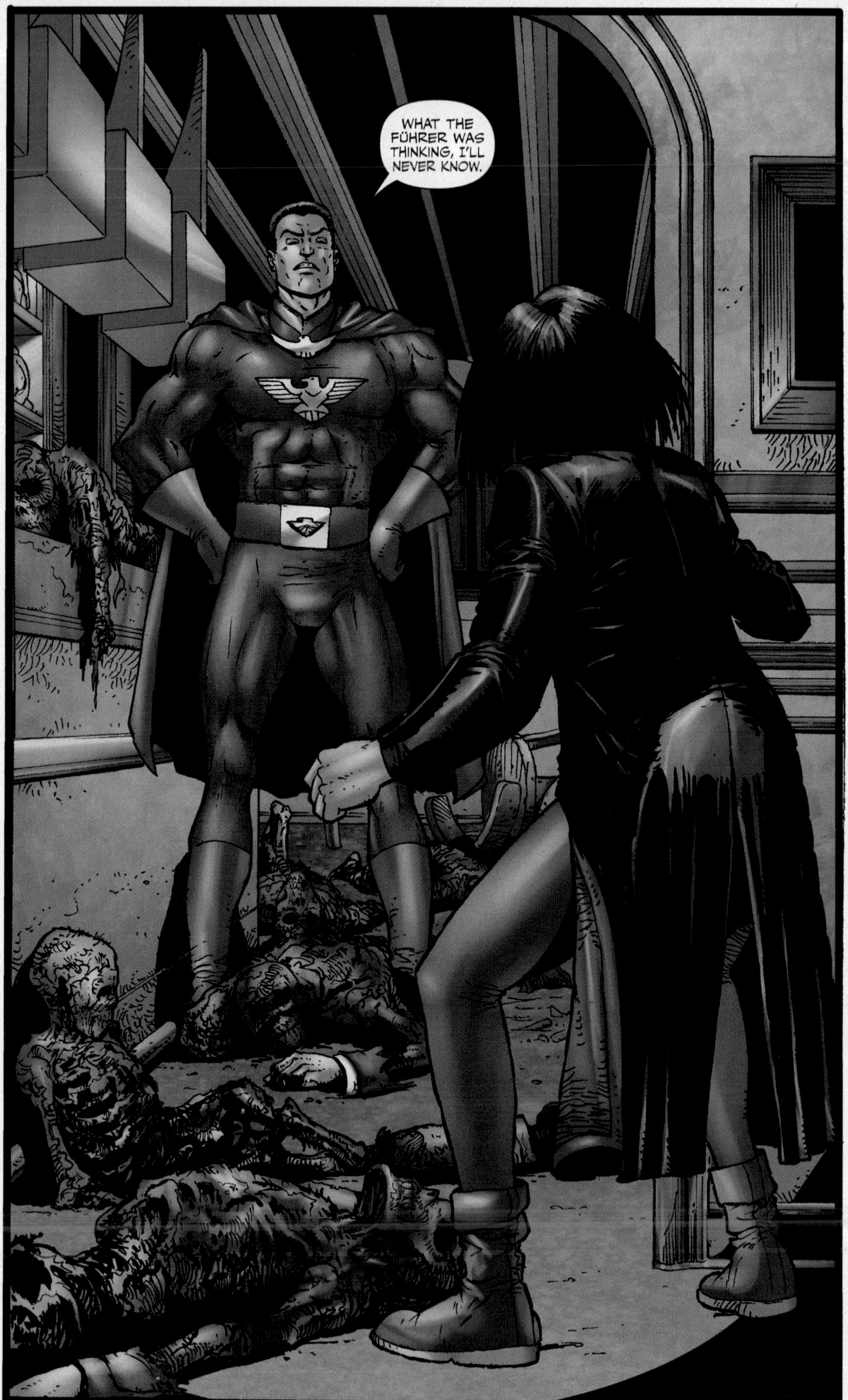
WHAT THE FÜHRER WAS THINKING, I'LL NEVER KNOW.

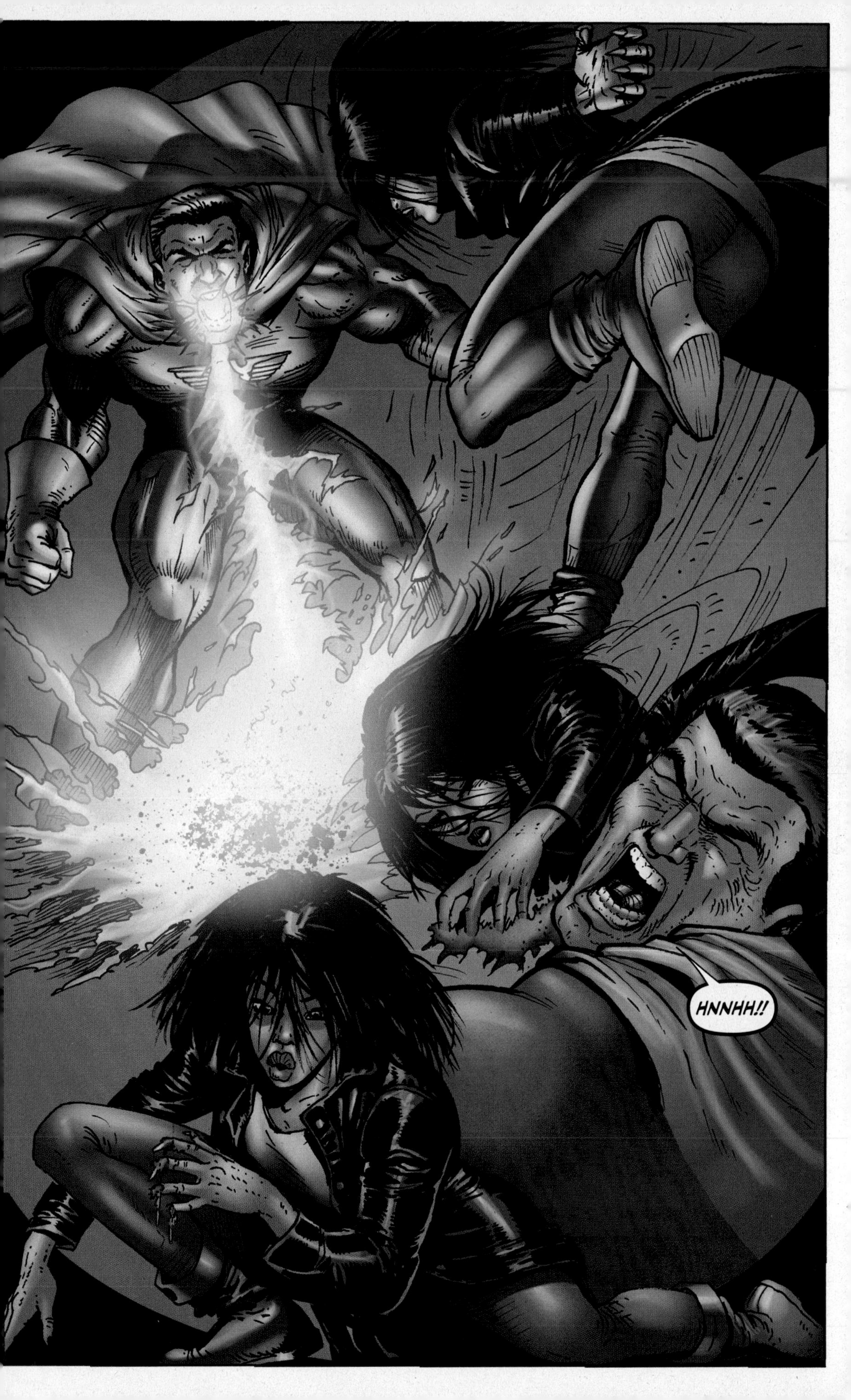
HNNHH!!

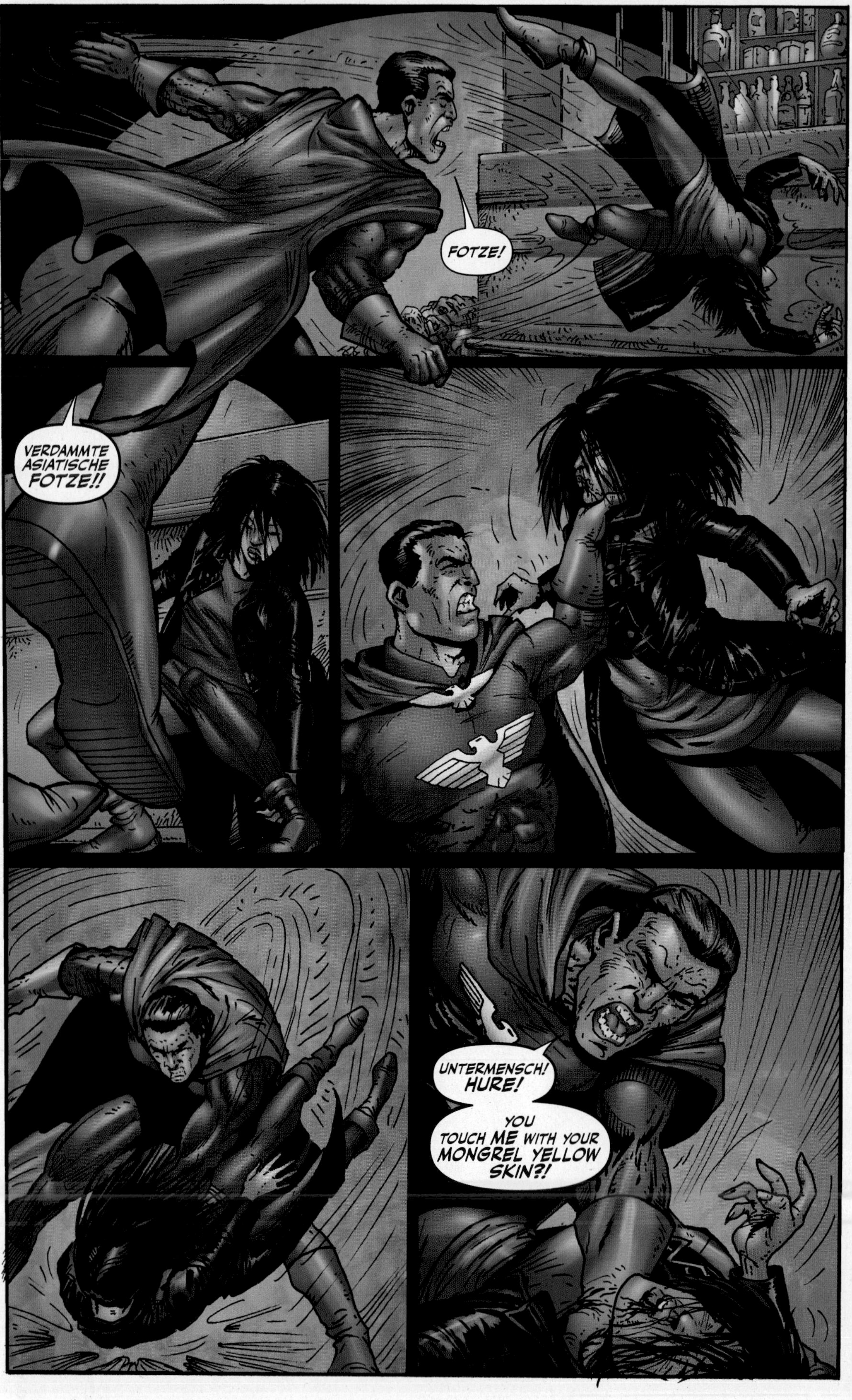
FOTZE!
VERDAMMTE ASIATISCHE FOTZE!!
UNTERMENSCH! HURE!
YOU TOUCH ME WITH YOUR MONGREL YELLOW SKIN?!

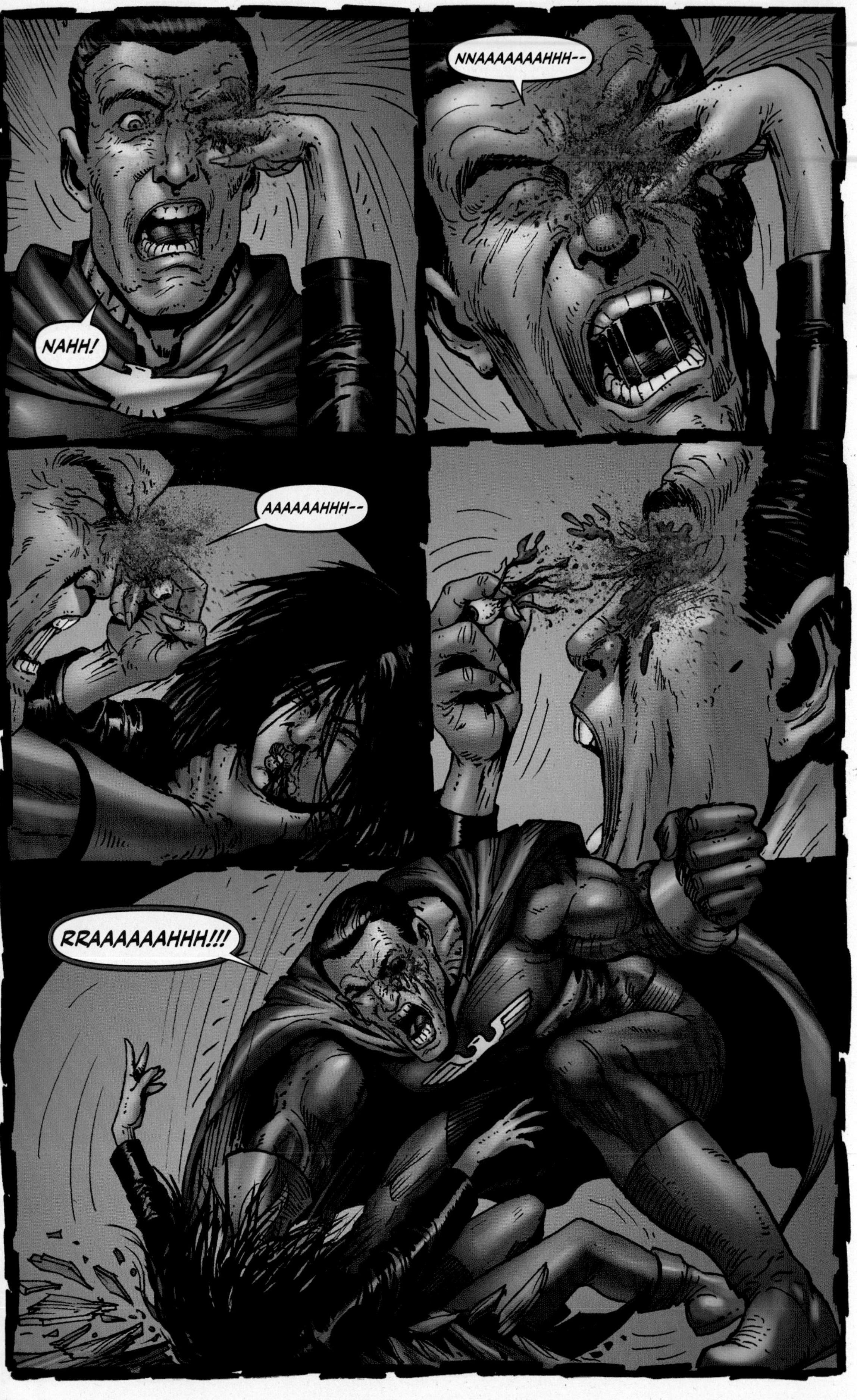
NAHH!
NNAAAAAAAAHHH--
AAAAAAHHH--
RRAAAAAAHHH!!!

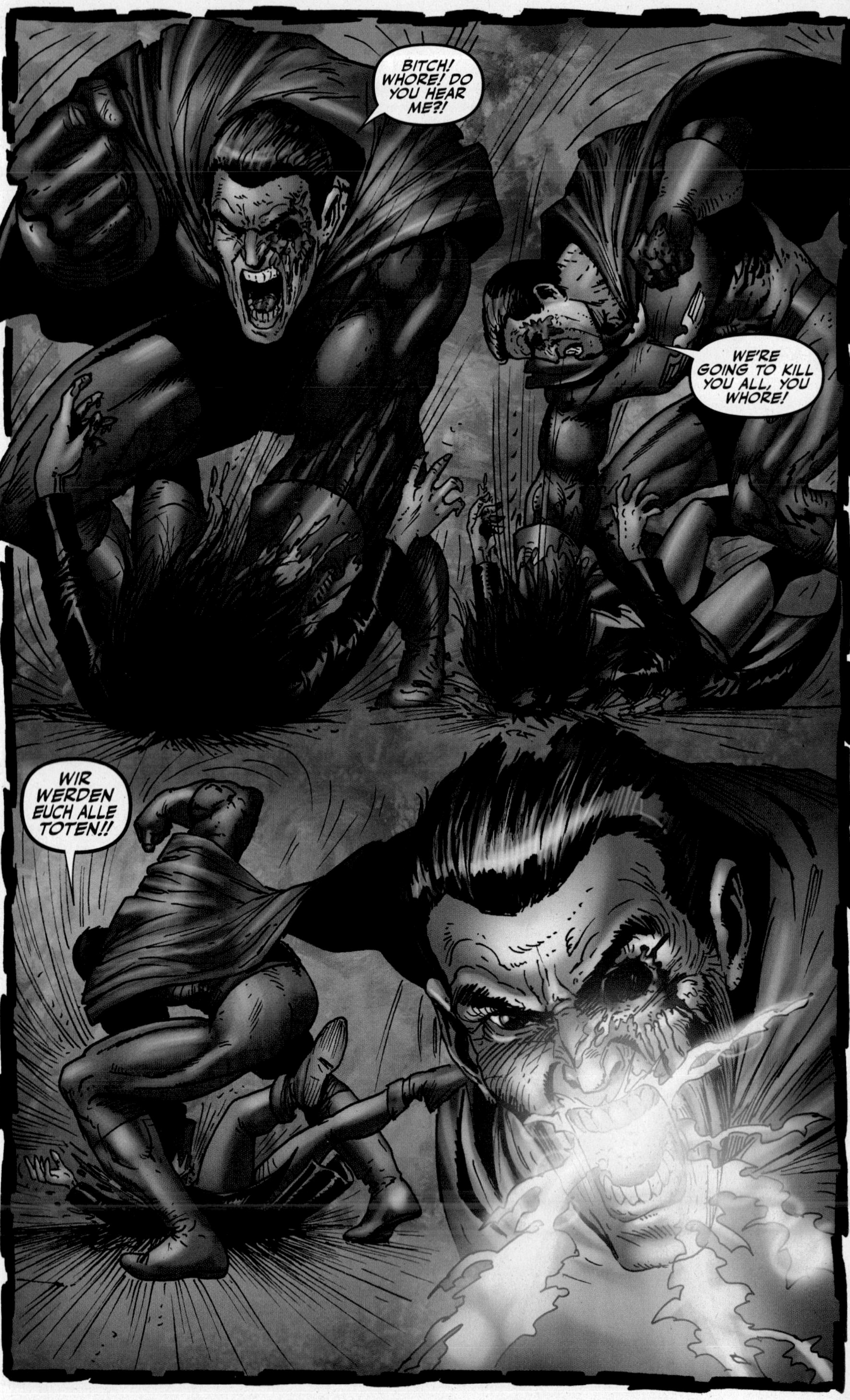
BITCH! WHORE! DO YOU HEAR ME?!
WE'RE GOING TO KILL YOU ALL, YOU WHORE!
WIR WERDEN EUCH ALLE TOTEN!!

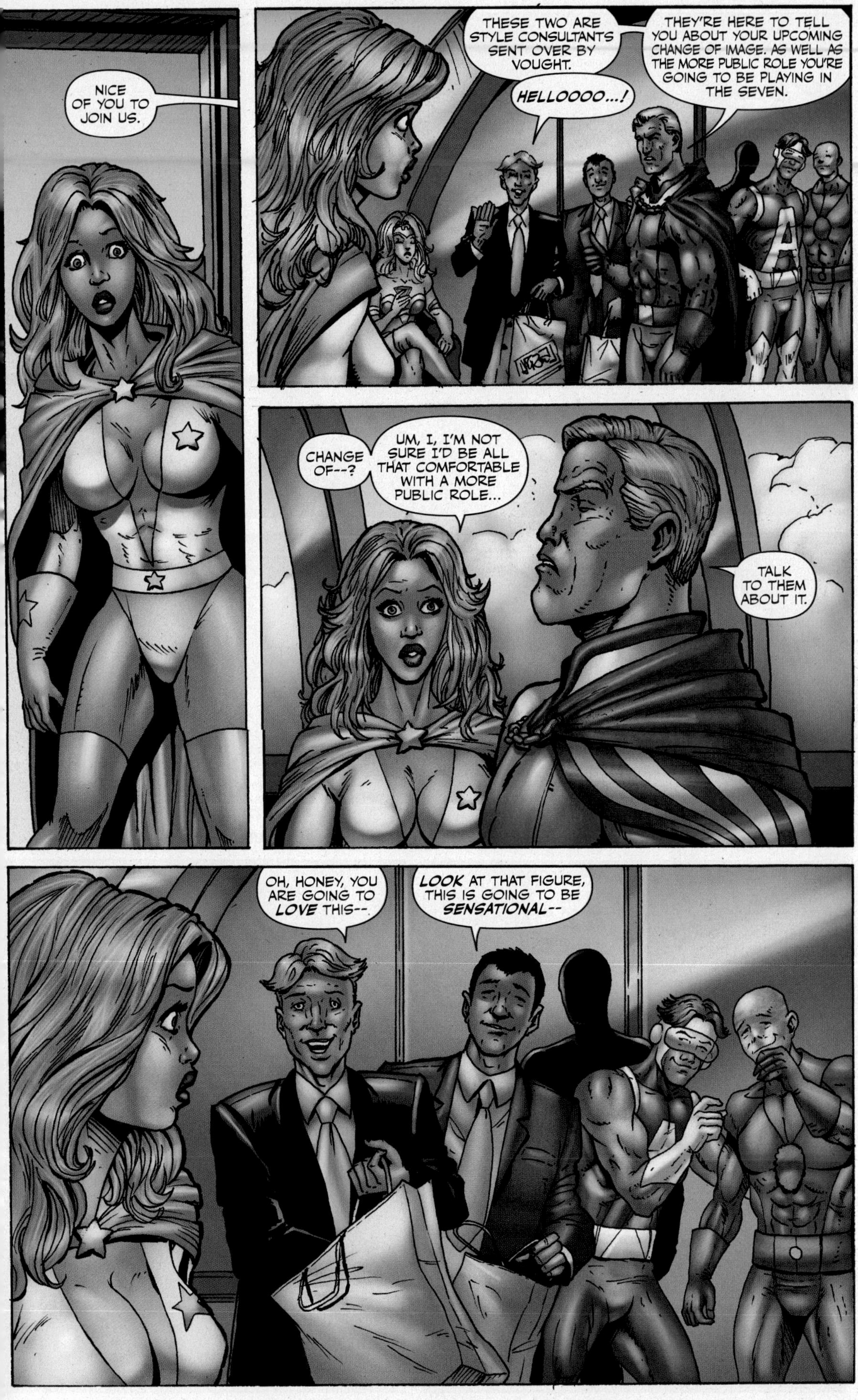
NICE OF YOU TO JOIN US.
THESE TWO ARE STYLE CONSULTANTS SENT OVER BY VOUGHT.
THEY'RE HERE TO TELL YOU ABOUT YOUR UPCOMING CHANGE OF IMAGE. AS WELL AS THE MORE PUBLIC ROLE YOU'RE GOING TO BE PLAYING IN THE SEVEN.
HELLOOOO...!
CHANGE OF--?
UM, I, I'M NOT SURE I'D BE ALL THAT COMFORTABLE WITH A MORE PUBLIC ROLE...
TALK TO THEM ABOUT IT.
OH, HONEY, YOU ARE GOING TO LOVE THIS--
LOOK AT THAT FIGURE, THIS IS GOING TO BE SENSATIONAL--

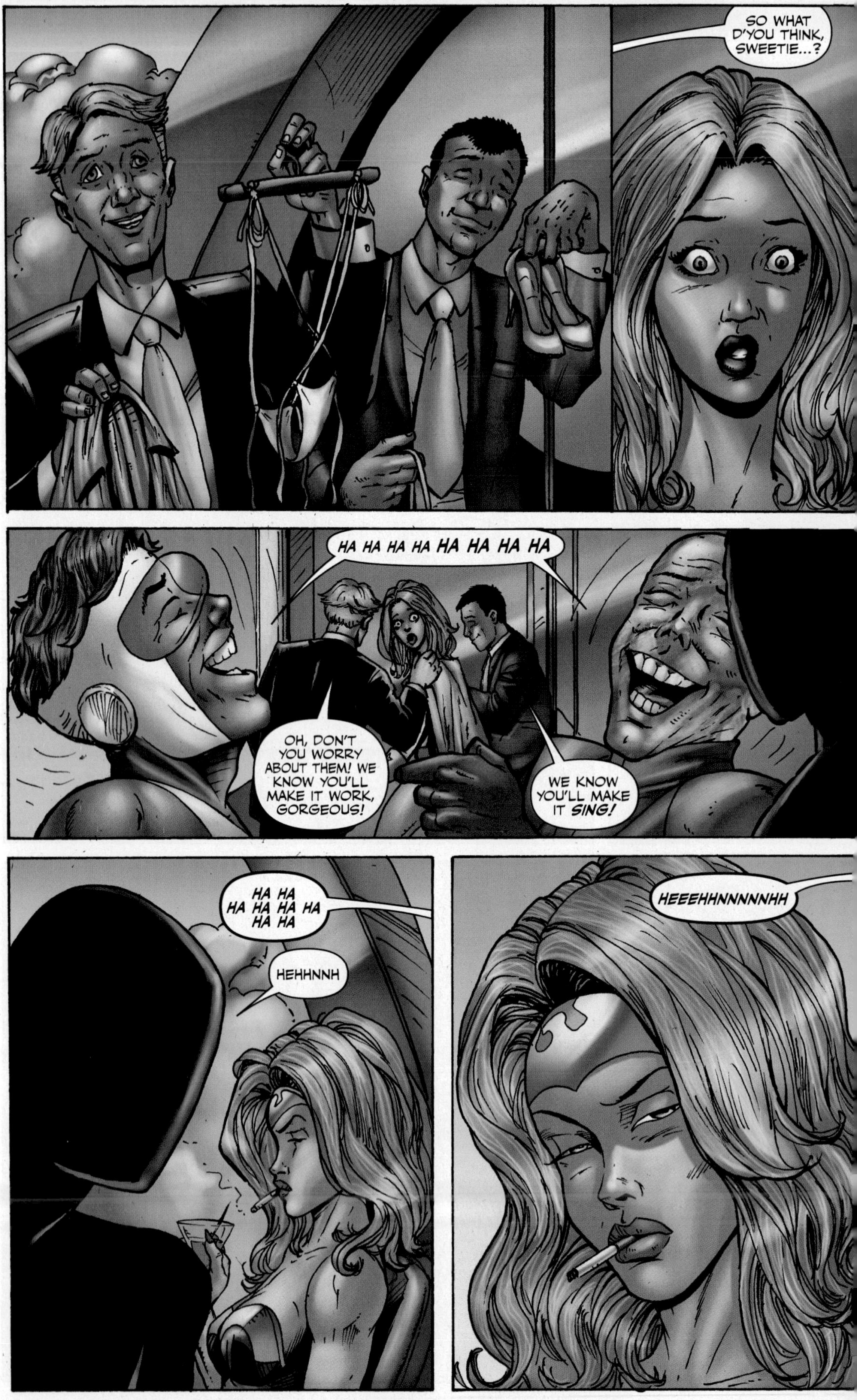
SO WHAT D'YOU THINK, SWEETIE...?
HA HA HA HA HA HA HA HA
OH, DON'T YOU WORRY ABOUT THEM! WE KNOW YOU'LL MAKE IT WORK, GORGEOUS!
WE KNOW YOU'LL MAKE IT SING!
HA HA HA HA HA HA HA HA
HEHHNNH
HEEEHHNNNNNHH

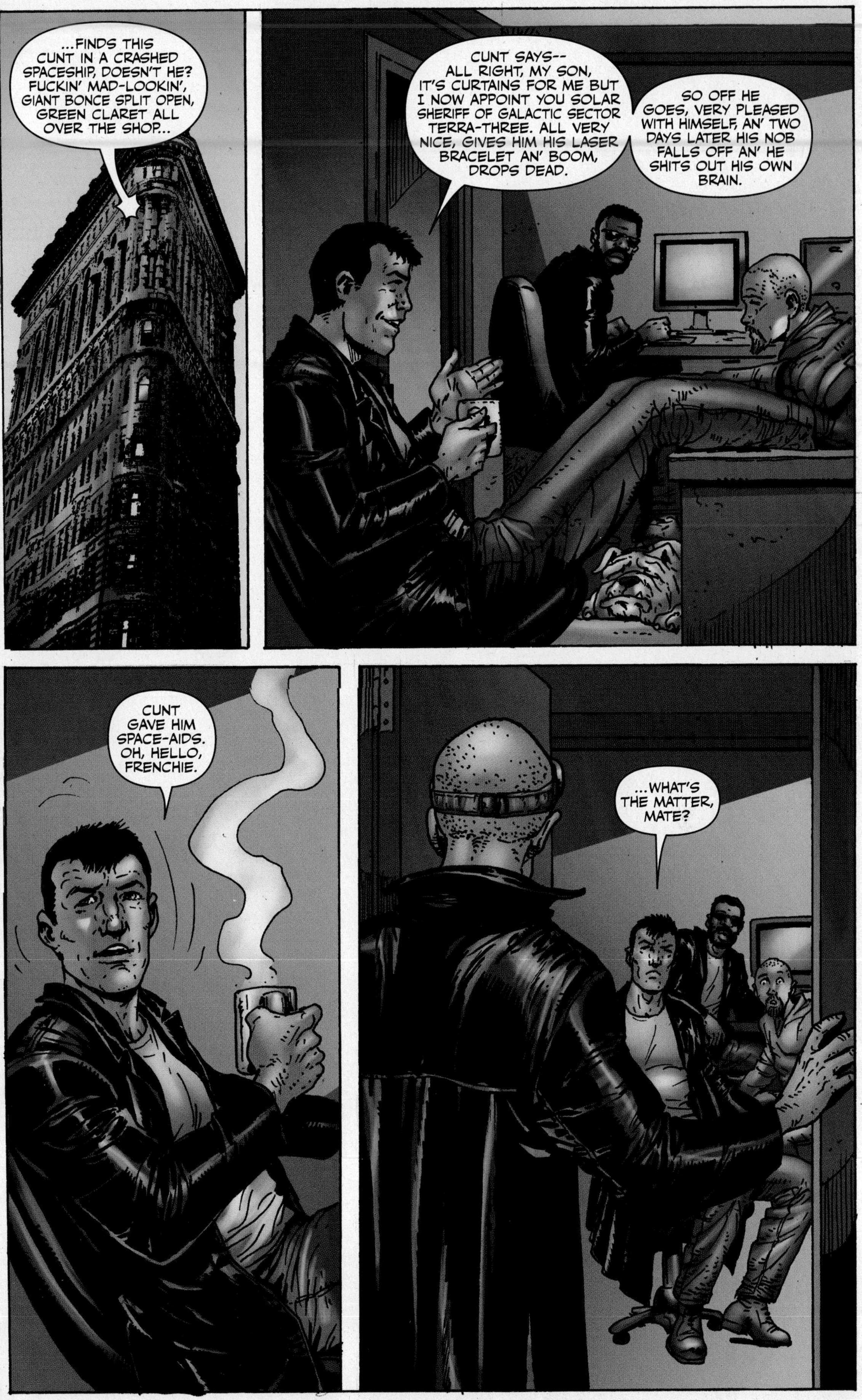
...FINDS THIS CUNT IN A CRASHED SPACESHIP, DOESN'T HE? FUCKIN' MAD-LOOKIN', GIANT BONCE SPLIT OPEN, GREEN CLARET ALL OVER THE SHOP...
CUNT SAYS-- ALL RIGHT, MY SON, IT'S CURTAINS FOR ME BUT I NOW APPOINT YOU SOLAR SHERIFF OF GALACTIC SECTOR TERRA-THREE. ALL VERY NICE, GIVES HIM HIS LASER BRACELET AN' BOOM, DROPS DEAD.
SO OFF HE GOES, VERY PLEASED WITH HIMSELF, AN' TWO DAYS LATER HIS NOB FALLS OFF AN' HE SHITS OUT HIS OWN BRAIN.
CUNT GAVE HIM SPACE-AIDS. OH, HELLO, FRENCHIE.
...WHAT'S THE MATTER, MATE?

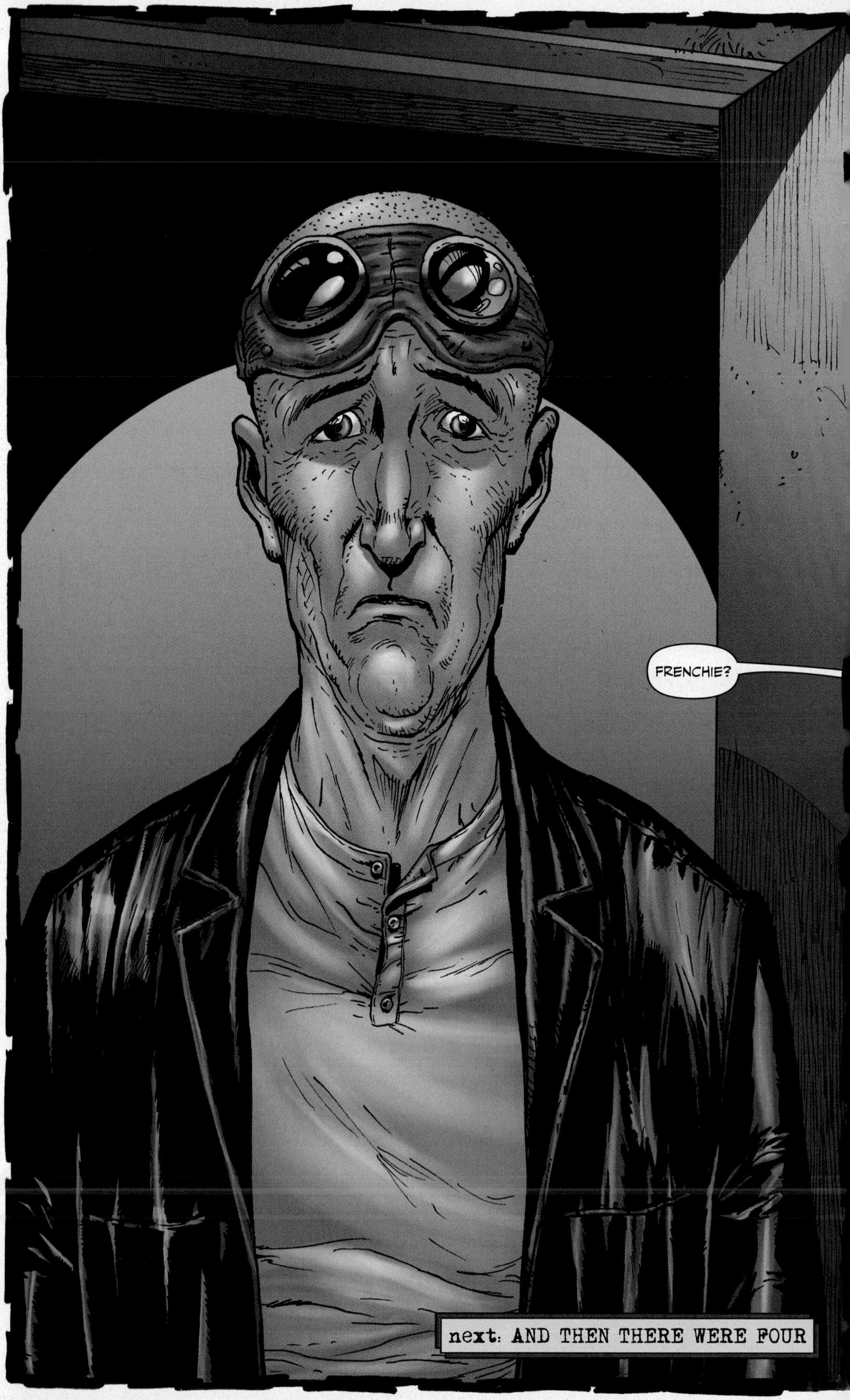

FRENCHIE?
next: AND THEN THERE WERE FOUR

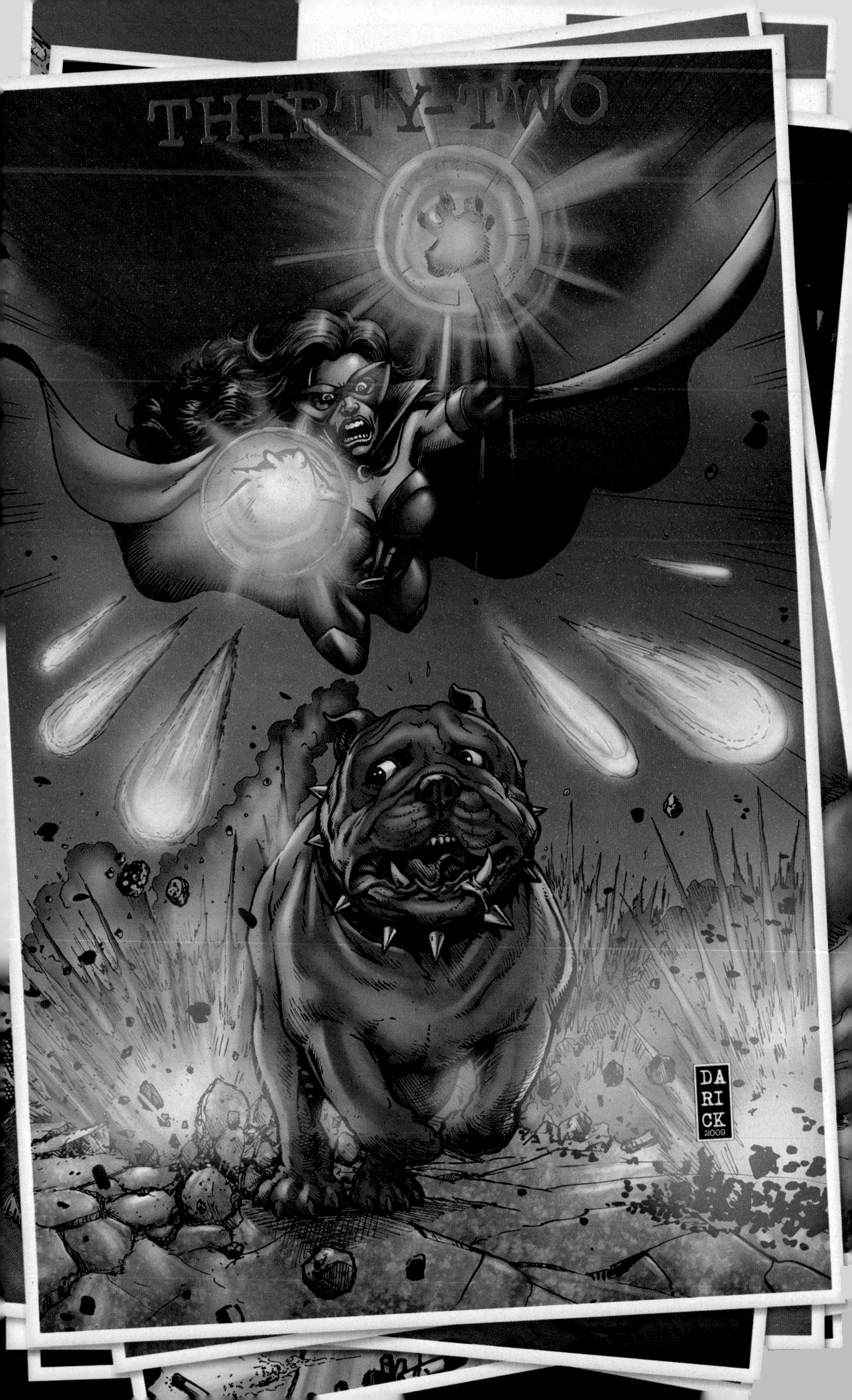
THIRTY-TWO
DA
RI
CK
2009

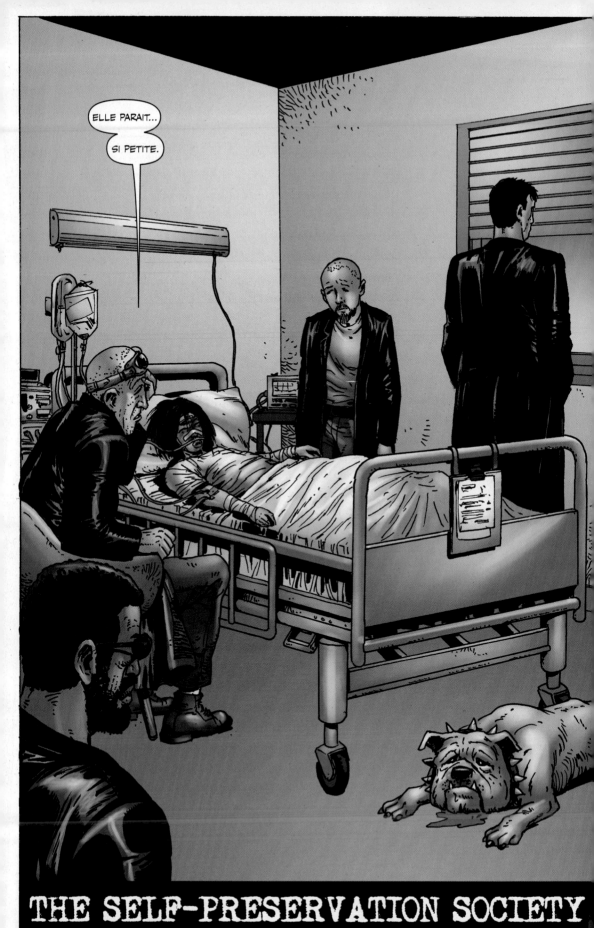

THE SELF-PRESERVATION SOCIETY
part two

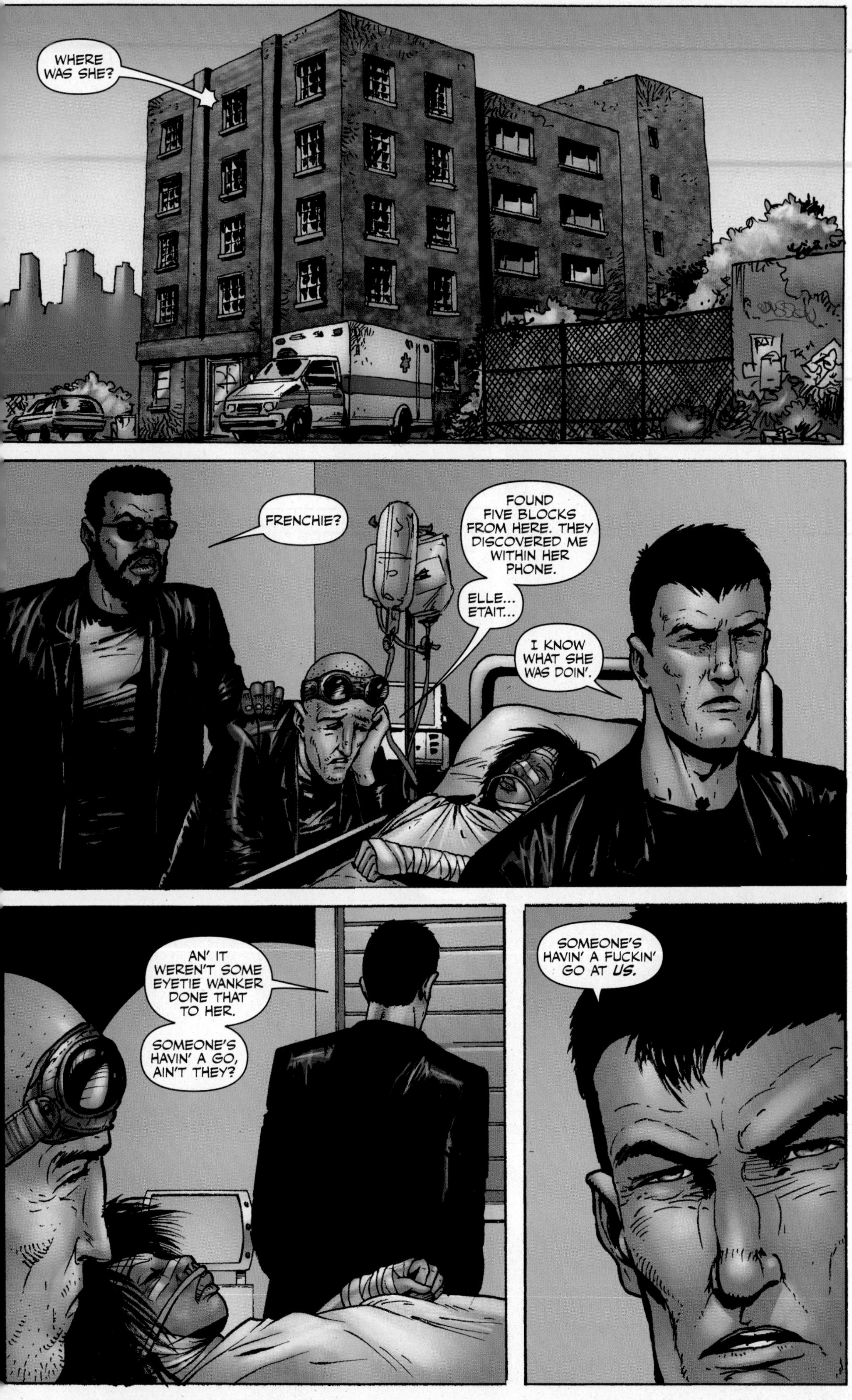
WHERE WAS SHE?
FRENCHIE?
FOUND FIVE BLOCKS FROM HERE. THEY DISCOVERED ME WITHIN HER PHONE.
ELLE... ETAIT...
I KNOW WHAT SHE WAS DOIN'.
AN' IT WEREN'T SOME EYETIE WANKER DONE THAT TO HER.
SOMEONE'S HAVIN' A GO, AIN'T THEY?
SOMEONE'S HAVIN' A FUCKIN' GO AT *US*.

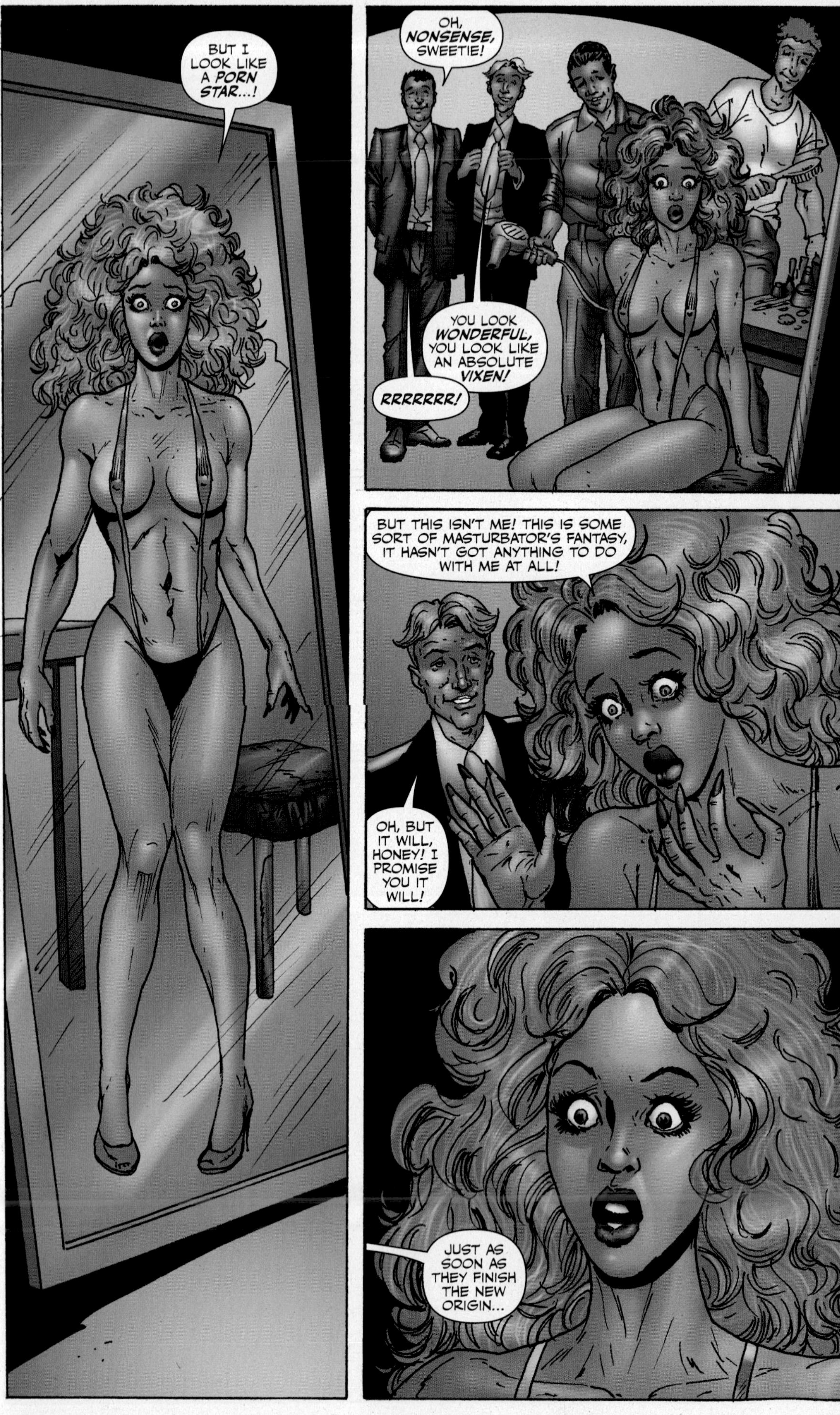
BUT I LOOK LIKE A PORN STAR...!
OH, NONSENSE, SWEETIE!
YOU LOOK WONDERFUL, YOU LOOK LIKE AN ABSOLUTE VIXEN!
RRRRRRR!
BUT THIS ISN'T ME! THIS IS SOME SORT OF MASTURBATOR'S FANTASY, IT HASN'T GOT ANYTHING TO DO WITH ME AT ALL!
OH, BUT IT WILL, HONEY! I PROMISE YOU IT WILL!
JUST AS SOON AS THEY FINISH THE NEW ORIGIN...

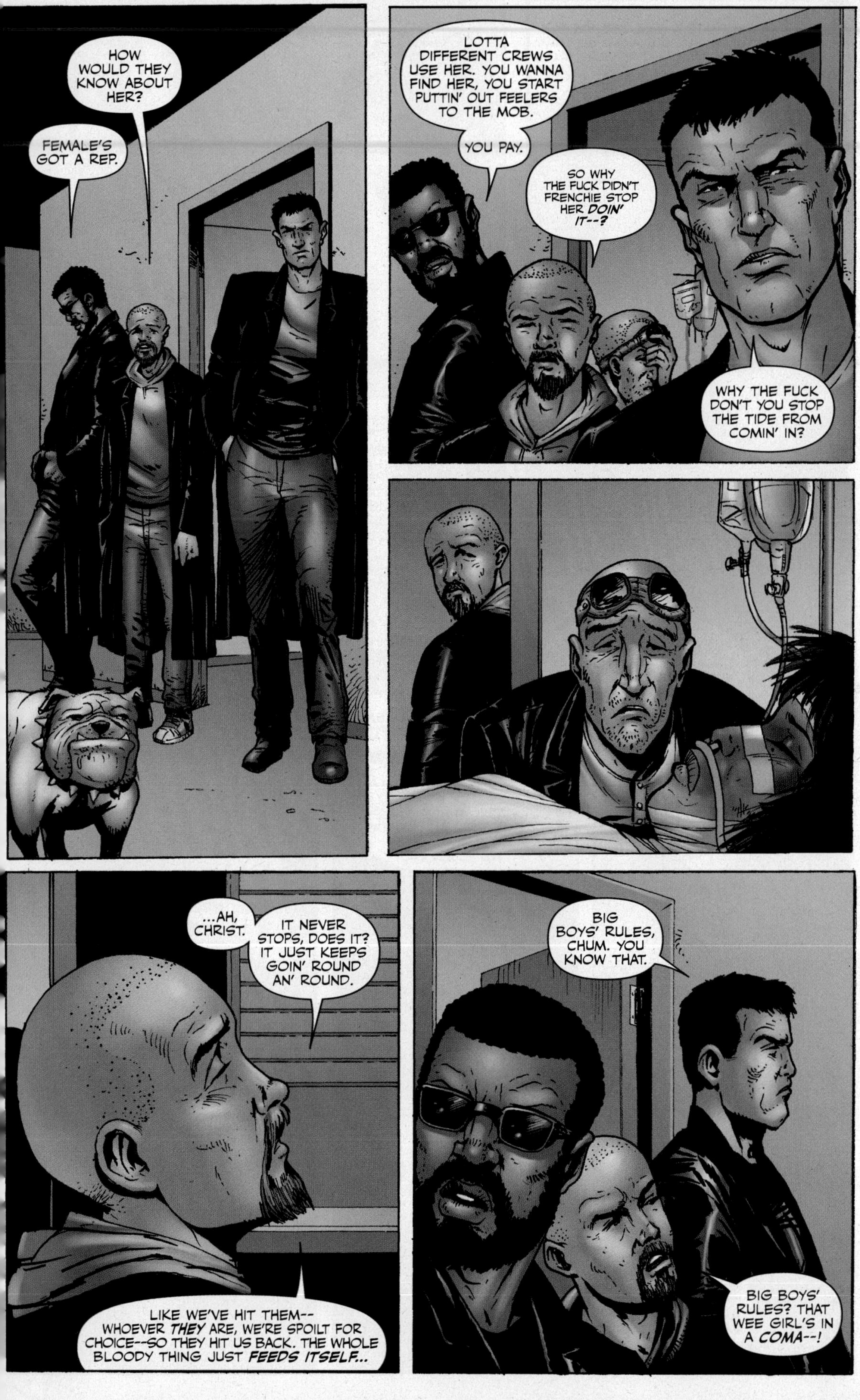
HOW WOULD THEY KNOW ABOUT HER?
FEMALE'S GOT A REP.
LOTTA DIFFERENT CREWS USE HER. YOU WANNA FIND HER, YOU START PUTTIN' OUT FEELERS TO THE MOB.
YOU PAY.
SO WHY THE FUCK DIDN'T FRENCHIE STOP HER *DOIN' IT*--?
WHY THE FUCK DON'T YOU STOP THE TIDE FROM COMIN' IN?
...AH, CHRIST.
IT NEVER STOPS, DOES IT? IT JUST KEEPS GOIN' ROUND AN' ROUND.
LIKE WE'VE HIT THEM-- WHOEVER *THEY* ARE, WE'RE SPOILT FOR CHOICE--SO THEY HIT US BACK. THE WHOLE BLOODY THING JUST *FEEDS ITSELF*...
BIG BOYS' RULES, CHUM. YOU KNOW THAT.
BIG BOYS' RULES? THAT WEE GIRL'S IN A *COMA*--!

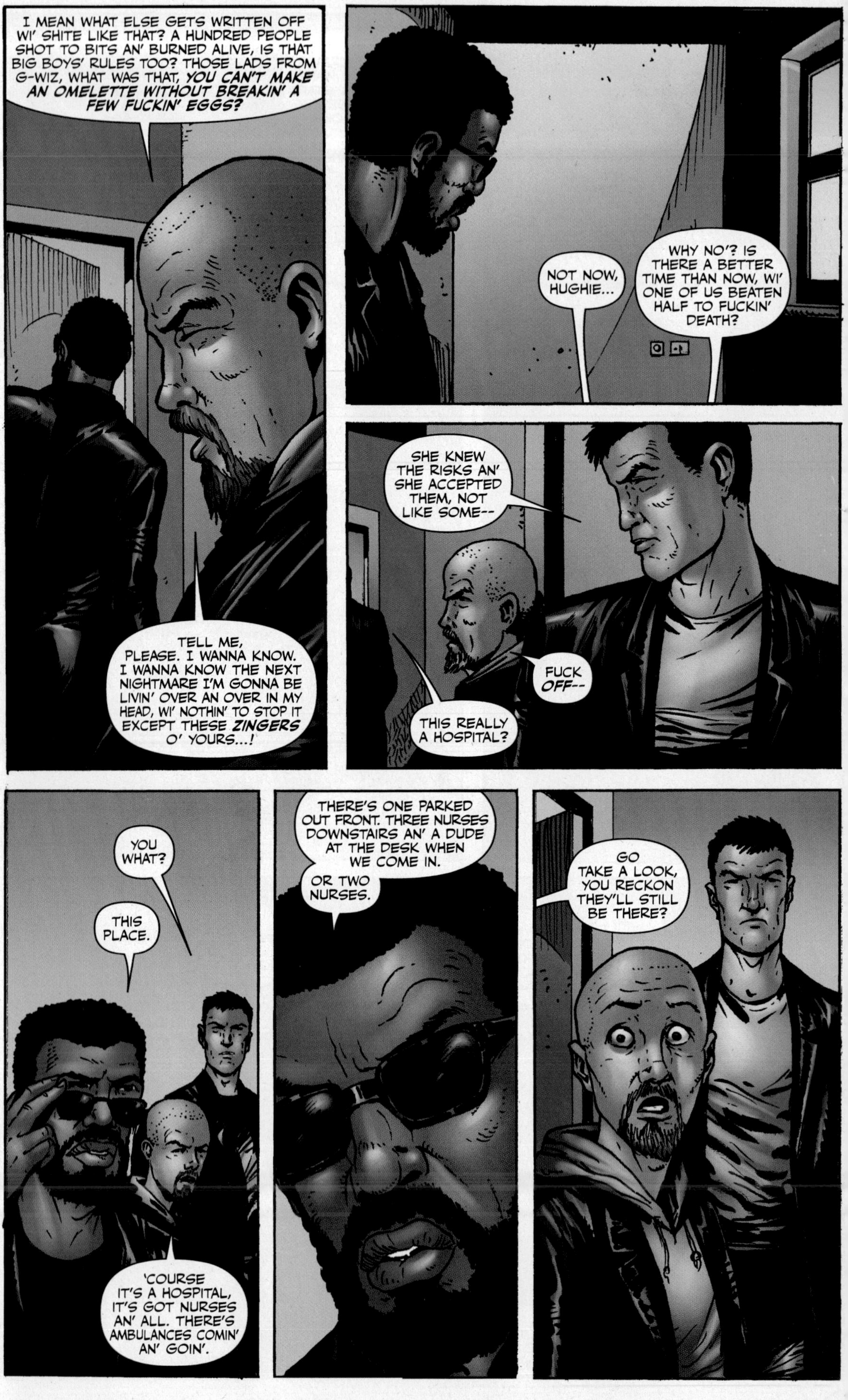
I MEAN WHAT ELSE GETS WRITTEN OFF WI' SHITE LIKE THAT? A HUNDRED PEOPLE SHOT TO BITS AN' BURNED ALIVE, IS THAT BIG BOYS' RULES TOO? THOSE LADS FROM G-WIZ, WHAT WAS THAT, *YOU CAN'T MAKE AN OMELETTE WITHOUT BREAKIN' A FEW FUCKIN' EGGS?*
TELL ME, PLEASE. I WANNA KNOW. I WANNA KNOW THE NEXT NIGHTMARE I'M GONNA BE LIVIN' OVER AN OVER IN MY HEAD, WI' NOTHIN' TO STOP IT EXCEPT THESE *ZINGERS* O' YOURS...!
NOT NOW, HUGHIE...
WHY NO'? IS THERE A BETTER TIME THAN NOW, WI' ONE OF US BEATEN HALF TO FUCKIN' DEATH?
SHE KNEW THE RISKS AN' SHE ACCEPTED THEM, NOT LIKE SOME--
FUCK *OFF*--
THIS REALLY A HOSPITAL?
YOU WHAT?
THIS PLACE.
'COURSE IT'S A HOSPITAL, IT'S GOT NURSES AN' ALL. THERE'S AMBULANCES COMIN' AN' GOIN'.
THERE'S ONE PARKED OUT FRONT. THREE NURSES DOWNSTAIRS AN' A DUDE AT THE DESK WHEN WE COME IN.
OR TWO NURSES.
GO TAKE A LOOK, YOU RECKON THEY'LL STILL BE THERE?

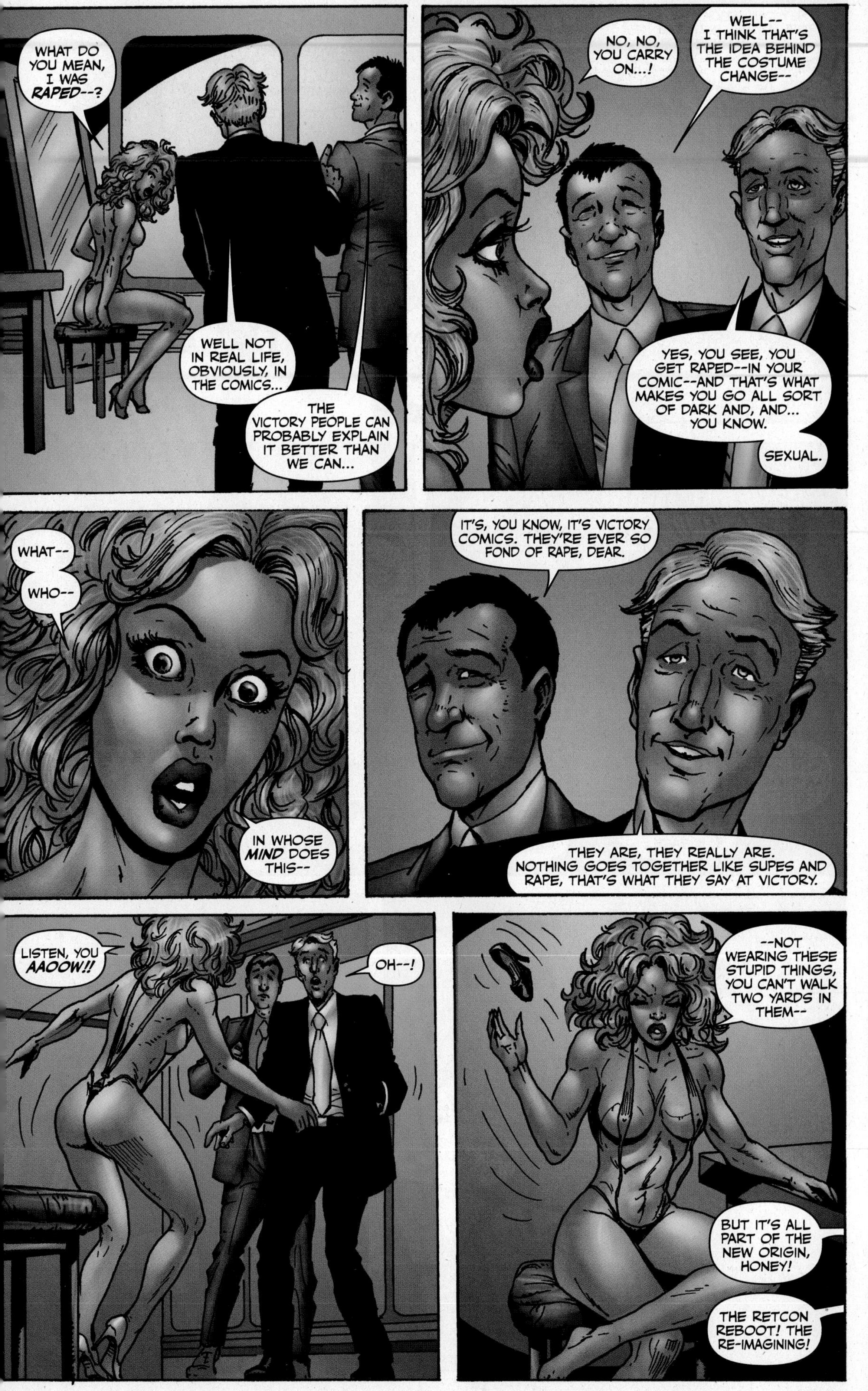
WHAT DO YOU MEAN, I WAS *RAPED*--?
WELL NOT IN REAL LIFE, OBVIOUSLY, IN THE COMICS...
THE VICTORY PEOPLE CAN PROBABLY EXPLAIN IT BETTER THAN WE CAN...
NO, NO, YOU CARRY ON...!
WELL-- I THINK THAT'S THE IDEA BEHIND THE COSTUME CHANGE--
YES, YOU SEE, YOU GET RAPED--IN YOUR COMIC--AND THAT'S WHAT MAKES YOU GO ALL SORT OF DARK AND, AND... YOU KNOW.
SEXUAL.
WHAT--
WHO--
IN WHOSE *MIND* DOES THIS--
IT'S, YOU KNOW, IT'S VICTORY COMICS. THEY'RE EVER SO FOND OF RAPE, DEAR.
THEY ARE, THEY REALLY ARE. NOTHING GOES TOGETHER LIKE SUPES AND RAPE, THAT'S WHAT THEY SAY AT VICTORY.
LISTEN, YOU *AAOOW!!*
OH--!
--NOT WEARING THESE STUPID THINGS, YOU CAN'T WALK TWO YARDS IN THEM--
BUT IT'S ALL PART OF THE NEW ORIGIN, HONEY!
THE RETCON REBOOT! THE RE-IMAGINING!

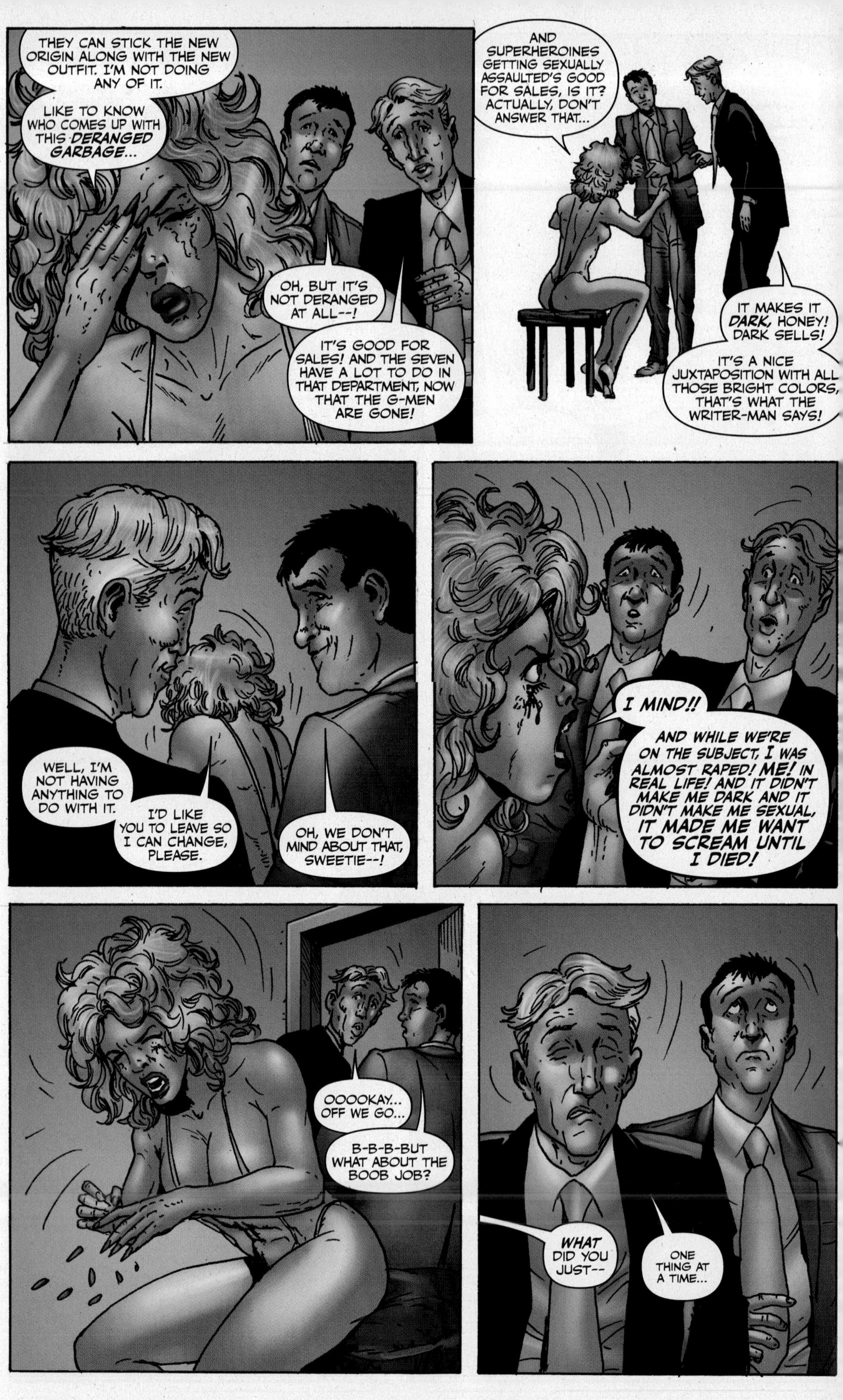
THEY CAN STICK THE NEW ORIGIN ALONG WITH THE NEW OUTFIT. I'M NOT DOING ANY OF IT.
LIKE TO KNOW WHO COMES UP WITH THIS *DERANGED GARBAGE*...
OH, BUT IT'S NOT DERANGED AT ALL--!
IT'S GOOD FOR SALES! AND THE SEVEN HAVE A LOT TO DO IN THAT DEPARTMENT, NOW THAT THE G-MEN ARE GONE!
AND SUPERHEROINES GETTING SEXUALLY ASSAULTED'S GOOD FOR SALES, IS IT? ACTUALLY, DON'T ANSWER THAT...
IT MAKES IT *DARK*, HONEY! DARK SELLS!
IT'S A NICE JUXTAPOSITION WITH ALL THOSE BRIGHT COLORS, THAT'S WHAT THE WRITER-MAN SAYS!
WELL, I'M NOT HAVING ANYTHING TO DO WITH IT.
I'D LIKE YOU TO LEAVE SO I CAN CHANGE, PLEASE.
OH, WE DON'T MIND ABOUT THAT, SWEETIE--!
I MIND!!
AND WHILE WE'RE ON THE SUBJECT, I WAS ALMOST RAPED! ME! IN REAL LIFE! AND IT DIDN'T MAKE ME DARK AND IT DIDN'T MAKE ME SEXUAL, IT MADE ME WANT TO SCREAM UNTIL I DIED!
OOOOKAY... OFF WE GO...
B-B-B-BUT WHAT ABOUT THE BOOB JOB?
WHAT DID YOU JUST--
ONE THING AT A TIME...

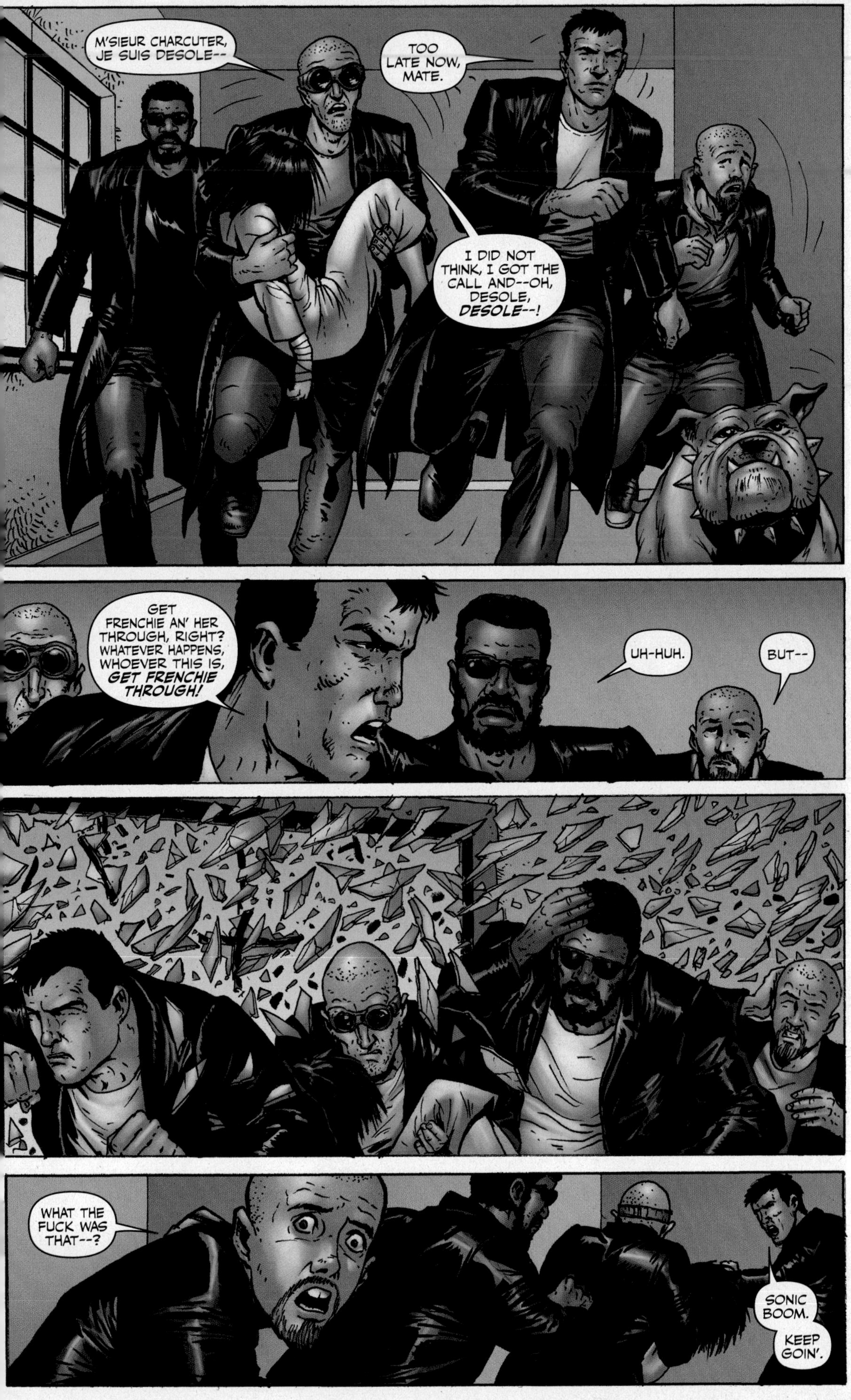
M'SIEUR CHARCUTER, JE SUIS DESOLE--
TOO LATE NOW, MATE.
I DID NOT THINK, I GOT THE CALL AND--OH, DESOLE, *DESOLE*--!
GET FRENCHIE AN' HER THROUGH, RIGHT? WHATEVER HAPPENS, WHOEVER THIS IS, *GET FRENCHIE THROUGH!*
UH-HUH.
BUT--
WHAT THE FUCK WAS THAT--?
SONIC BOOM.
KEEP GOIN'.

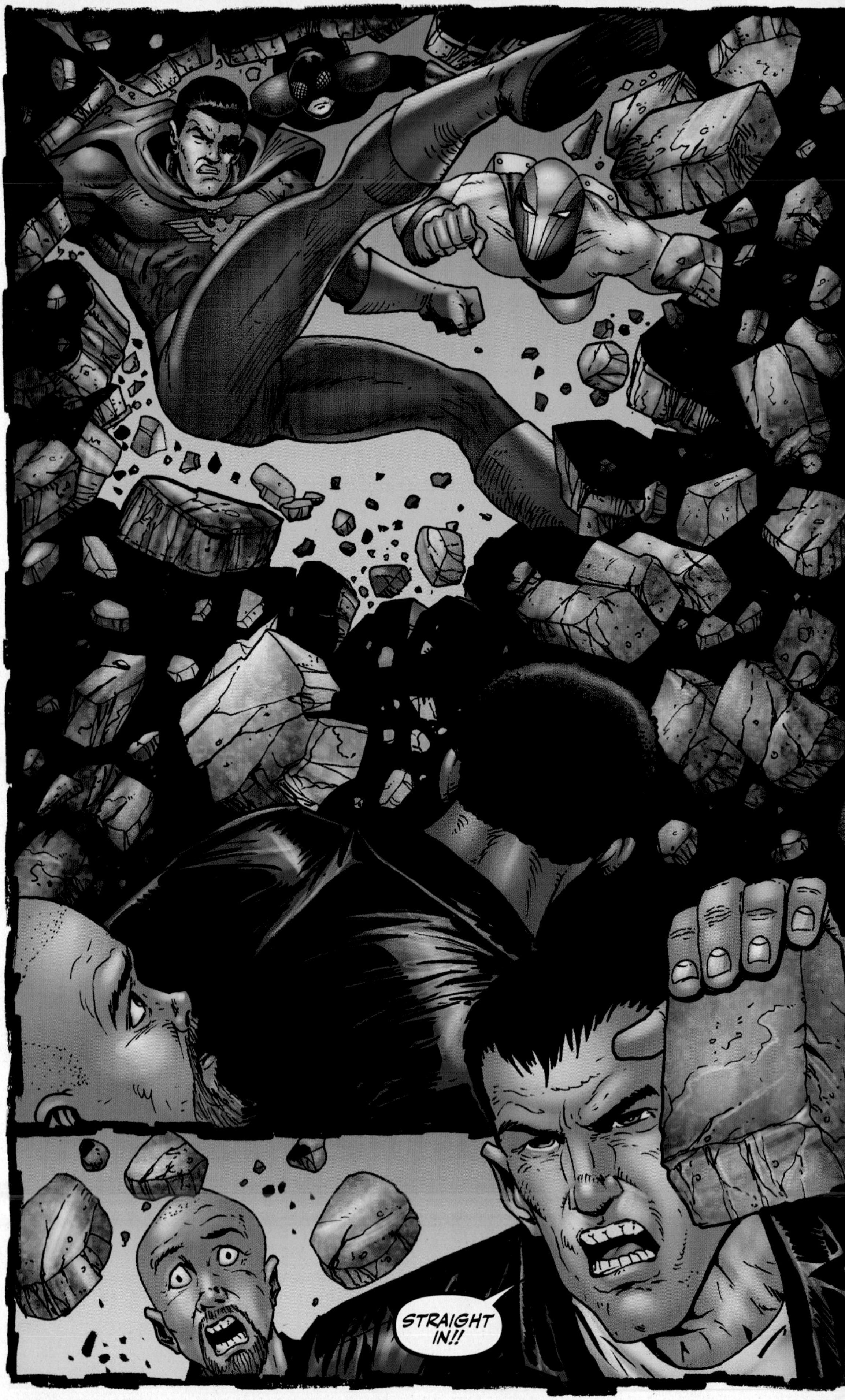
STRAIGHT IN!!

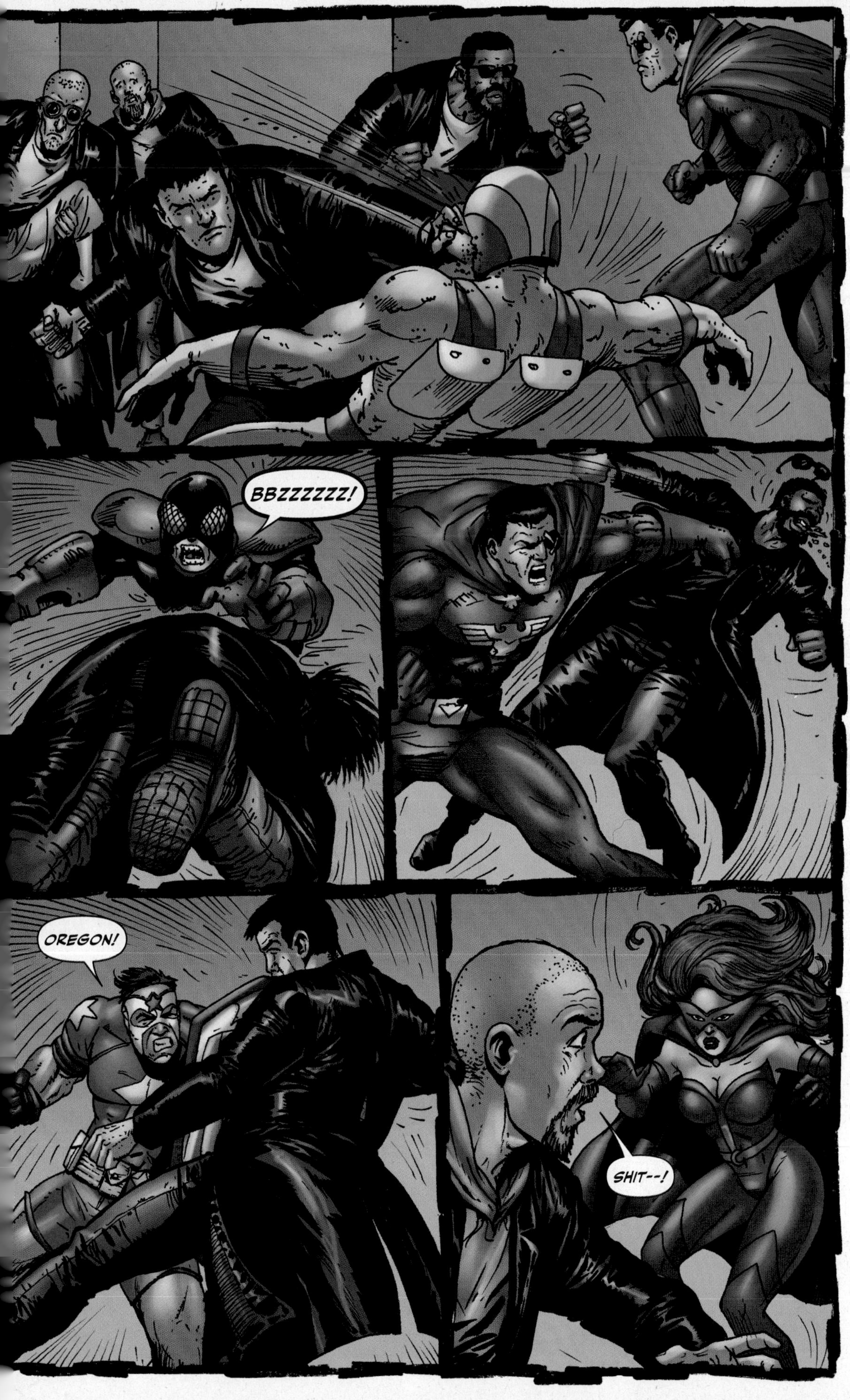
BBZZZZZZ!
OREGON!
SHIT--!

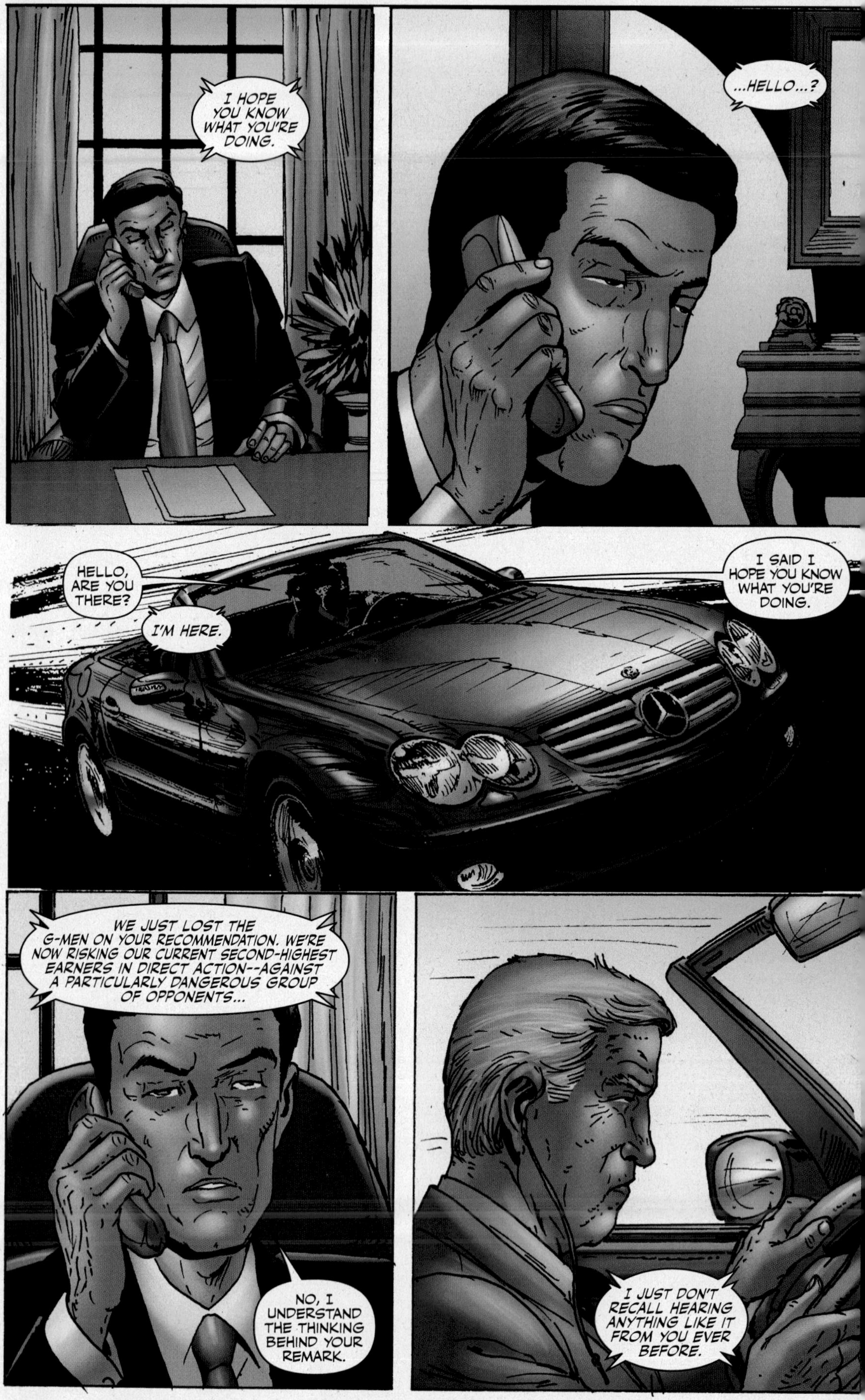
I HOPE YOU KNOW WHAT YOU'RE DOING.
...HELLO...?
HELLO, ARE YOU THERE?
I'M HERE.
I SAID I HOPE YOU KNOW WHAT YOU'RE DOING.
WE JUST LOST THE G-MEN ON YOUR RECOMMENDATION. WE'RE NOW RISKING OUR CURRENT SECOND-HIGHEST EARNERS IN DIRECT ACTION--AGAINST A PARTICULARLY DANGEROUS GROUP OF OPPONENTS...
NO, I UNDERSTAND THE THINKING BEHIND YOUR REMARK.
I JUST DON'T RECALL HEARING ANYTHING LIKE IT FROM YOU EVER BEFORE.

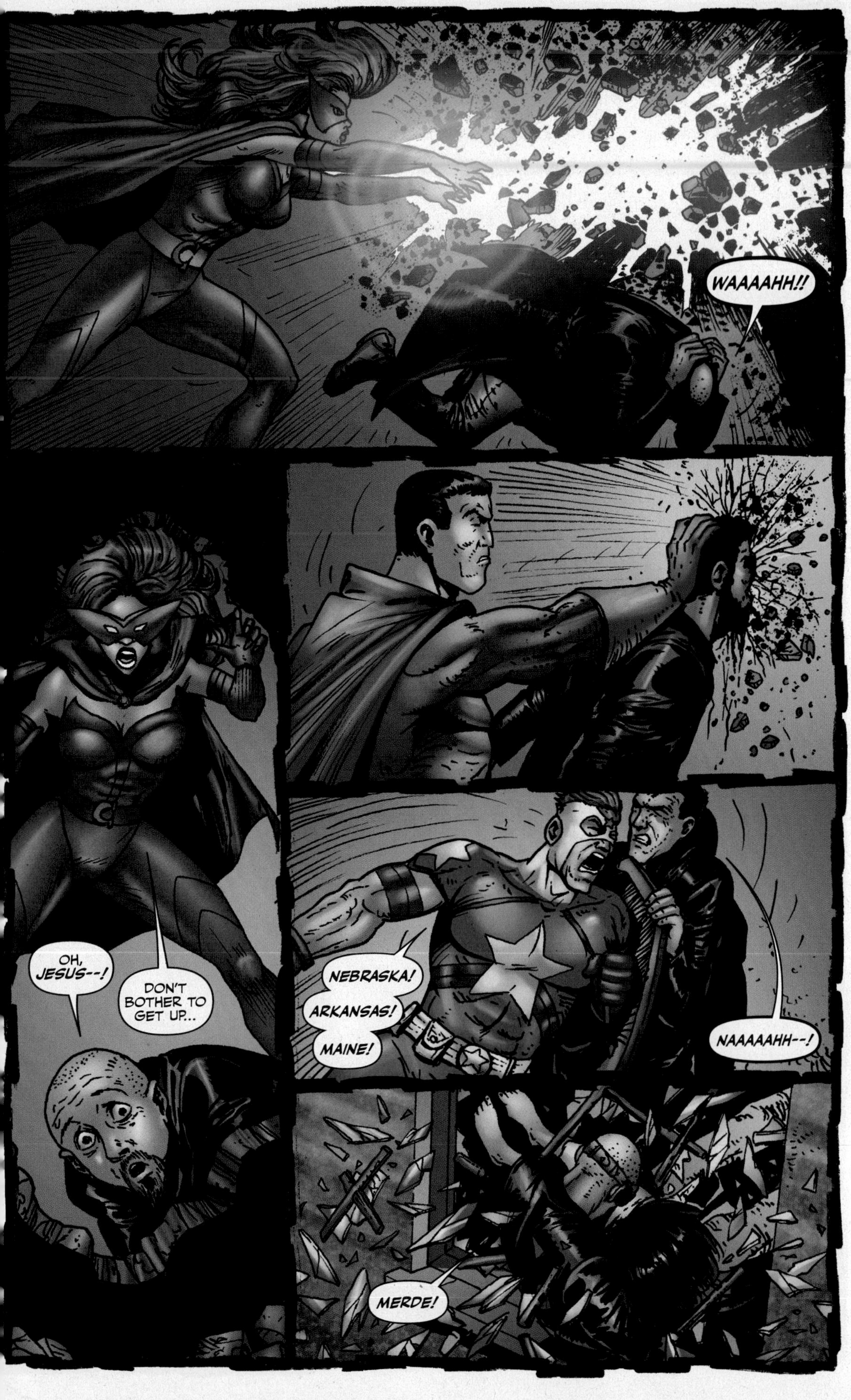
WAAAAHH!!
OH, JESUS--!
DON'T BOTHER TO GET UP...
NEBRASKA!
ARKANSAS!
MAINE!
NAAAAAHH--!
MERDE!

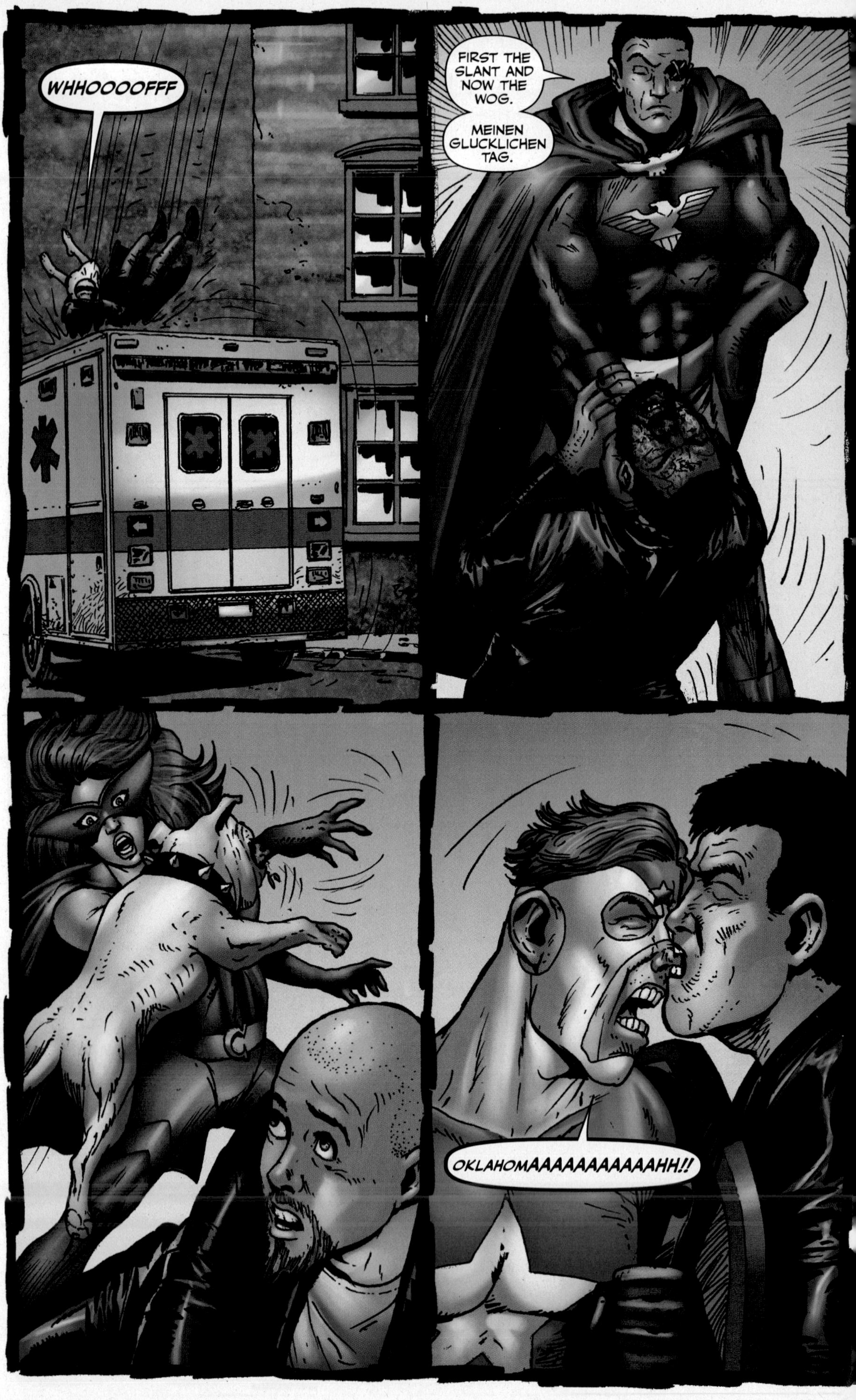
WHHOOOOFFF
FIRST THE SLANT AND NOW THE WOG.
MEINEN GLUCKLICHEN TAG.
OKLAHOMAAAAAAAAAAAAHH!!

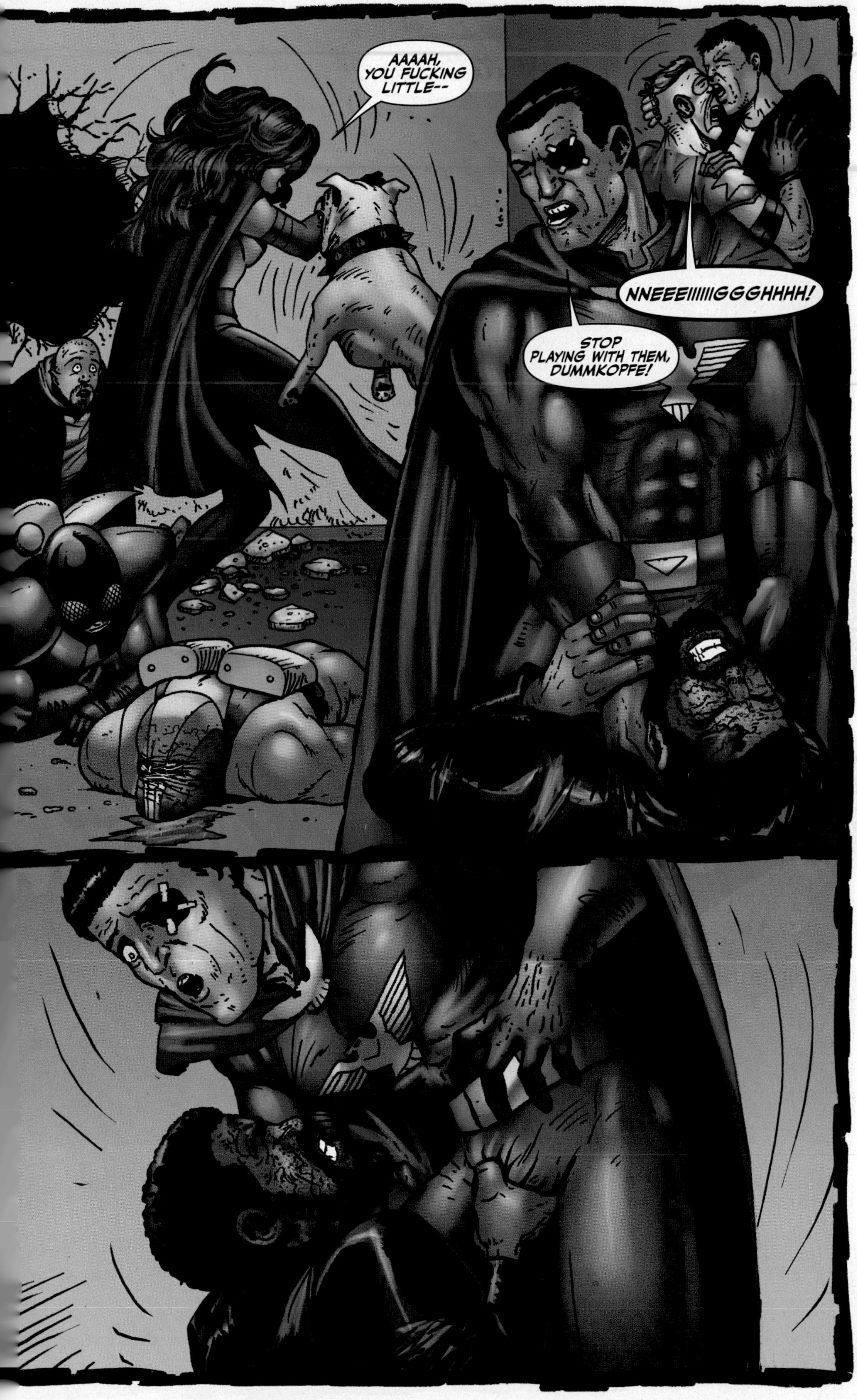
AAAAH, YOU FUCKING LITTLE--
NNEEEIIIIIIGGGHHHH!
STOP PLAYING WITH THEM, DUMMKOPFE!

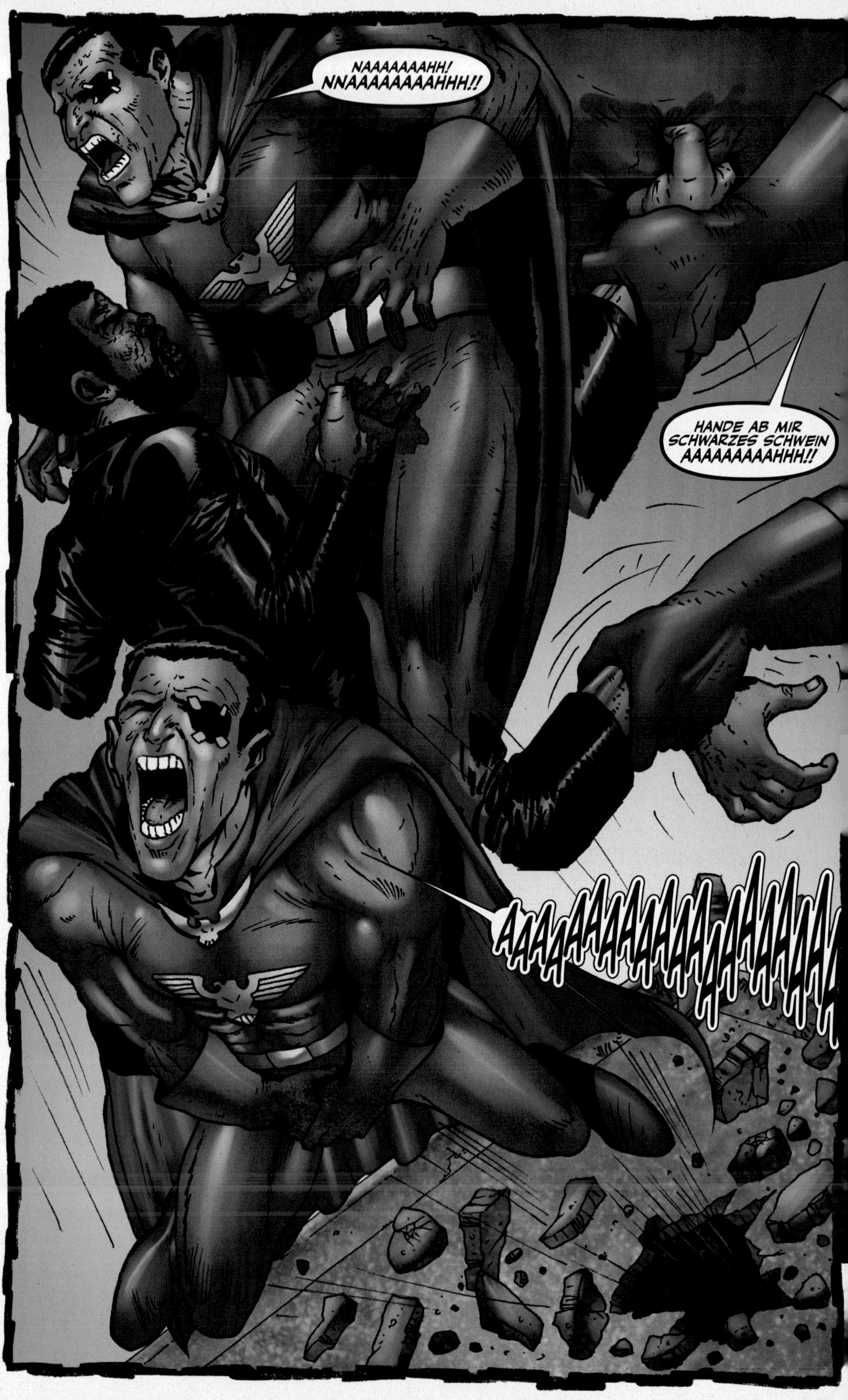
NAAAAAAAAHH!
NNAAAAAAAAAHHH!!
HANDE AB MIR
SCHWARZES SCHWEIN
AAAAAAAAAAHHH!!
AAAAAAAAAAAAAAAAAAA

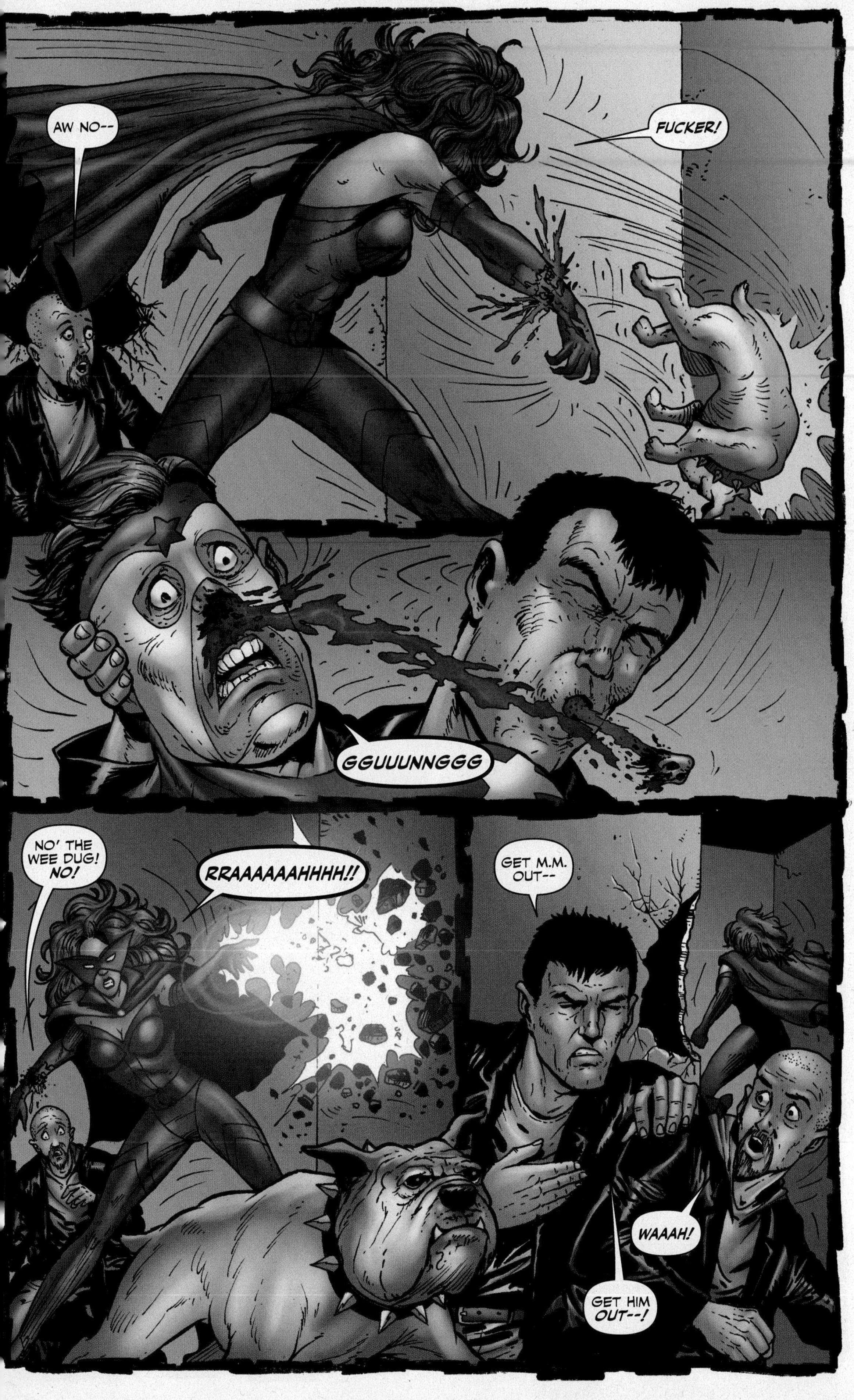
AW NO--
FUCKER!
GGUUUNNGGG
NO' THE WEE DUG! NO!
RRAAAAAAHHHH!!
GET M.M. OUT--
WAAAH!
GET HIM OUT--!

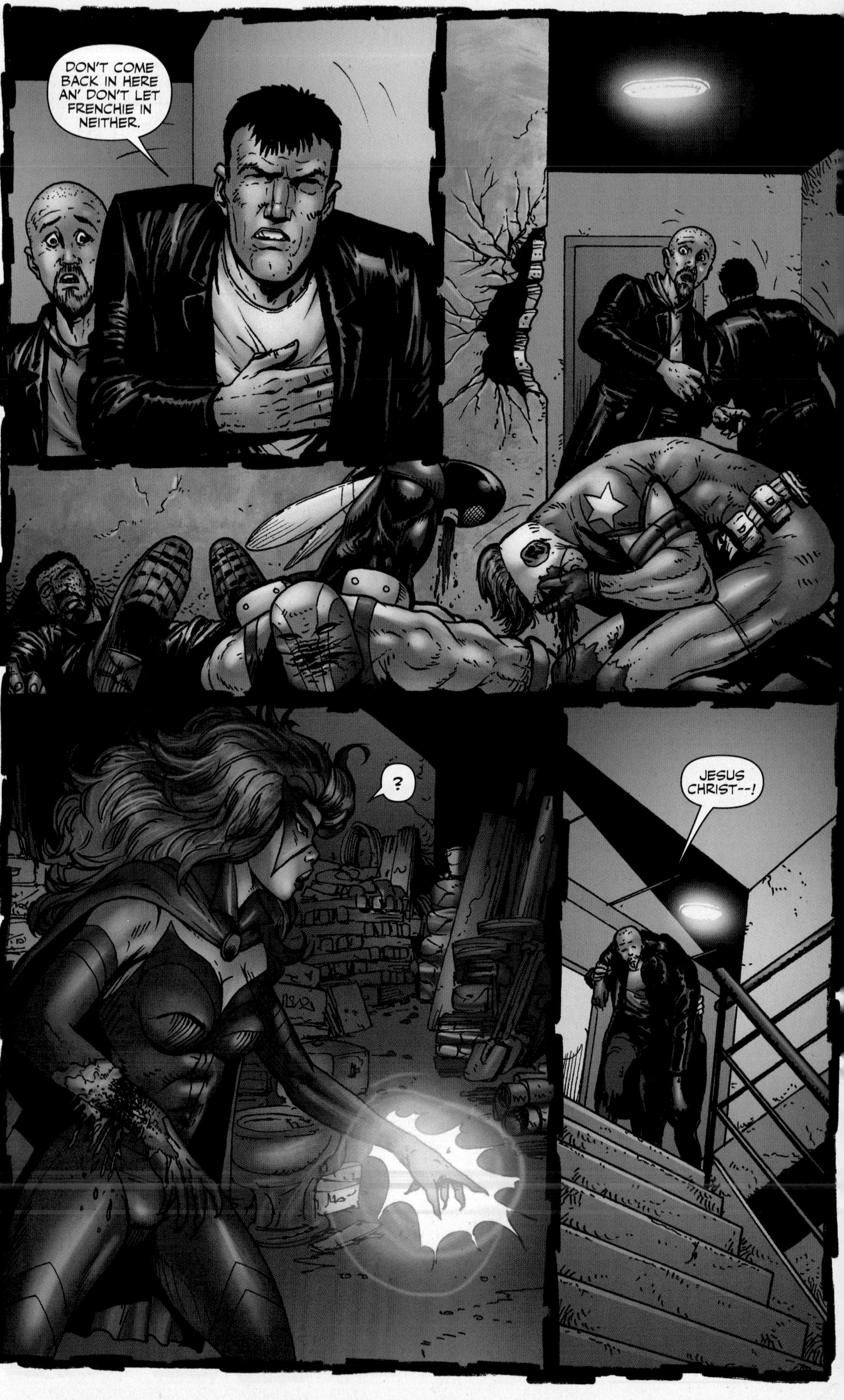
DON'T COME BACK IN HERE AN' DON'T LET FRENCHIE IN NEITHER.
?
JESUS CHRIST--!

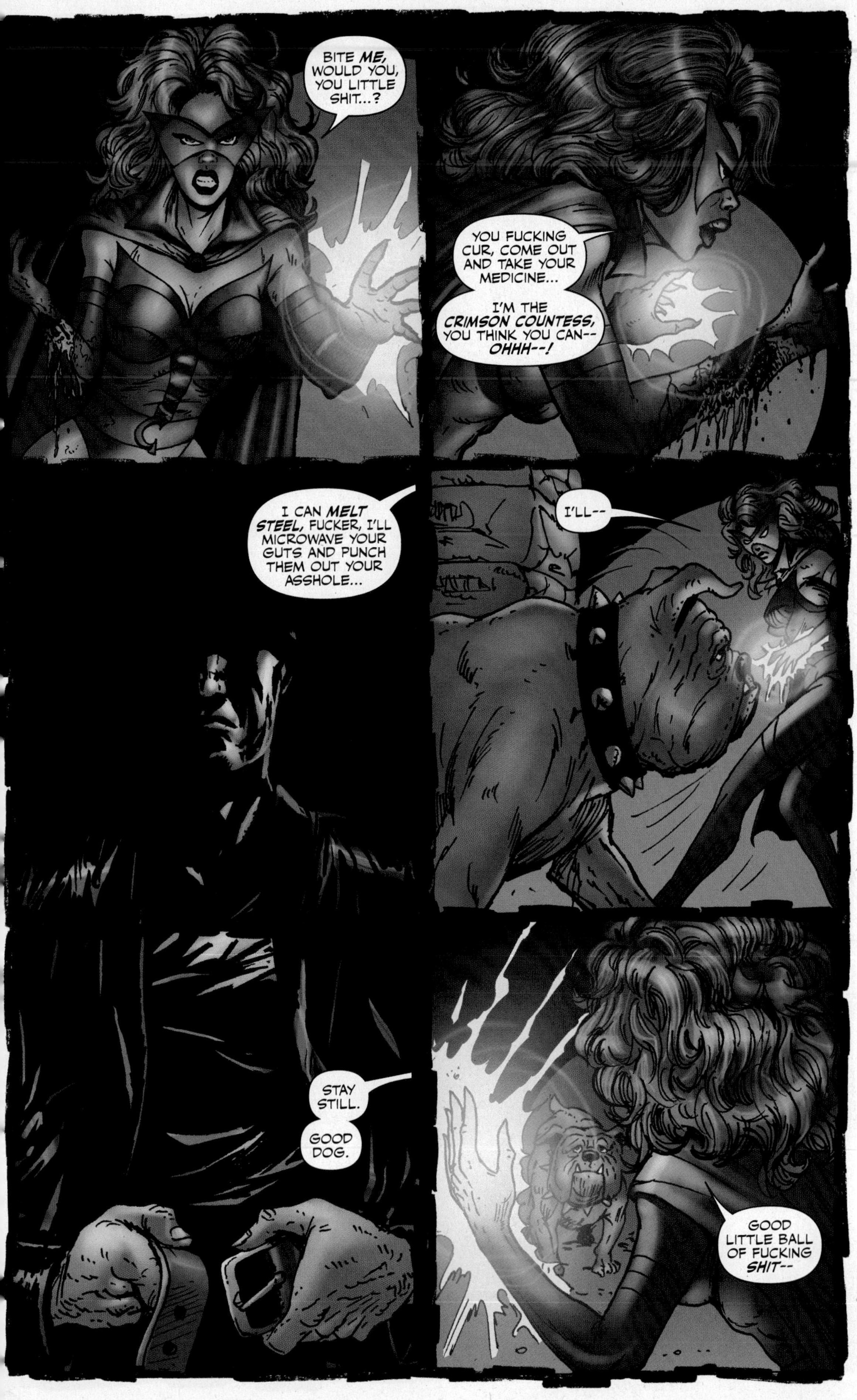
BITE ME, WOULD YOU, YOU LITTLE SHIT...?
YOU FUCKING CUR, COME OUT AND TAKE YOUR MEDICINE...
I'M THE CRIMSON COUNTESS, YOU THINK YOU CAN-- OHHH--!
I CAN MELT STEEL, FUCKER, I'LL MICROWAVE YOUR GUTS AND PUNCH THEM OUT YOUR ASSHOLE...
I'LL--
STAY STILL.
GOOD DOG.
GOOD LITTLE BALL OF FUCKING SHIT--

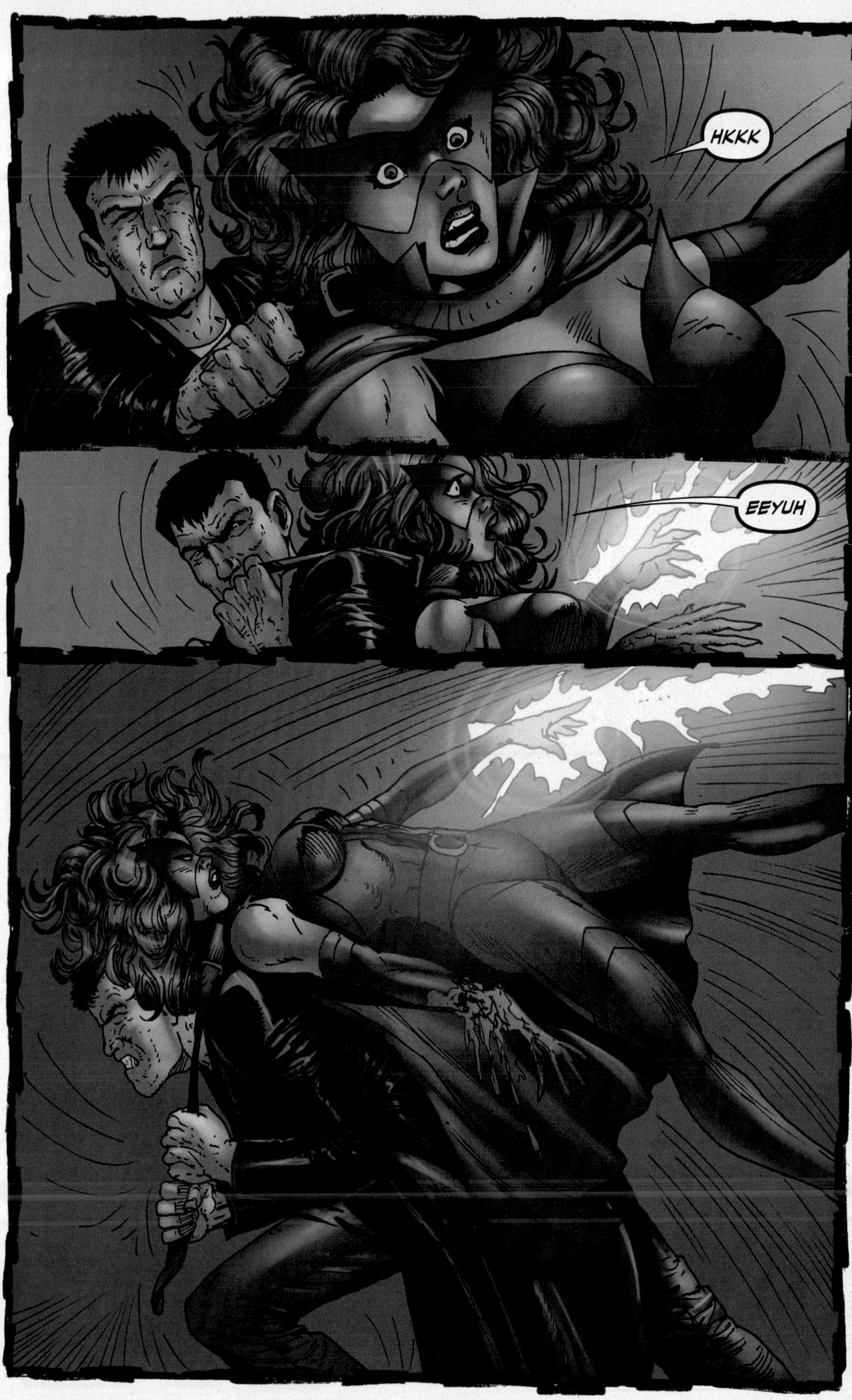
HKKK
EEYUH

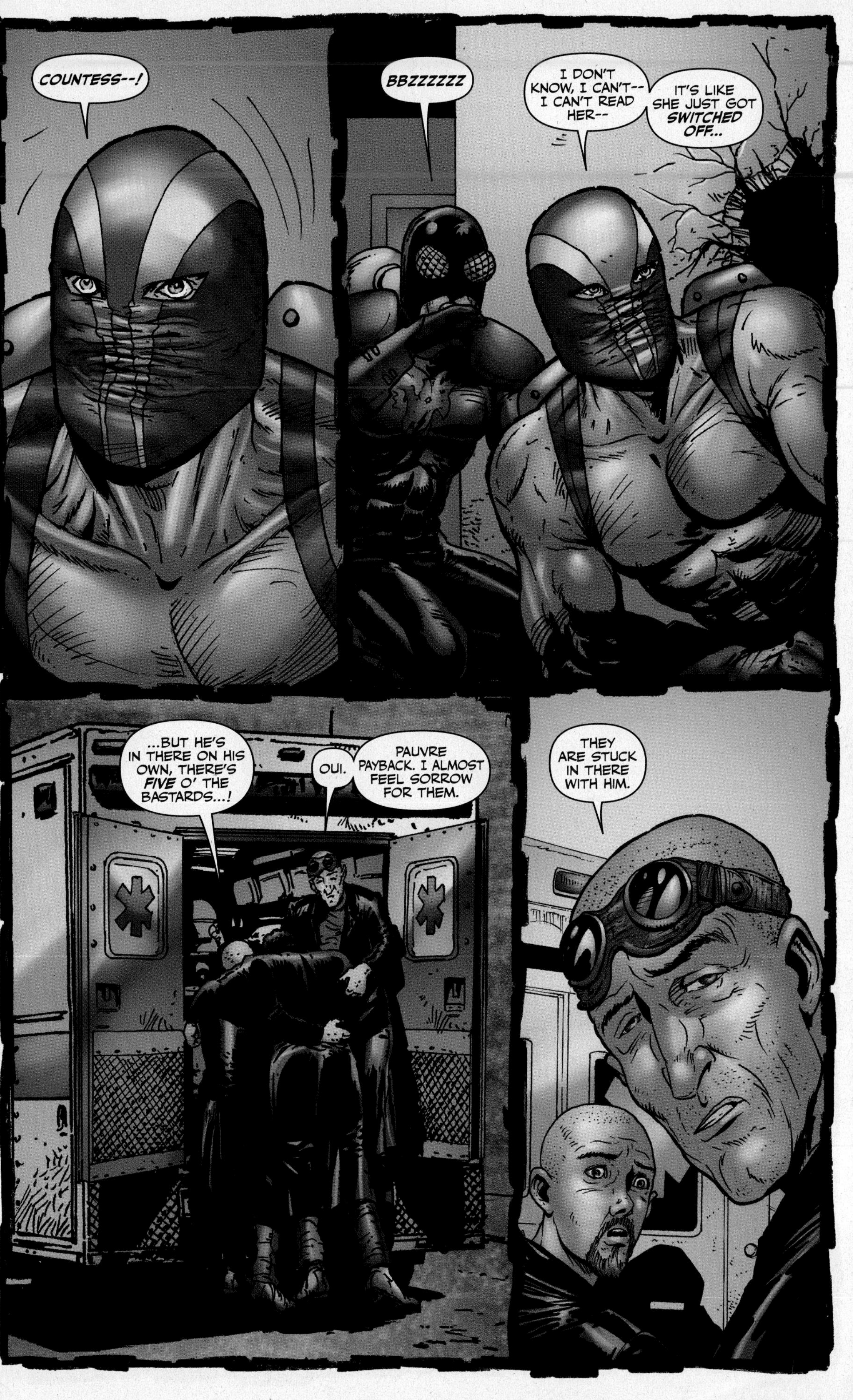

COUNTESS--!
BBZZZZZZ
I DON'T KNOW, I CAN'T-- I CAN'T READ HER--
IT'S LIKE SHE JUST GOT *SWITCHED OFF...*
...BUT HE'S IN THERE ON HIS OWN, THERE'S *FIVE* O' THE BASTARDS...!
OUI.
PAUVRE PAYBACK. I ALMOST FEEL SORROW FOR THEM.
THEY ARE STUCK IN THERE WITH HIM.

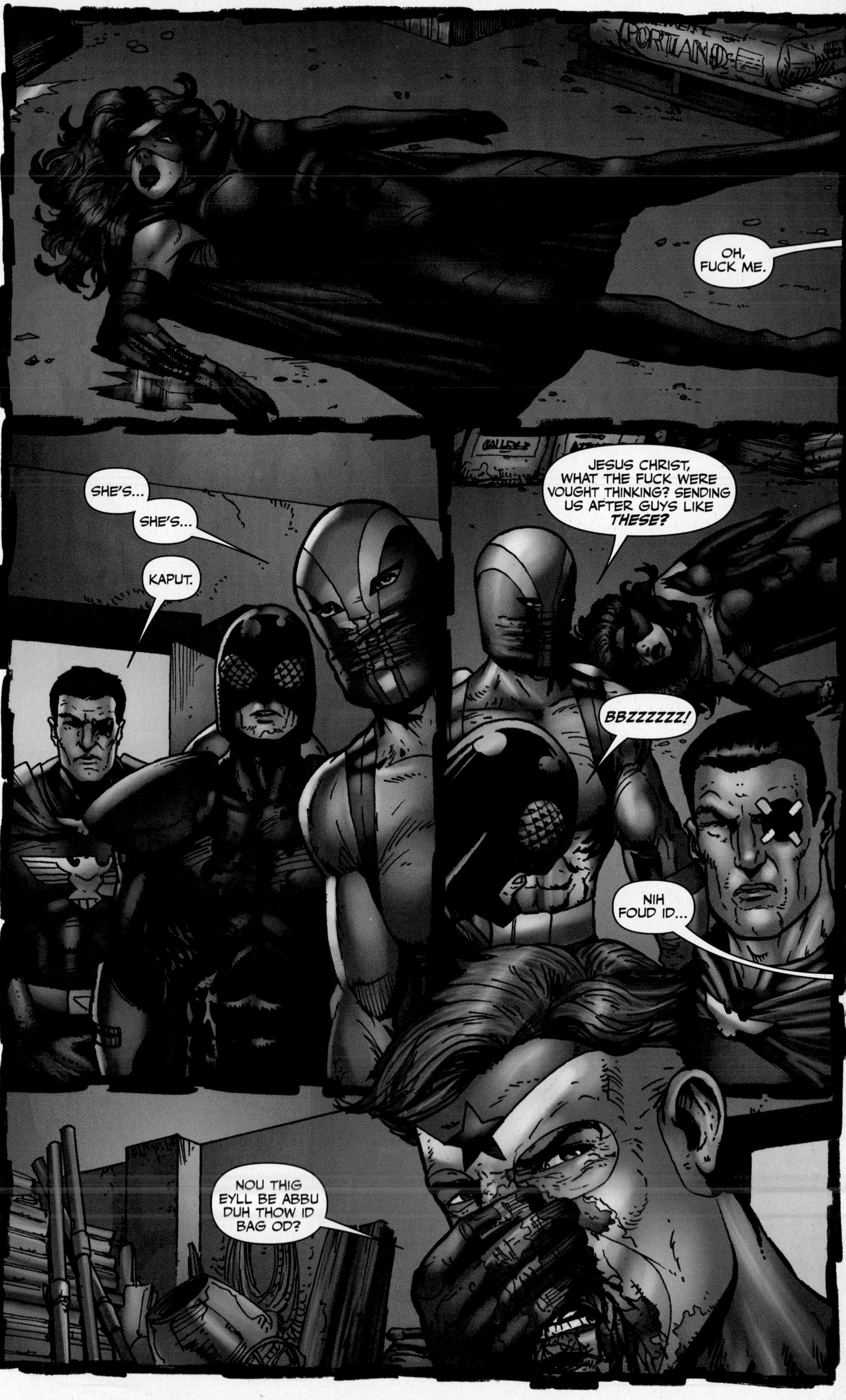
PORTLAND
OH, FUCK ME.
SHE'S...
SHE'S...
KAPUT.
JESUS CHRIST, WHAT THE FUCK WERE VOUGHT THINKING? SENDING US AFTER GUYS LIKE *THESE?*
BBZZZZZZ!
NIH FOUD ID...
NOU THIG EYLL BE ABBU DUH THOW ID BAG OD?

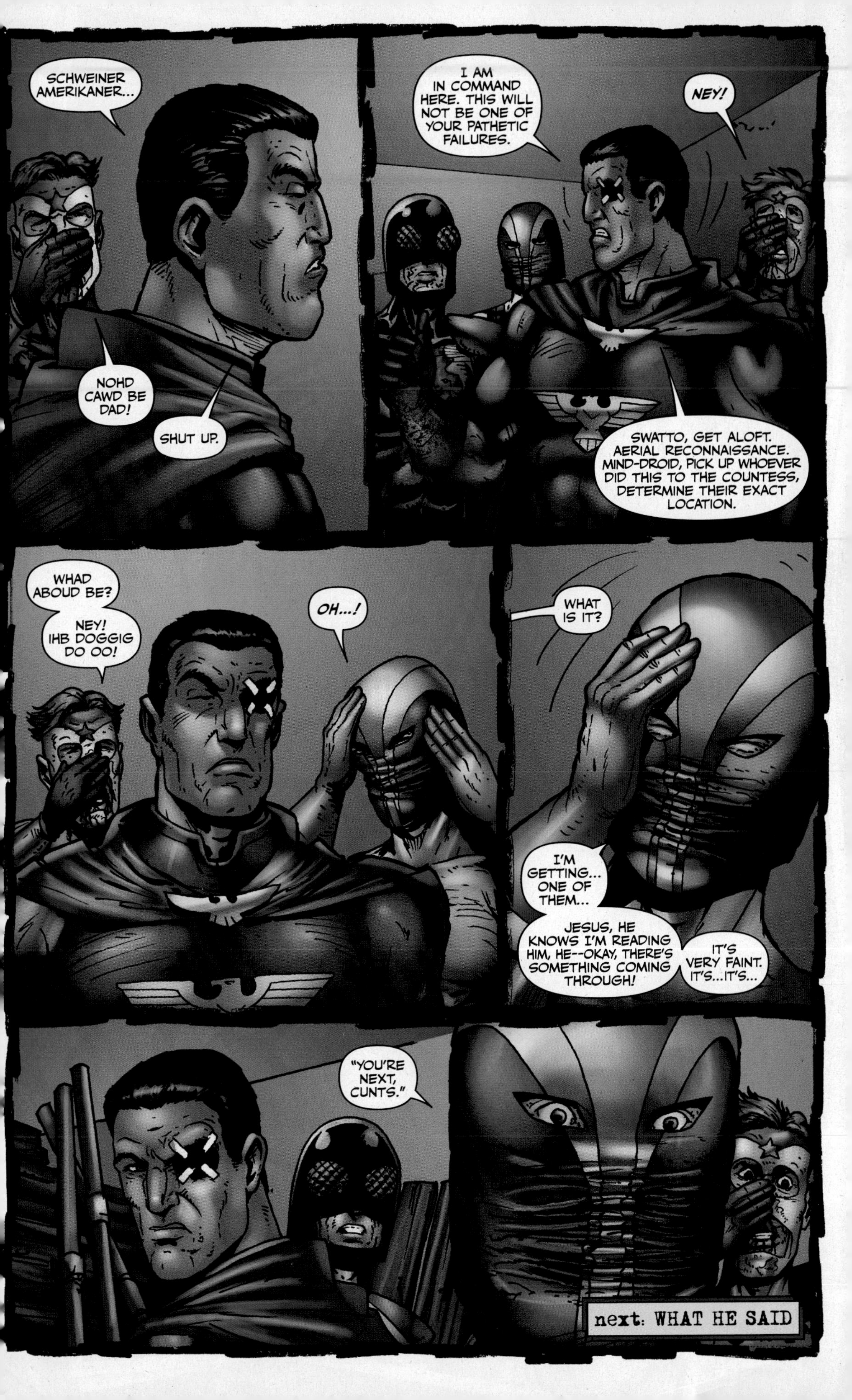
SCHWEINER AMERIKANER...
NOHD CAWD BE DAD!
SHUT UP.
I AM IN COMMAND HERE. THIS WILL NOT BE ONE OF YOUR PATHETIC FAILURES.
NEY!
SWATTO, GET ALOFT. AERIAL RECONNAISSANCE. MIND-DROID, PICK UP WHOEVER DID THIS TO THE COUNTESS, DETERMINE THEIR EXACT LOCATION.
WHAD ABOUD BE?
NEY! IHB DOGGIG DO OO!
OH...!
WHAT IS IT?
I'M GETTING... ONE OF THEM...
JESUS, HE KNOWS I'M READING HIM, HE--OKAY, THERE'S SOMETHING COMING THROUGH!
IT'S VERY FAINT. IT'S...IT'S...
"YOU'RE NEXT, CUNTS."
next: WHAT HE SAID

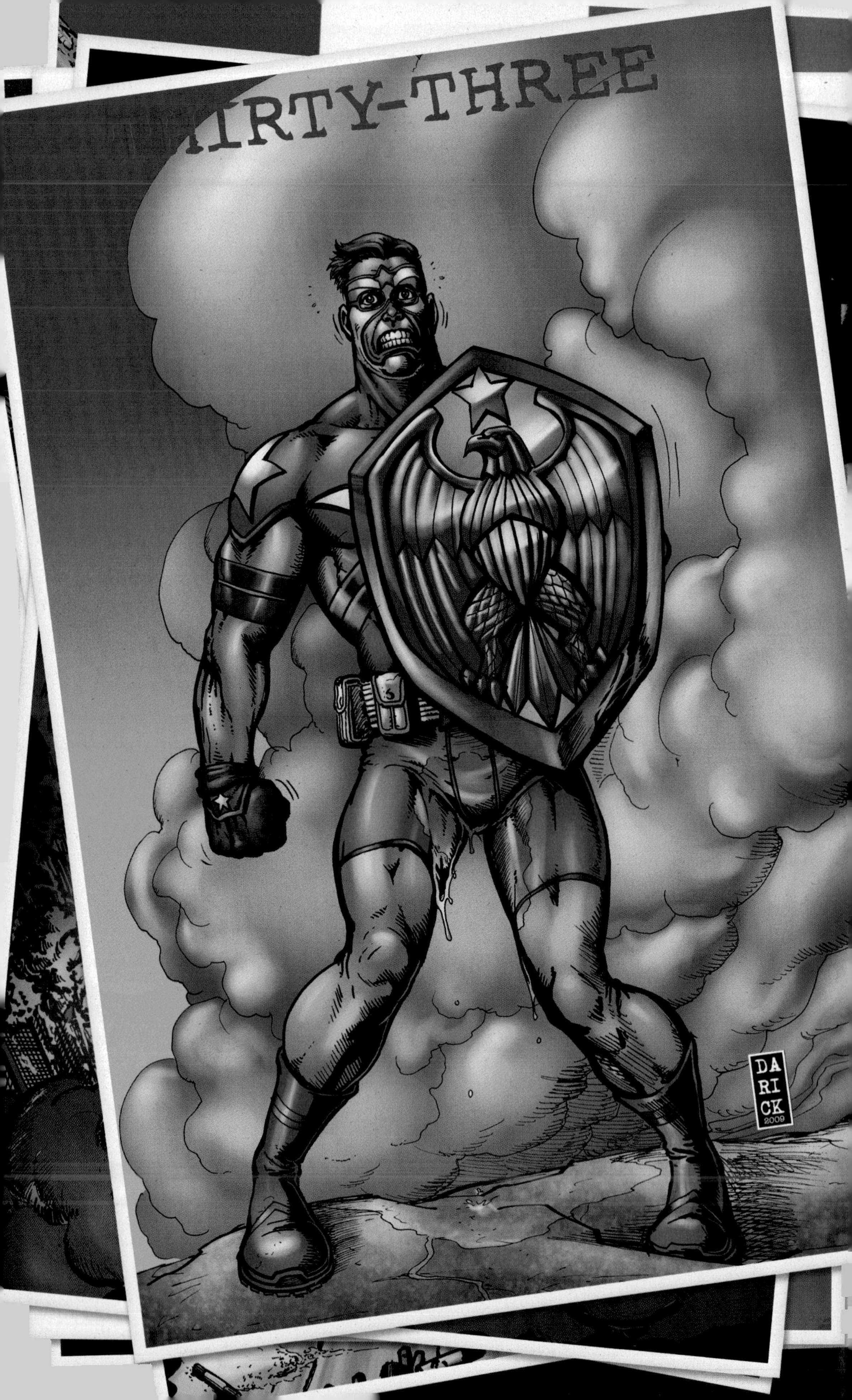

IRTY-THREE
DA
RI
CK
2009

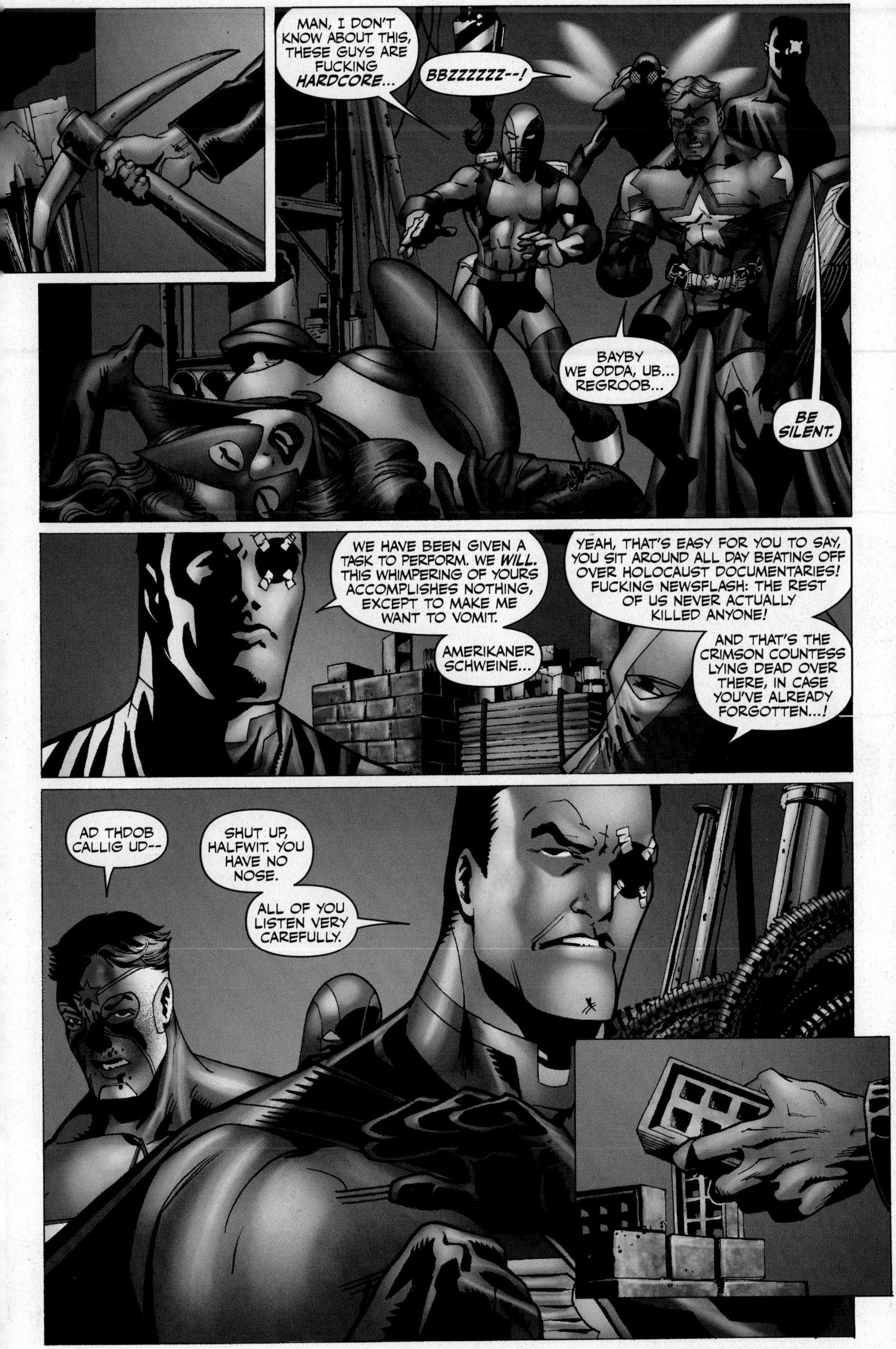

MAN, I DON'T KNOW ABOUT THIS, THESE GUYS ARE FUCKING HARDCORE...
BBZZZZZZ--!
BAYBY WE ODDA, UB... REGROOB...
BE SILENT.
WE HAVE BEEN GIVEN A TASK TO PERFORM. WE WILL. THIS WHIMPERING OF YOURS ACCOMPLISHES NOTHING, EXCEPT TO MAKE ME WANT TO VOMIT.
AMERIKANER SCHWEINE...
YEAH, THAT'S EASY FOR YOU TO SAY, YOU SIT AROUND ALL DAY BEATING OFF OVER HOLOCAUST DOCUMENTARIES! FUCKING NEWSFLASH: THE REST OF US NEVER ACTUALLY KILLED ANYONE!
AND THAT'S THE CRIMSON COUNTESS LYING DEAD OVER THERE, IN CASE YOU'VE ALREADY FORGOTTEN...!
AD THDOB CALLIG UD--
SHUT UP, HALFWIT. YOU HAVE NO NOSE.
ALL OF YOU LISTEN VERY CAREFULLY.

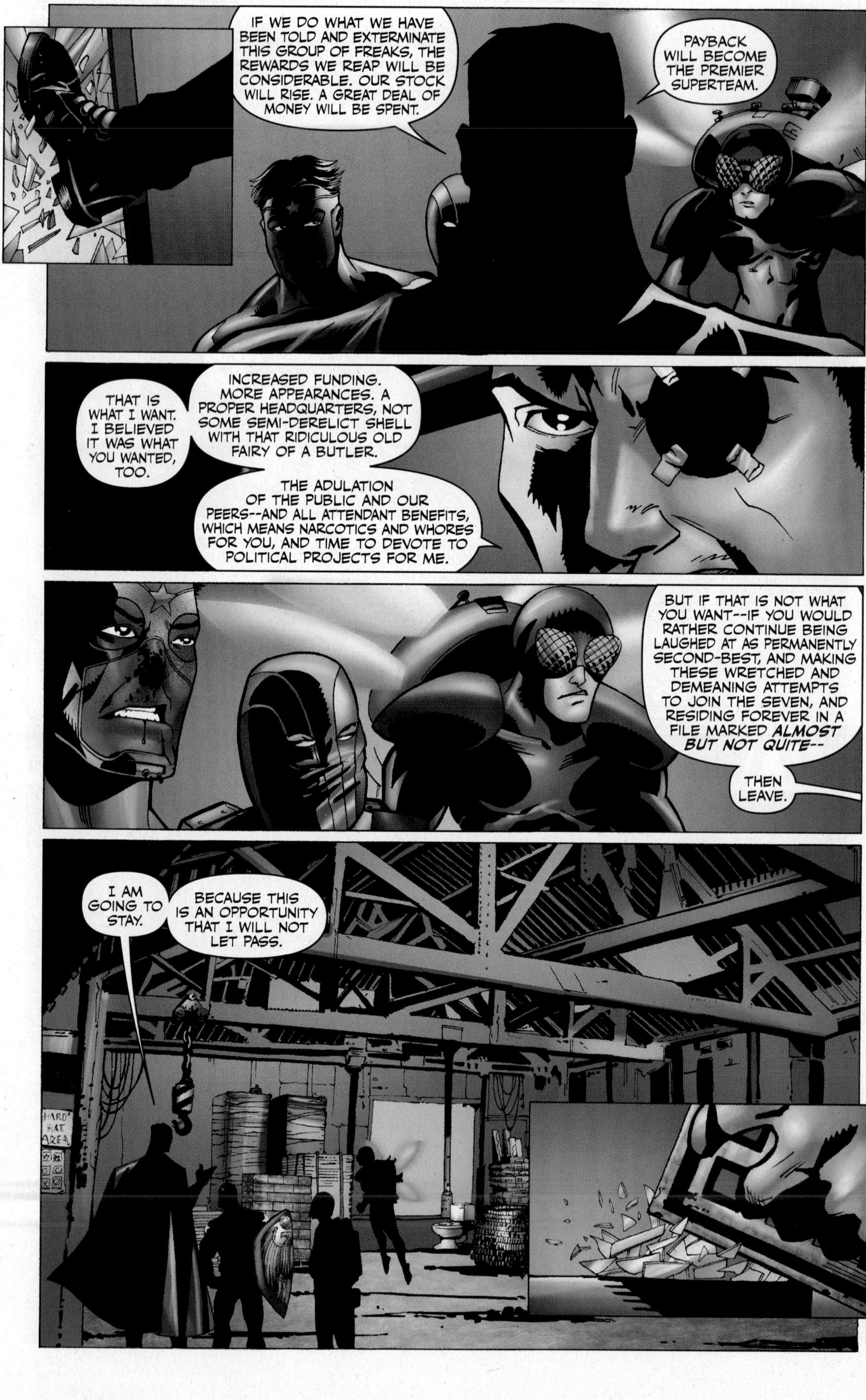
IF WE DO WHAT WE HAVE BEEN TOLD AND EXTERMINATE THIS GROUP OF FREAKS, THE REWARDS WE REAP WILL BE CONSIDERABLE. OUR STOCK WILL RISE. A GREAT DEAL OF MONEY WILL BE SPENT.
PAYBACK WILL BECOME THE PREMIER SUPERTEAM.
INCREASED FUNDING. MORE APPEARANCES. A PROPER HEADQUARTERS, NOT SOME SEMI-DERELICT SHELL WITH THAT RIDICULOUS OLD FAIRY OF A BUTLER.
THE ADULATION OF THE PUBLIC AND OUR PEERS--AND ALL ATTENDANT BENEFITS, WHICH MEANS NARCOTICS AND WHORES FOR YOU, AND TIME TO DEVOTE TO POLITICAL PROJECTS FOR ME.
THAT IS WHAT I WANT. I BELIEVED IT WAS WHAT YOU WANTED, TOO.
BUT IF THAT IS NOT WHAT YOU WANT--IF YOU WOULD RATHER CONTINUE BEING LAUGHED AT AS PERMANENTLY SECOND-BEST, AND MAKING THESE WRETCHED AND DEMEANING ATTEMPTS TO JOIN THE SEVEN, AND RESIDING FOREVER IN A FILE MARKED ***ALMOST BUT NOT QUITE***--
THEN LEAVE.
I AM GOING TO STAY.
BECAUSE THIS IS AN OPPORTUNITY THAT I WILL NOT LET PASS.

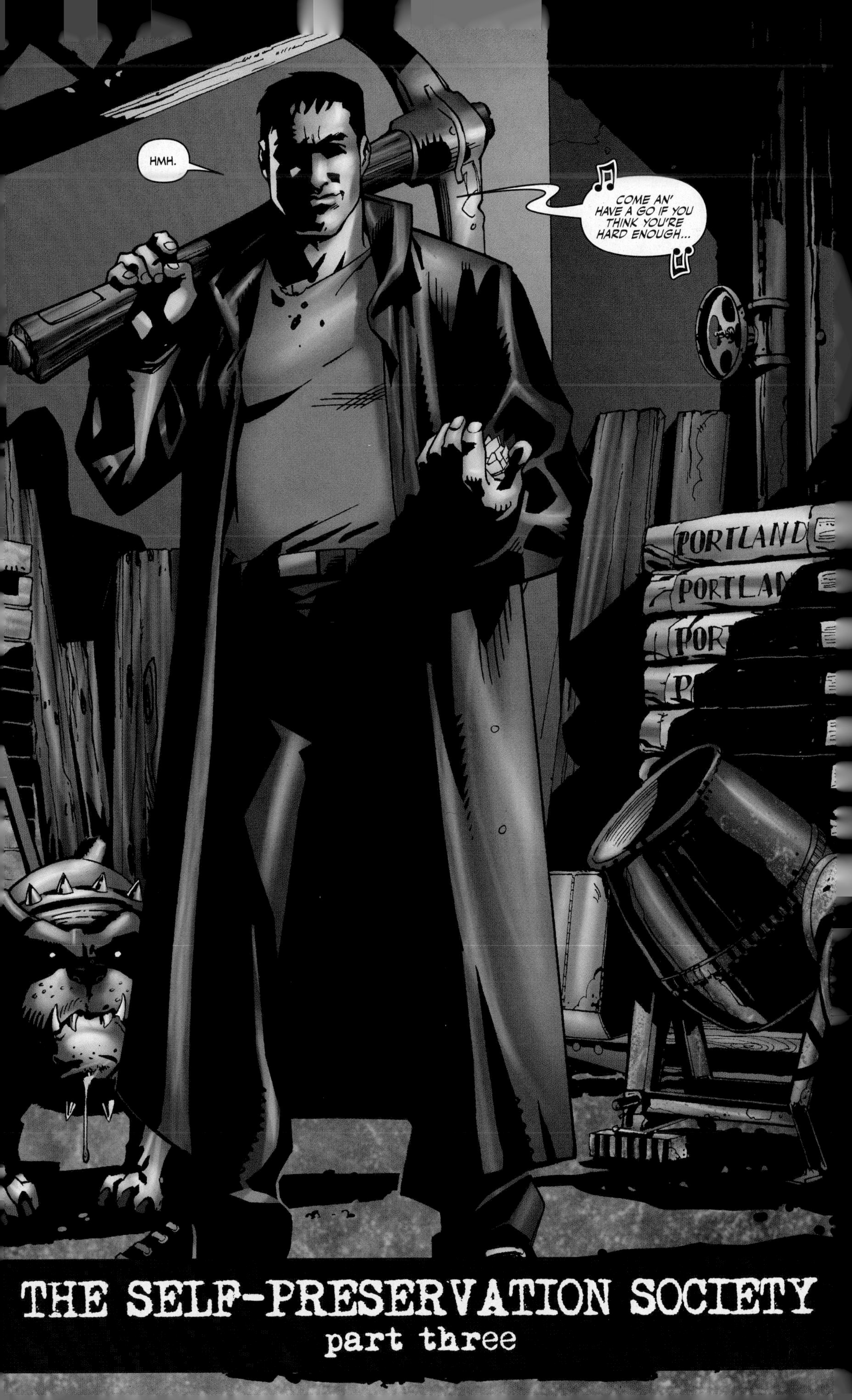
HMH.
COME AN' HAVE A GO IF YOU THINK YOU'RE HARD ENOUGH...
PORTLAND
THE SELF-PRESERVATION SOCIETY
part three

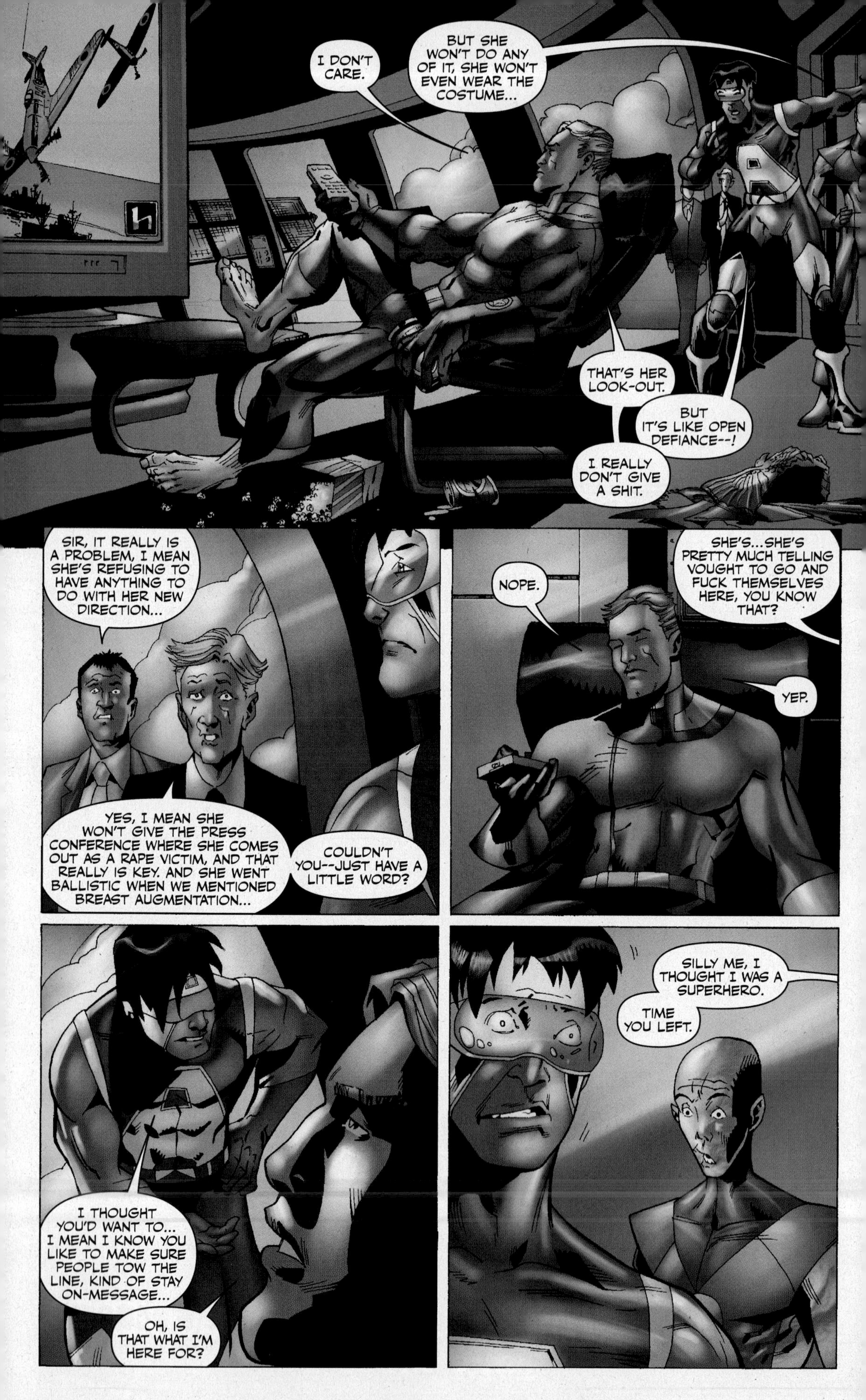
BUT SHE WON'T DO ANY OF IT, SHE WON'T EVEN WEAR THE COSTUME...
I DON'T CARE.
THAT'S HER LOOK-OUT.
BUT IT'S LIKE OPEN DEFIANCE--!
I REALLY DON'T GIVE A SHIT.
SIR, IT REALLY IS A PROBLEM, I MEAN SHE'S REFUSING TO HAVE ANYTHING TO DO WITH HER NEW DIRECTION...
YES, I MEAN SHE WON'T GIVE THE PRESS CONFERENCE WHERE SHE COMES OUT AS A RAPE VICTIM, AND THAT REALLY IS KEY. AND SHE WENT BALLISTIC WHEN WE MENTIONED BREAST AUGMENTATION...
COULDN'T YOU--JUST HAVE A LITTLE WORD?
NOPE.
SHE'S...SHE'S PRETTY MUCH TELLING VOUGHT TO GO AND FUCK THEMSELVES HERE, YOU KNOW THAT?
YEP.
I THOUGHT YOU'D WANT TO... I MEAN I KNOW YOU LIKE TO MAKE SURE PEOPLE TOW THE LINE, KIND OF STAY ON-MESSAGE...
OH, IS THAT WHAT I'M HERE FOR?
SILLY ME, I THOUGHT I WAS A SUPERHERO.
TIME YOU LEFT.

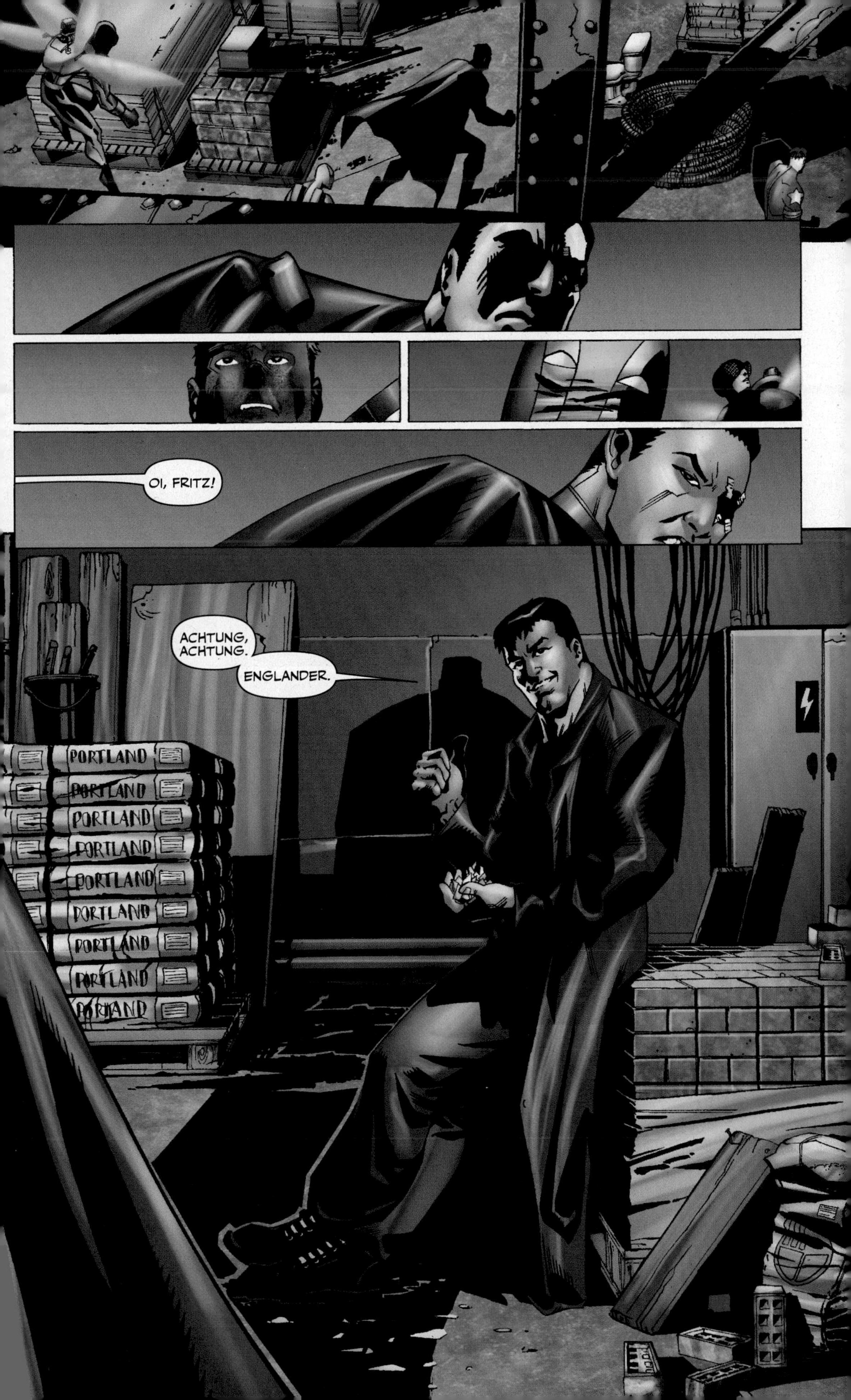
OI, FRITZ!
ACHTUNG, ACHTUNG.
ENGLANDER.
PORTLAND
PORTLAND
PORTLAND
PORTLAND
PORTLAND
PORTLAND
PORTLAND
PORTLAND
PORTLAND

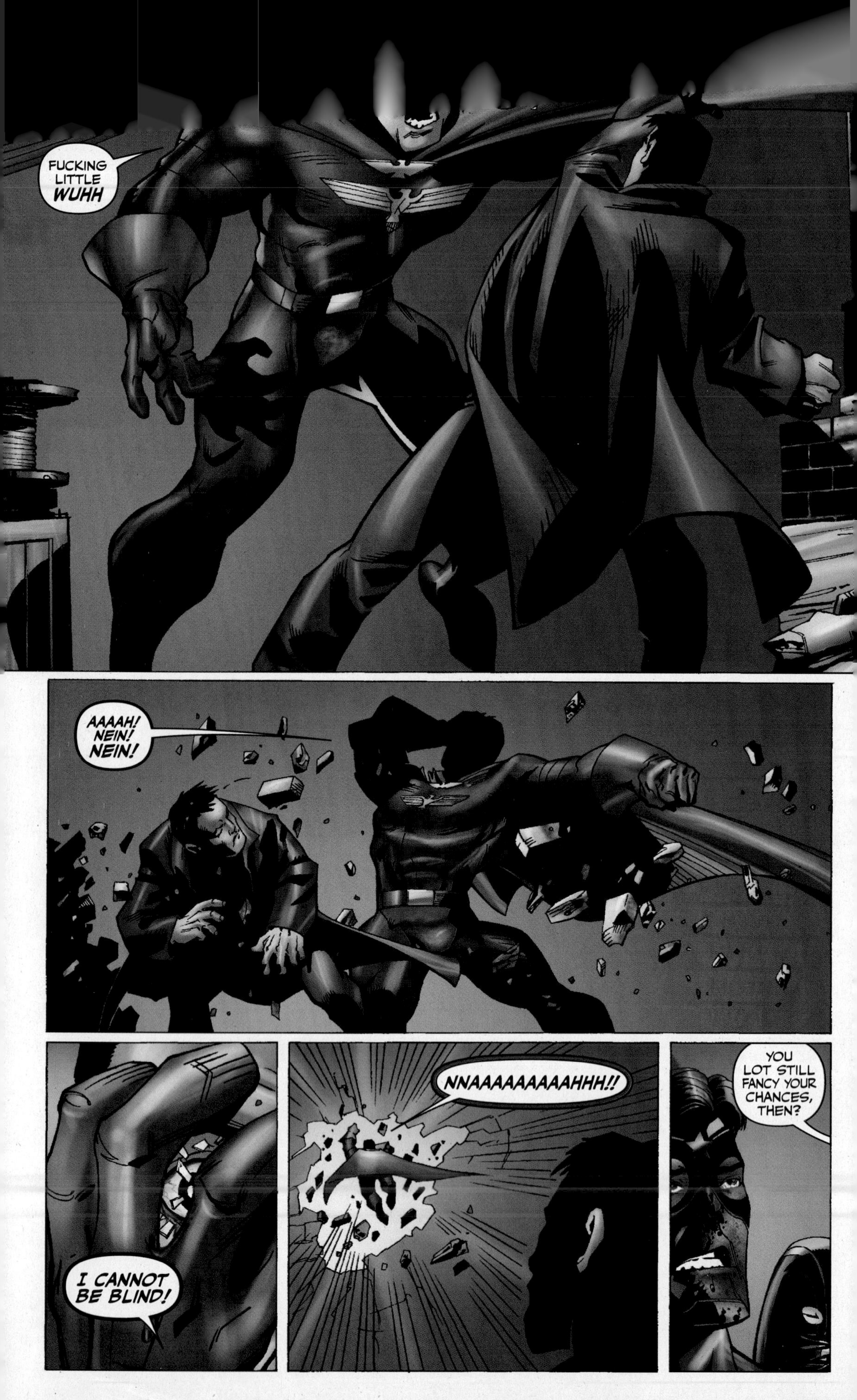
FUCKING LITTLE WUHH
AAAAH! NEIN! NEIN!
I CANNOT BE BLIND!
NNAAAAAAAAAAHHH!!
YOU LOT STILL FANCY YOUR CHANCES, THEN?

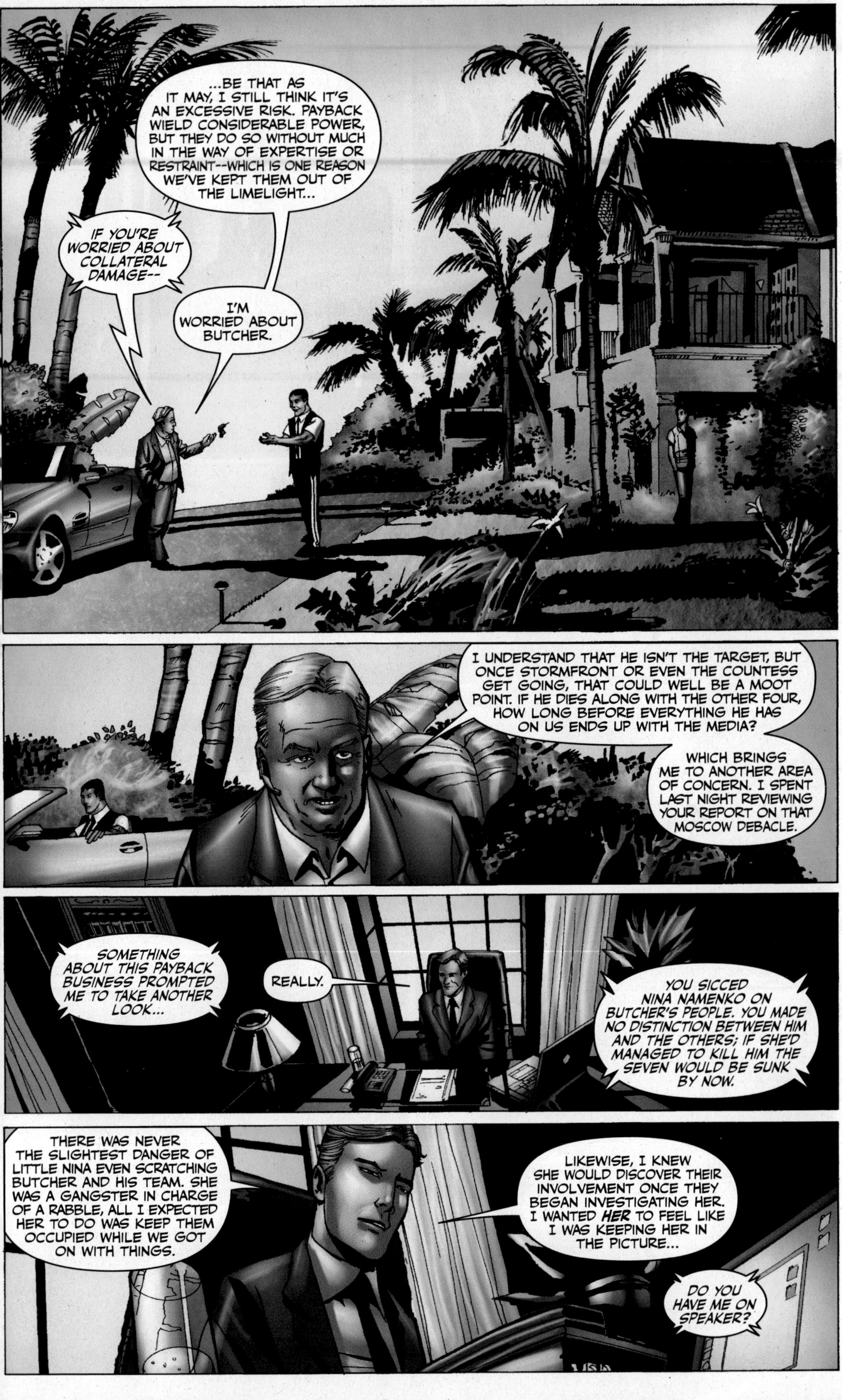
...BE THAT AS IT MAY, I STILL THINK IT'S AN EXCESSIVE RISK. PAYBACK WIELD CONSIDERABLE POWER, BUT THEY DO SO WITHOUT MUCH IN THE WAY OF EXPERTISE OR RESTRAINT--WHICH IS ONE REASON WE'VE KEPT THEM OUT OF THE LIMELIGHT...
IF YOU'RE WORRIED ABOUT COLLATERAL DAMAGE--
I'M WORRIED ABOUT BUTCHER.
I UNDERSTAND THAT HE ISN'T THE TARGET, BUT ONCE STORMFRONT OR EVEN THE COUNTESS GET GOING, THAT COULD WELL BE A MOOT POINT. IF HE DIES ALONG WITH THE OTHER FOUR, HOW LONG BEFORE EVERYTHING HE HAS ON US ENDS UP WITH THE MEDIA?
WHICH BRINGS ME TO ANOTHER AREA OF CONCERN. I SPENT LAST NIGHT REVIEWING YOUR REPORT ON THAT MOSCOW DEBACLE.
SOMETHING ABOUT THIS PAYBACK BUSINESS PROMPTED ME TO TAKE ANOTHER LOOK...
REALLY.
YOU SICCED NINA NAMENKO ON BUTCHER'S PEOPLE. YOU MADE NO DISTINCTION BETWEEN HIM AND THE OTHERS; IF SHE'D MANAGED TO KILL HIM THE SEVEN WOULD BE SUNK BY NOW.
THERE WAS NEVER THE SLIGHTEST DANGER OF LITTLE NINA EVEN SCRATCHING BUTCHER AND HIS TEAM. SHE WAS A GANGSTER IN CHARGE OF A RABBLE, ALL I EXPECTED HER TO DO WAS KEEP THEM OCCUPIED WHILE WE GOT ON WITH THINGS.
LIKEWISE, I KNEW SHE WOULD DISCOVER THEIR INVOLVEMENT ONCE THEY BEGAN INVESTIGATING HER. I WANTED **HER** TO FEEL LIKE I WAS KEEPING HER IN THE PICTURE...
DO YOU HAVE ME ON SPEAKER?

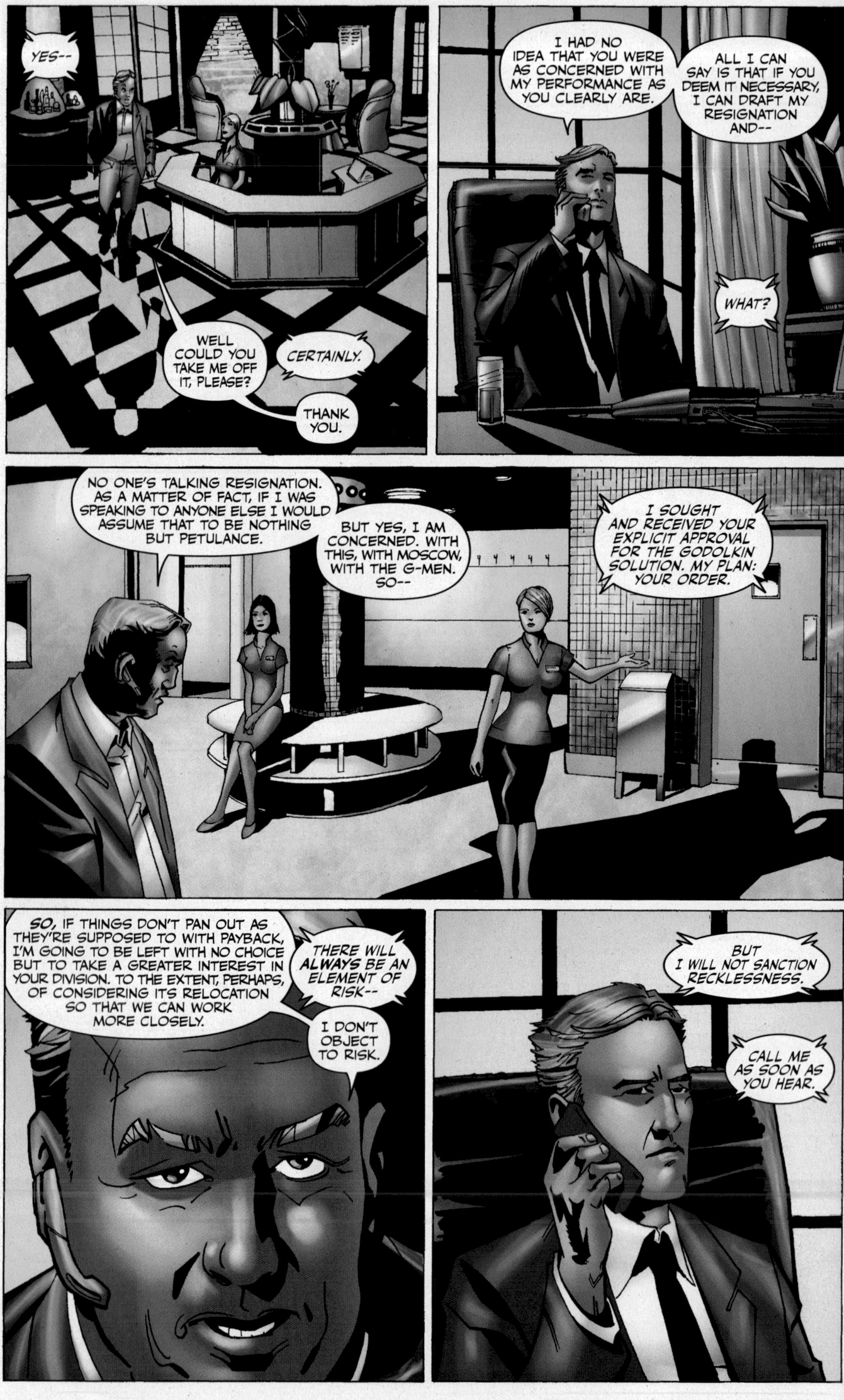
YES--
WELL COULD YOU TAKE ME OFF IT, PLEASE?
CERTAINLY.
THANK YOU.
I HAD NO IDEA THAT YOU WERE AS CONCERNED WITH MY PERFORMANCE AS YOU CLEARLY ARE.
ALL I CAN SAY IS THAT IF YOU DEEM IT NECESSARY, I CAN DRAFT MY RESIGNATION AND--
WHAT?
NO ONE'S TALKING RESIGNATION. AS A MATTER OF FACT, IF I WAS SPEAKING TO ANYONE ELSE I WOULD ASSUME THAT TO BE NOTHING BUT PETULANCE.
BUT YES, I AM CONCERNED. WITH THIS, WITH MOSCOW, WITH THE G-MEN. SO--
I SOUGHT AND RECEIVED YOUR EXPLICIT APPROVAL FOR THE GODOLKIN SOLUTION. MY PLAN: YOUR ORDER.
SO, IF THINGS DON'T PAN OUT AS THEY'RE SUPPOSED TO WITH PAYBACK, I'M GOING TO BE LEFT WITH NO CHOICE BUT TO TAKE A GREATER INTEREST IN YOUR DIVISION. TO THE EXTENT, PERHAPS, OF CONSIDERING ITS RELOCATION SO THAT WE CAN WORK MORE CLOSELY.
THERE WILL ALWAYS BE AN ELEMENT OF RISK--
I DON'T OBJECT TO RISK.
BUT I WILL NOT SANCTION RECKLESSNESS.
CALL ME AS SOON AS YOU HEAR.

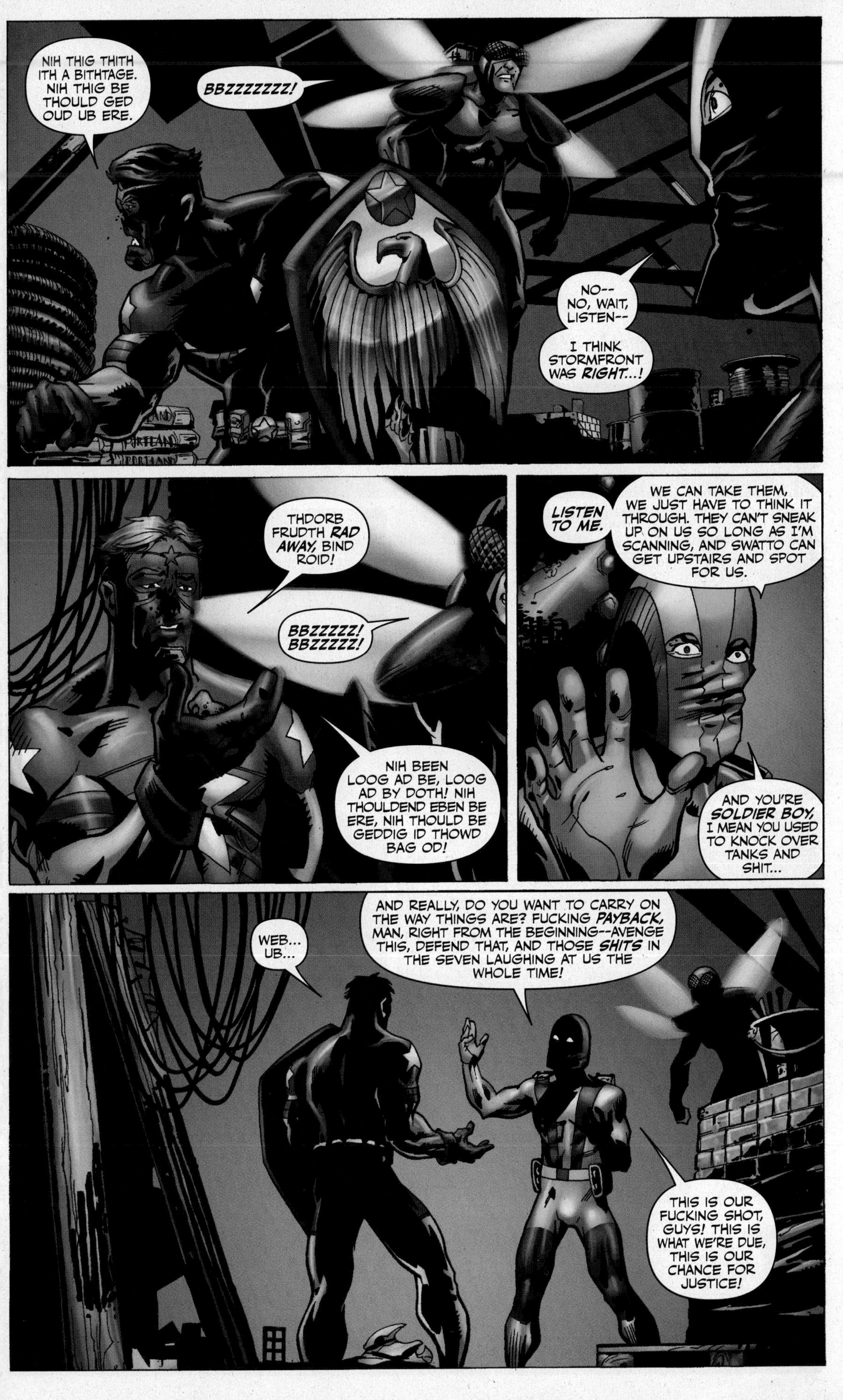
NIH THIG THITH ITH A BITHTAGE. NIH THIG BE THOULD GED OUD UB ERE.
BBZZZZZZZ!
NO-- NO, WAIT, LISTEN--
I THINK STORMFRONT WAS RIGHT...!
THDORB FRUDTH RAD AWAY, BIND ROID!
BBZZZZZ! BBZZZZZ!
NIH BEEN LOOG AD BE, LOOG AD BY DOTH! NIH THOULDEND EBEN BE ERE, NIH THOULD BE GEDDIG ID THOWD BAG OD!
LISTEN TO ME.
WE CAN TAKE THEM, WE JUST HAVE TO THINK IT THROUGH. THEY CAN'T SNEAK UP ON US SO LONG AS I'M SCANNING, AND SWATTO CAN GET UPSTAIRS AND SPOT FOR US.
AND YOU'RE SOLDIER BOY, I MEAN YOU USED TO KNOCK OVER TANKS AND SHIT...
WEB... UB...
AND REALLY, DO YOU WANT TO CARRY ON THE WAY THINGS ARE? FUCKING PAYBACK, MAN, RIGHT FROM THE BEGINNING--AVENGE THIS, DEFEND THAT, AND THOSE SHITS IN THE SEVEN LAUGHING AT US THE WHOLE TIME!
THIS IS OUR FUCKING SHOT, GUYS! THIS IS WHAT WE'RE DUE, THIS IS OUR CHANCE FOR JUSTICE!

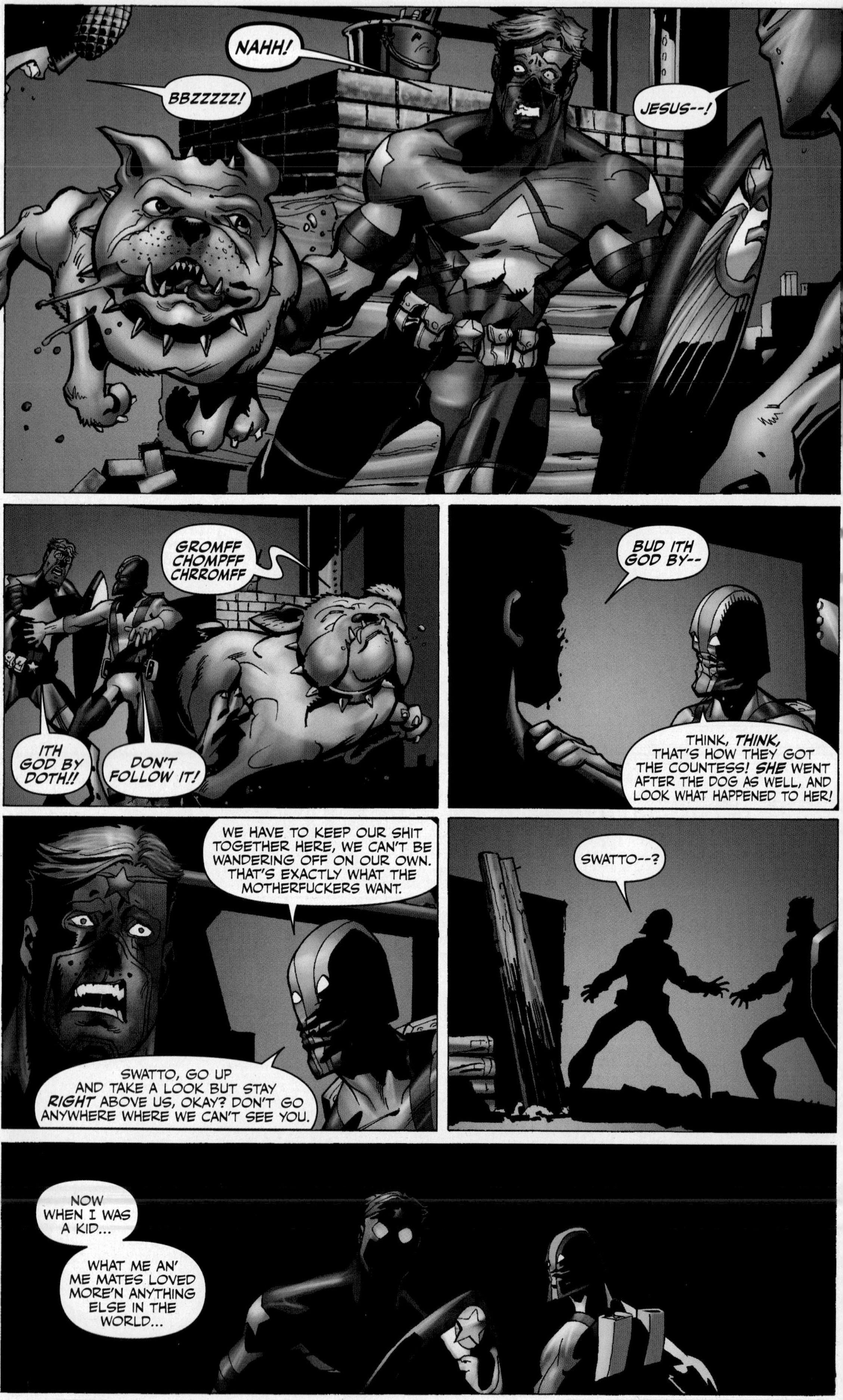
NAHH!
BBZZZZZ!
JESUS--!
GROMFF CHOMPFF CHRROMFF
ITH GOD BY DOTH!!
DON'T FOLLOW IT!
BUD ITH GOD BY--
THINK, THINK, THAT'S HOW THEY GOT THE COUNTESS! SHE WENT AFTER THE DOG AS WELL, AND LOOK WHAT HAPPENED TO HER!
WE HAVE TO KEEP OUR SHIT TOGETHER HERE, WE CAN'T BE WANDERING OFF ON OUR OWN. THAT'S EXACTLY WHAT THE MOTHERFUCKERS WANT.
SWATTO, GO UP AND TAKE A LOOK BUT STAY RIGHT ABOVE US, OKAY? DON'T GO ANYWHERE WHERE WE CAN'T SEE YOU.
SWATTO--?
NOW WHEN I WAS A KID...
WHAT ME AN' ME MATES LOVED MORE'N ANYTHING ELSE IN THE WORLD...

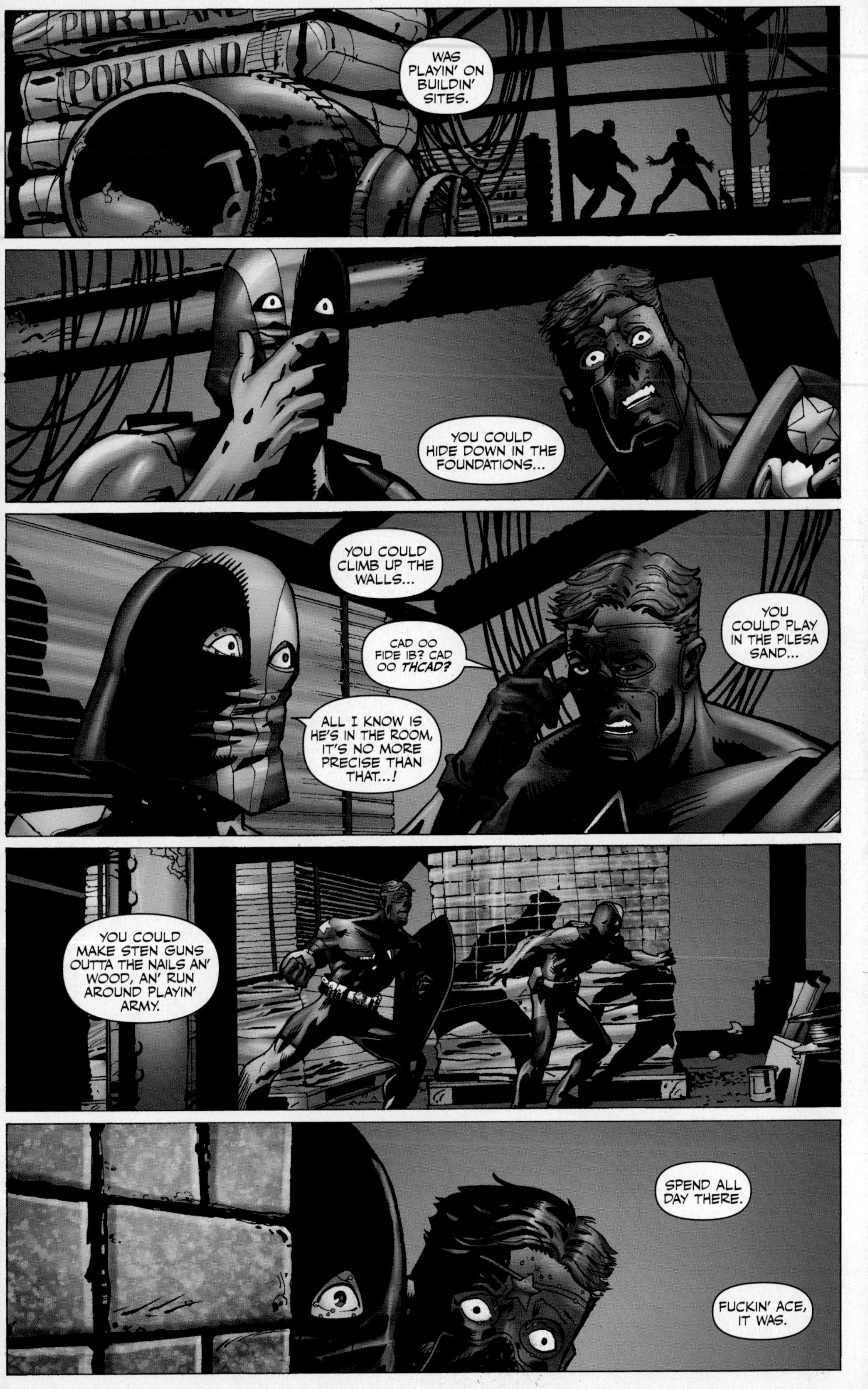
PORTLAND
WAS PLAYIN' ON BUILDIN' SITES.
YOU COULD HIDE DOWN IN THE FOUNDATIONS...
YOU COULD CLIMB UP THE WALLS...
CAD OO FIDE IB? CAD OO THCAD?
ALL I KNOW IS HE'S IN THE ROOM, IT'S NO MORE PRECISE THAN THAT...!
YOU COULD PLAY IN THE PILESA SAND...
YOU COULD MAKE STEN GUNS OUTTA THE NAILS AN' WOOD, AN' RUN AROUND PLAYIN' ARMY.
SPEND ALL DAY THERE.
FUCKIN' ACE, IT WAS.

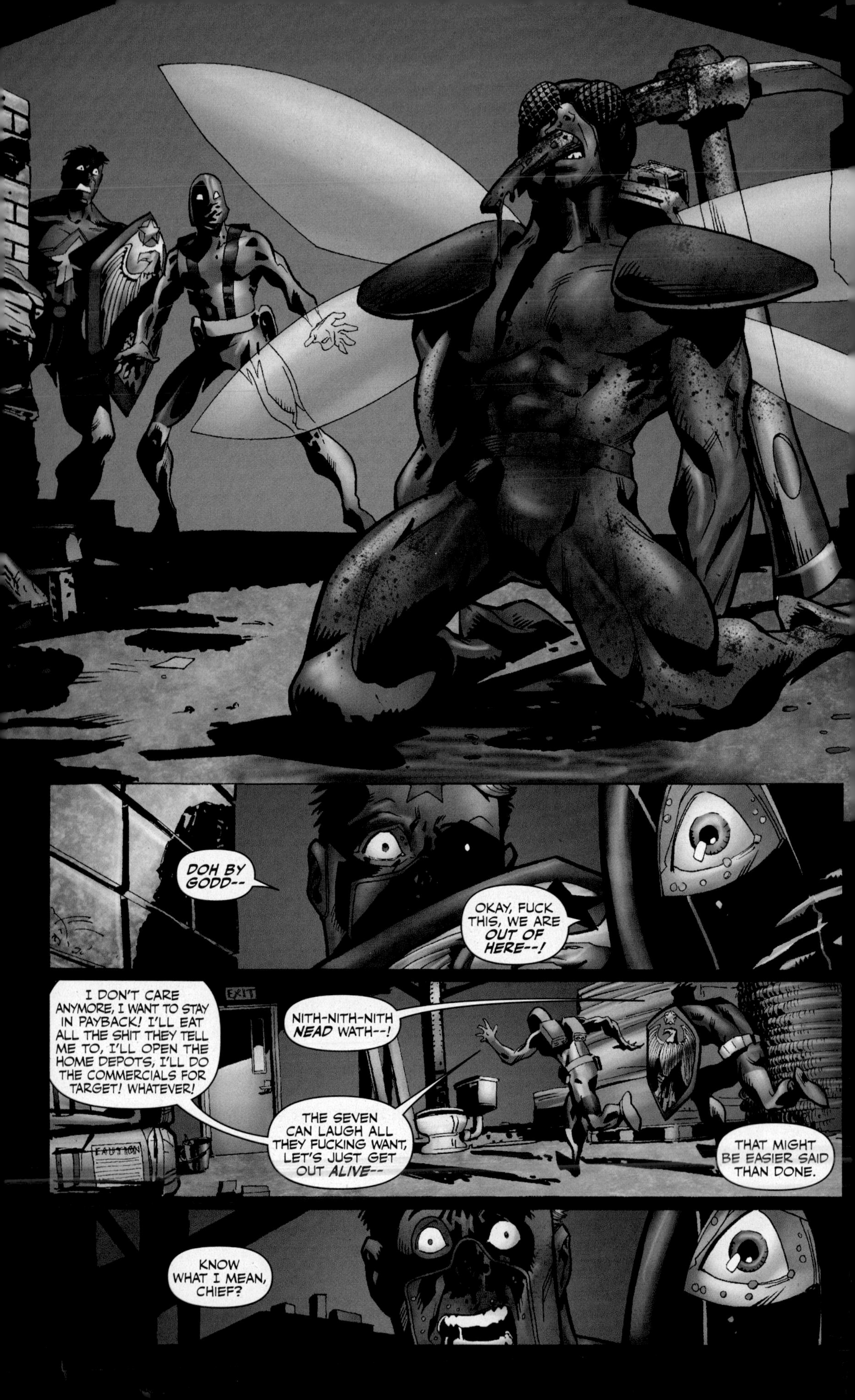
DOH BY GODD--
OKAY, FUCK THIS, WE ARE OUT OF HERE--!
I DON'T CARE ANYMORE, I WANT TO STAY IN PAYBACK! I'LL EAT ALL THE SHIT THEY TELL ME TO, I'LL OPEN THE HOME DEPOTS, I'LL DO THE COMMERCIALS FOR TARGET! WHATEVER!
NITH-NITH-NITH NEAD WATH--!
THE SEVEN CAN LAUGH ALL THEY FUCKING WANT, LET'S JUST GET OUT ALIVE--
THAT MIGHT BE EASIER SAID THAN DONE.
KNOW WHAT I MEAN, CHIEF?

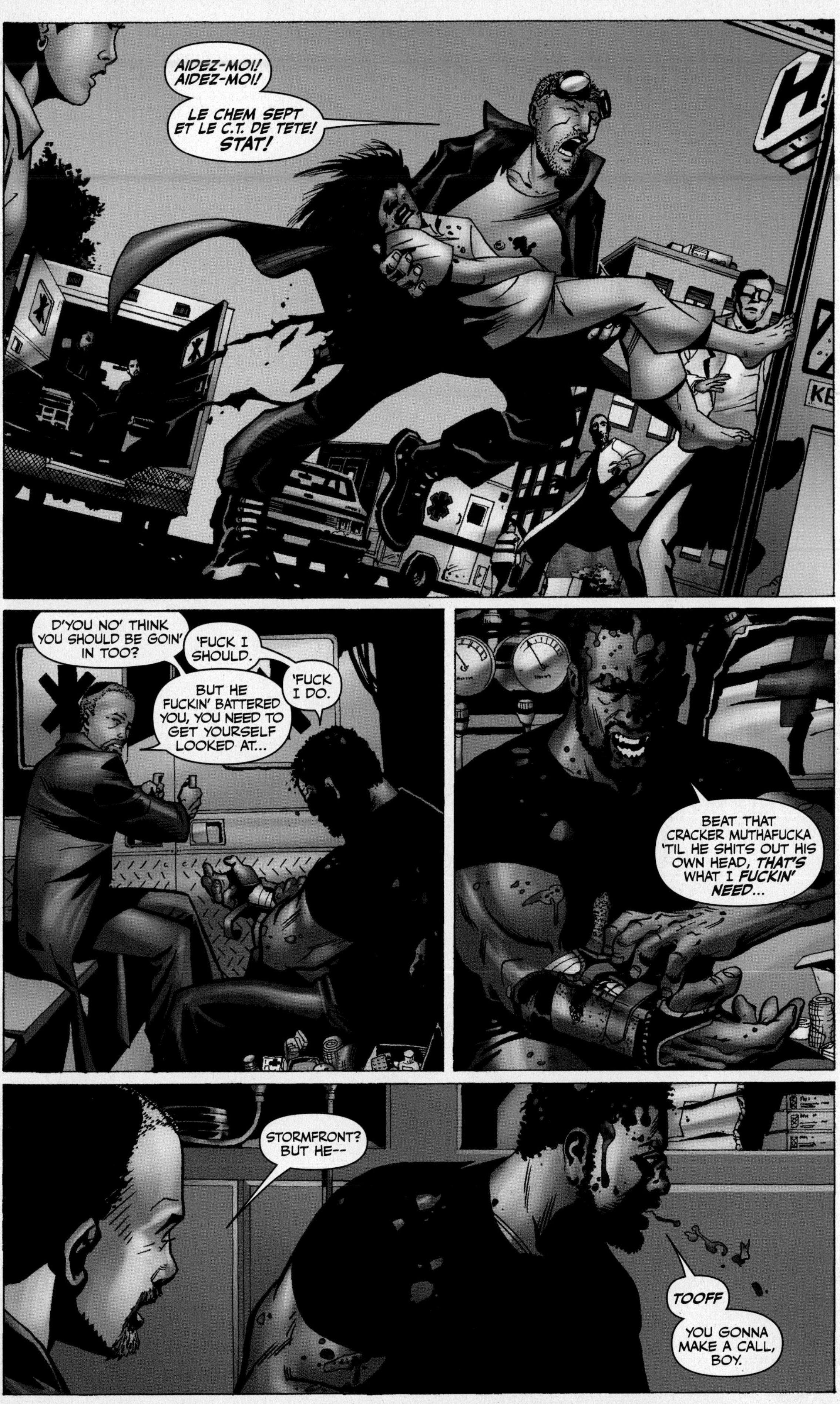
AIDEZ-MOI! AIDEZ-MOI!
LE CHEM SEPT ET LE C.T. DE TETE! STAT!
D'YOU NO' THINK YOU SHOULD BE GOIN' IN TOO?
'FUCK I SHOULD.
BUT HE FUCKIN' BATTERED YOU, YOU NEED TO GET YOURSELF LOOKED AT...
'FUCK I DO.
BEAT THAT CRACKER MUTHAFUCKA 'TIL HE SHITS OUT HIS OWN HEAD, THAT'S WHAT I FUCKIN' NEED...
STORMFRONT? BUT HE--
TOOFF
YOU GONNA MAKE A CALL, BOY.

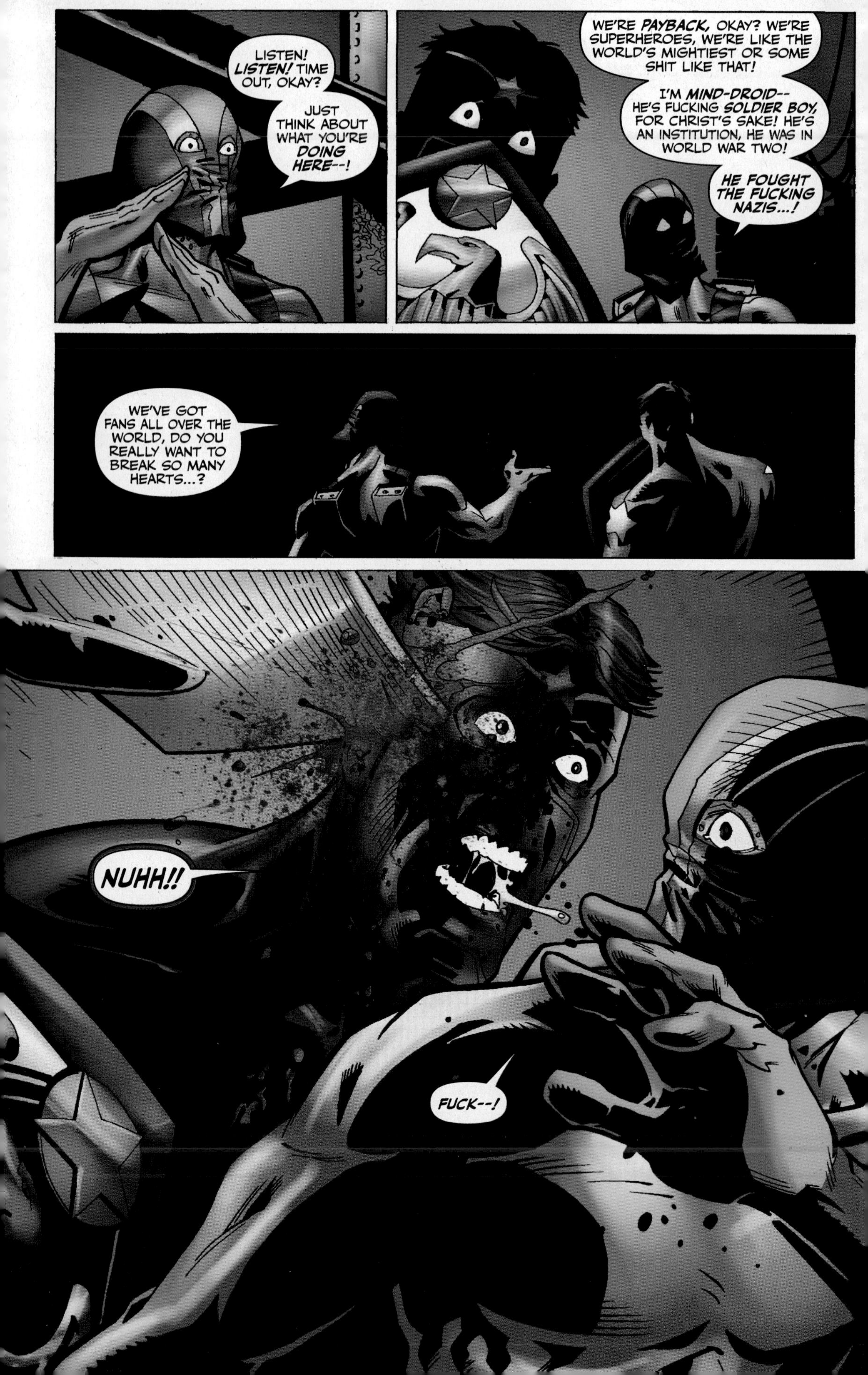
LISTEN! LISTEN! TIME OUT, OKAY?
JUST THINK ABOUT WHAT YOU'RE DOING HERE--!
WE'RE PAYBACK, OKAY? WE'RE SUPERHEROES, WE'RE LIKE THE WORLD'S MIGHTIEST OR SOME SHIT LIKE THAT!
I'M MIND-DROID-- HE'S FUCKING SOLDIER BOY, FOR CHRIST'S SAKE! HE'S AN INSTITUTION, HE WAS IN WORLD WAR TWO!
HE FOUGHT THE FUCKING NAZIS...!
WE'VE GOT FANS ALL OVER THE WORLD, DO YOU REALLY WANT TO BREAK SO MANY HEARTS...?
NUHH!!
FUCK--!

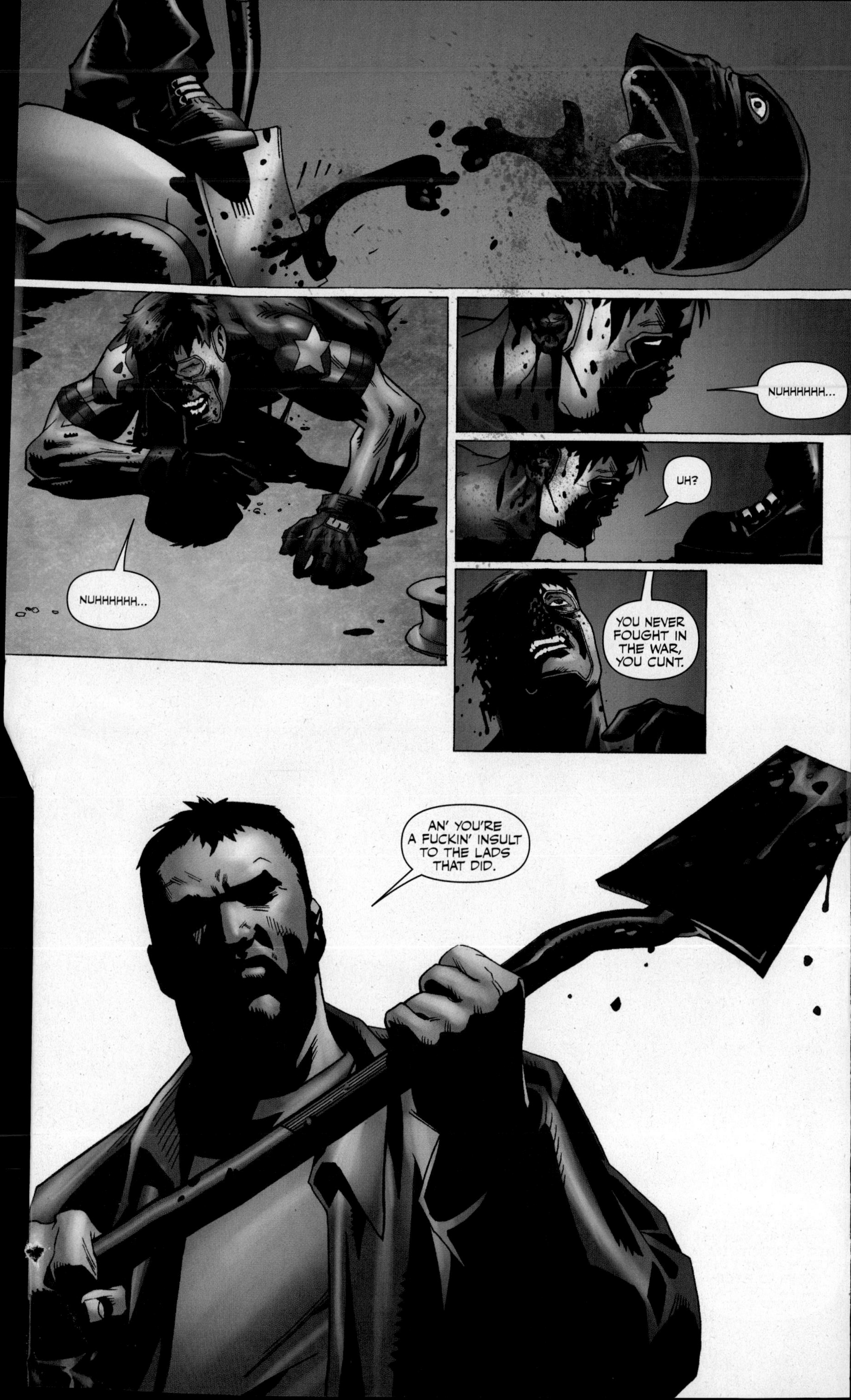
NUHHHHHH...
NUHHHHHH...
UH?
YOU NEVER FOUGHT IN THE WAR, YOU CUNT.
AN' YOU'RE A FUCKIN' INSULT TO THE LADS THAT DID.

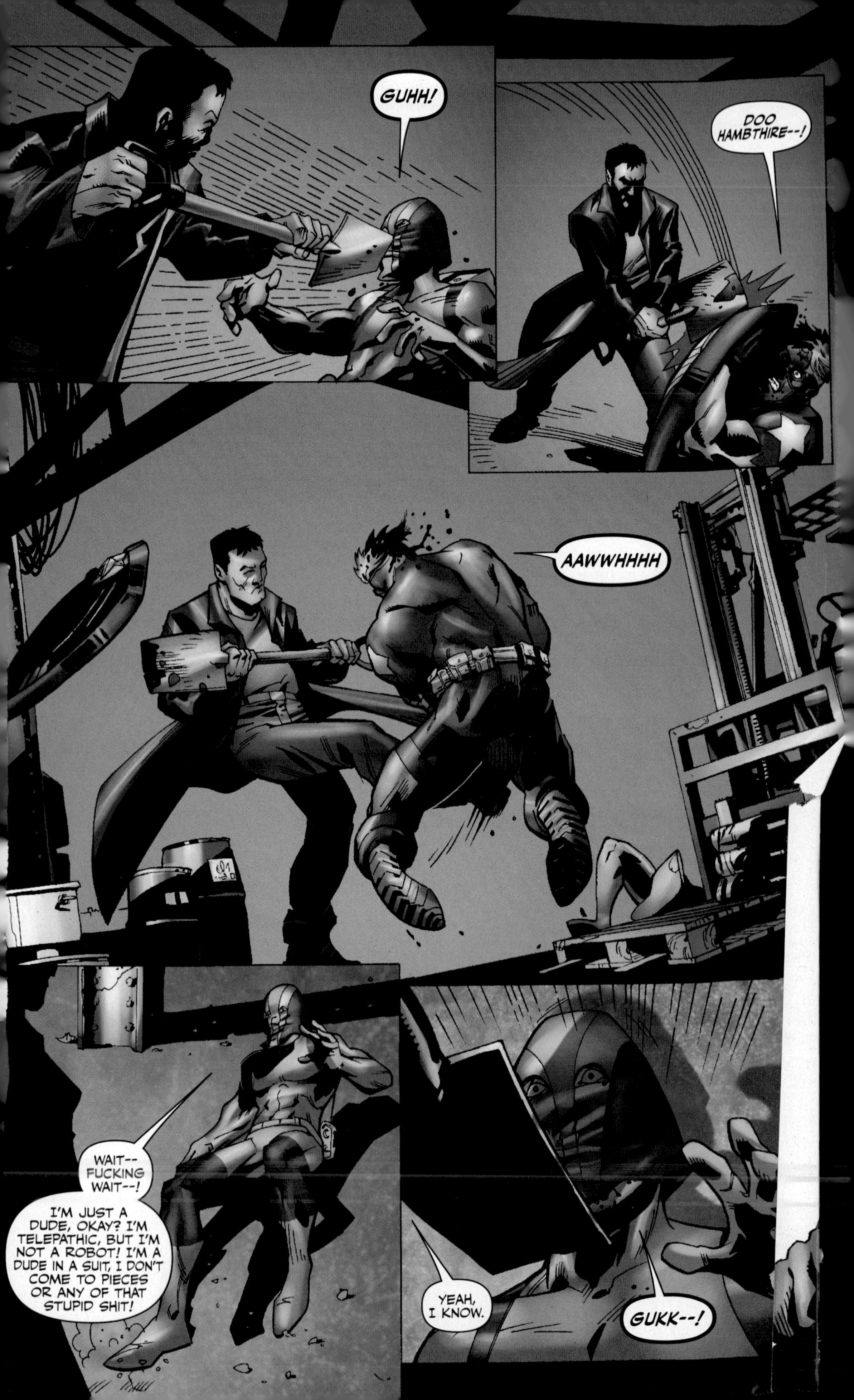
GUHH!
DOO HAMBTHIRE--!
AAWWHHHH
WAIT-- FUCKING WAIT--!
I'M JUST A DUDE, OKAY? I'M TELEPATHIC, BUT I'M NOT A ROBOT! I'M A DUDE IN A SUIT, I DON'T COME TO PIECES OR ANY OF THAT STUPID SHIT!
YEAH, I KNOW.
GUKK--!

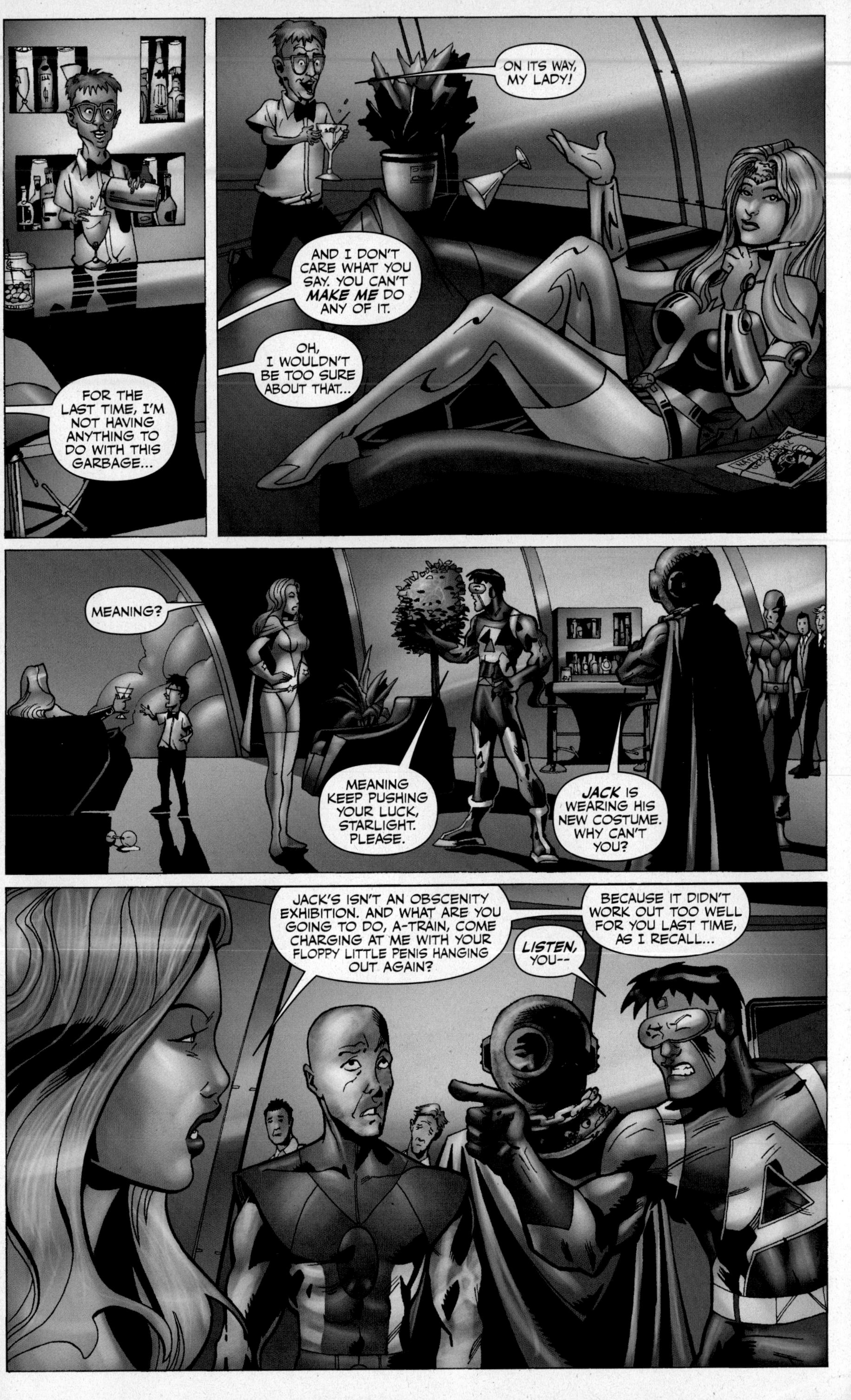

ON ITS WAY, MY LADY!
FOR THE LAST TIME, I'M NOT HAVING ANYTHING TO DO WITH THIS GARBAGE...
AND I DON'T CARE WHAT YOU SAY. YOU CAN'T *MAKE ME* DO ANY OF IT.
OH, I WOULDN'T BE TOO SURE ABOUT THAT...
MEANING?
MEANING KEEP PUSHING YOUR LUCK, STARLIGHT. PLEASE.
JACK IS WEARING HIS NEW COSTUME. WHY CAN'T YOU?
JACK'S ISN'T AN OBSCENITY EXHIBITION. AND WHAT ARE YOU GOING TO DO, A-TRAIN, COME CHARGING AT ME WITH YOUR FLOPPY LITTLE PENIS HANGING OUT AGAIN?
LISTEN, YOU--
BECAUSE IT DIDN'T WORK OUT TOO WELL FOR YOU LAST TIME, AS I RECALL...

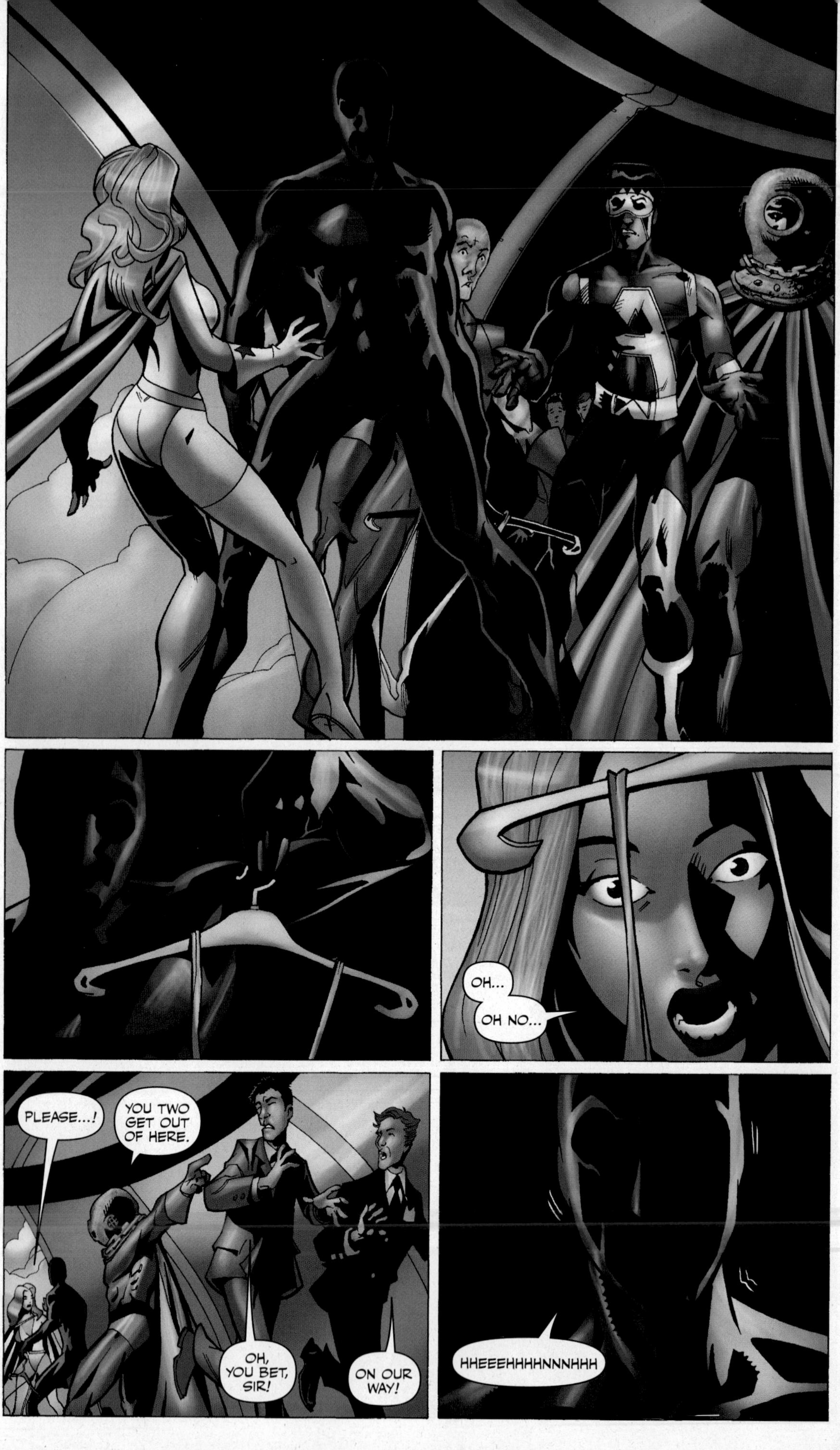
OH...
OH NO...
PLEASE...!
YOU TWO GET OUT OF HERE.
OH, YOU BET, SIR!
ON OUR WAY!
HHEEEHHHHNNNHHH

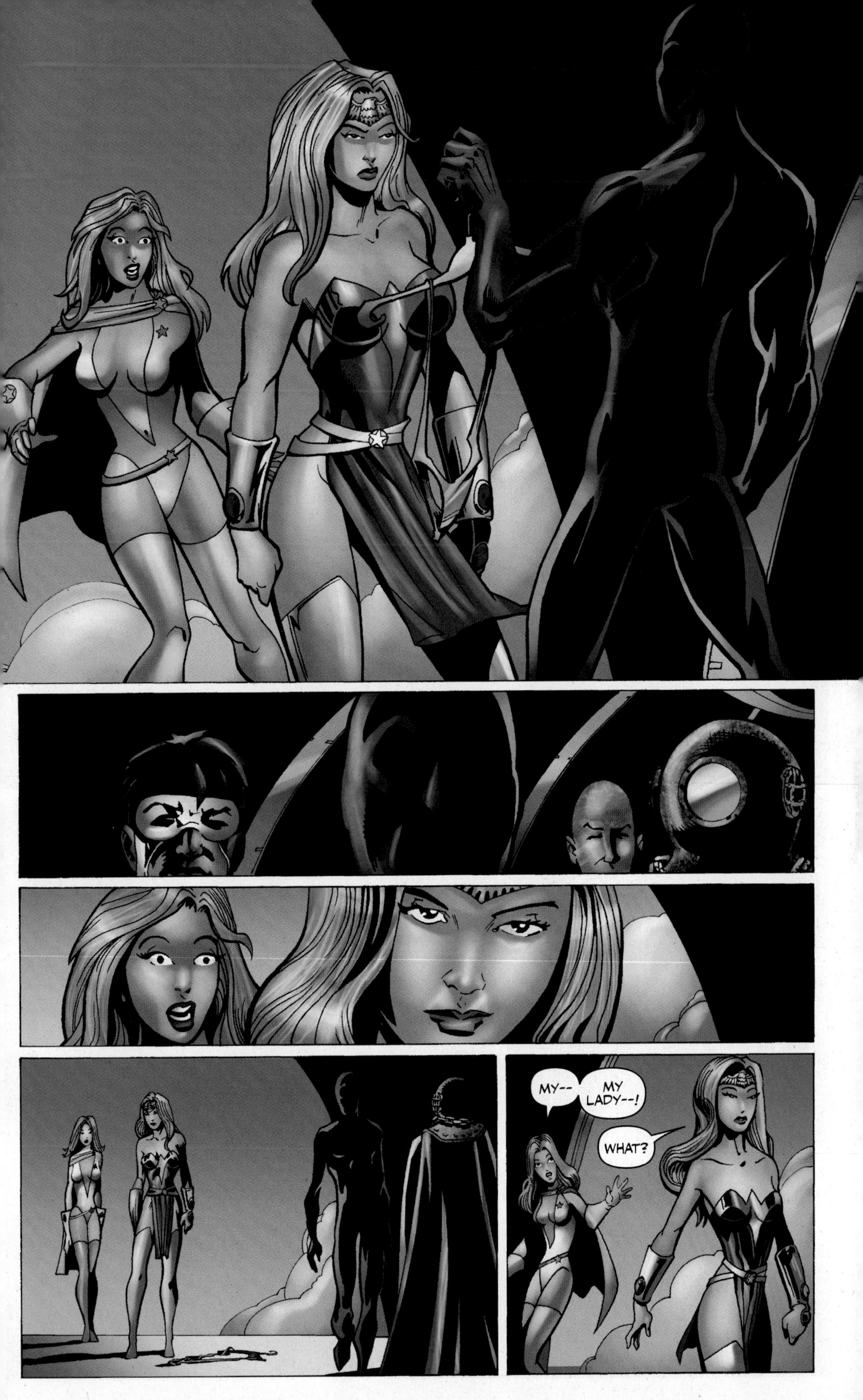
MY--
MY LADY--!
WHAT?

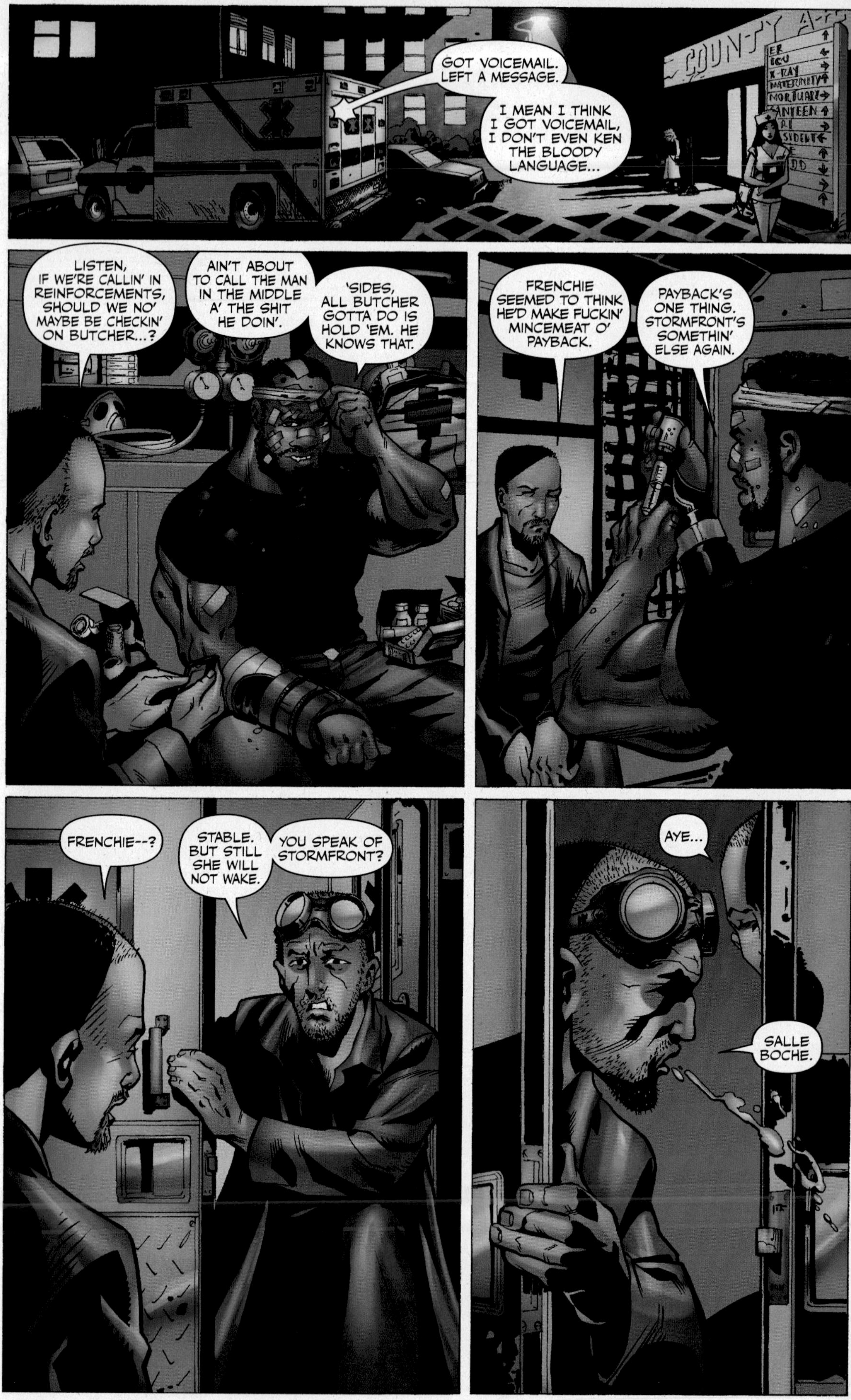

GOT VOICEMAIL. LEFT A MESSAGE.
I MEAN I THINK I GOT VOICEMAIL, I DON'T EVEN KEN THE BLOODY LANGUAGE...
COUNTY
ER
ICU
X-RAY
MATERNITY
MORTUARY
CANTEEN
LISTEN, IF WE'RE CALLIN' IN REINFORCEMENTS, SHOULD WE NO' MAYBE BE CHECKIN' ON BUTCHER...?
AIN'T ABOUT TO CALL THE MAN IN THE MIDDLE A' THE SHIT HE DOIN'.
'SIDES, ALL BUTCHER GOTTA DO IS HOLD 'EM. HE KNOWS THAT.
FRENCHIE SEEMED TO THINK HE'D MAKE FUCKIN' MINCEMEAT O' PAYBACK.
PAYBACK'S ONE THING. STORMFRONT'S SOMETHIN' ELSE AGAIN.
FRENCHIE--?
STABLE. BUT STILL SHE WILL NOT WAKE.
YOU SPEAK OF STORMFRONT?
AYE...
SALLE BOCHE.

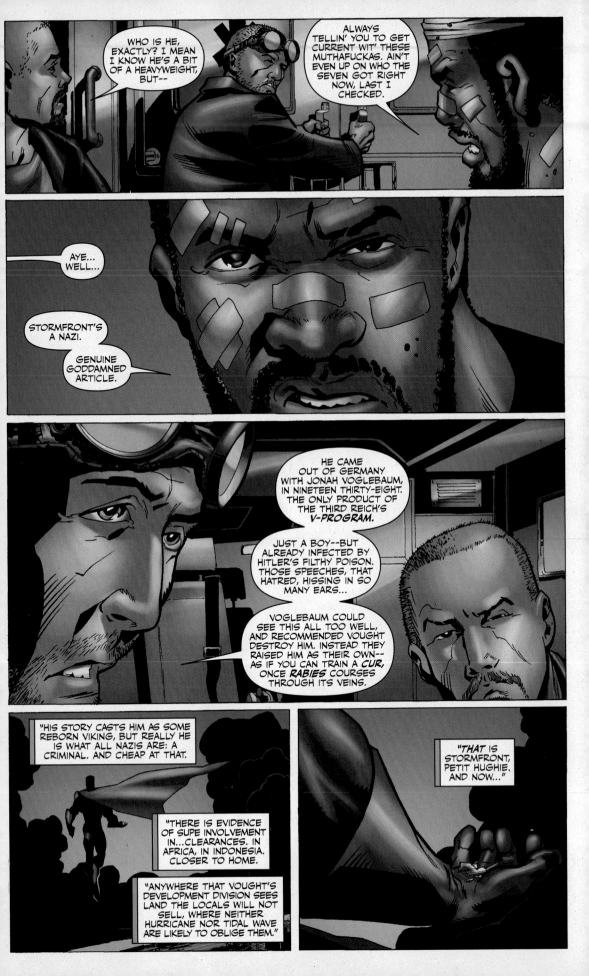

WHO IS HE, EXACTLY? I MEAN I KNOW HE'S A BIT OF A HEAVYWEIGHT, BUT--

ALWAYS TELLIN' YOU TO GET CURRENT WIT' THESE MUTHAFUCKAS. AIN'T EVEN UP ON WHO THE SEVEN GOT RIGHT NOW, LAST I CHECKED.

AYE... WELL...

STORMFRONT'S A NAZI.

GENUINE GODDAMNED ARTICLE.

HE CAME OUT OF GERMANY WITH JONAH VOGLEBAUM, IN NINETEEN THIRTY-EIGHT. THE ONLY PRODUCT OF THE THIRD REICH'S *V-PROGRAM.*

JUST A BOY--BUT ALREADY INFECTED BY HITLER'S FILTHY POISON. THOSE SPEECHES, THAT HATRED, HISSING IN SO MANY EARS...

VOGLEBAUM COULD SEE THIS ALL TOO WELL, AND RECOMMENDED VOUGHT DESTROY HIM. INSTEAD THEY RAISED HIM AS THEIR OWN-- AS IF YOU CAN TRAIN A *CUR,* ONCE *RABIES* COURSES THROUGH ITS VEINS.

"HIS STORY CASTS HIM AS SOME REBORN VIKING, BUT REALLY HE IS WHAT ALL NAZIS ARE: A CRIMINAL. AND CHEAP AT THAT.

"THERE IS EVIDENCE OF SUPE INVOLVEMENT IN...CLEARANCES. IN AFRICA, IN INDONESIA. CLOSER TO HOME.

"ANYWHERE THAT VOUGHT'S DEVELOPMENT DIVISION SEES LAND THE LOCALS WILL NOT SELL, WHERE NEITHER HURRICANE NOR TIDAL WAVE ARE LIKELY TO OBLIGE THEM."

"*THAT* IS STORMFRONT, PETIT HUGHIE, AND NOW..."

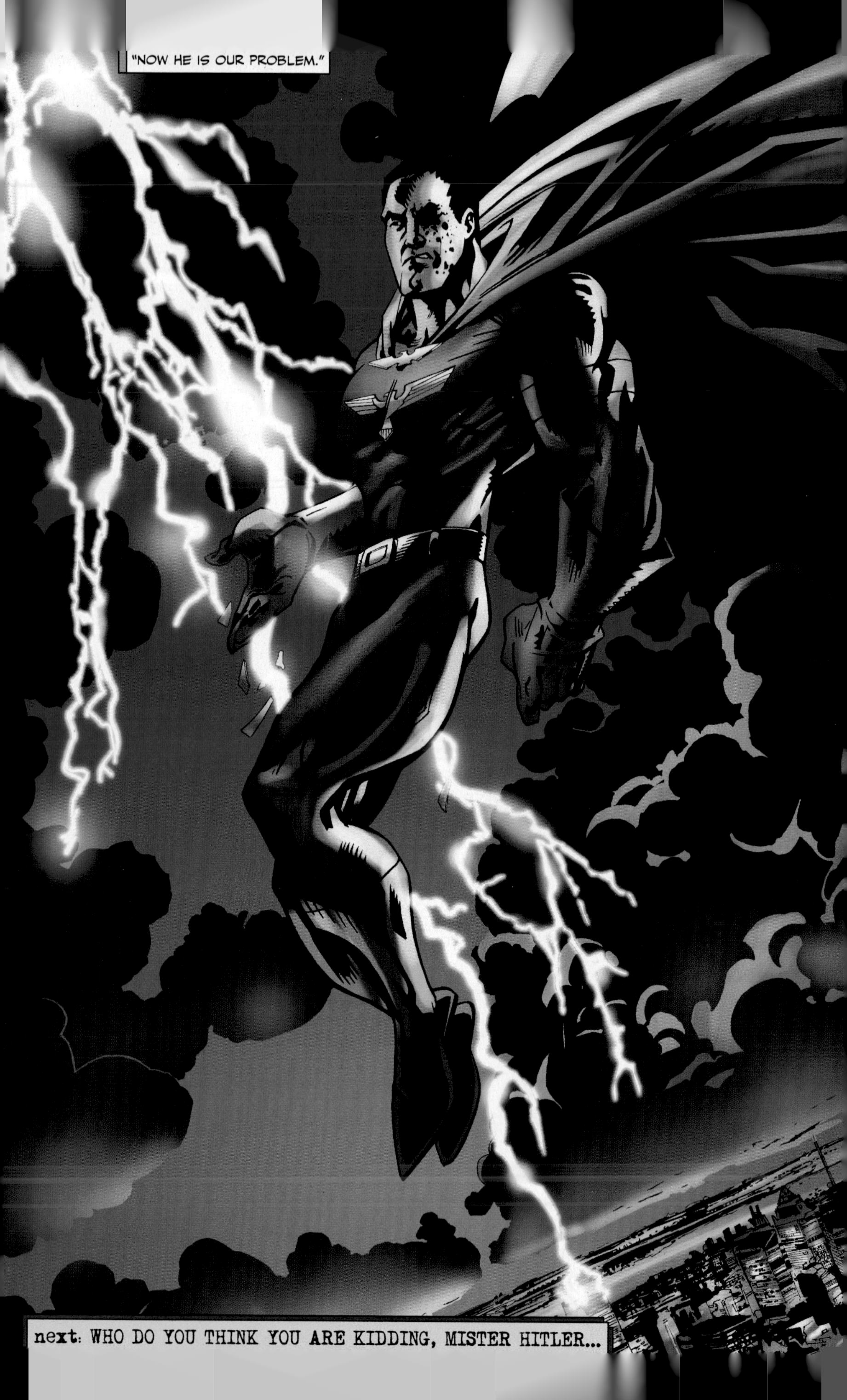
"NOW HE IS OUR PROBLEM."
next: WHO DO YOU THINK YOU ARE KIDDING, MISTER HITLER...

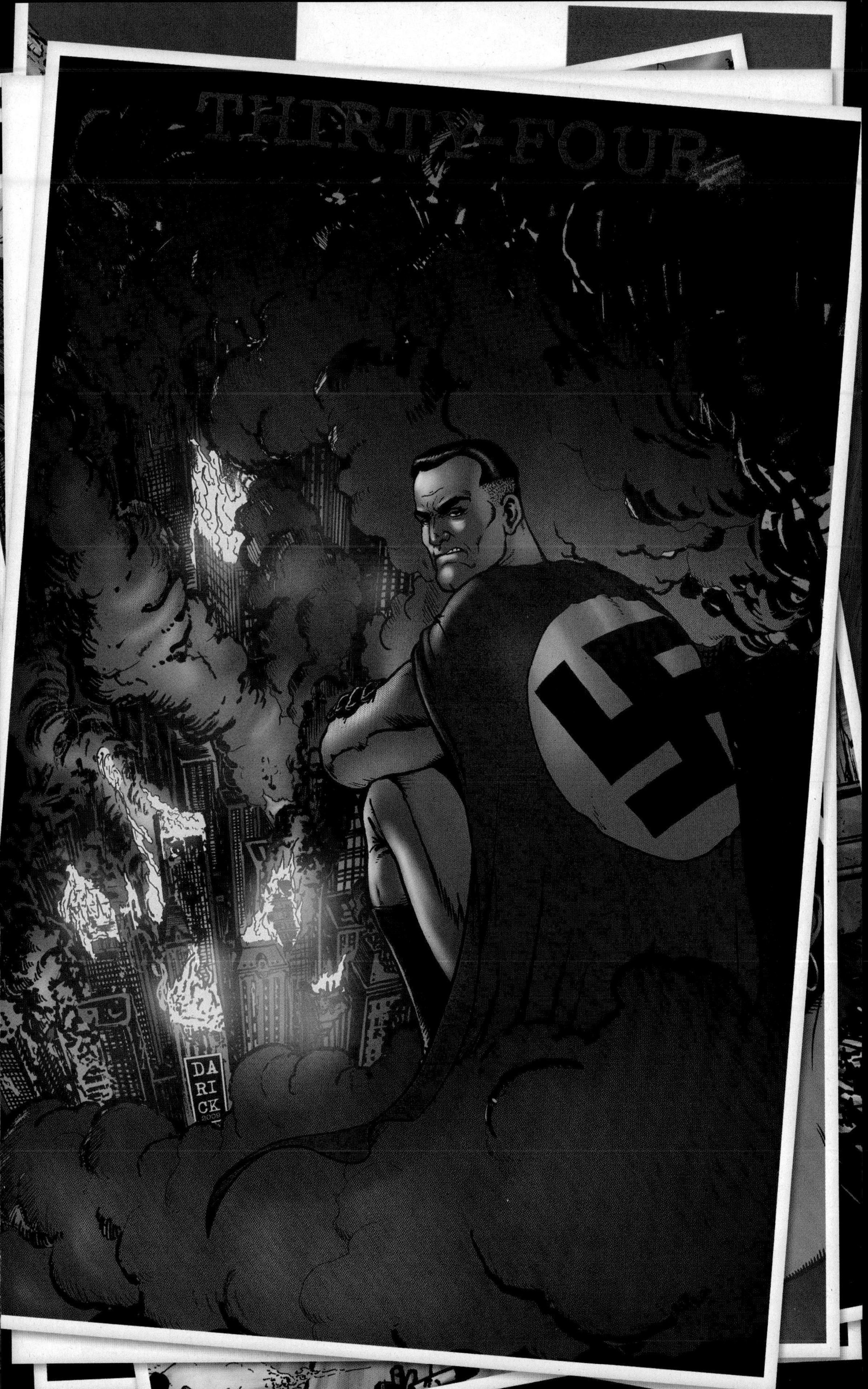
THIRTY-FOUR
DA
RI
CK
2009

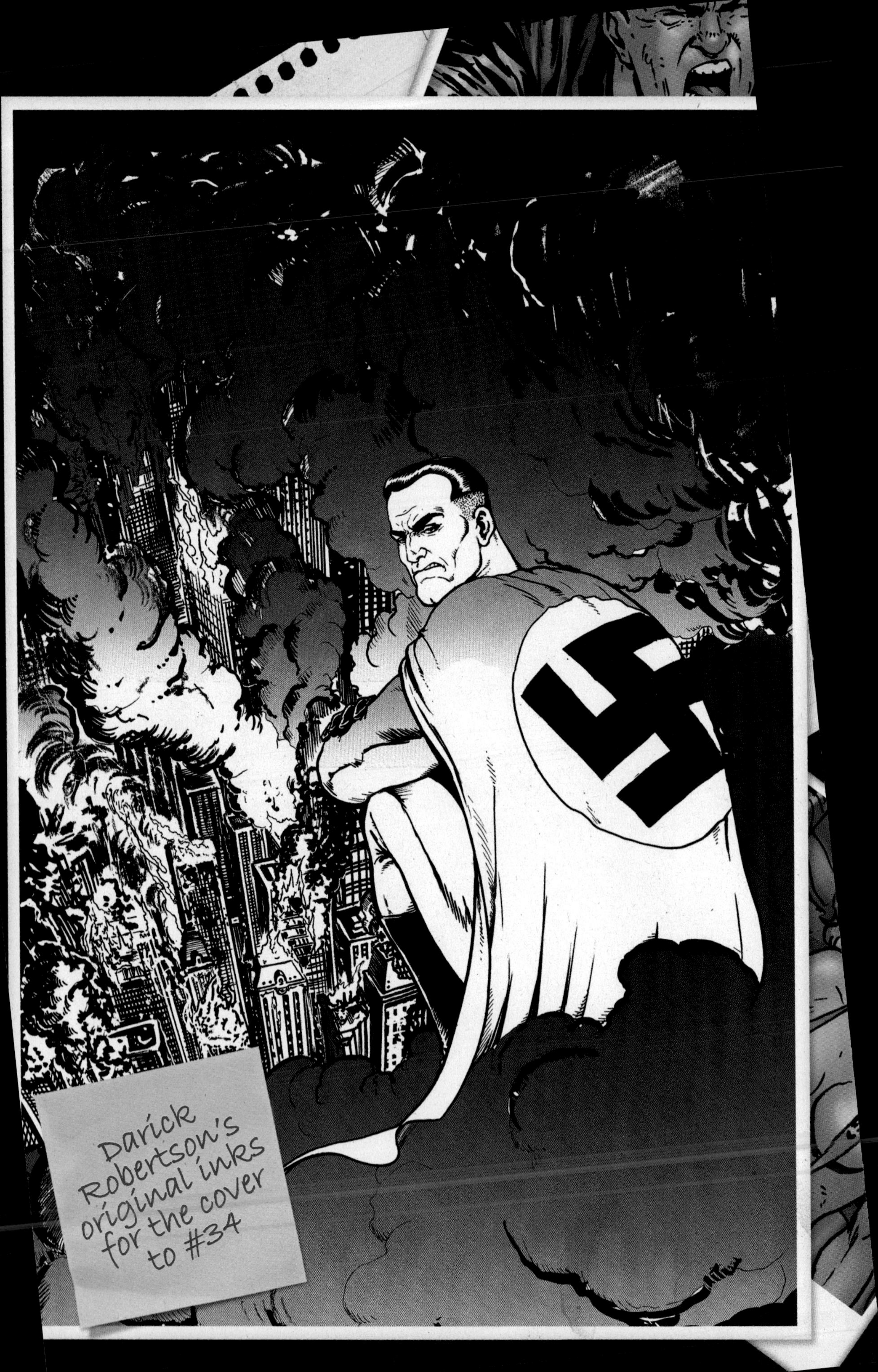

Darick Robertson's original inks for the cover to #34

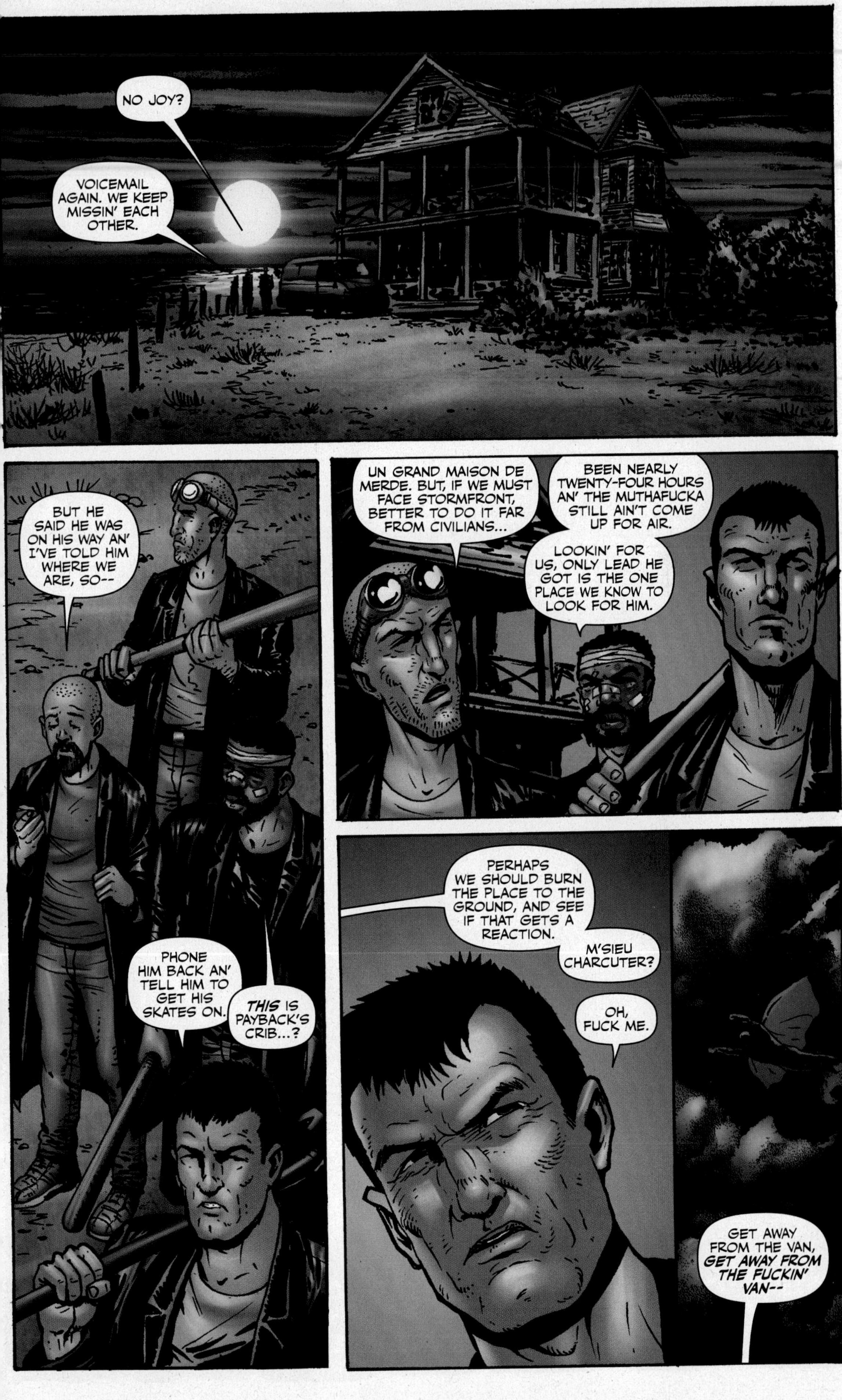
NO JOY?
VOICEMAIL AGAIN. WE KEEP MISSIN' EACH OTHER.
BUT HE SAID HE WAS ON HIS WAY AN' I'VE TOLD HIM WHERE WE ARE, SO--
PHONE HIM BACK AN' TELL HIM TO GET HIS SKATES ON.
THIS IS PAYBACK'S CRIB...?
UN GRAND MAISON DE MERDE. BUT, IF WE MUST FACE STORMFRONT, BETTER TO DO IT FAR FROM CIVILIANS...
BEEN NEARLY TWENTY-FOUR HOURS AN' THE MUTHAFUCKA STILL AIN'T COME UP FOR AIR.
LOOKIN' FOR US, ONLY LEAD HE GOT IS THE ONE PLACE WE KNOW TO LOOK FOR HIM.
PERHAPS WE SHOULD BURN THE PLACE TO THE GROUND, AND SEE IF THAT GETS A REACTION.
M'SIEU CHARCUTER?
OH, FUCK ME.
GET AWAY FROM THE VAN, *GET AWAY FROM THE FUCKIN' VAN--*

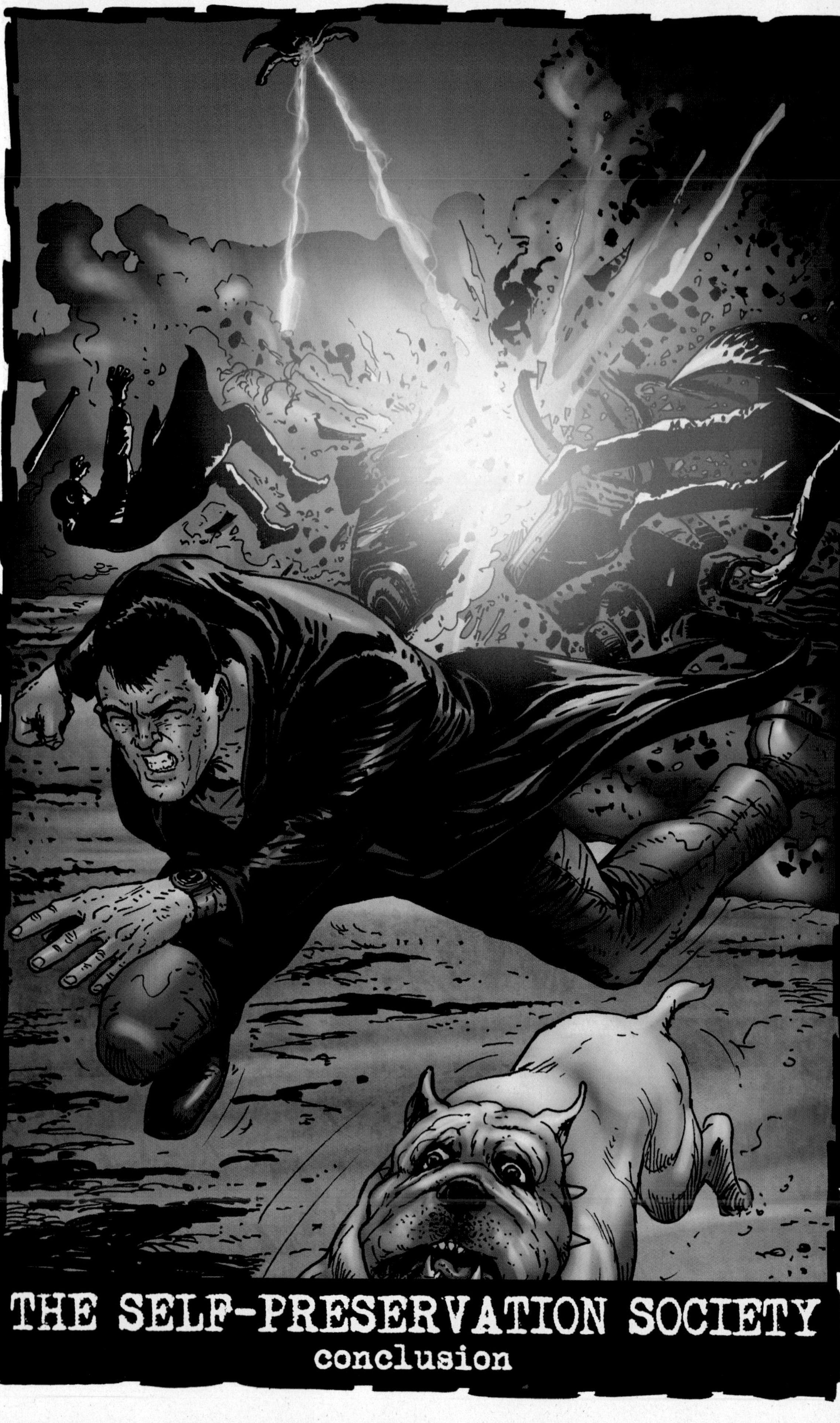
THE SELF-PRESERVATION SOCIETY
conclusion

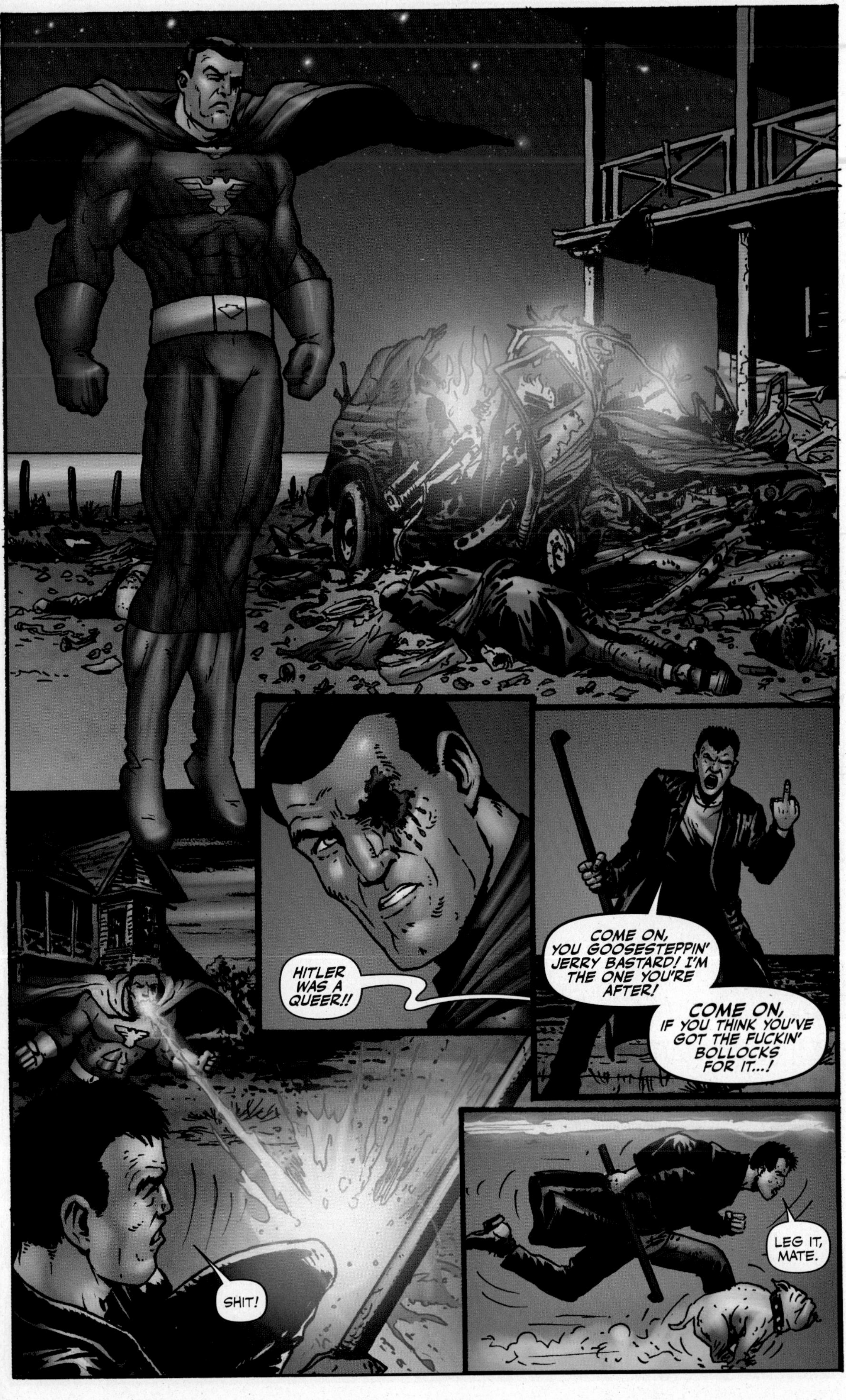
HITLER WAS A QUEER!!
COME ON, YOU GOOSESTEPPIN' JERRY BASTARD! I'M THE ONE YOU'RE AFTER!
COME ON, IF YOU THINK YOU'VE GOT THE FUCKIN' BOLLOCKS FOR IT...!
SHIT!
LEG IT, MATE.

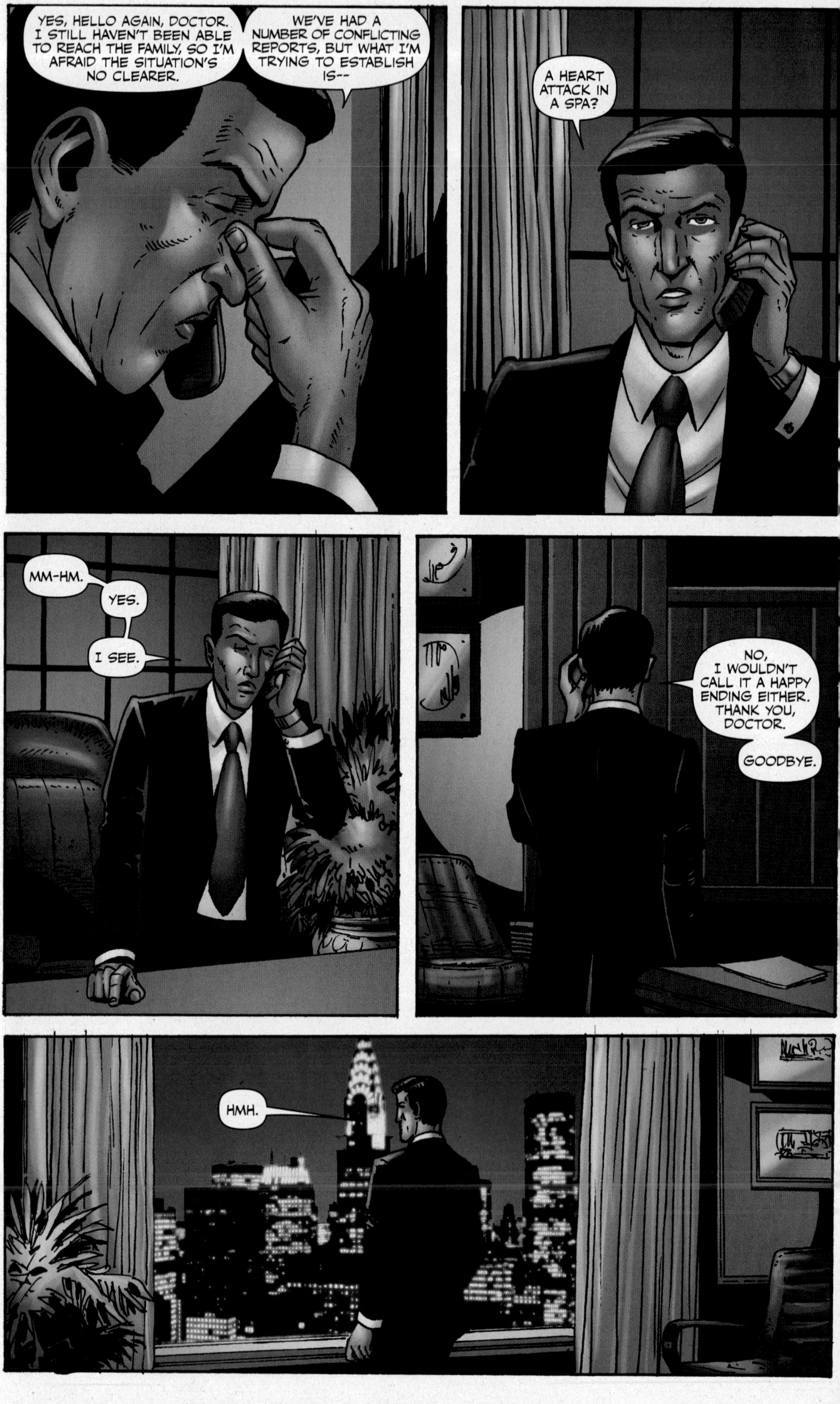
YES, HELLO AGAIN, DOCTOR. I STILL HAVEN'T BEEN ABLE TO REACH THE FAMILY, SO I'M AFRAID THE SITUATION'S NO CLEARER.
WE'VE HAD A NUMBER OF CONFLICTING REPORTS, BUT WHAT I'M TRYING TO ESTABLISH IS--
A HEART ATTACK IN A SPA?
MM-HM.
YES.
I SEE.
NO, I WOULDN'T CALL IT A HAPPY ENDING EITHER. THANK YOU, DOCTOR.
GOODBYE.
HMH.

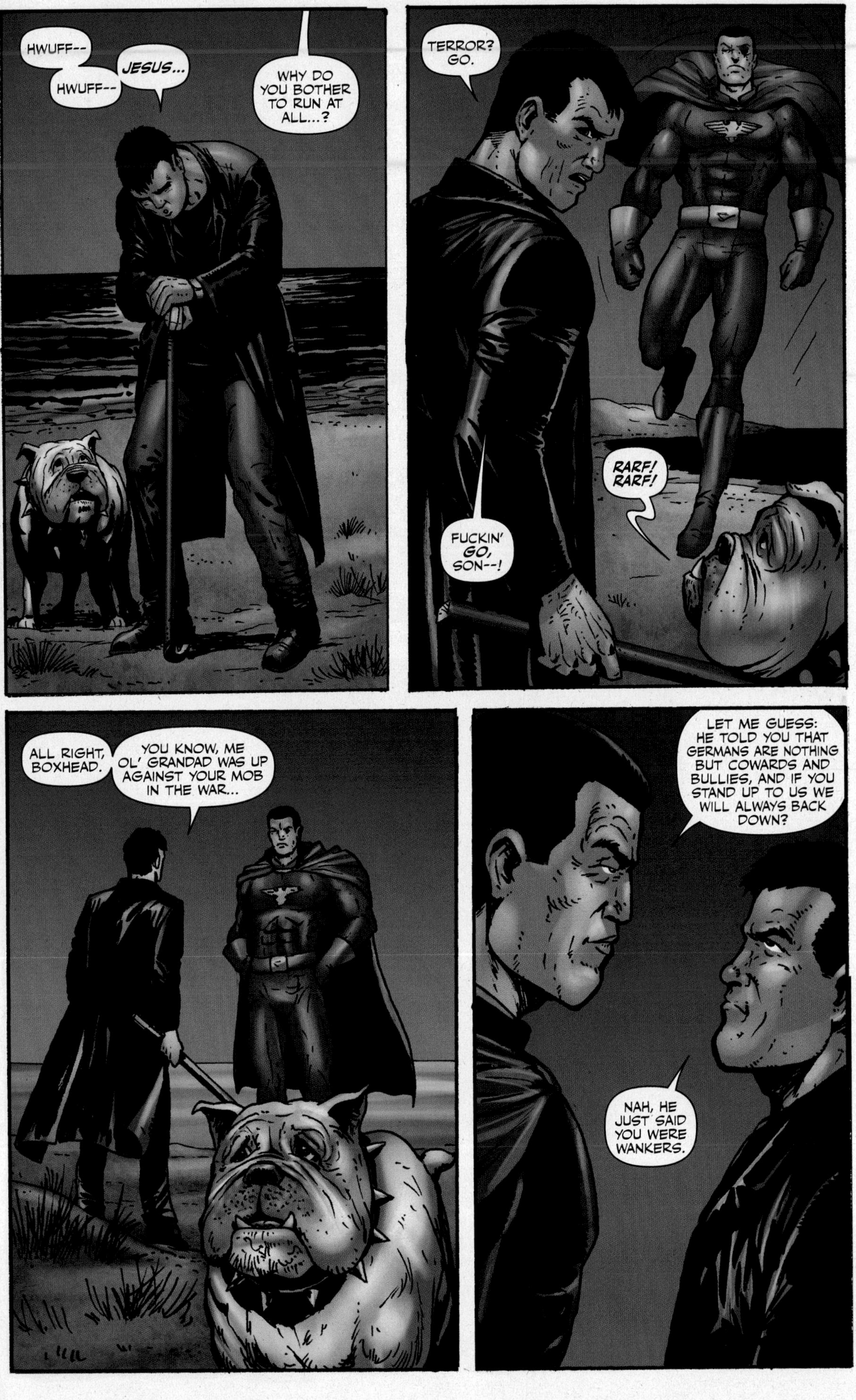
HWUFF--
HWUFF--
JESUS...
WHY DO YOU BOTHER TO RUN AT ALL...?
TERROR? GO.
RARF! RARF!
FUCKIN' GO, SON--!
ALL RIGHT, BOXHEAD.
YOU KNOW, ME OL' GRANDAD WAS UP AGAINST YOUR MOB IN THE WAR...
LET ME GUESS: HE TOLD YOU THAT GERMANS ARE NOTHING BUT COWARDS AND BULLIES, AND IF YOU STAND UP TO US WE WILL ALWAYS BACK DOWN?
NAH, HE JUST SAID YOU WERE WANKERS.

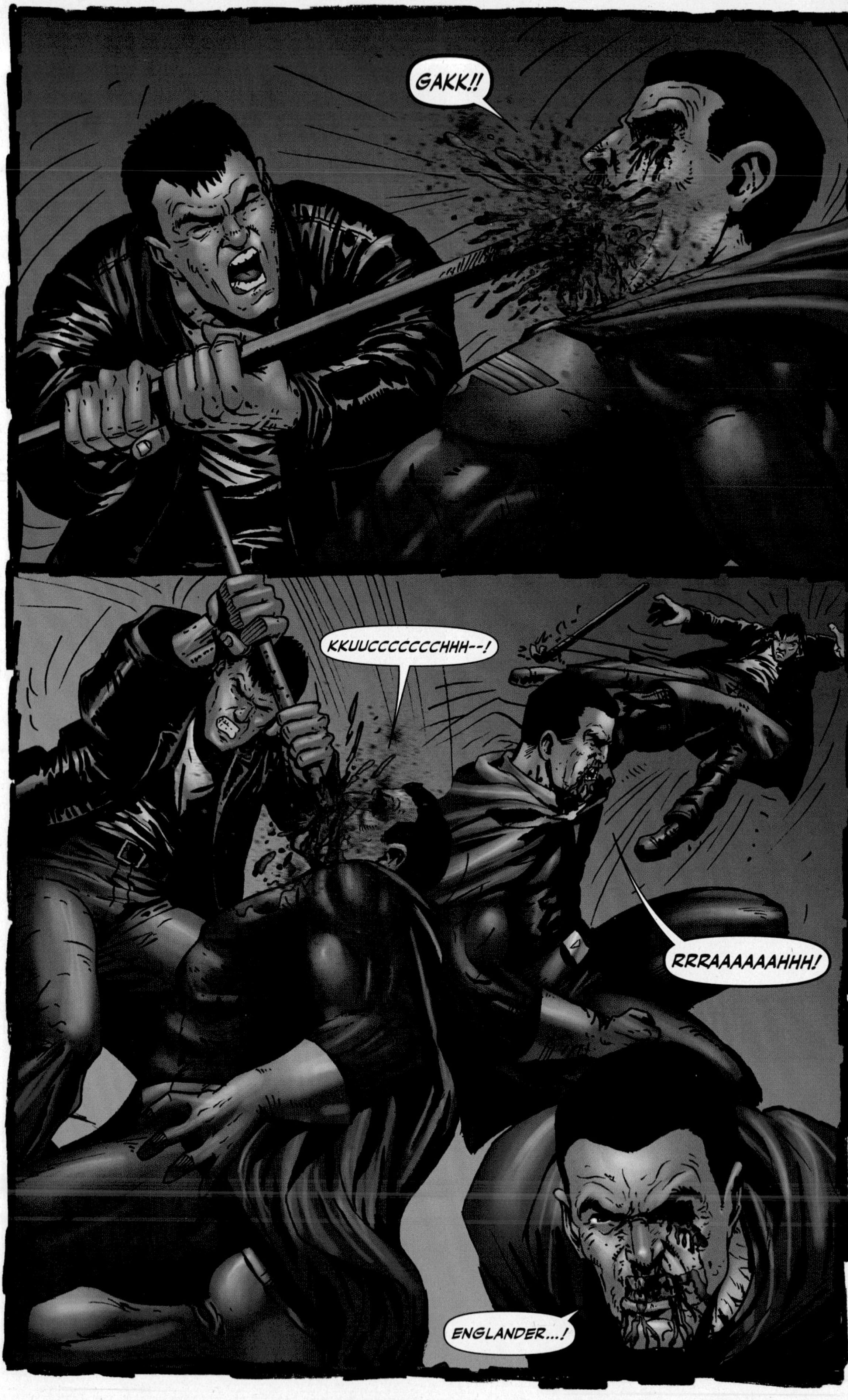
GAKK!!
KKUUCCCCCCCHHH--!
RRRAAAAAAHHH!
ENGLANDER...!

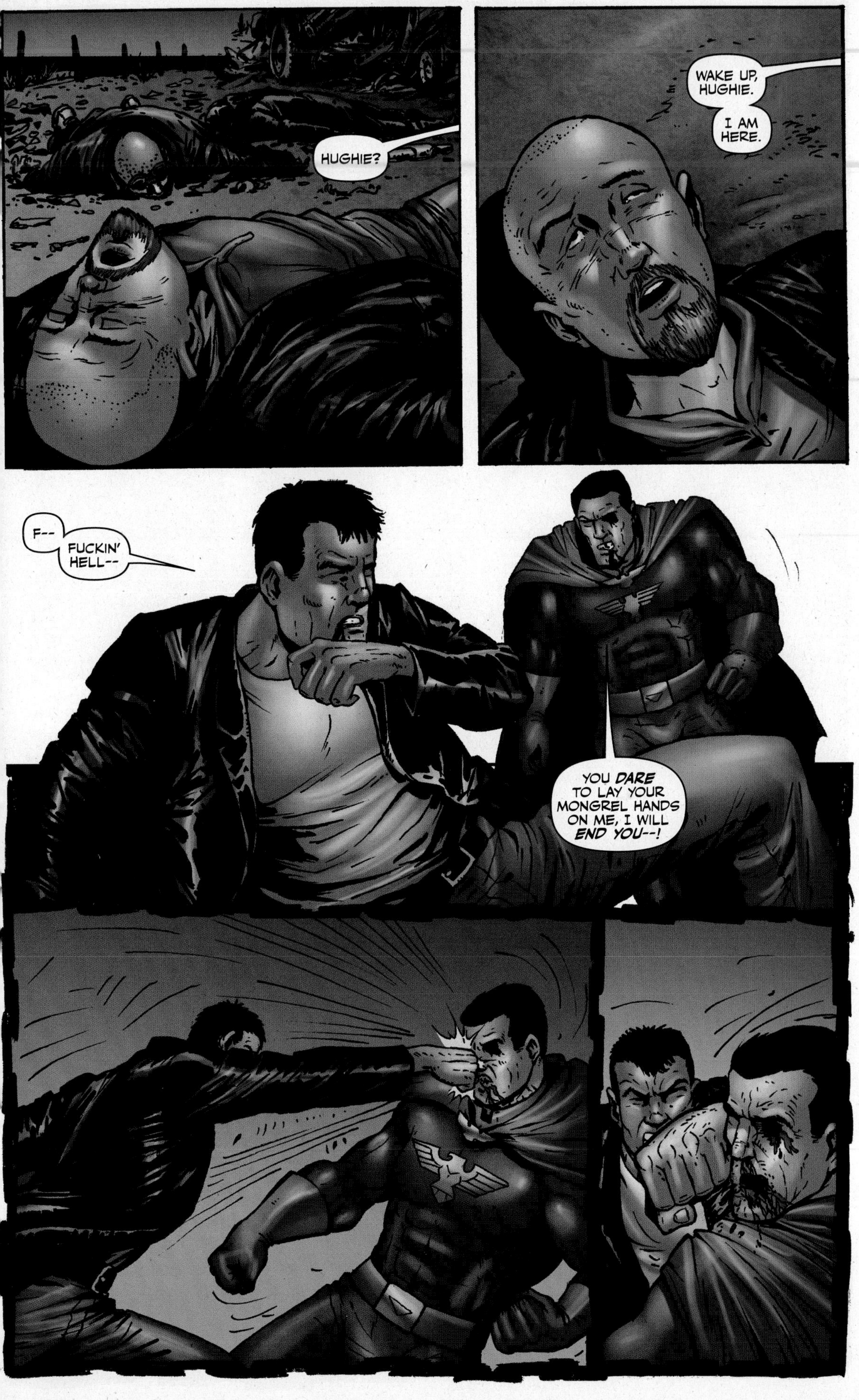
HUGHIE?
WAKE UP, HUGHIE.
I AM HERE.
F--
FUCKIN' HELL--
YOU DARE TO LAY YOUR MONGREL HANDS ON ME, I WILL END YOU--!

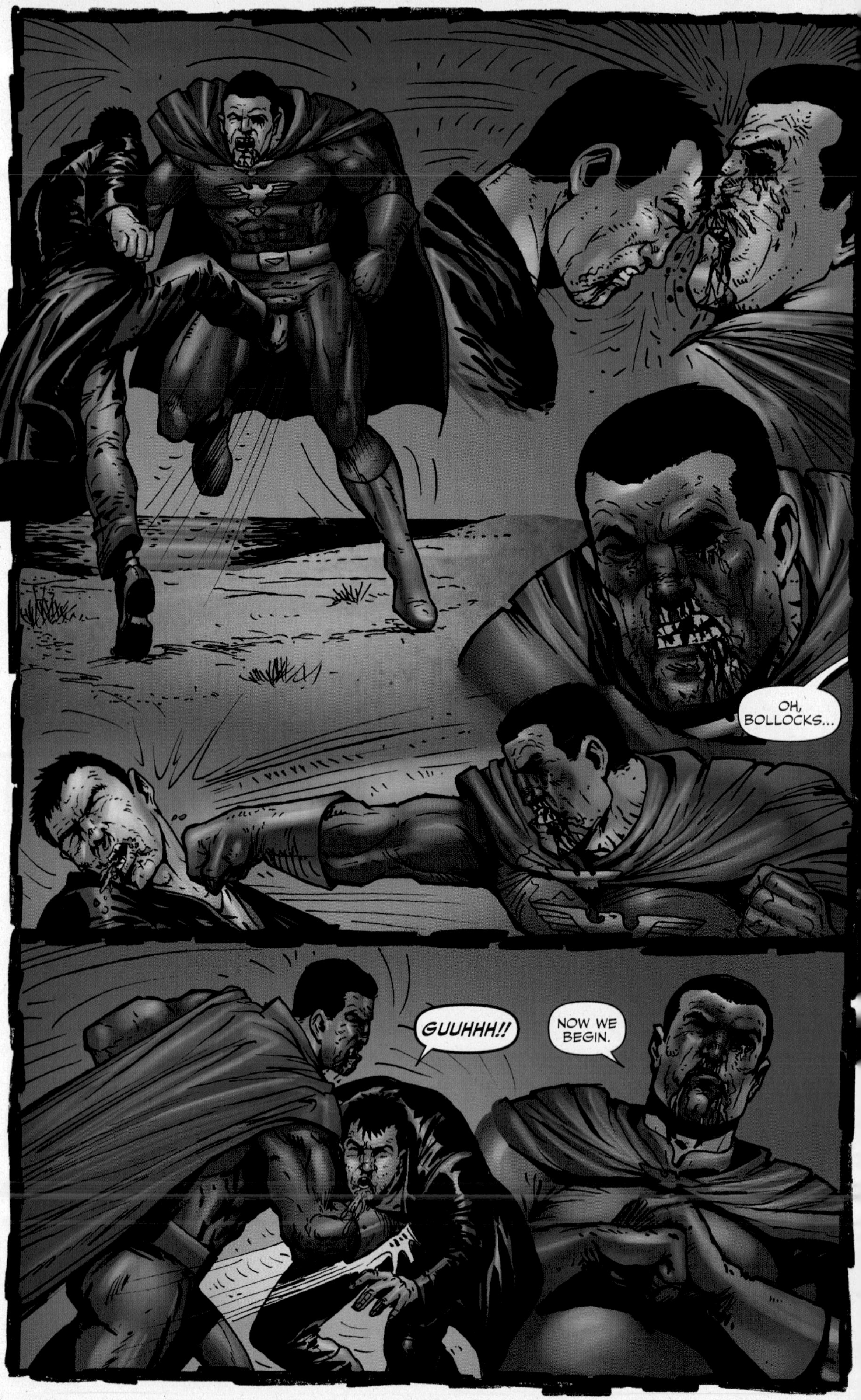
OH, BOLLOCKS...
GUUHHH!!
NOW WE BEGIN.

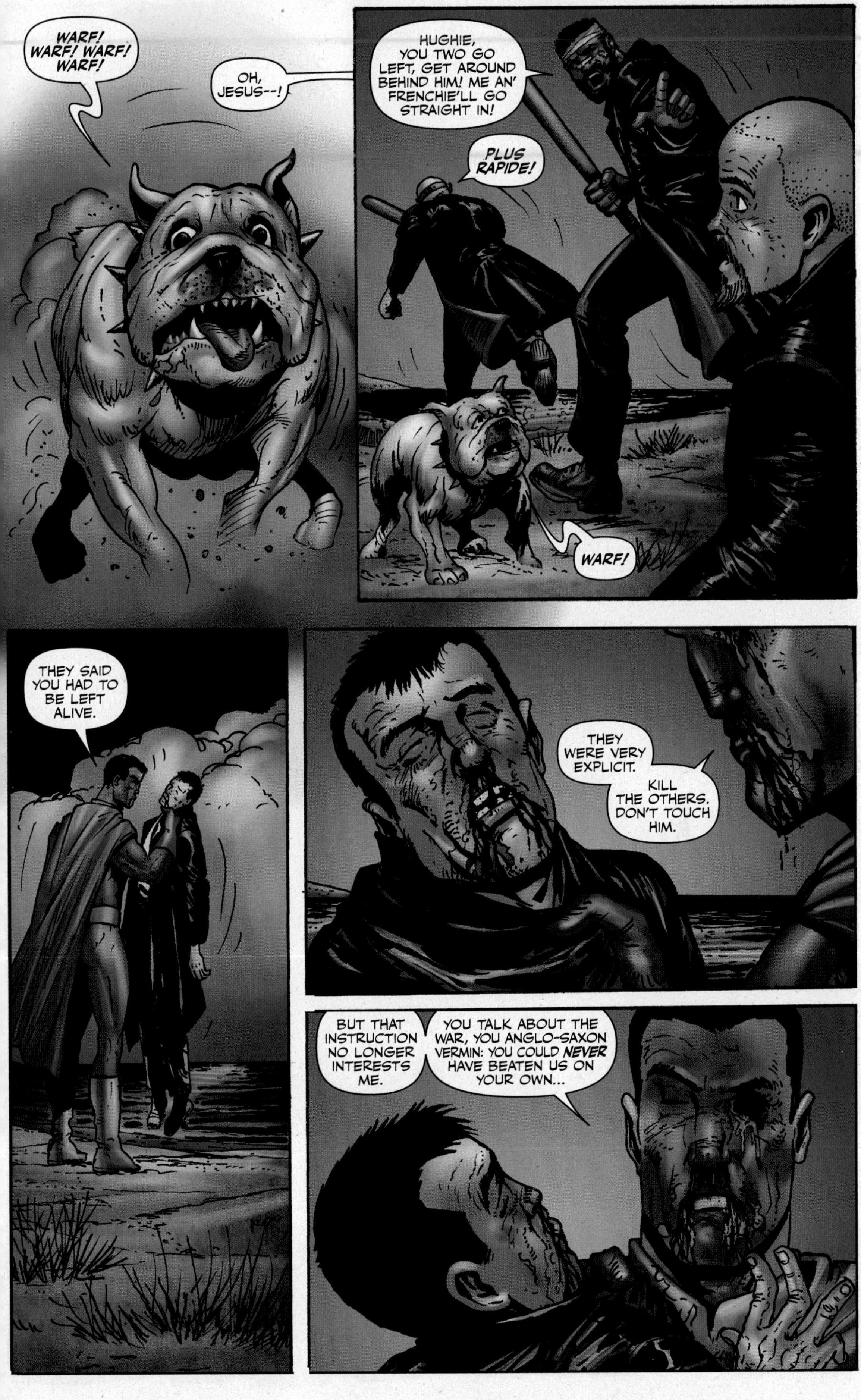
WARF! WARF! WARF! WARF!
OH, JESUS--!
HUGHIE, YOU TWO GO LEFT, GET AROUND BEHIND HIM! ME AN' FRENCHIE'LL GO STRAIGHT IN!
PLUS RAPIDE!
WARF!
THEY SAID YOU HAD TO BE LEFT ALIVE.
THEY WERE VERY EXPLICIT.
KILL THE OTHERS. DON'T TOUCH HIM.
BUT THAT INSTRUCTION NO LONGER INTERESTS ME.
YOU TALK ABOUT THE WAR, YOU ANGLO-SAXON VERMIN: YOU COULD NEVER HAVE BEATEN US ON YOUR OWN...

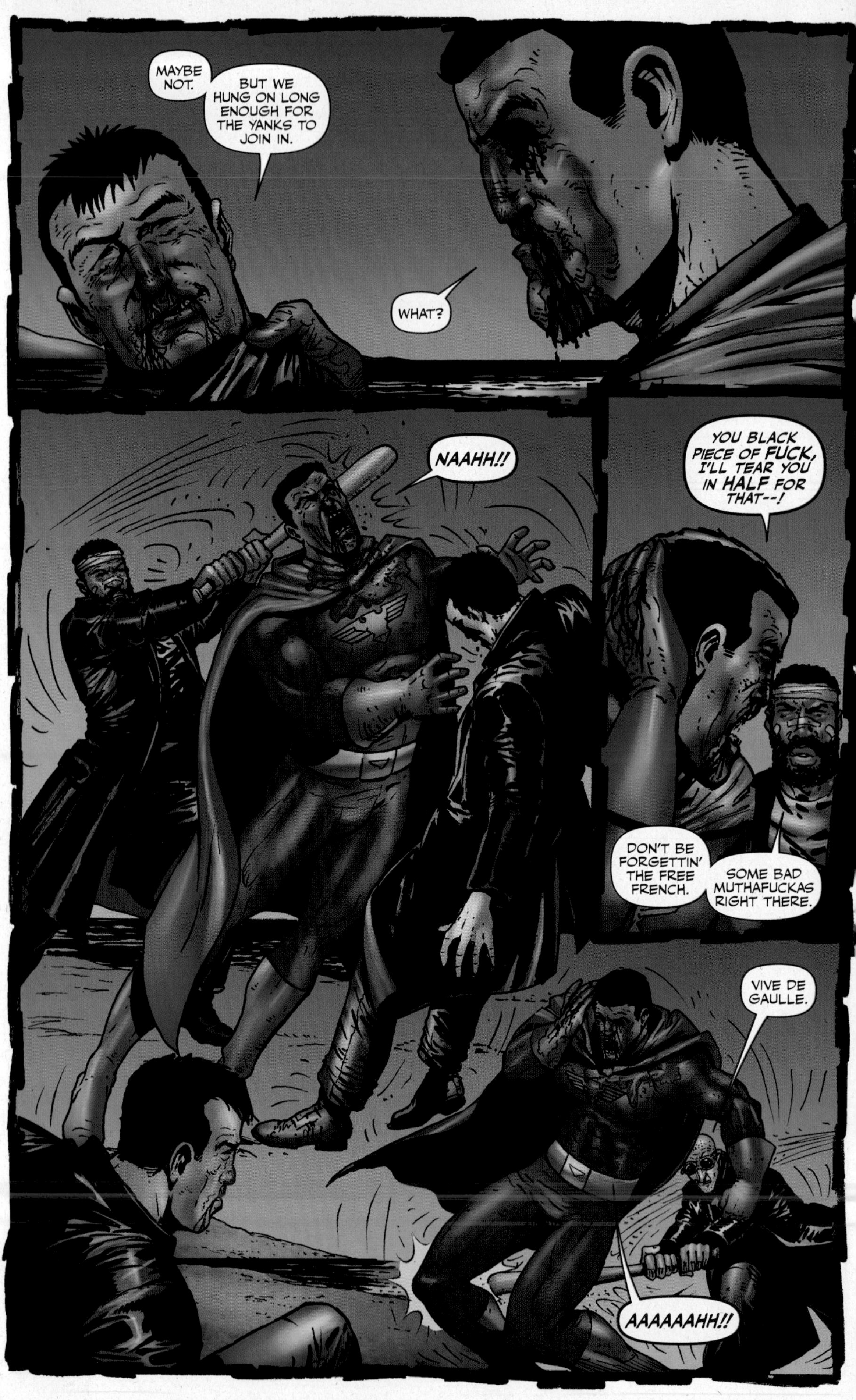
MAYBE NOT.
BUT WE HUNG ON LONG ENOUGH FOR THE YANKS TO JOIN IN.
WHAT?
NAAHH!!
YOU BLACK PIECE OF FUCK, I'LL TEAR YOU IN HALF FOR THAT--!
DON'T BE FORGETTIN' THE FREE FRENCH.
SOME BAD MUTHAFUCKAS RIGHT THERE.
VIVE DE GAULLE.
AAAAAAHH!!

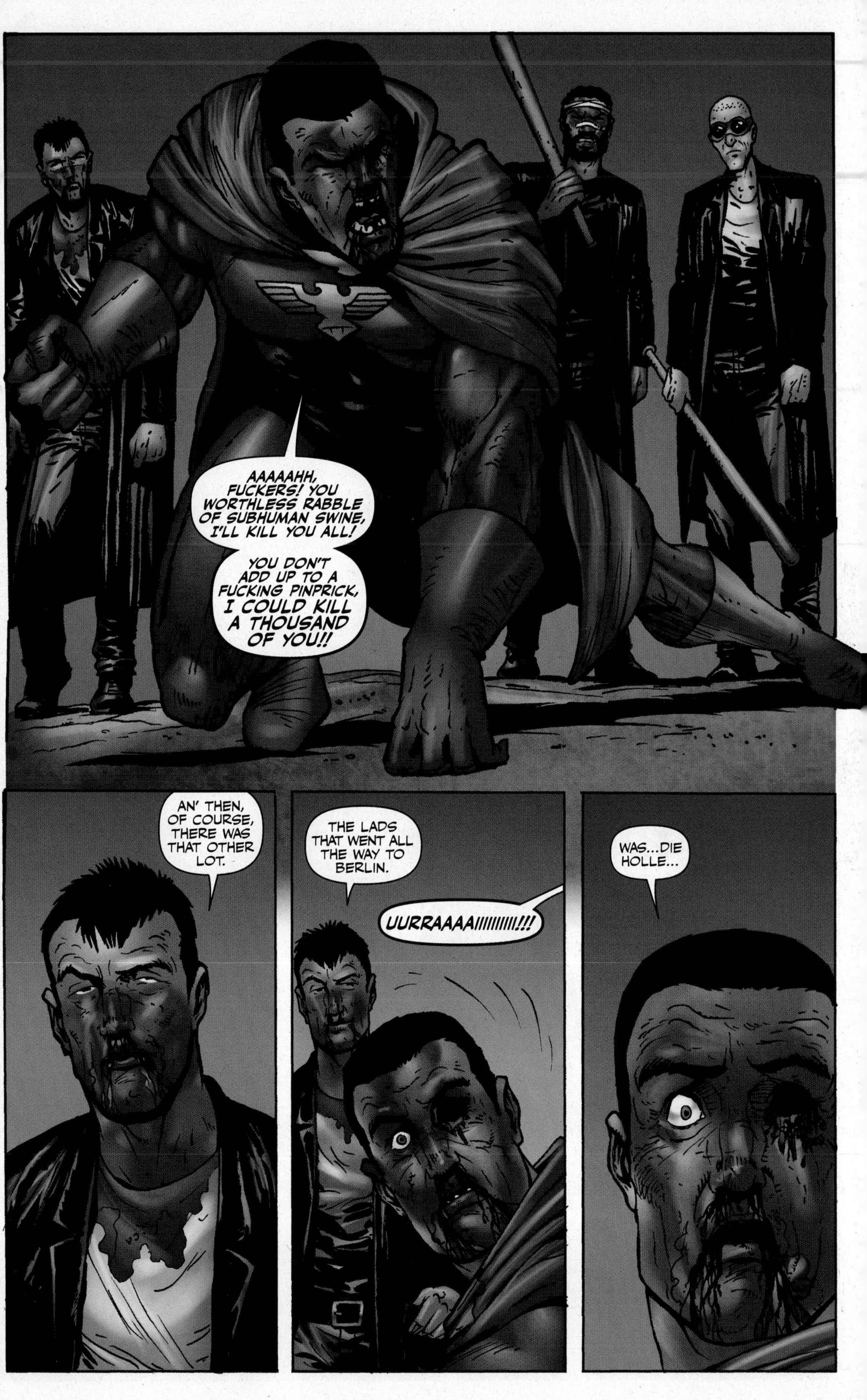
AAAAAHH, FUCKERS! YOU WORTHLESS RABBLE OF SUBHUMAN SWINE, I'LL KILL YOU ALL!
YOU DON'T ADD UP TO A FUCKING PINPRICK, I COULD KILL A THOUSAND OF YOU!!
AN' THEN, OF COURSE, THERE WAS THAT OTHER LOT.
THE LADS THAT WENT ALL THE WAY TO BERLIN.
UURRAAAAIIIIIIIIIII!!!
WAS...DIE HOLLE...

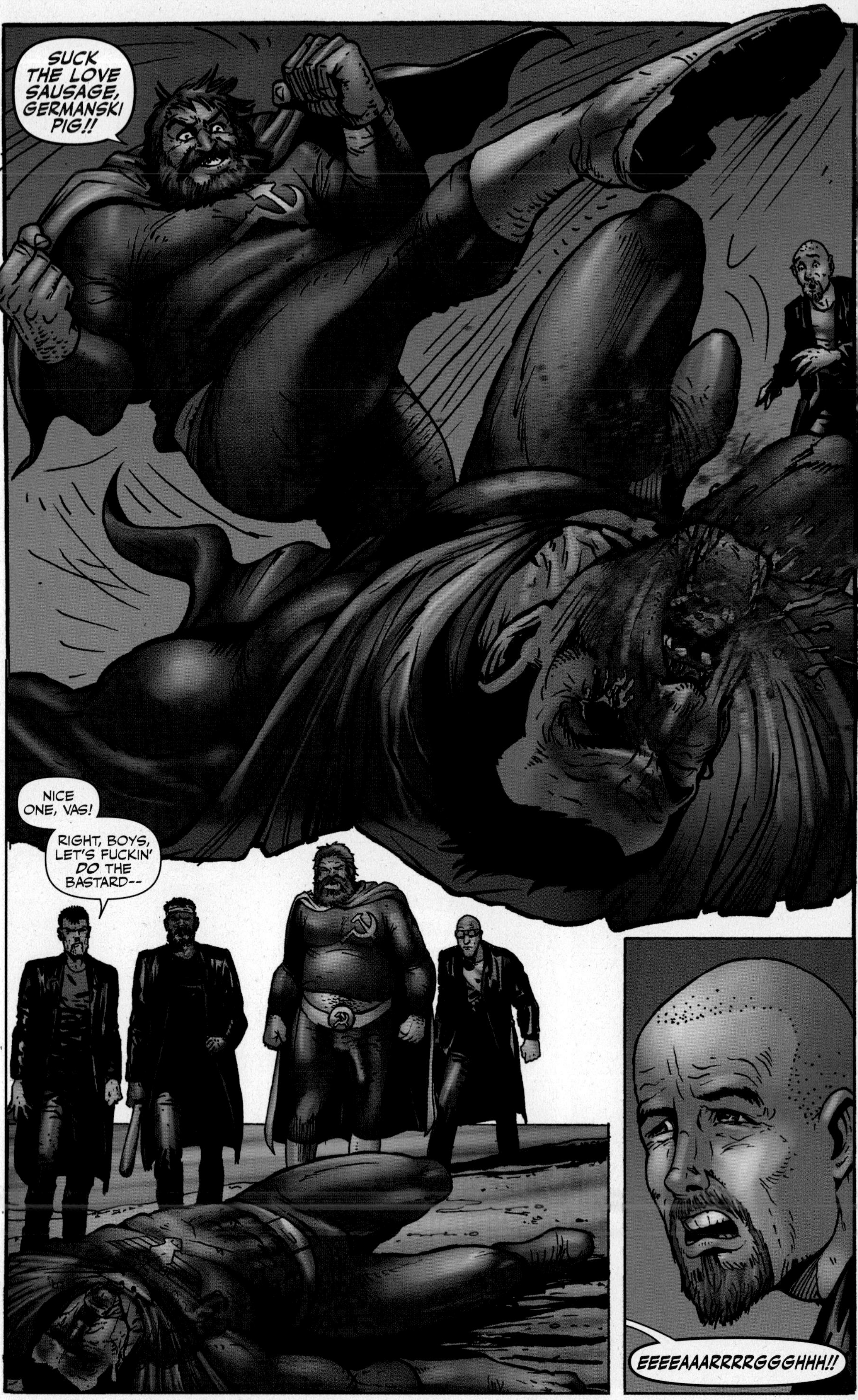
SUCK THE LOVE SAUSAGE, GERMANSKI PIG!!
NICE ONE, VAS!
RIGHT, BOYS, LET'S FUCKIN' DO THE BASTARD--
EEEEAAARRRRGGGHHH!!

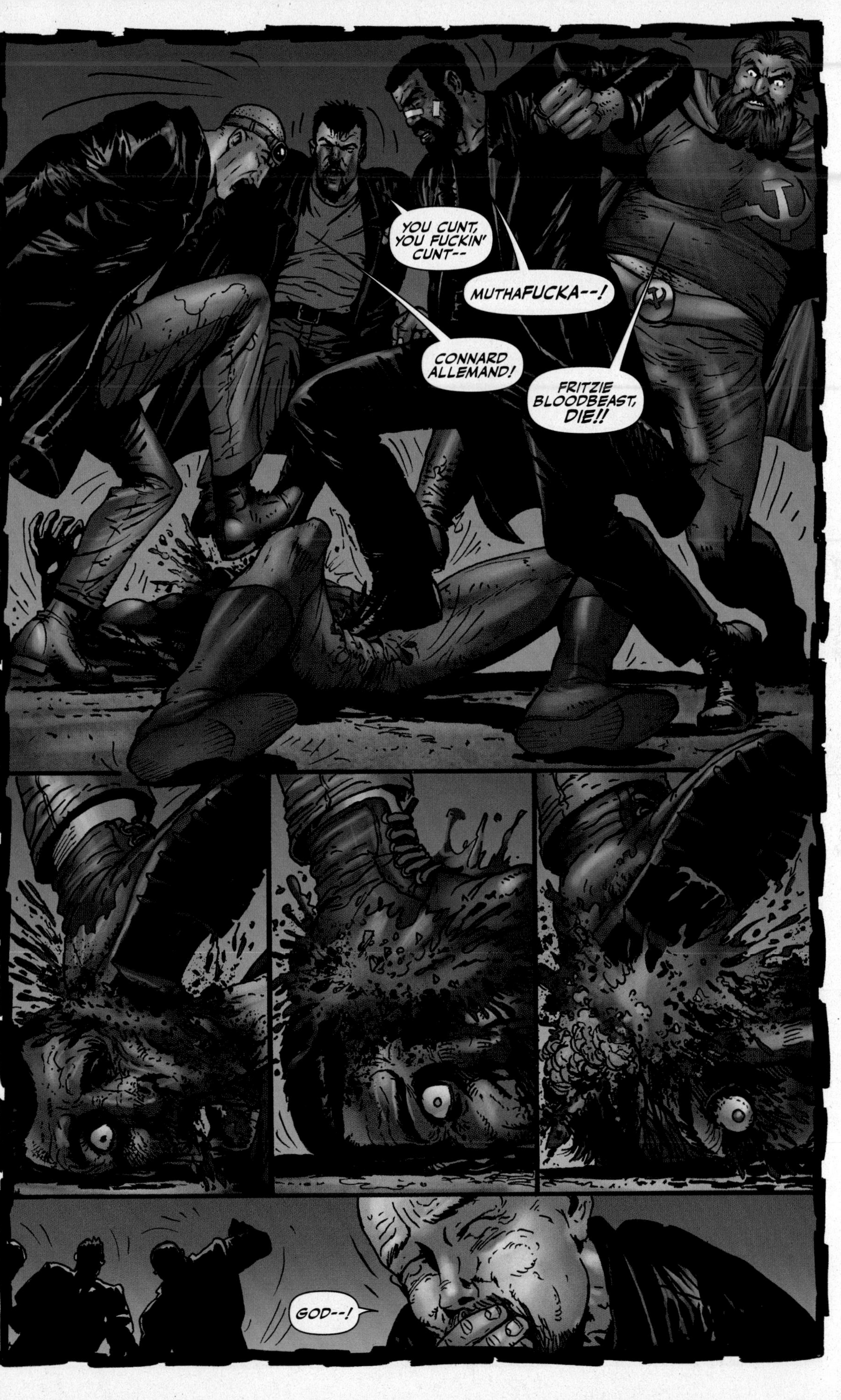
YOU CUNT, YOU FUCKIN' CUNT--
MUTHAFUCKA--!
CONNARD ALLEMAND!
FRITZIE BLOODBEAST, DIE!!
GOD--!

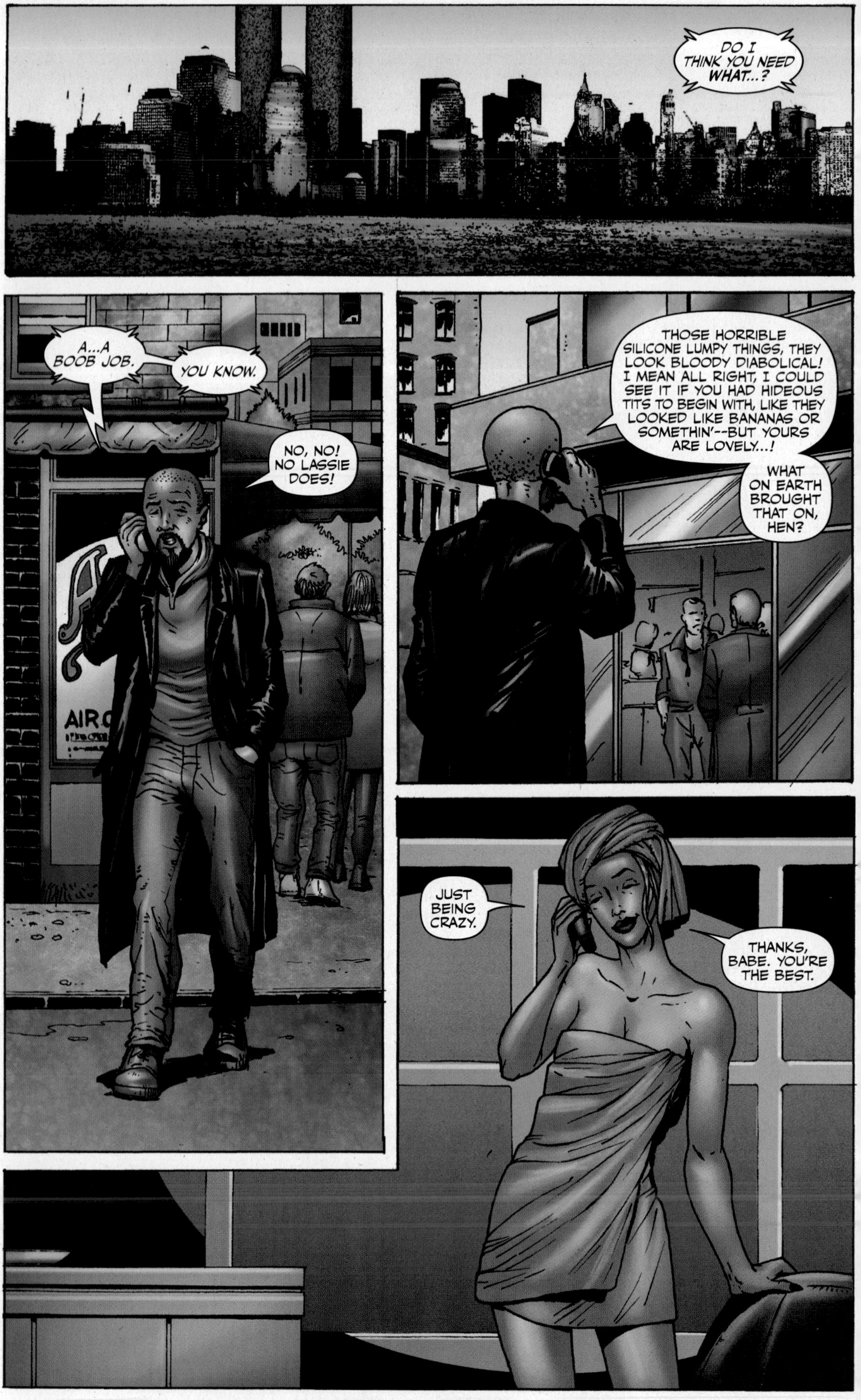
DO I THINK YOU NEED WHAT...?
A...A BOOB JOB.
YOU KNOW.
NO, NO! NO LASSIE DOES!
THOSE HORRIBLE SILICONE LUMPY THINGS, THEY LOOK BLOODY DIABOLICAL! I MEAN ALL RIGHT, I COULD SEE IT IF YOU HAD HIDEOUS TITS TO BEGIN WITH, LIKE THEY LOOKED LIKE BANANAS OR SOMETHIN'--BUT YOURS ARE LOVELY...!
WHAT ON EARTH BROUGHT THAT ON, HEN?
JUST BEING CRAZY.
THANKS, BABE. YOU'RE THE BEST.

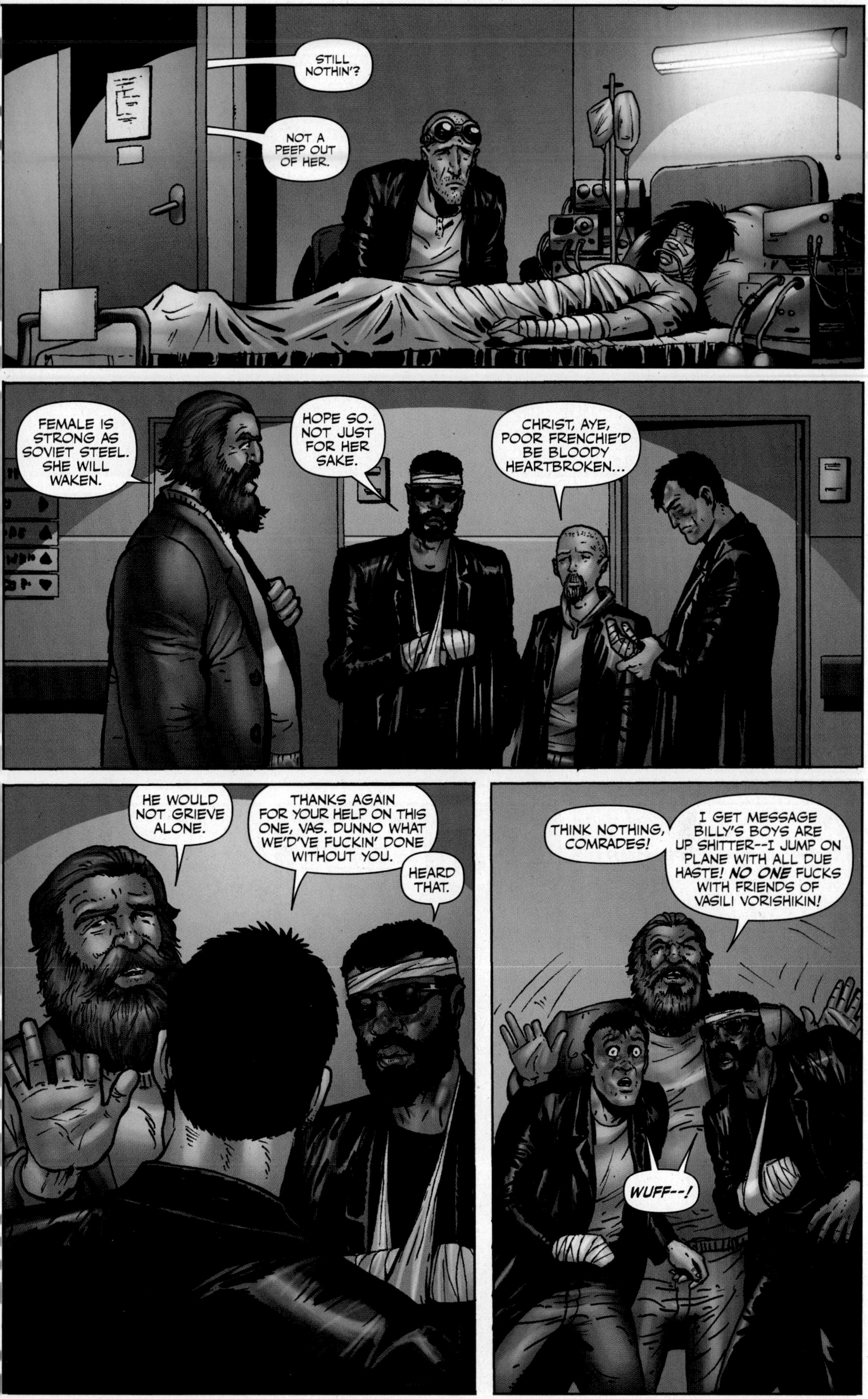
STILL NOTHIN'?
NOT A PEEP OUT OF HER.
FEMALE IS STRONG AS SOVIET STEEL. SHE WILL WAKEN.
HOPE SO. NOT JUST FOR HER SAKE.
CHRIST, AYE, POOR FRENCHIE'D BE BLOODY HEARTBROKEN...
HE WOULD NOT GRIEVE ALONE.
THANKS AGAIN FOR YOUR HELP ON THIS ONE, VAS. DUNNO WHAT WE'D'VE FUCKIN' DONE WITHOUT YOU.
HEARD THAT.
THINK NOTHING, COMRADES!
I GET MESSAGE BILLY'S BOYS ARE UP SHITTER--I JUMP ON PLANE WITH ALL DUE HASTE! NO ONE FUCKS WITH FRIENDS OF VASILI VORISHIKIN!
WUFF--!

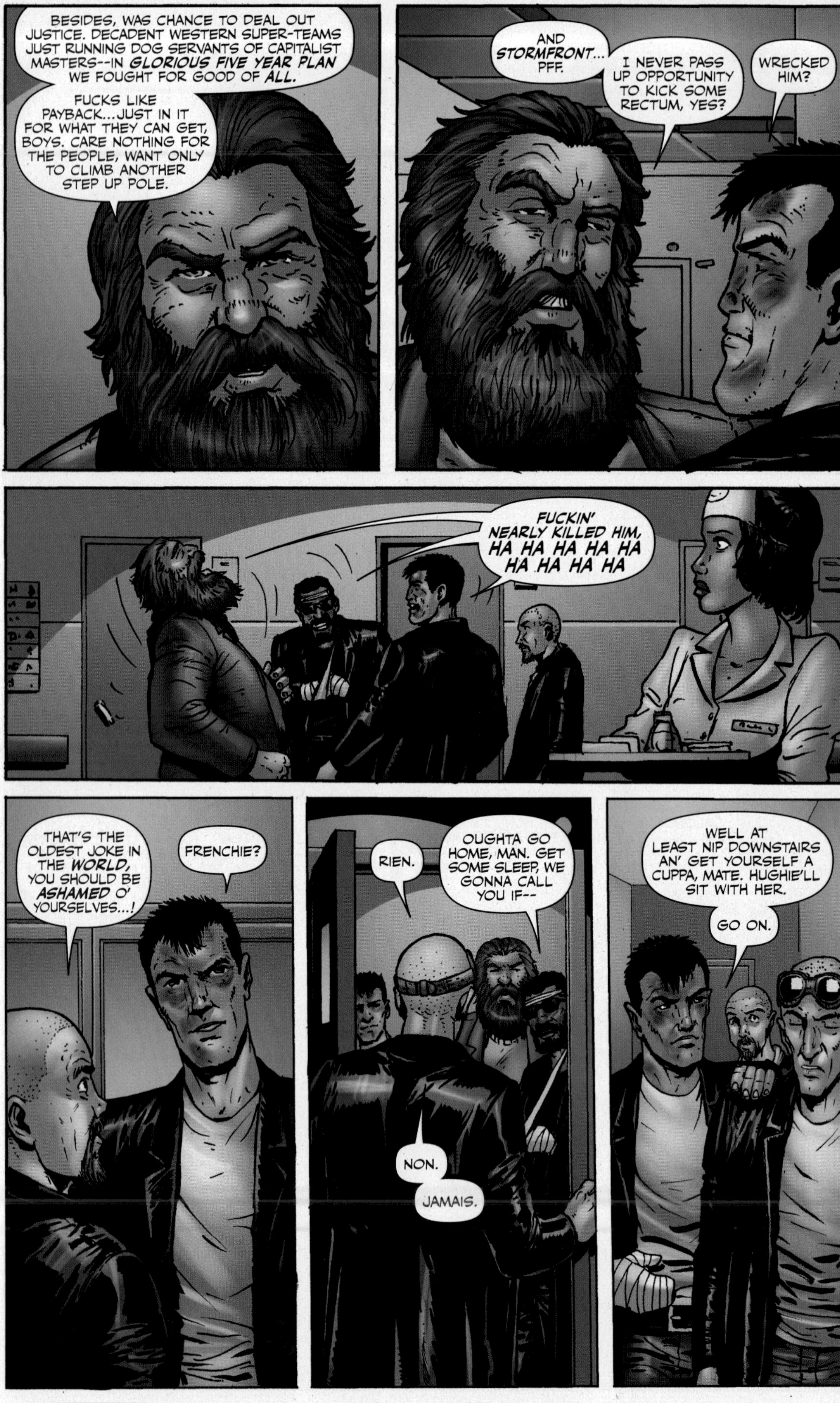

BESIDES, WAS CHANCE TO DEAL OUT JUSTICE. DECADENT WESTERN SUPER-TEAMS JUST RUNNING DOG SERVANTS OF CAPITALIST MASTERS--IN *GLORIOUS FIVE YEAR PLAN* WE FOUGHT FOR GOOD OF *ALL.*
FUCKS LIKE PAYBACK...JUST IN IT FOR WHAT THEY CAN GET, BOYS. CARE NOTHING FOR THE PEOPLE, WANT ONLY TO CLIMB ANOTHER STEP UP POLE.
AND *STORMFRONT*... PFF.
I NEVER PASS UP OPPORTUNITY TO KICK SOME RECTUM, YES?
WRECKED HIM?
FUCKIN' NEARLY KILLED HIM, **HA HA HA HA HA HA HA HA HA HA**
THAT'S THE OLDEST JOKE IN THE *WORLD,* YOU SHOULD BE *ASHAMED* O' YOURSELVES...!
FRENCHIE?
RIEN.
OUGHTA GO HOME, MAN. GET SOME SLEEP, WE GONNA CALL YOU IF--
NON.
JAMAIS.
WELL AT LEAST NIP DOWNSTAIRS AN' GET YOURSELF A CUPPA, MATE. HUGHIE'LL SIT WITH HER.
GO ON.

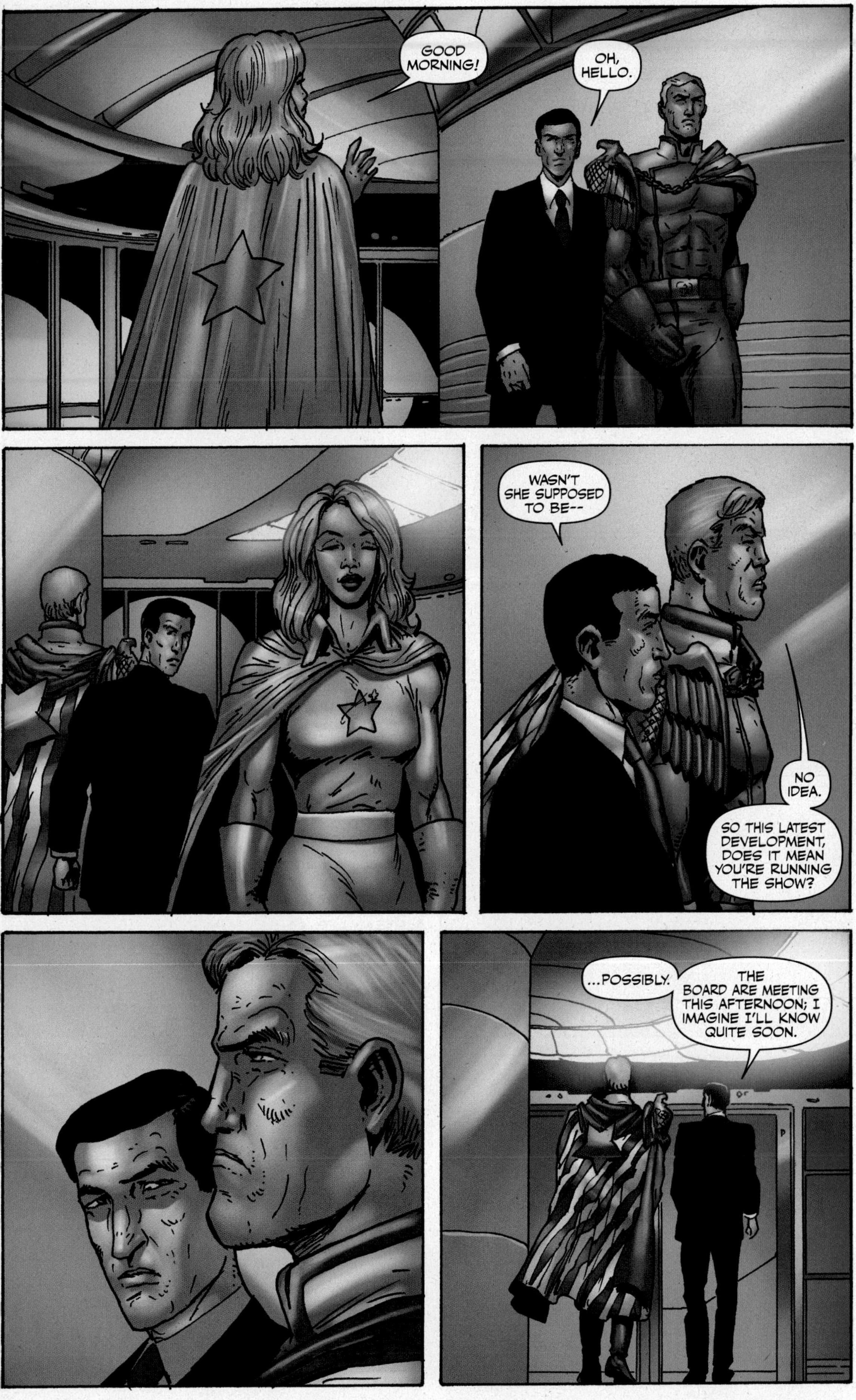
GOOD MORNING!
OH, HELLO.
WASN'T SHE SUPPOSED TO BE--
NO IDEA.
SO THIS LATEST DEVELOPMENT, DOES IT MEAN YOU'RE RUNNING THE SHOW?
...POSSIBLY.
THE BOARD ARE MEETING THIS AFTERNOON; I IMAGINE I'LL KNOW QUITE SOON.

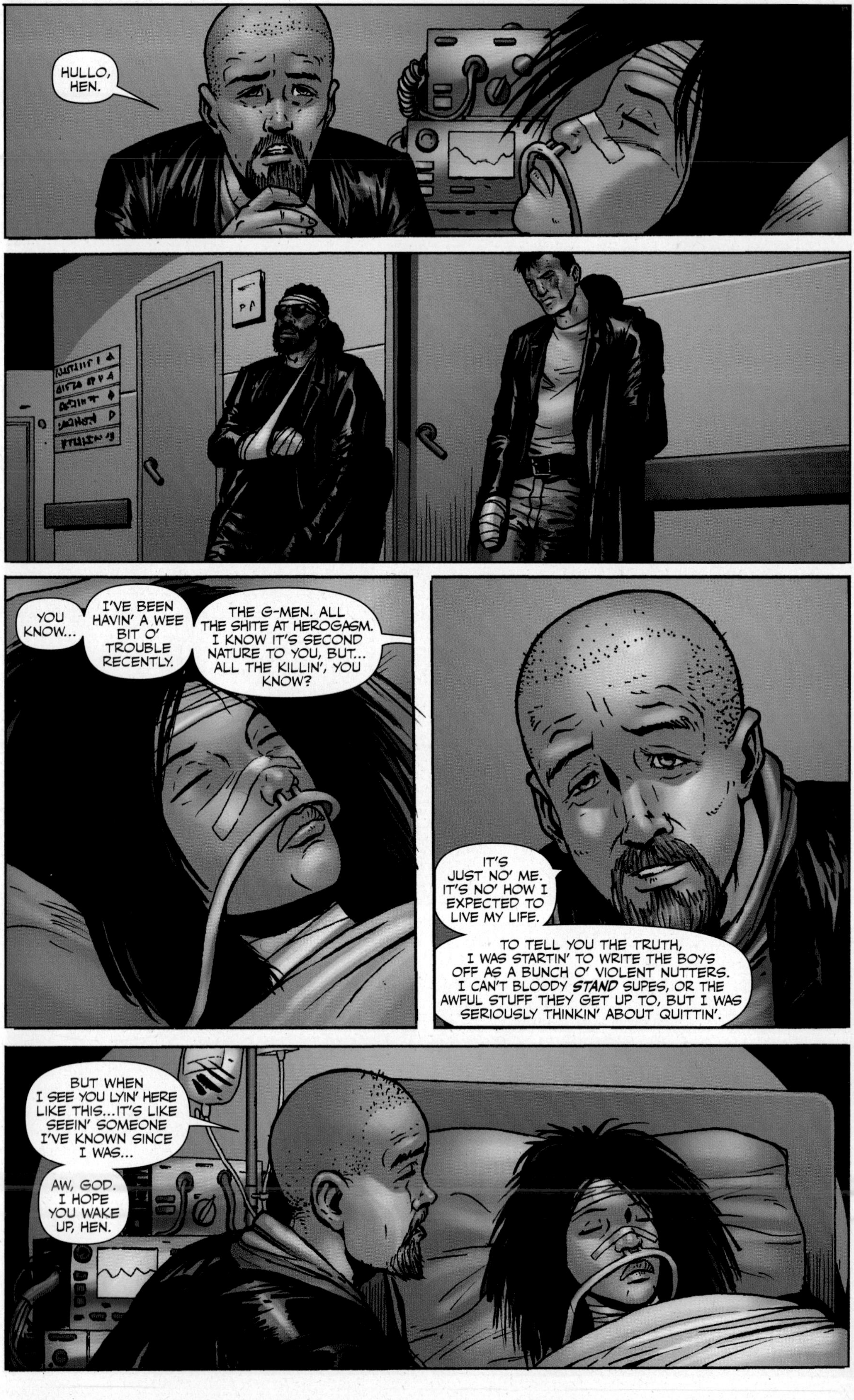
HULLO, HEN.
YOU KNOW...
I'VE BEEN HAVIN' A WEE BIT O' TROUBLE RECENTLY.
THE G-MEN. ALL THE SHITE AT HEROGASM. I KNOW IT'S SECOND NATURE TO YOU, BUT... ALL THE KILLIN', YOU KNOW?
IT'S JUST NO' ME. IT'S NO' HOW I EXPECTED TO LIVE MY LIFE.
TO TELL YOU THE TRUTH, I WAS STARTIN' TO WRITE THE BOYS OFF AS A BUNCH O' VIOLENT NUTTERS. I CAN'T BLOODY STAND SUPES, OR THE AWFUL STUFF THEY GET UP TO, BUT I WAS SERIOUSLY THINKIN' ABOUT QUITTIN'.
BUT WHEN I SEE YOU LYIN' HERE LIKE THIS...IT'S LIKE SEEIN' SOMEONE I'VE KNOWN SINCE I WAS...
AW, GOD. I HOPE YOU WAKE UP, HEN.

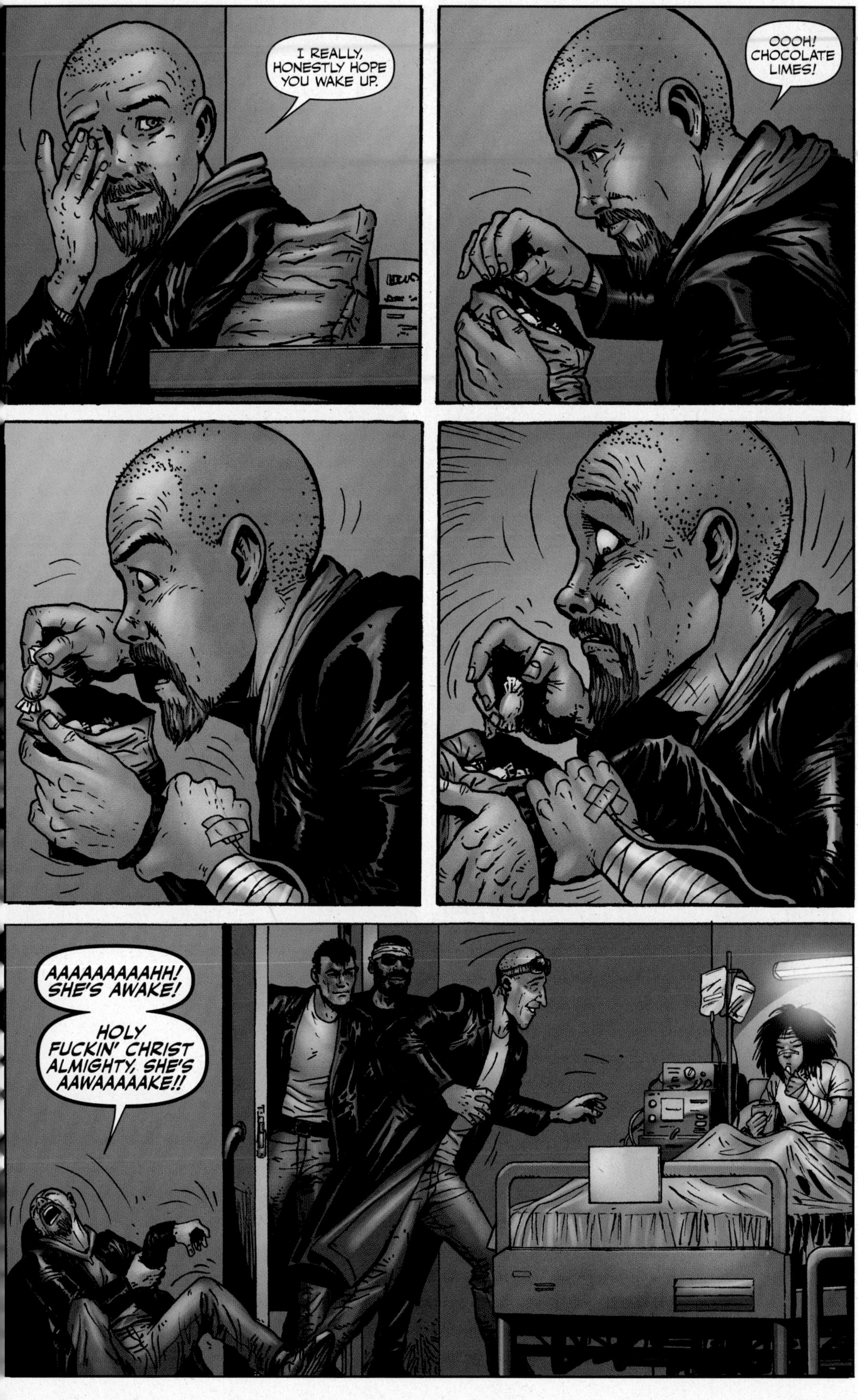
I REALLY, HONESTLY HOPE YOU WAKE UP.
OOOH! CHOCOLATE LIMES!
AAAAAAAAAHH! SHE'S AWAKE!
HOLY FUCKIN' CHRIST ALMIGHTY, SHE'S AAWAAAAAKE!!

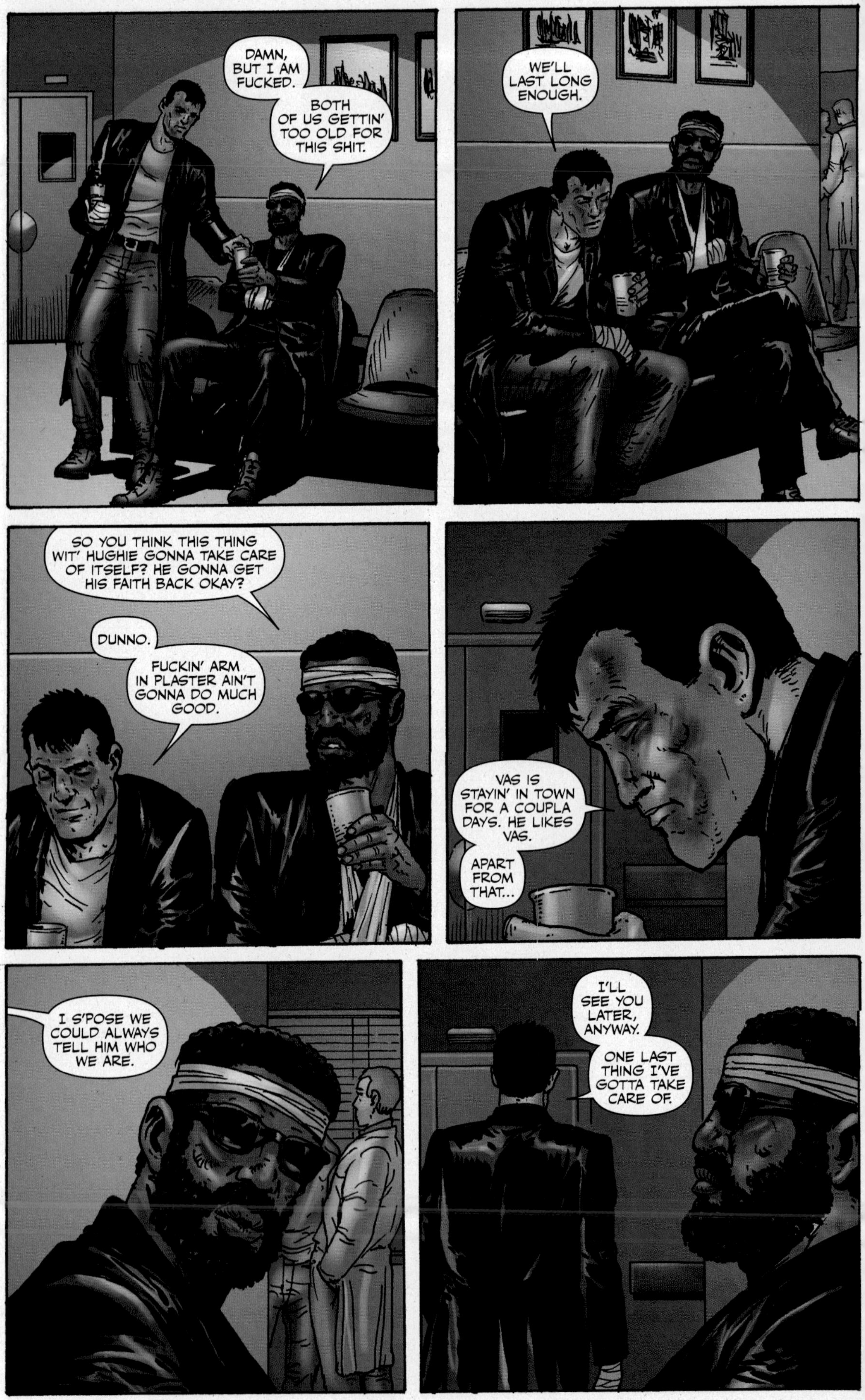
DAMN, BUT I AM FUCKED.
BOTH OF US GETTIN' TOO OLD FOR THIS SHIT.
WE'LL LAST LONG ENOUGH.
SO YOU THINK THIS THING WIT' HUGHIE GONNA TAKE CARE OF ITSELF? HE GONNA GET HIS FAITH BACK OKAY?
DUNNO.
FUCKIN' ARM IN PLASTER AIN'T GONNA DO MUCH GOOD.
VAS IS STAYIN' IN TOWN FOR A COUPLA DAYS. HE LIKES VAS.
APART FROM THAT...
I S'POSE WE COULD ALWAYS TELL HIM WHO WE ARE.
I'LL SEE YOU LATER, ANYWAY.
ONE LAST THING I'VE GOTTA TAKE CARE OF.

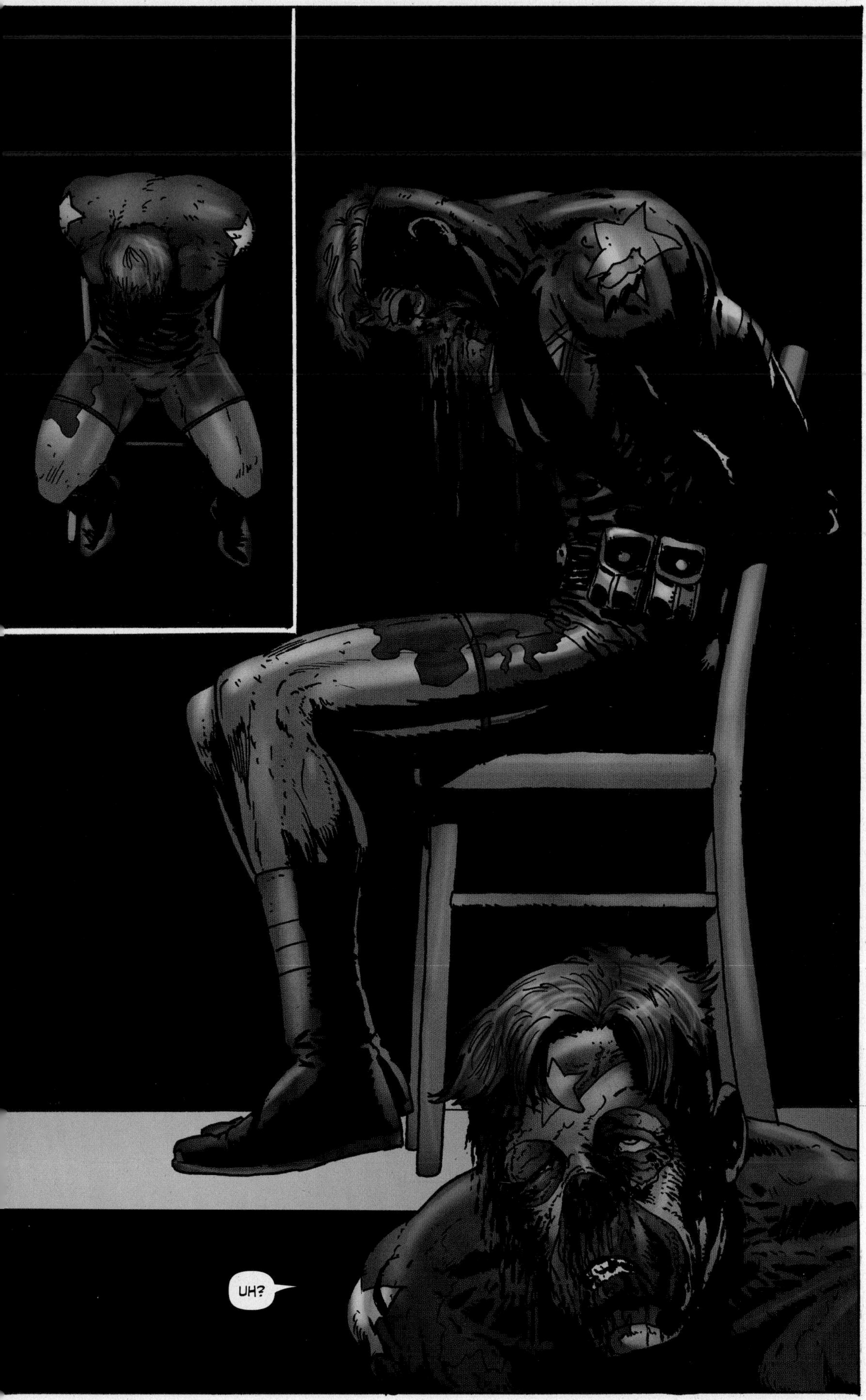
UH?

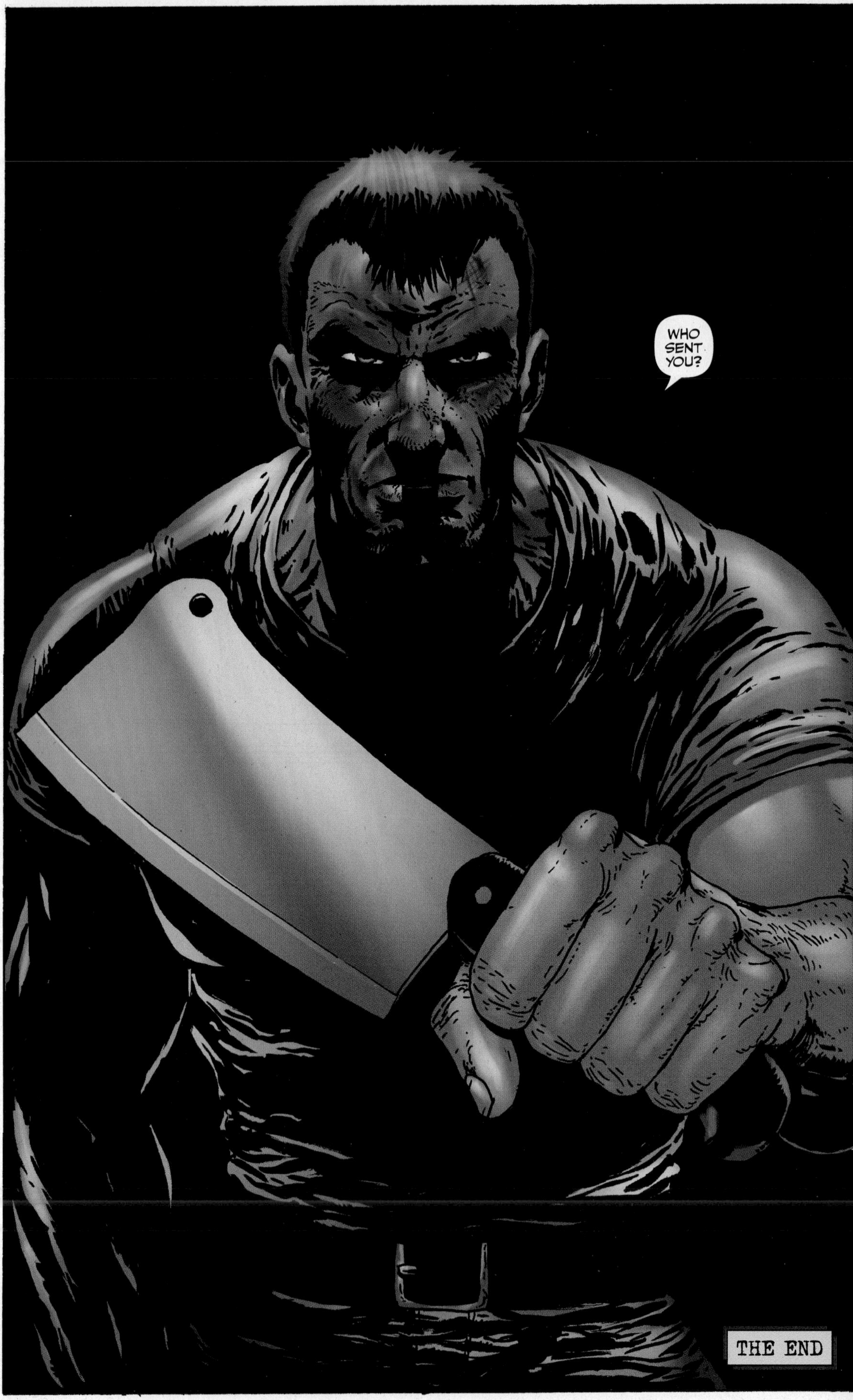
WHO SENT YOU?
THE END

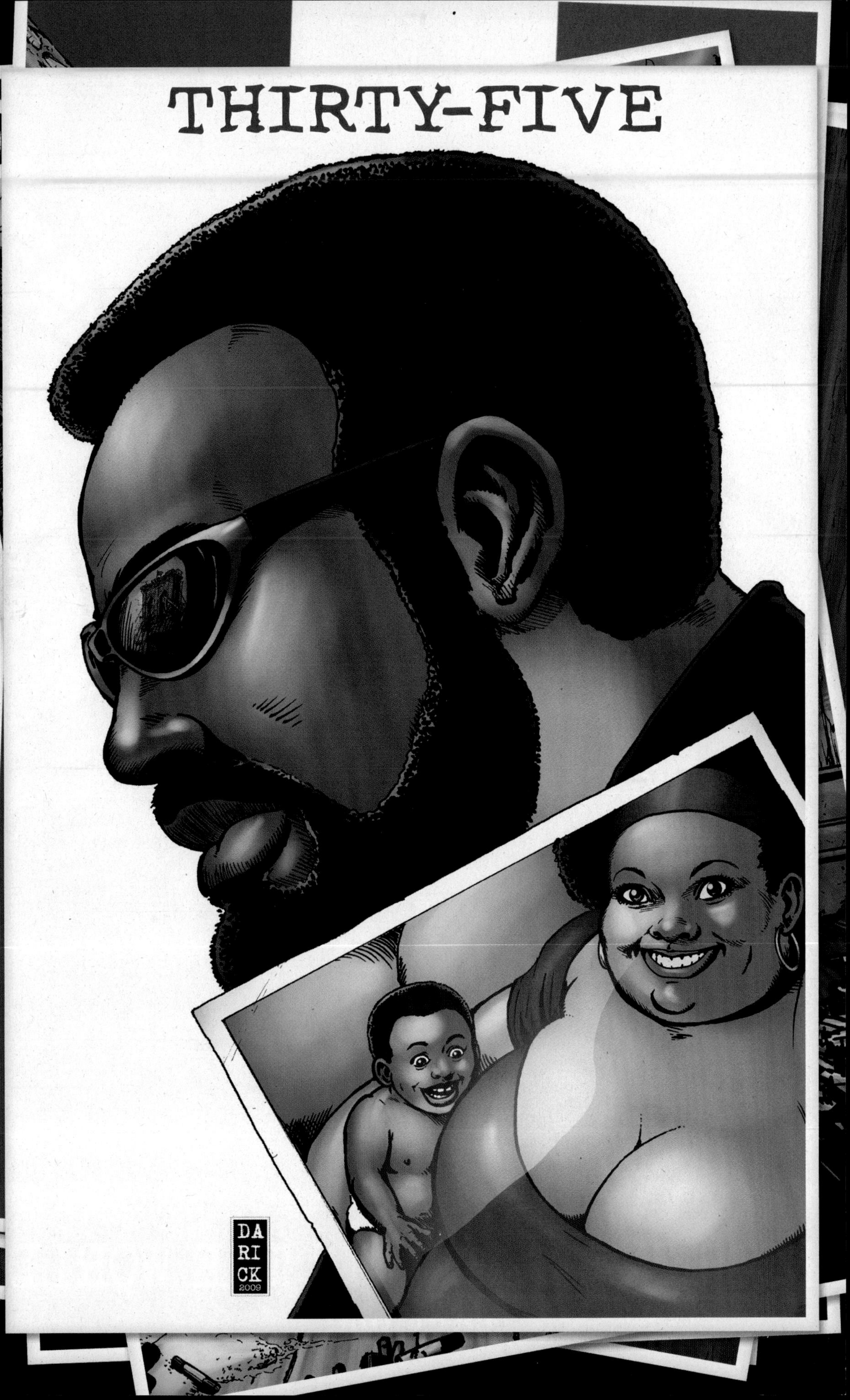
THIRTY-FIVE
DA
RI
CK
2009

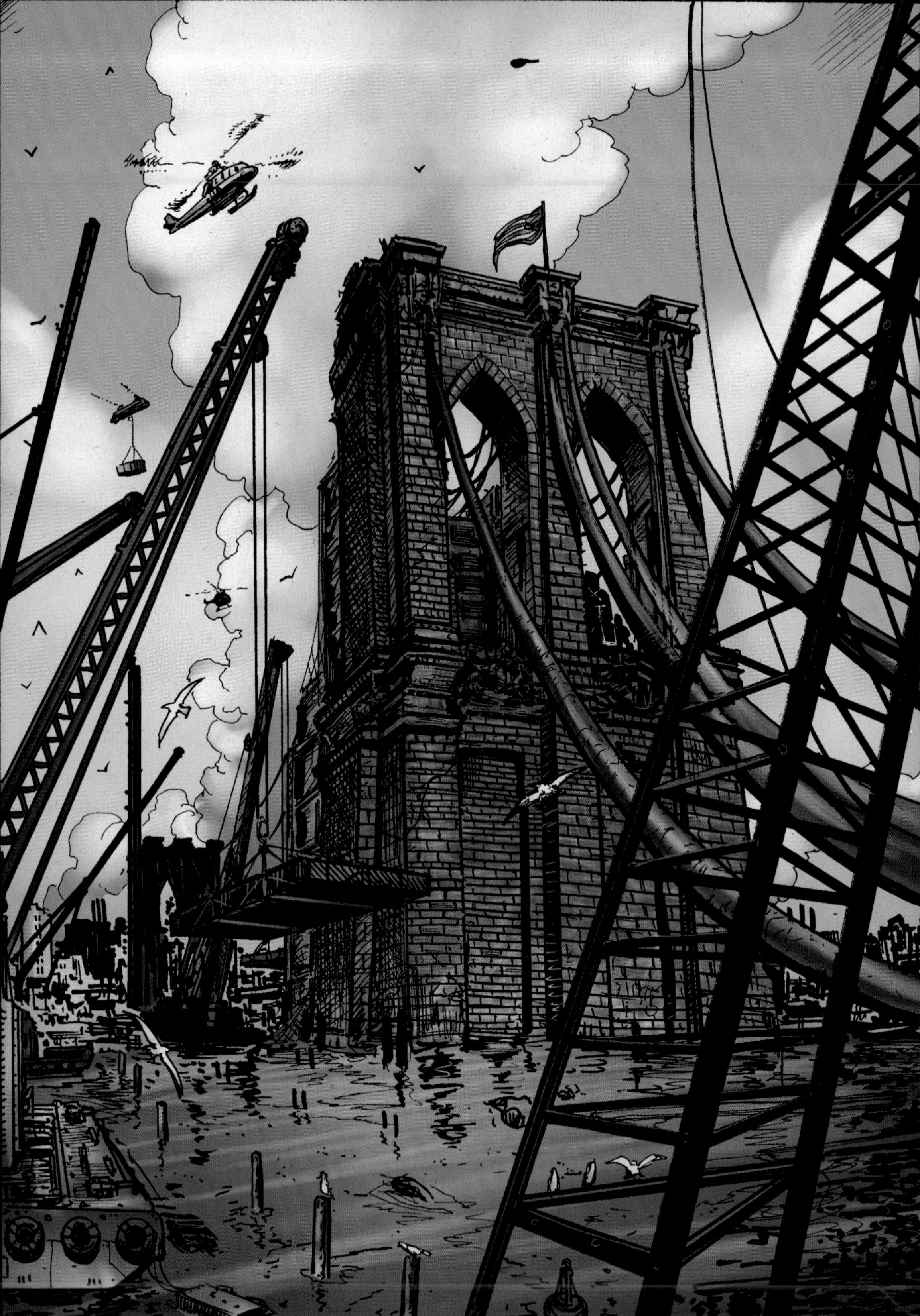

NOTHING LIKE IT IN THE WORLD

part one

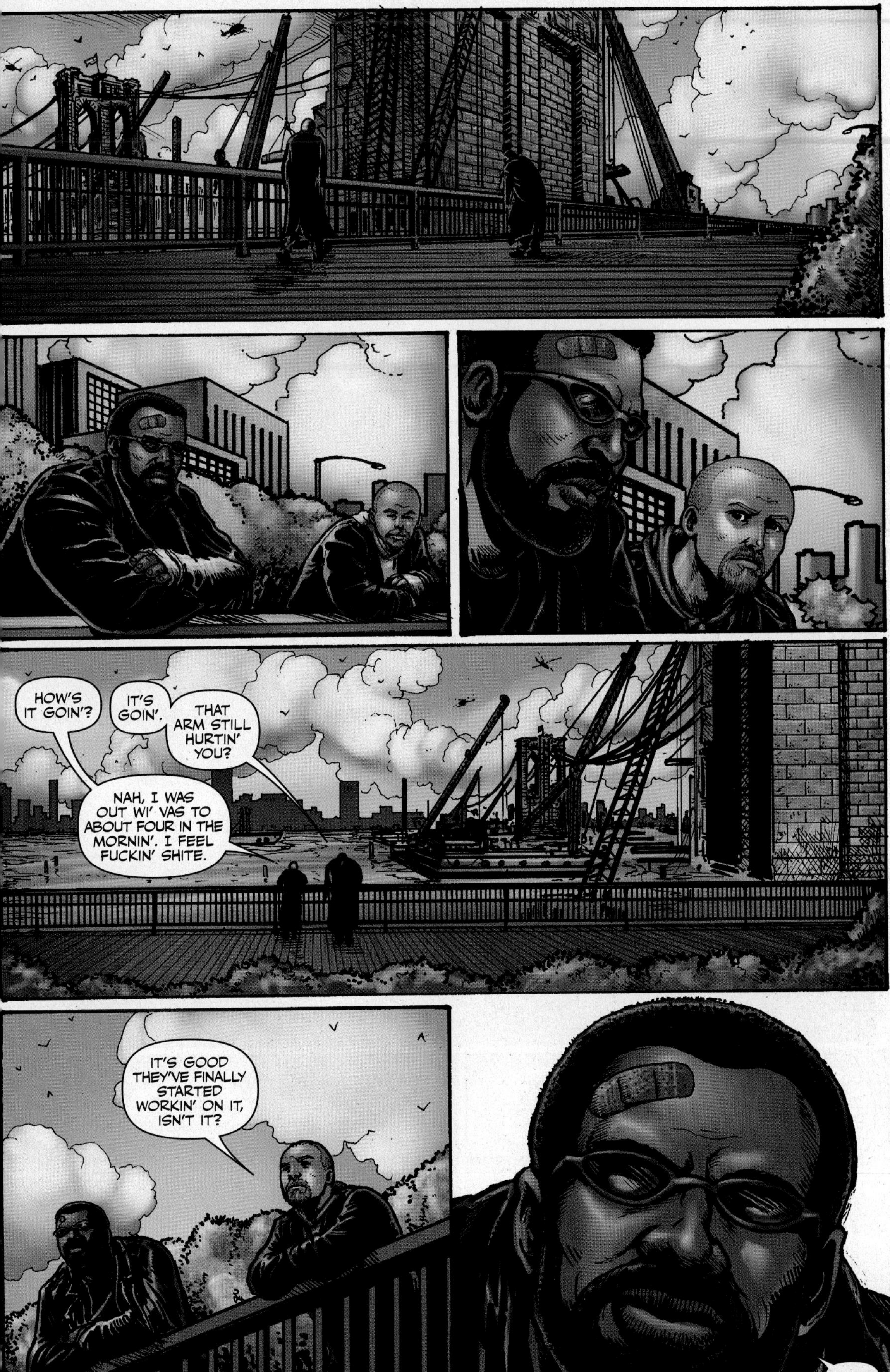
HOW'S IT GOIN'?
IT'S GOIN'.
THAT ARM STILL HURTIN' YOU?
NAH, I WAS OUT WI' VAS TO ABOUT FOUR IN THE MORNIN'. I FEEL FUCKIN' SHITE.
IT'S GOOD THEY'VE FINALLY STARTED WORKIN' ON IT, ISN'T IT?
YEAH.

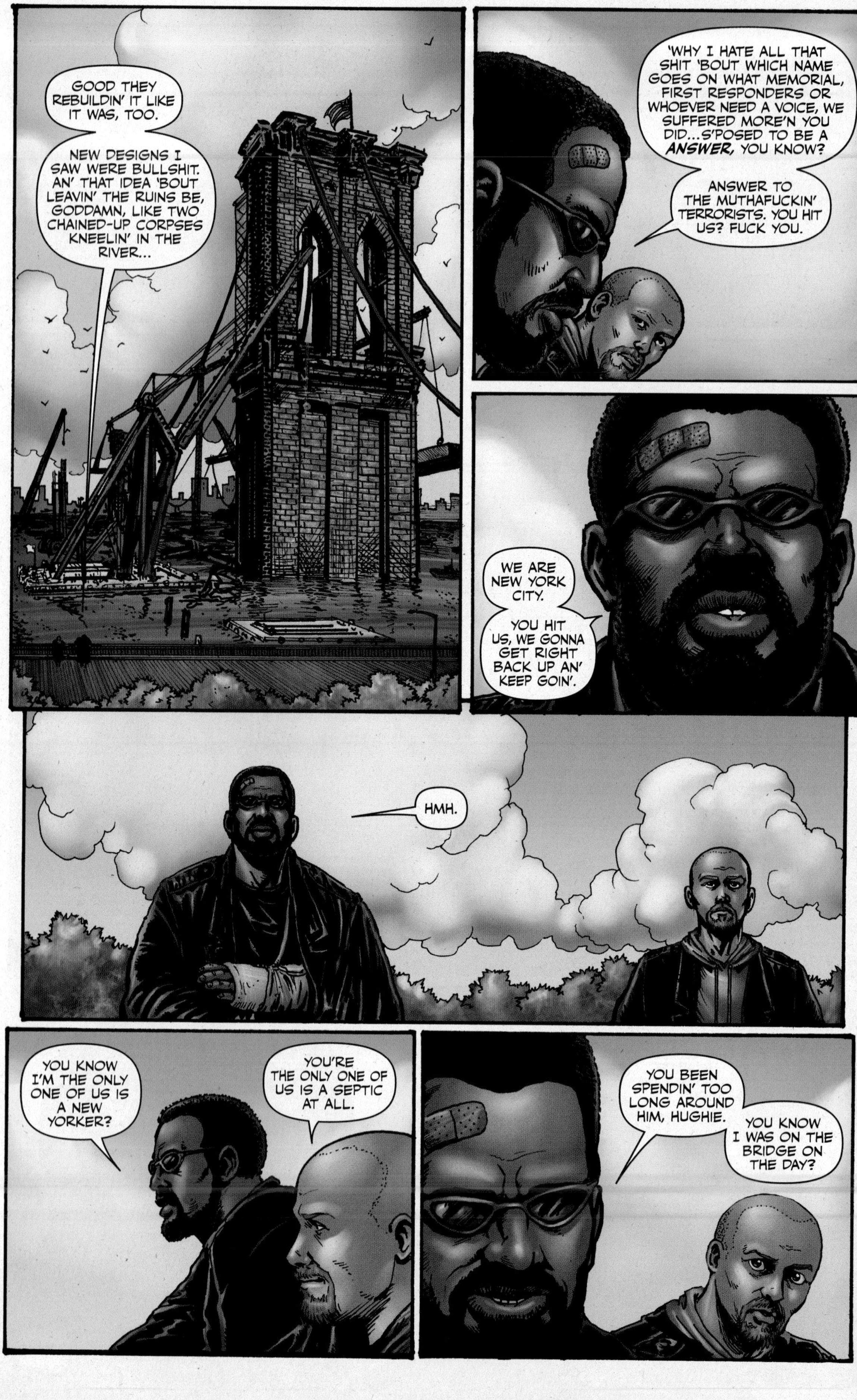
GOOD THEY REBUILDIN' IT LIKE IT WAS, TOO.
NEW DESIGNS I SAW WERE BULLSHIT. AN' THAT IDEA 'BOUT LEAVIN' THE RUINS BE, GODDAMN, LIKE TWO CHAINED-UP CORPSES KNEELIN' IN THE RIVER...
'WHY I HATE ALL THAT SHIT 'BOUT WHICH NAME GOES ON WHAT MEMORIAL, FIRST RESPONDERS OR WHOEVER NEED A VOICE, WE SUFFERED MORE'N YOU DID...S'POSED TO BE A ANSWER, YOU KNOW?
ANSWER TO THE MUTHAFUCKIN' TERRORISTS. YOU HIT US? FUCK YOU.
WE ARE NEW YORK CITY.
YOU HIT US, WE GONNA GET RIGHT BACK UP AN' KEEP GOIN'.
HMH.
YOU KNOW I'M THE ONLY ONE OF US IS A NEW YORKER?
YOU'RE THE ONLY ONE OF US IS A SEPTIC AT ALL.
YOU BEEN SPENDIN' TOO LONG AROUND HIM, HUGHIE.
YOU KNOW I WAS ON THE BRIDGE ON THE DAY?

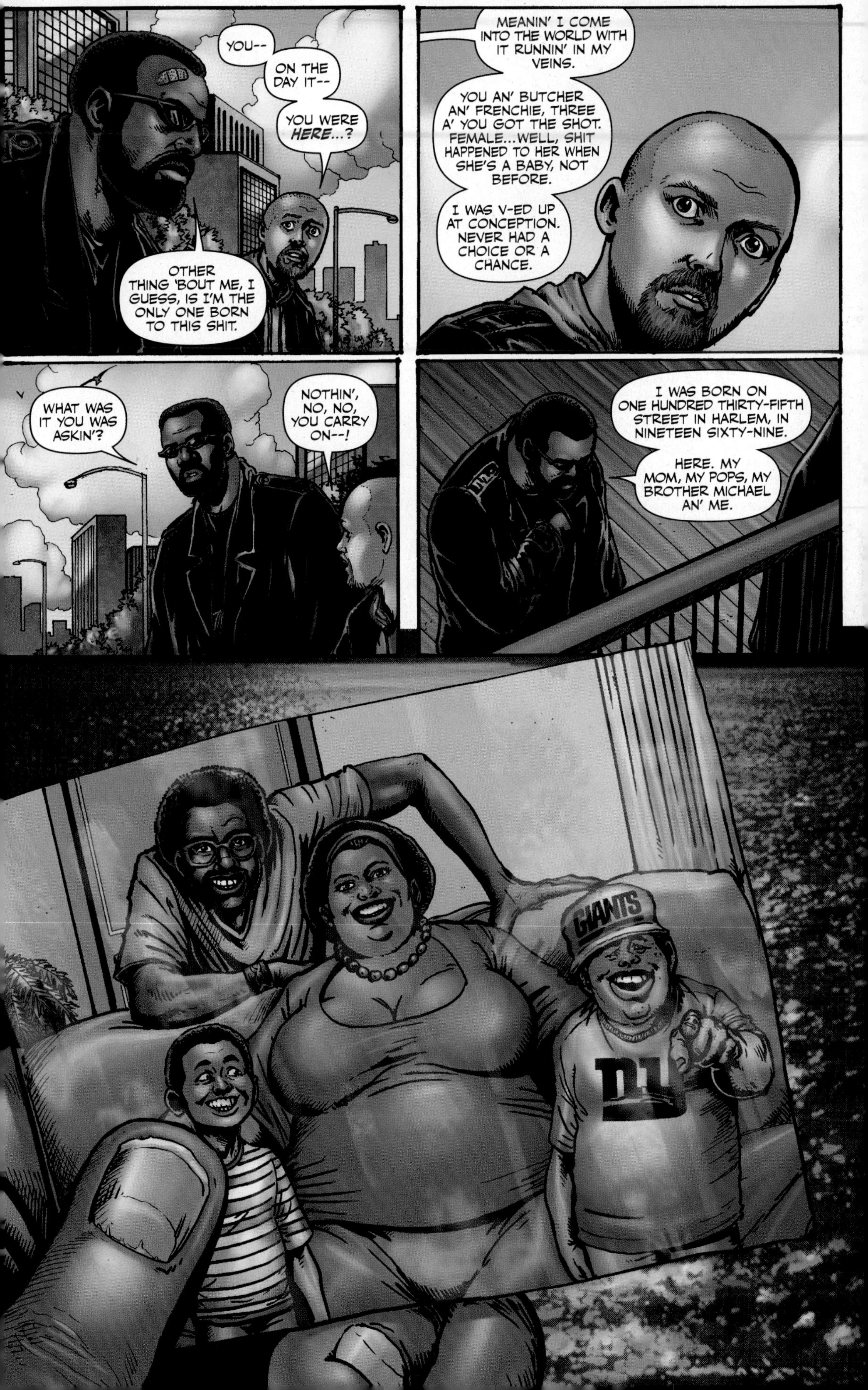

YOU--
ON THE DAY IT--
YOU WERE *HERE*...?
OTHER THING 'BOUT ME, I GUESS, IS I'M THE ONLY ONE BORN TO THIS SHIT.
MEANIN' I COME INTO THE WORLD WITH IT RUNNIN' IN MY VEINS.
YOU AN' BUTCHER AN' FRENCHIE, THREE A' YOU GOT THE SHOT. FEMALE...WELL, SHIT HAPPENED TO HER WHEN SHE'S A BABY, NOT BEFORE.
I WAS V-ED UP AT CONCEPTION. NEVER HAD A CHOICE OR A CHANCE.
WHAT WAS IT YOU WAS ASKIN'?
NOTHIN', NO, NO, YOU CARRY ON--!
I WAS BORN ON ONE HUNDRED THIRTY-FIFTH STREET IN HARLEM, IN NINETEEN SIXTY-NINE.
HERE. MY MOM, MY POPS, MY BROTHER MICHAEL AN' ME.
GIANTS

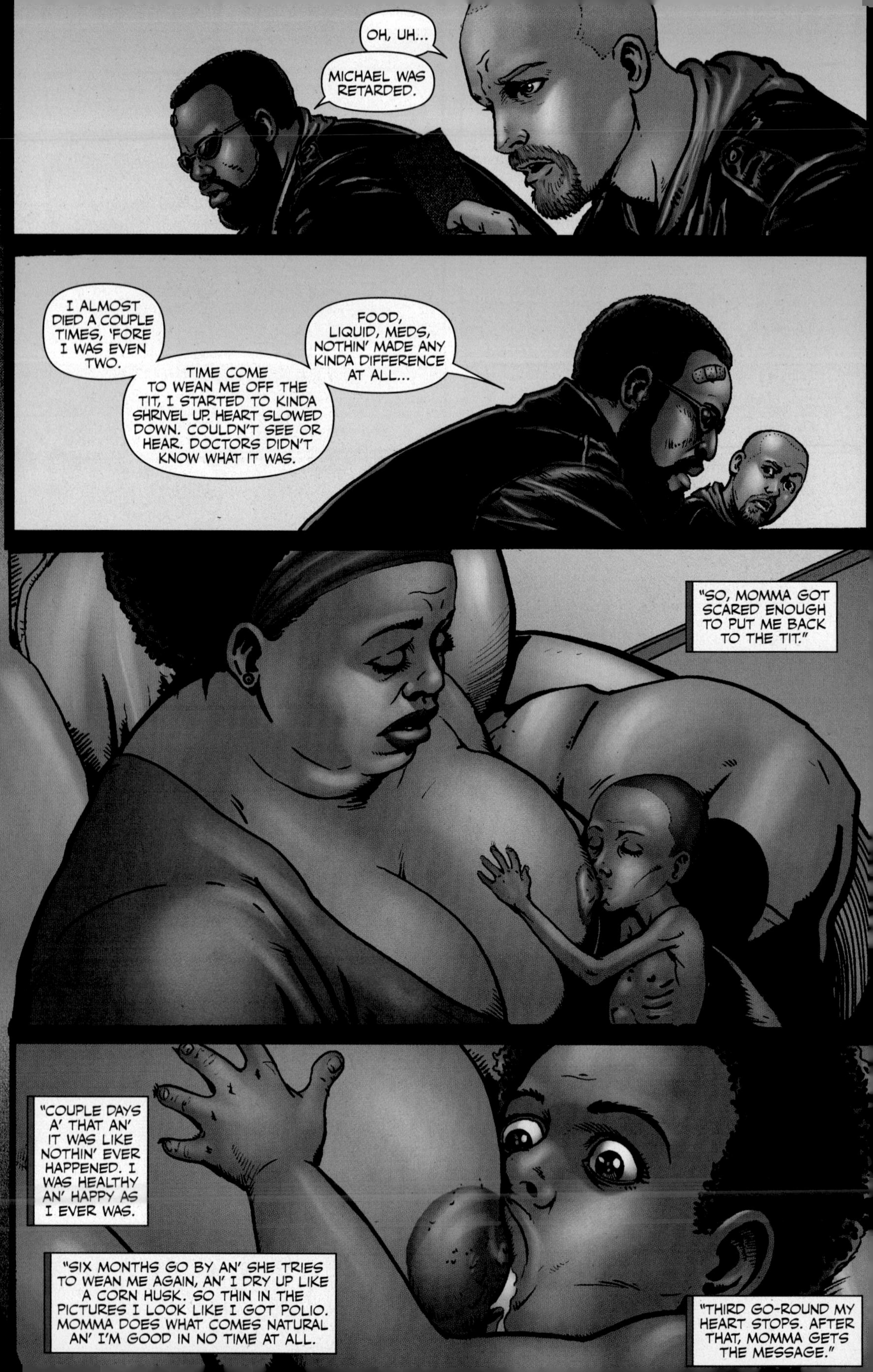
OH, UH...
MICHAEL WAS RETARDED.
I ALMOST DIED A COUPLE TIMES, 'FORE I WAS EVEN TWO.
TIME COME TO WEAN ME OFF THE TIT, I STARTED TO KINDA SHRIVEL UP. HEART SLOWED DOWN. COULDN'T SEE OR HEAR. DOCTORS DIDN'T KNOW WHAT IT WAS.
FOOD, LIQUID, MEDS, NOTHIN' MADE ANY KINDA DIFFERENCE AT ALL...
"SO, MOMMA GOT SCARED ENOUGH TO PUT ME BACK TO THE TIT."
"COUPLE DAYS A' THAT AN' IT WAS LIKE NOTHIN' EVER HAPPENED. I WAS HEALTHY AN' HAPPY AS I EVER WAS.
"SIX MONTHS GO BY AN' SHE TRIES TO WEAN ME AGAIN, AN' I DRY UP LIKE A CORN HUSK. SO THIN IN THE PICTURES I LOOK LIKE I GOT POLIO. MOMMA DOES WHAT COMES NATURAL AN' I'M GOOD IN NO TIME AT ALL.
"THIRD GO-ROUND MY HEART STOPS. AFTER THAT, MOMMA GETS THE MESSAGE."

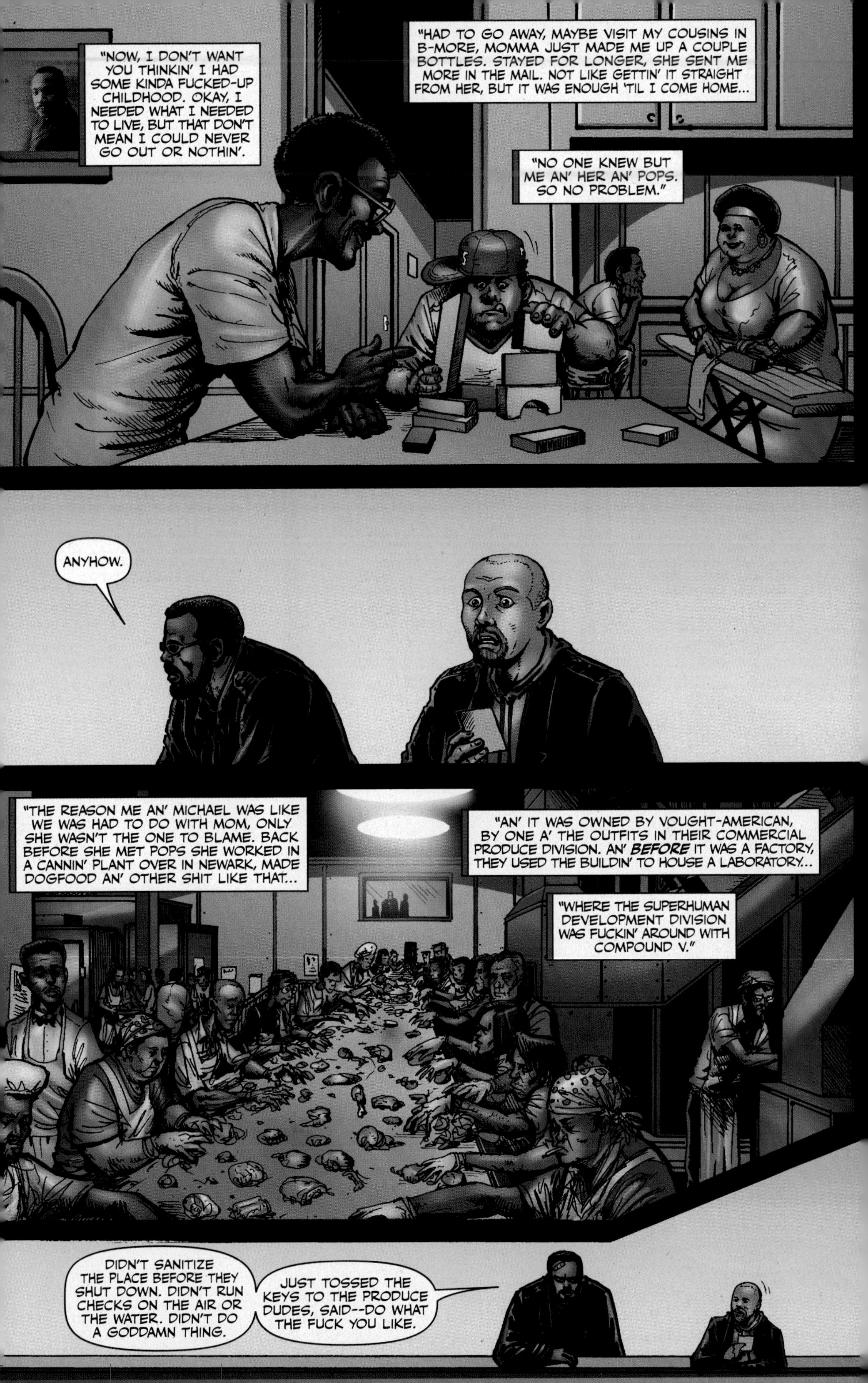
"NOW, I DON'T WANT YOU THINKIN' I HAD SOME KINDA FUCKED-UP CHILDHOOD. OKAY, I NEEDED WHAT I NEEDED TO LIVE, BUT THAT DON'T MEAN I COULD NEVER GO OUT OR NOTHIN'.
"HAD TO GO AWAY, MAYBE VISIT MY COUSINS IN B-MORE, MOMMA JUST MADE ME UP A COUPLE BOTTLES. STAYED FOR LONGER, SHE SENT ME MORE IN THE MAIL. NOT LIKE GETTIN' IT STRAIGHT FROM HER, BUT IT WAS ENOUGH 'TIL I COME HOME...
"NO ONE KNEW BUT ME AN' HER AN' POPS. SO NO PROBLEM."
ANYHOW.
"THE REASON ME AN' MICHAEL WAS LIKE WE WAS HAD TO DO WITH MOM, ONLY SHE WASN'T THE ONE TO BLAME. BACK BEFORE SHE MET POPS SHE WORKED IN A CANNIN' PLANT OVER IN NEWARK, MADE DOGFOOD AN' OTHER SHIT LIKE THAT...
"AN' IT WAS OWNED BY VOUGHT-AMERICAN, BY ONE A' THE OUTFITS IN THEIR COMMERCIAL PRODUCE DIVISION. AN' BEFORE IT WAS A FACTORY, THEY USED THE BUILDIN' TO HOUSE A LABORATORY...
"WHERE THE SUPERHUMAN DEVELOPMENT DIVISION WAS FUCKIN' AROUND WITH COMPOUND V."
DIDN'T SANITIZE THE PLACE BEFORE THEY SHUT DOWN. DIDN'T RUN CHECKS ON THE AIR OR THE WATER. DIDN'T DO A GODDAMN THING.
JUST TOSSED THE KEYS TO THE PRODUCE DUDES, SAID--DO WHAT THE FUCK YOU LIKE.

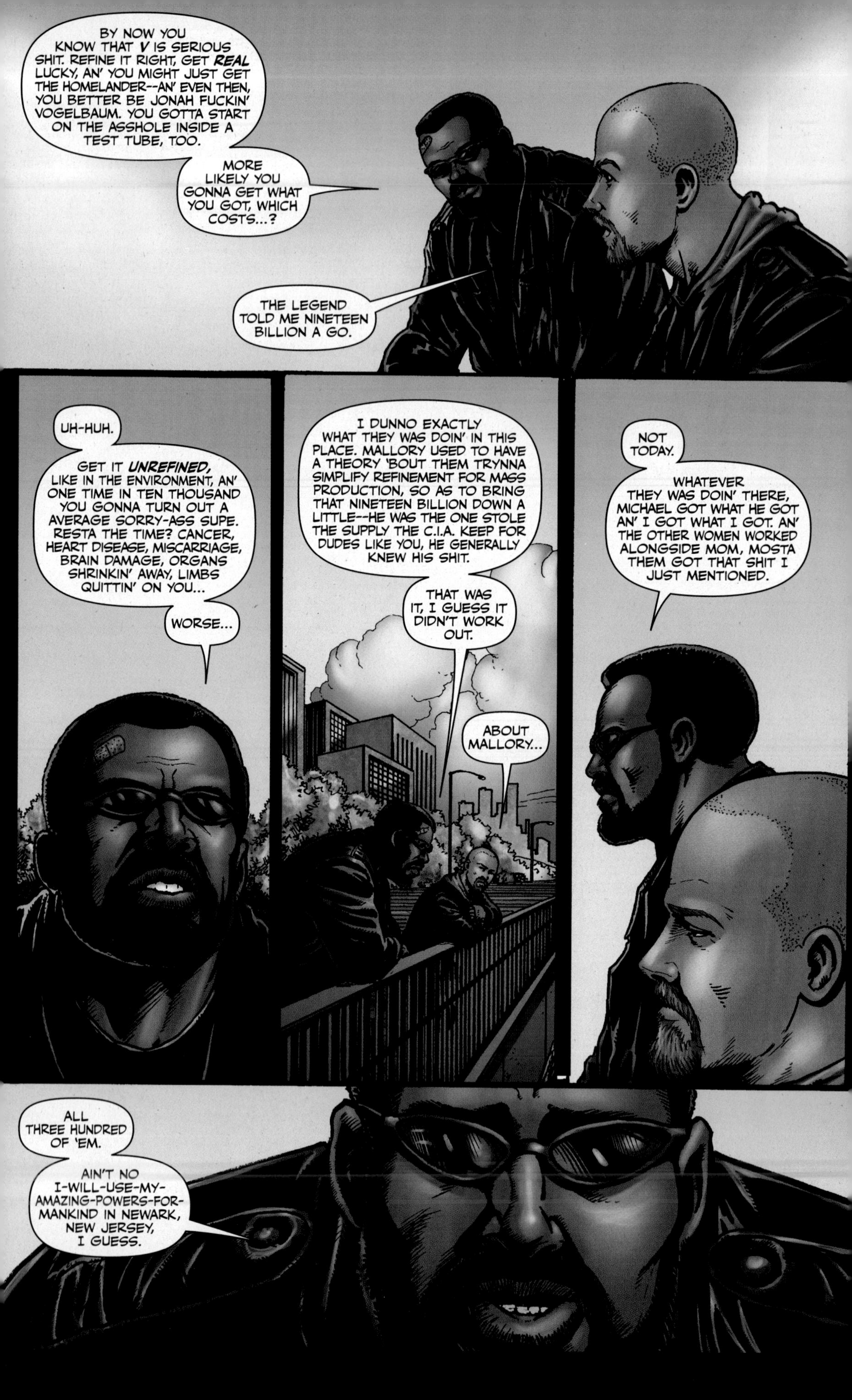
BY NOW YOU KNOW THAT V IS SERIOUS SHIT. REFINE IT RIGHT, GET REAL LUCKY, AN' YOU MIGHT JUST GET THE HOMELANDER--AN' EVEN THEN, YOU BETTER BE JONAH FUCKIN' VOGELBAUM. YOU GOTTA START ON THE ASSHOLE INSIDE A TEST TUBE, TOO.
MORE LIKELY YOU GONNA GET WHAT YOU GOT, WHICH COSTS...?
THE LEGEND TOLD ME NINETEEN BILLION A GO.
UH-HUH.
GET IT UNREFINED, LIKE IN THE ENVIRONMENT, AN' ONE TIME IN TEN THOUSAND YOU GONNA TURN OUT A AVERAGE SORRY-ASS SUPE. RESTA THE TIME? CANCER, HEART DISEASE, MISCARRIAGE, BRAIN DAMAGE, ORGANS SHRINKIN' AWAY, LIMBS QUITTIN' ON YOU...
WORSE...
I DUNNO EXACTLY WHAT THEY WAS DOIN' IN THIS PLACE. MALLORY USED TO HAVE A THEORY 'BOUT THEM TRYNNA SIMPLIFY REFINEMENT FOR MASS PRODUCTION, SO AS TO BRING THAT NINETEEN BILLION DOWN A LITTLE--HE WAS THE ONE STOLE THE SUPPLY THE C.I.A. KEEP FOR DUDES LIKE YOU, HE GENERALLY KNEW HIS SHIT.
THAT WAS IT, I GUESS IT DIDN'T WORK OUT.
ABOUT MALLORY...
NOT TODAY.
WHATEVER THEY WAS DOIN' THERE, MICHAEL GOT WHAT HE GOT AN' I GOT WHAT I GOT. AN' THE OTHER WOMEN WORKED ALONGSIDE MOM, MOSTA THEM GOT THAT SHIT I JUST MENTIONED.
ALL THREE HUNDRED OF 'EM.
AIN'T NO I-WILL-USE-MY-AMAZING-POWERS-FOR-MANKIND IN NEWARK, NEW JERSEY, I GUESS.

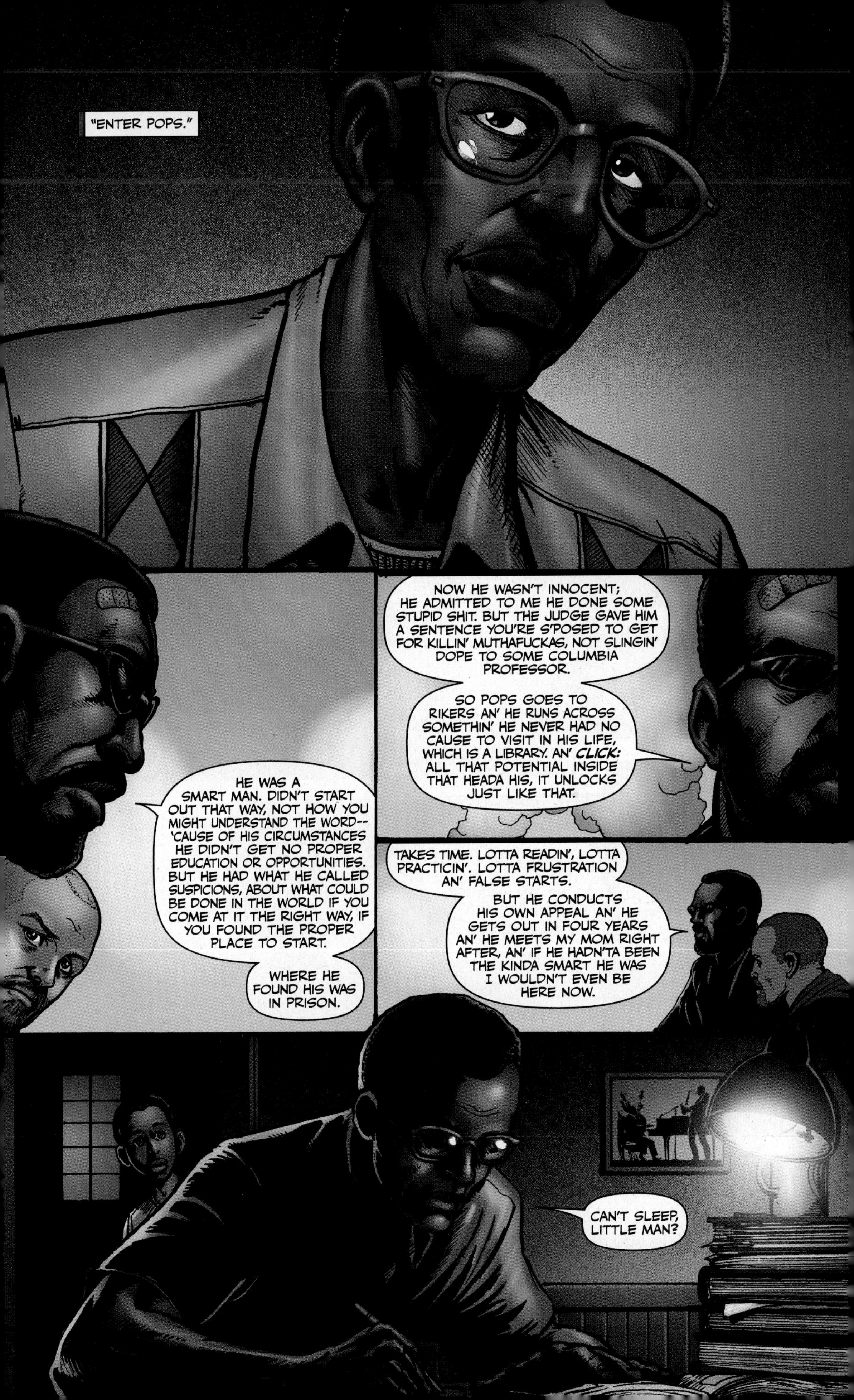
"ENTER POPS."
HE WAS A SMART MAN. DIDN'T START OUT THAT WAY, NOT HOW YOU MIGHT UNDERSTAND THE WORD-- 'CAUSE OF HIS CIRCUMSTANCES HE DIDN'T GET NO PROPER EDUCATION OR OPPORTUNITIES. BUT HE HAD WHAT HE CALLED SUSPICIONS, ABOUT WHAT COULD BE DONE IN THE WORLD IF YOU COME AT IT THE RIGHT WAY, IF YOU FOUND THE PROPER PLACE TO START.
WHERE HE FOUND HIS WAS IN PRISON.
NOW HE WASN'T INNOCENT; HE ADMITTED TO ME HE DONE SOME STUPID SHIT. BUT THE JUDGE GAVE HIM A SENTENCE YOU'RE S'POSED TO GET FOR KILLIN' MUTHAFUCKAS, NOT SLINGIN' DOPE TO SOME COLUMBIA PROFESSOR.
SO POPS GOES TO RIKERS AN' HE RUNS ACROSS SOMETHIN' HE NEVER HAD NO CAUSE TO VISIT IN HIS LIFE, WHICH IS A LIBRARY. AN' *CLICK:* ALL THAT POTENTIAL INSIDE THAT HEADA HIS, IT UNLOCKS JUST LIKE THAT.
TAKES TIME. LOTTA READIN', LOTTA PRACTICIN'. LOTTA FRUSTRATION AN' FALSE STARTS.
BUT HE CONDUCTS HIS OWN APPEAL AN' HE GETS OUT IN FOUR YEARS AN' HE MEETS MY MOM RIGHT AFTER, AN' IF HE HADN'TA BEEN THE KINDA SMART HE WAS I WOULDN'T EVEN BE HERE NOW.
CAN'T SLEEP, LITTLE MAN?

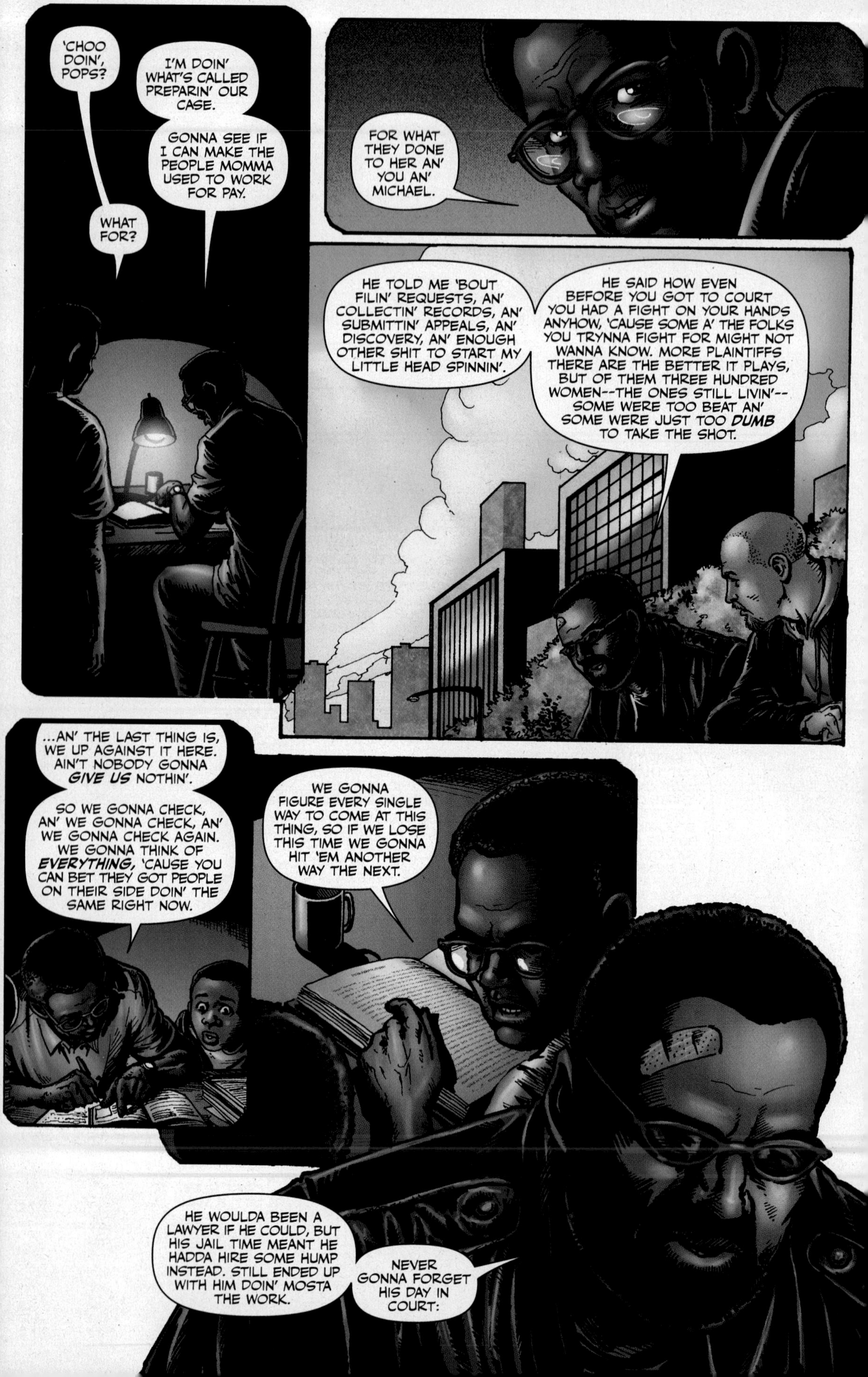
'CHOO DOIN', POPS?
I'M DOIN' WHAT'S CALLED PREPARIN' OUR CASE.
GONNA SEE IF I CAN MAKE THE PEOPLE MOMMA USED TO WORK FOR PAY.
WHAT FOR?
FOR WHAT THEY DONE TO HER AN' YOU AN' MICHAEL.
HE TOLD ME 'BOUT FILIN' REQUESTS, AN' COLLECTIN' RECORDS, AN' SUBMITTIN' APPEALS, AN' DISCOVERY, AN' ENOUGH OTHER SHIT TO START MY LITTLE HEAD SPINNIN'.
HE SAID HOW EVEN BEFORE YOU GOT TO COURT YOU HAD A FIGHT ON YOUR HANDS ANYHOW, 'CAUSE SOME A' THE FOLKS YOU TRYNNA FIGHT FOR MIGHT NOT WANNA KNOW. MORE PLAINTIFFS THERE ARE THE BETTER IT PLAYS, BUT OF THEM THREE HUNDRED WOMEN--THE ONES STILL LIVIN'--SOME WERE TOO BEAT AN' SOME WERE JUST TOO *DUMB* TO TAKE THE SHOT.
...AN' THE LAST THING IS, WE UP AGAINST IT HERE. AIN'T NOBODY GONNA *GIVE US* NOTHIN'.
SO WE GONNA CHECK, AN' WE GONNA CHECK, AN' WE GONNA CHECK AGAIN. WE GONNA THINK OF *EVERYTHING,* 'CAUSE YOU CAN BET THEY GOT PEOPLE ON THEIR SIDE DOIN' THE SAME RIGHT NOW.
WE GONNA FIGURE EVERY SINGLE WAY TO COME AT THIS THING, SO IF WE LOSE THIS TIME WE GONNA HIT 'EM ANOTHER WAY THE NEXT.
HE WOULDA BEEN A LAWYER IF HE COULD, BUT HIS JAIL TIME MEANT HE HADDA HIRE SOME HUMP INSTEAD. STILL ENDED UP WITH HIM DOIN' MOSTA THE WORK.
NEVER GONNA FORGET HIS DAY IN COURT:

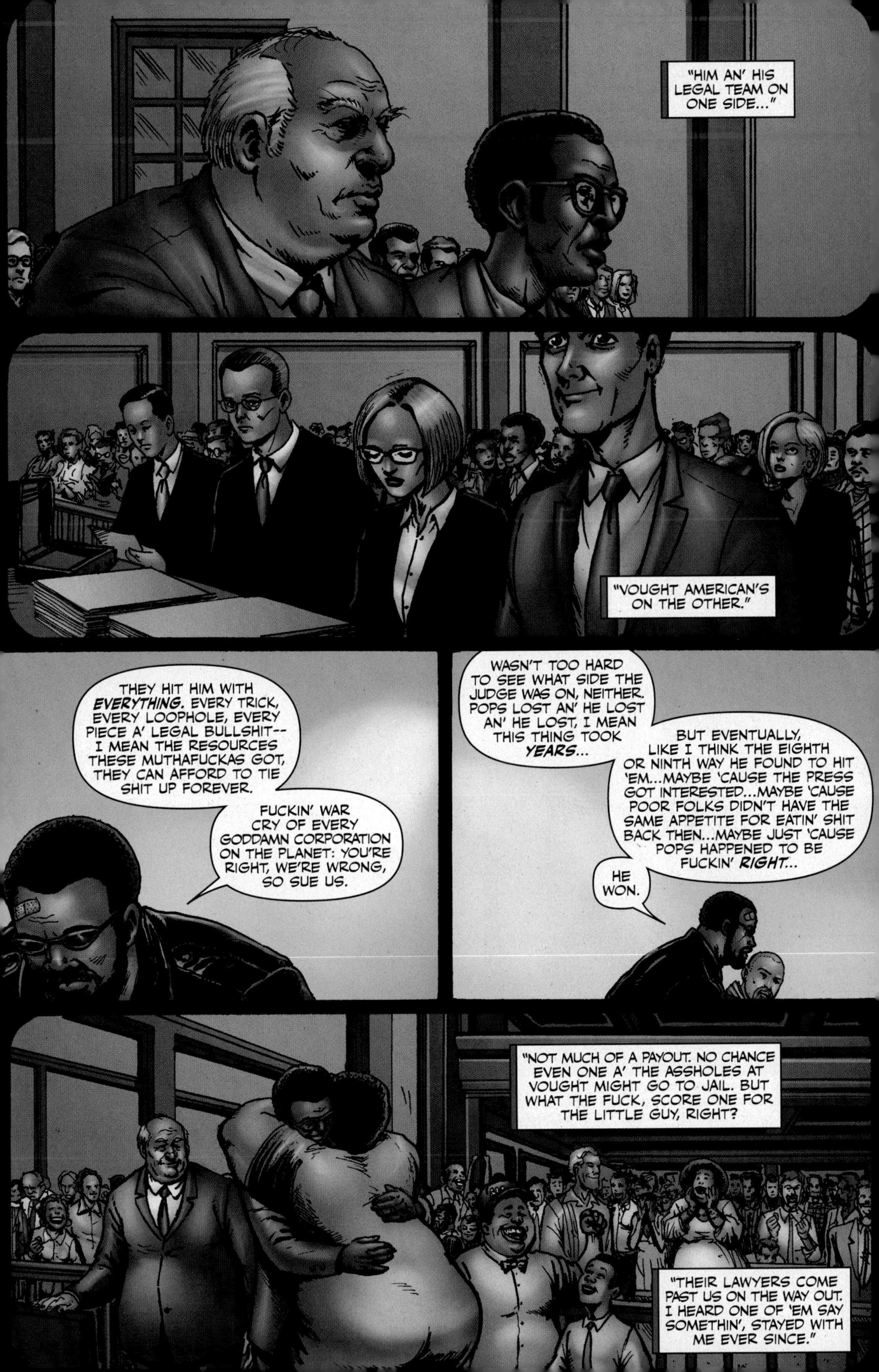
"HIM AN' HIS LEGAL TEAM ON ONE SIDE..."
"VOUGHT AMERICAN'S ON THE OTHER."
THEY HIT HIM WITH EVERYTHING. EVERY TRICK, EVERY LOOPHOLE, EVERY PIECE A' LEGAL BULLSHIT-- I MEAN THE RESOURCES THESE MUTHAFUCKAS GOT, THEY CAN AFFORD TO TIE SHIT UP FOREVER.
FUCKIN' WAR CRY OF EVERY GODDAMN CORPORATION ON THE PLANET: YOU'RE RIGHT, WE'RE WRONG, SO SUE US.
WASN'T TOO HARD TO SEE WHAT SIDE THE JUDGE WAS ON, NEITHER. POPS LOST AN' HE LOST AN' HE LOST, I MEAN THIS THING TOOK YEARS...
BUT EVENTUALLY, LIKE I THINK THE EIGHTH OR NINTH WAY HE FOUND TO HIT 'EM...MAYBE 'CAUSE THE PRESS GOT INTERESTED...MAYBE 'CAUSE POOR FOLKS DIDN'T HAVE THE SAME APPETITE FOR EATIN' SHIT BACK THEN...MAYBE JUST 'CAUSE POPS HAPPENED TO BE FUCKIN' RIGHT...
HE WON.
"NOT MUCH OF A PAYOUT. NO CHANCE EVEN ONE A' THE ASSHOLES AT VOUGHT MIGHT GO TO JAIL. BUT WHAT THE FUCK, SCORE ONE FOR THE LITTLE GUY, RIGHT?
"THEIR LAWYERS COME PAST US ON THE WAY OUT. I HEARD ONE OF 'EM SAY SOMETHIN', STAYED WITH ME EVER SINCE."

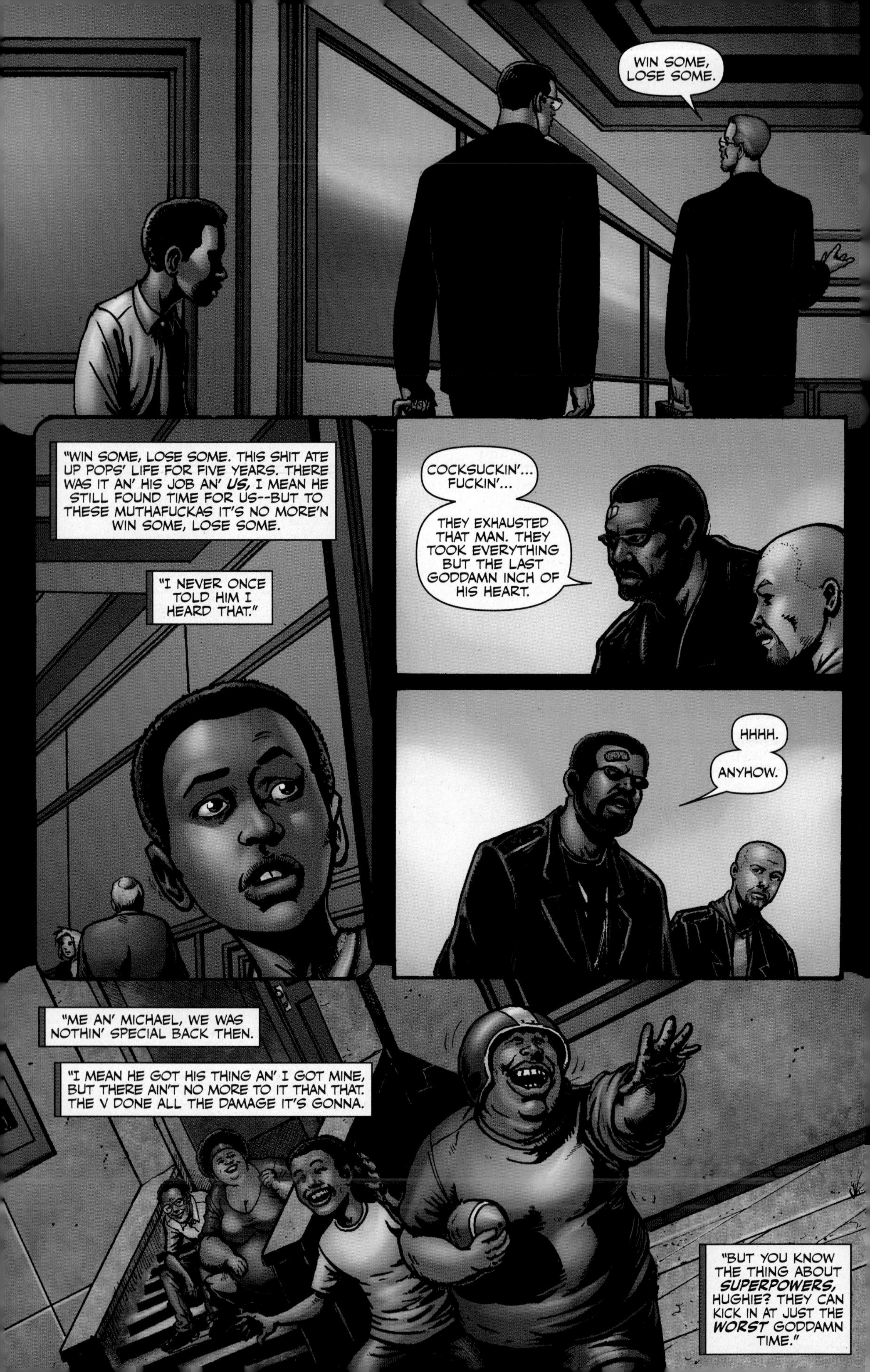
WIN SOME, LOSE SOME.
"WIN SOME, LOSE SOME. THIS SHIT ATE UP POPS' LIFE FOR FIVE YEARS. THERE WAS IT AN' HIS JOB AN' *US*, I MEAN HE STILL FOUND TIME FOR US--BUT TO THESE MUTHAFUCKAS IT'S NO MORE'N WIN SOME, LOSE SOME.
"I NEVER ONCE TOLD HIM I HEARD THAT."
COCKSUCKIN'... FUCKIN'...
THEY EXHAUSTED THAT MAN. THEY TOOK EVERYTHING BUT THE LAST GODDAMN INCH OF HIS HEART.
HHHH.
ANYHOW.
"ME AN' MICHAEL, WE WAS NOTHIN' SPECIAL BACK THEN.
"I MEAN HE GOT HIS THING AN' I GOT MINE, BUT THERE AIN'T NO MORE TO IT THAN THAT. THE V DONE ALL THE DAMAGE IT'S GONNA.
"BUT YOU KNOW THE THING ABOUT *SUPERPOWERS*, HUGHIE? THEY CAN KICK IN AT JUST THE *WORST* GODDAMN TIME."

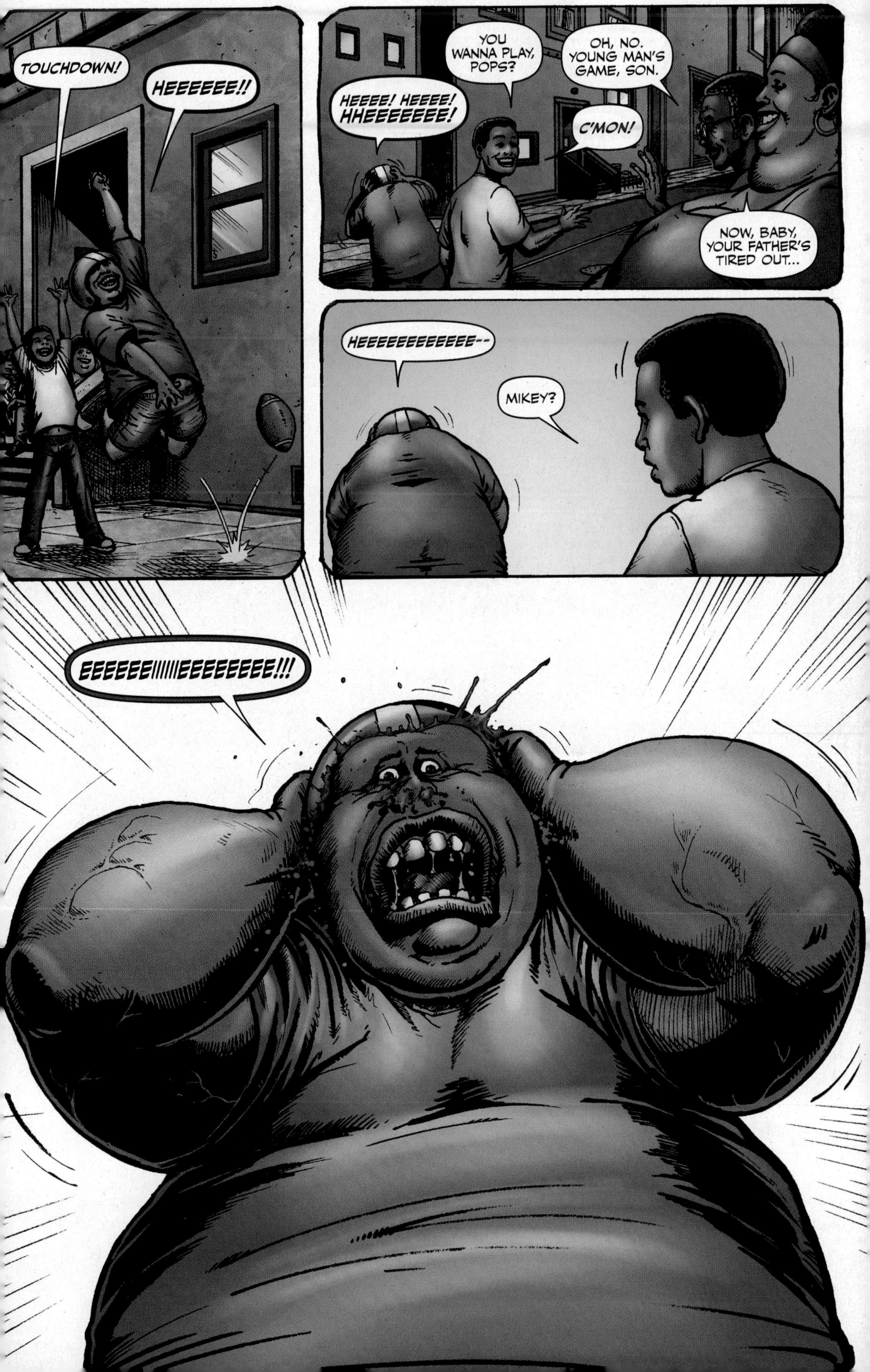
TOUCHDOWN!
HEEEEEE!!
YOU WANNA PLAY, POPS?
OH, NO. YOUNG MAN'S GAME, SON.
HEEEE! HEEEE! HHEEEEEEE!
C'MON!
NOW, BABY, YOUR FATHER'S TIRED OUT...
HEEEEEEEEEEE--
MIKEY?
EEEEEEIIIIIIEEEEEEEE!!!

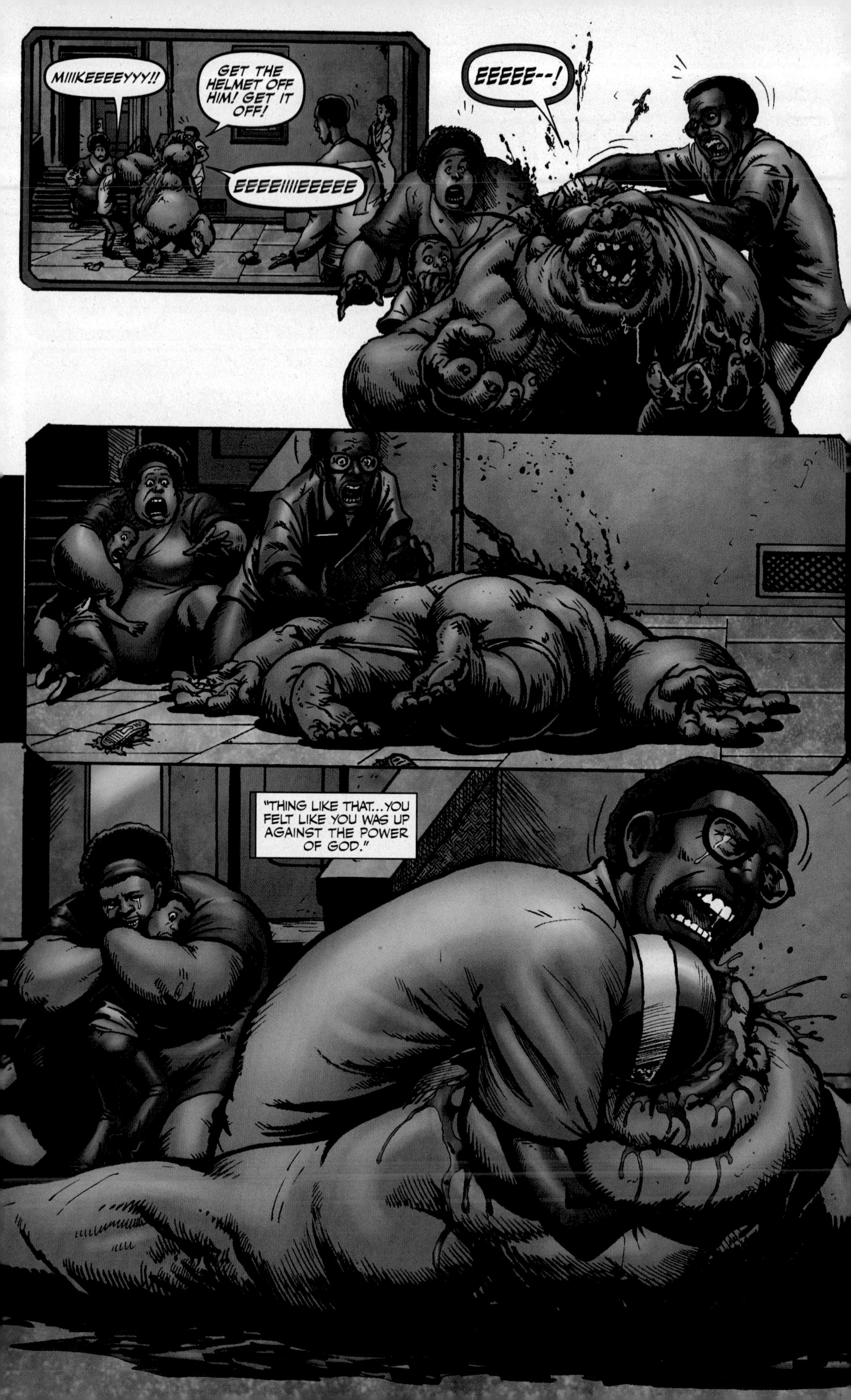

MIIIKEEEEYYY!!
GET THE HELMET OFF HIM! GET IT OFF!
EEEEIIIIEEEEE
EEEEE--!
"THING LIKE THAT...YOU FELT LIKE YOU WAS UP AGAINST THE POWER OF GOD."

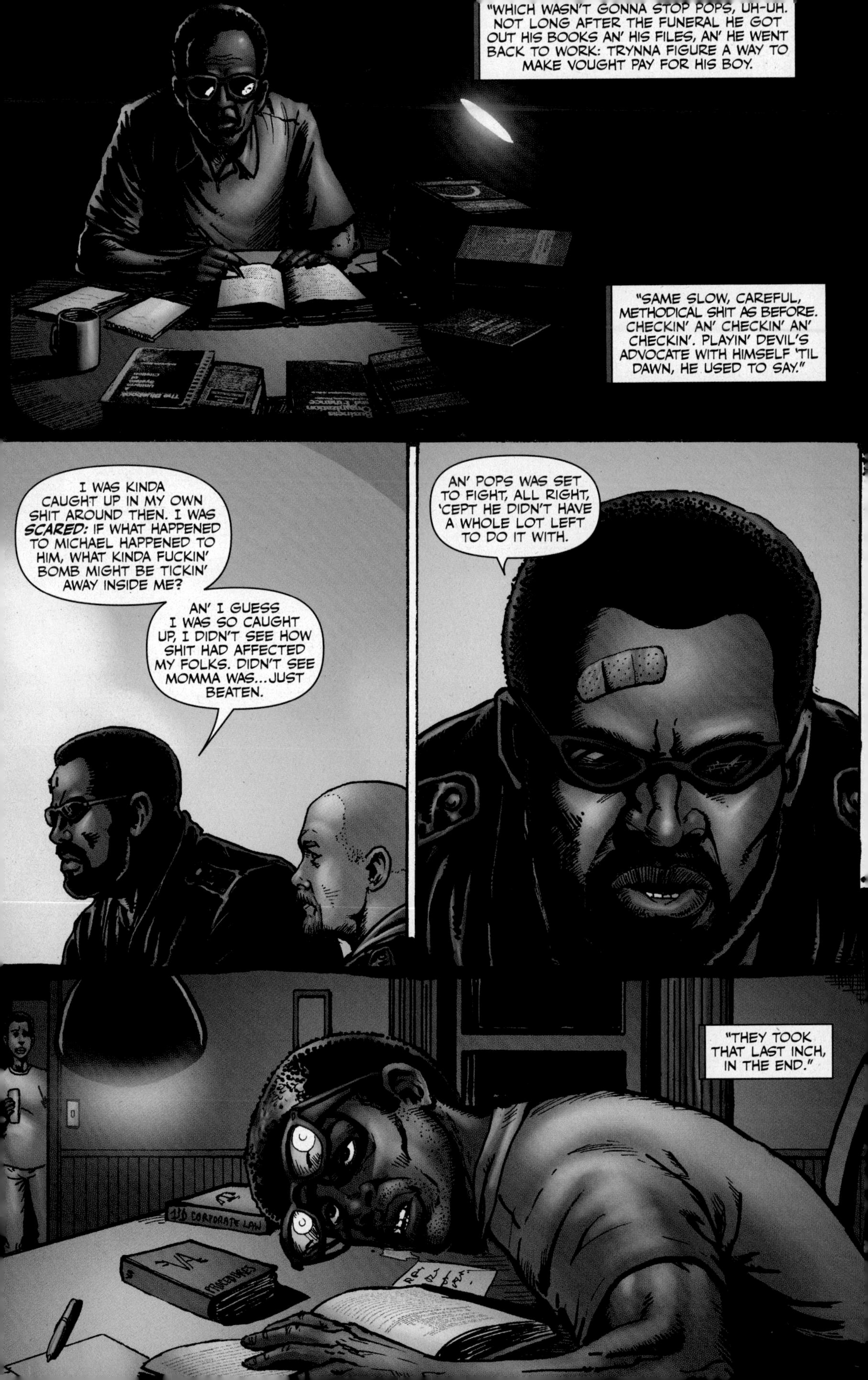
"WHICH WASN'T GONNA STOP POPS, UH-UH. NOT LONG AFTER THE FUNERAL HE GOT OUT HIS BOOKS AN' HIS FILES, AN' HE WENT BACK TO WORK: TRYNNA FIGURE A WAY TO MAKE VOUGHT PAY FOR HIS BOY.
"SAME SLOW, CAREFUL, METHODICAL SHIT AS BEFORE. CHECKIN' AN' CHECKIN' AN' CHECKIN'. PLAYIN' DEVIL'S ADVOCATE WITH HIMSELF 'TIL DAWN, HE USED TO SAY."
I WAS KINDA CAUGHT UP IN MY OWN SHIT AROUND THEN. I WAS *SCARED:* IF WHAT HAPPENED TO MICHAEL HAPPENED TO HIM, WHAT KINDA FUCKIN' BOMB MIGHT BE TICKIN' AWAY INSIDE ME?
AN' I GUESS I WAS SO CAUGHT UP, I DIDN'T SEE HOW SHIT HAD AFFECTED MY FOLKS. DIDN'T SEE MOMMA WAS... JUST BEATEN.
AN' POPS WAS SET TO FIGHT, ALL RIGHT, 'CEPT HE DIDN'T HAVE A WHOLE LOT LEFT TO DO IT WITH.
"THEY TOOK THAT LAST INCH, IN THE END."
CORPORATE LAW

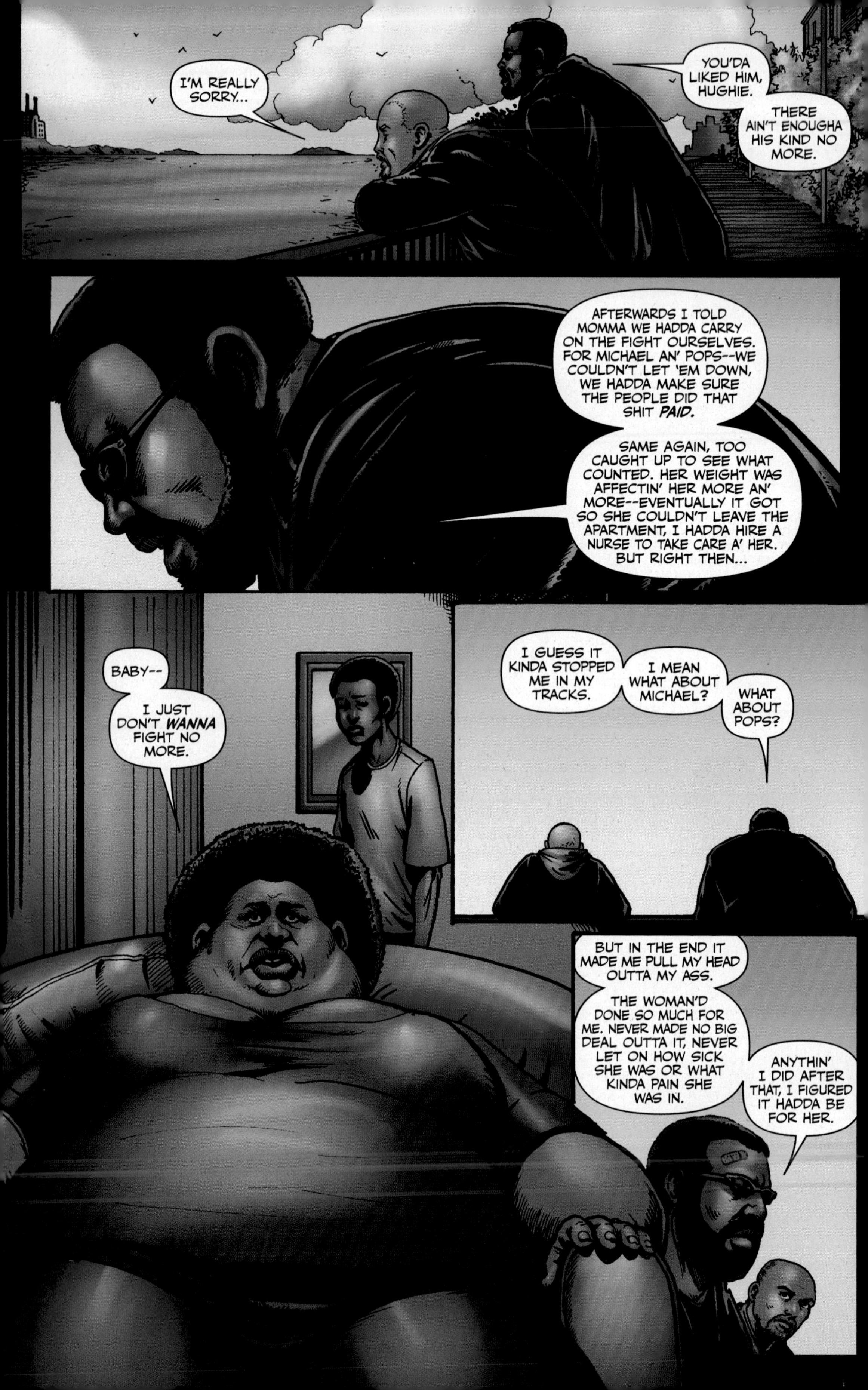
I'M REALLY SORRY...
YOU'DA LIKED HIM, HUGHIE.
THERE AIN'T ENOUGHA HIS KIND NO MORE.
AFTERWARDS I TOLD MOMMA WE HADDA CARRY ON THE FIGHT OURSELVES. FOR MICHAEL AN' POPS--WE COULDN'T LET 'EM DOWN, WE HADDA MAKE SURE THE PEOPLE DID THAT SHIT *PAID.*
SAME AGAIN, TOO CAUGHT UP TO SEE WHAT COUNTED. HER WEIGHT WAS AFFECTIN' HER MORE AN' MORE--EVENTUALLY IT GOT SO SHE COULDN'T LEAVE THE APARTMENT, I HADDA HIRE A NURSE TO TAKE CARE A' HER. BUT RIGHT THEN...
BABY--
I JUST DON'T *WANNA* FIGHT NO MORE.
I GUESS IT KINDA STOPPED ME IN MY TRACKS.
I MEAN WHAT ABOUT MICHAEL?
WHAT ABOUT POPS?
BUT IN THE END IT MADE ME PULL MY HEAD OUTTA MY ASS.
THE WOMAN'D DONE SO MUCH FOR ME. NEVER MADE NO BIG DEAL OUTTA IT, NEVER LET ON HOW SICK SHE WAS OR WHAT KINDA PAIN SHE WAS IN.
ANYTHIN' I DID AFTER THAT, I FIGURED IT HADDA BE FOR HER.

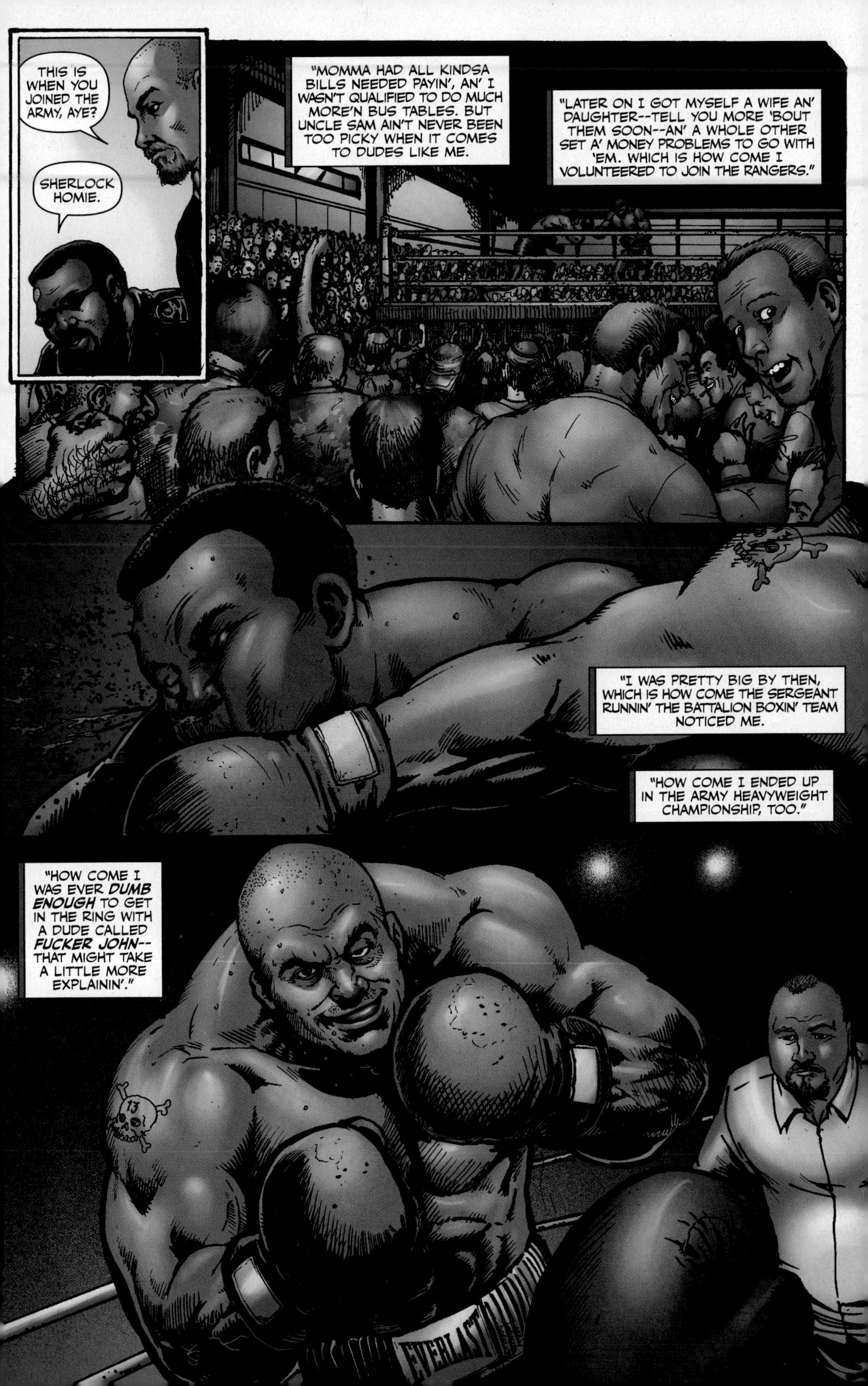
THIS IS WHEN YOU JOINED THE ARMY, AYE?
SHERLOCK HOMIE.
"MOMMA HAD ALL KINDSA BILLS NEEDED PAYIN', AN' I WASN'T QUALIFIED TO DO MUCH MORE'N BUS TABLES. BUT UNCLE SAM AIN'T NEVER BEEN TOO PICKY WHEN IT COMES TO DUDES LIKE ME.
"LATER ON I GOT MYSELF A WIFE AN' DAUGHTER--TELL YOU MORE 'BOUT THEM SOON--AN' A WHOLE OTHER SET A' MONEY PROBLEMS TO GO WITH 'EM. WHICH IS HOW COME I VOLUNTEERED TO JOIN THE RANGERS."
"I WAS PRETTY BIG BY THEN, WHICH IS HOW COME THE SERGEANT RUNNIN' THE BATTALION BOXIN' TEAM NOTICED ME.
"HOW COME I ENDED UP IN THE ARMY HEAVYWEIGHT CHAMPIONSHIP, TOO."
"HOW COME I WAS EVER DUMB ENOUGH TO GET IN THE RING WITH A DUDE CALLED FUCKER JOHN--THAT MIGHT TAKE A LITTLE MORE EXPLAININ'."
13
EVERLAST

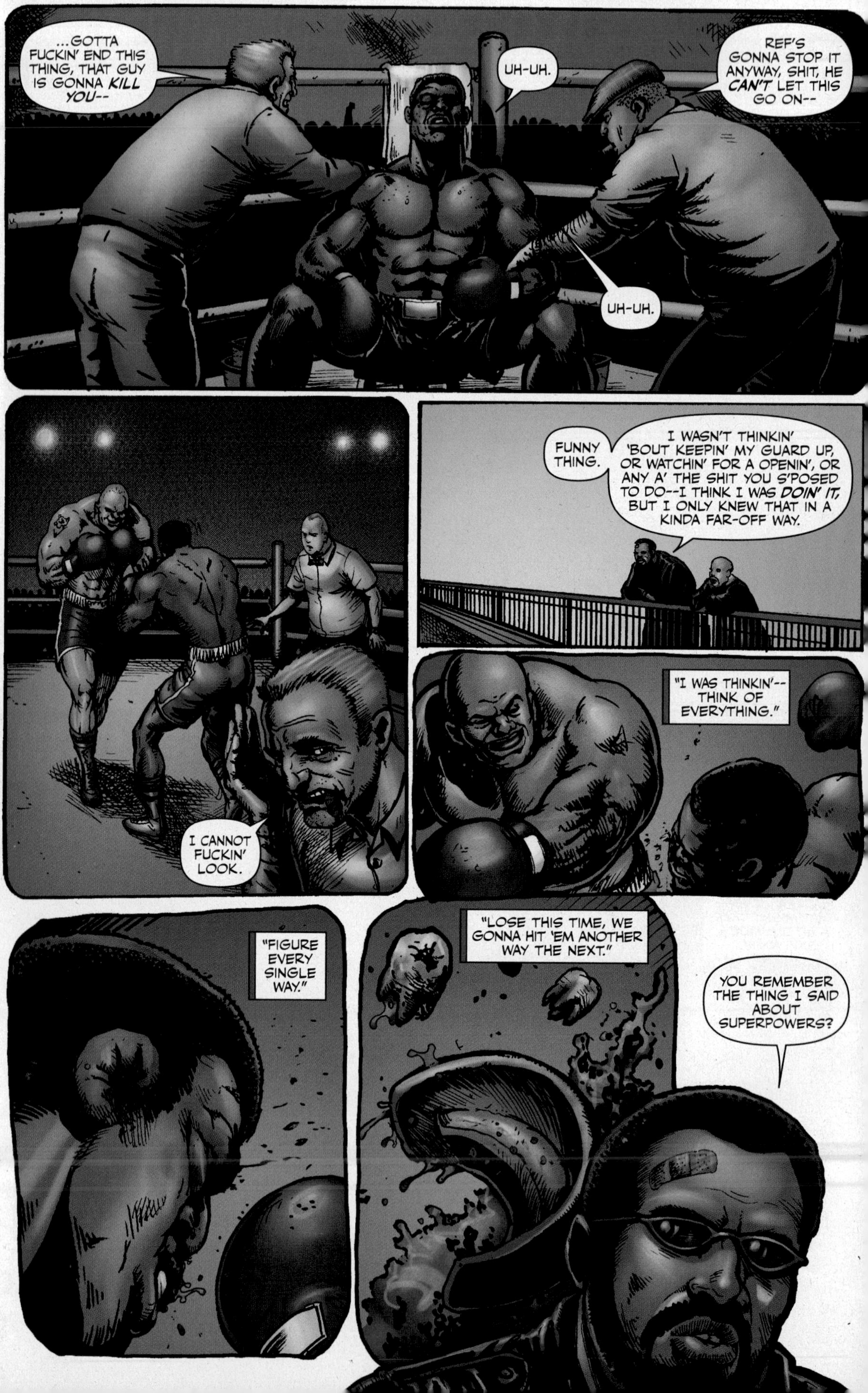
...GOTTA FUCKIN' END THIS THING, THAT GUY IS GONNA *KILL YOU*--
UH-UH.
REF'S GONNA STOP IT ANYWAY, SHIT, HE *CAN'T* LET THIS GO ON--
UH-UH.
I CANNOT FUCKIN' LOOK.
FUNNY THING.
I WASN'T THINKIN' 'BOUT KEEPIN' MY GUARD UP, OR WATCHIN' FOR A OPENIN', OR ANY A' THE SHIT YOU S'POSED TO DO--I THINK I WAS *DOIN' IT,* BUT I ONLY KNEW THAT IN A KINDA FAR-OFF WAY.
"I WAS THINKIN'--THINK OF EVERYTHING."
"FIGURE EVERY SINGLE WAY."
"LOSE THIS TIME, WE GONNA HIT 'EM ANOTHER WAY THE NEXT."
YOU REMEMBER THE THING I SAID ABOUT SUPERPOWERS?

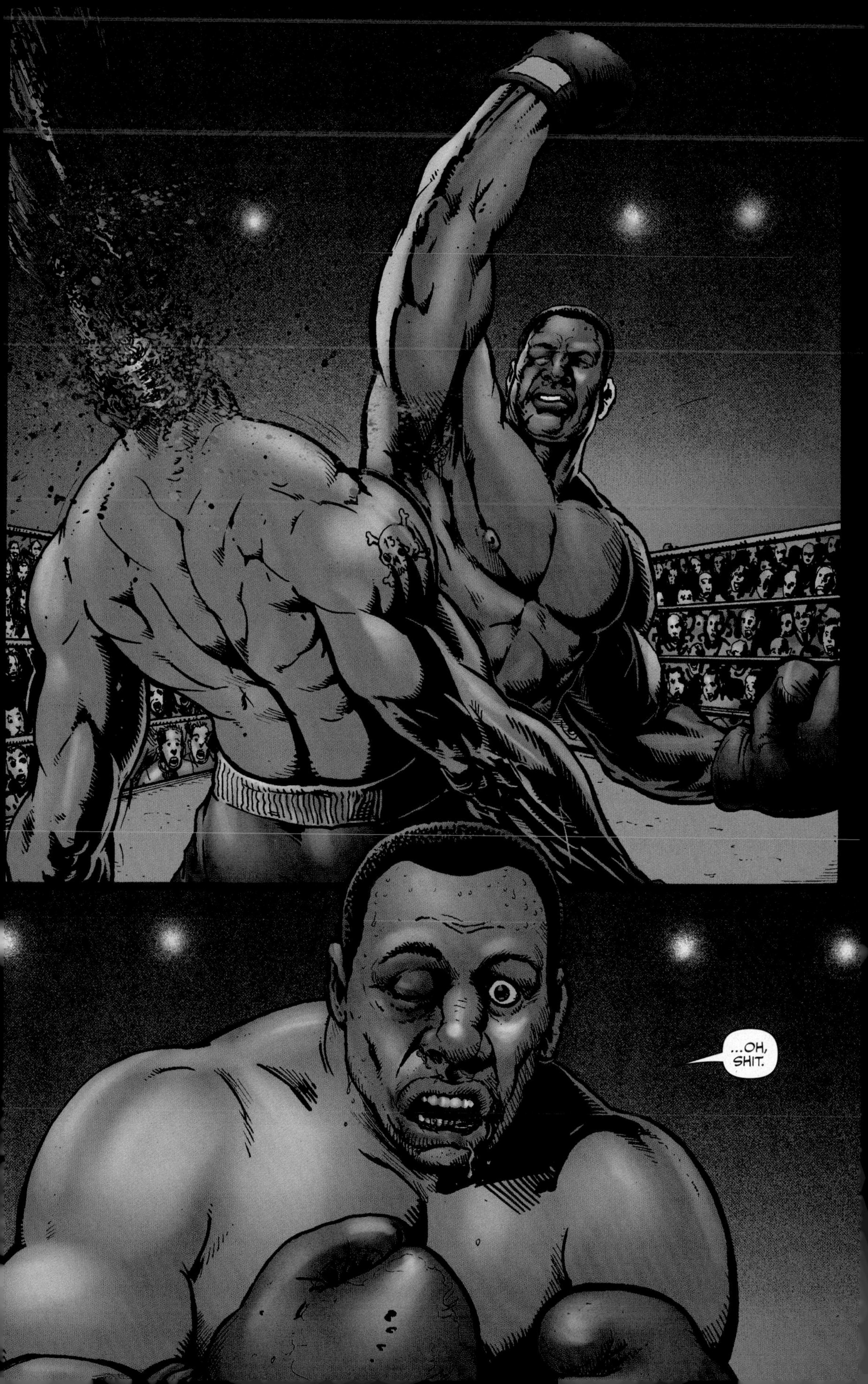
...OH, SHIT.

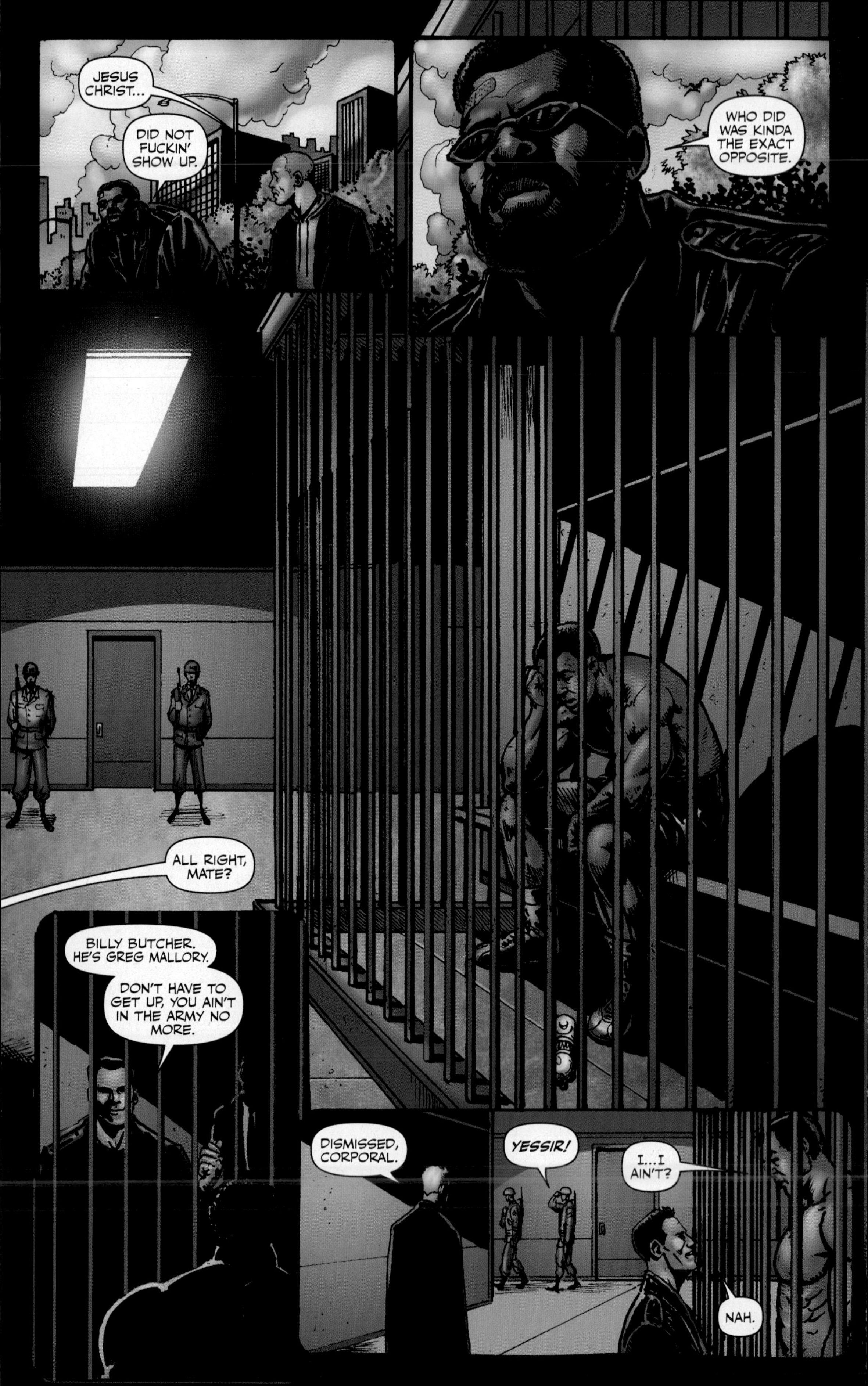
JESUS CHRIST...
DID NOT FUCKIN' SHOW UP.
WHO DID WAS KINDA THE EXACT OPPOSITE.
ALL RIGHT, MATE?
BILLY BUTCHER. HE'S GREG MALLORY.
DON'T HAVE TO GET UP, YOU AIN'T IN THE ARMY NO MORE.
DISMISSED, CORPORAL.
YESSIR!
I...I AIN'T?
NAH.

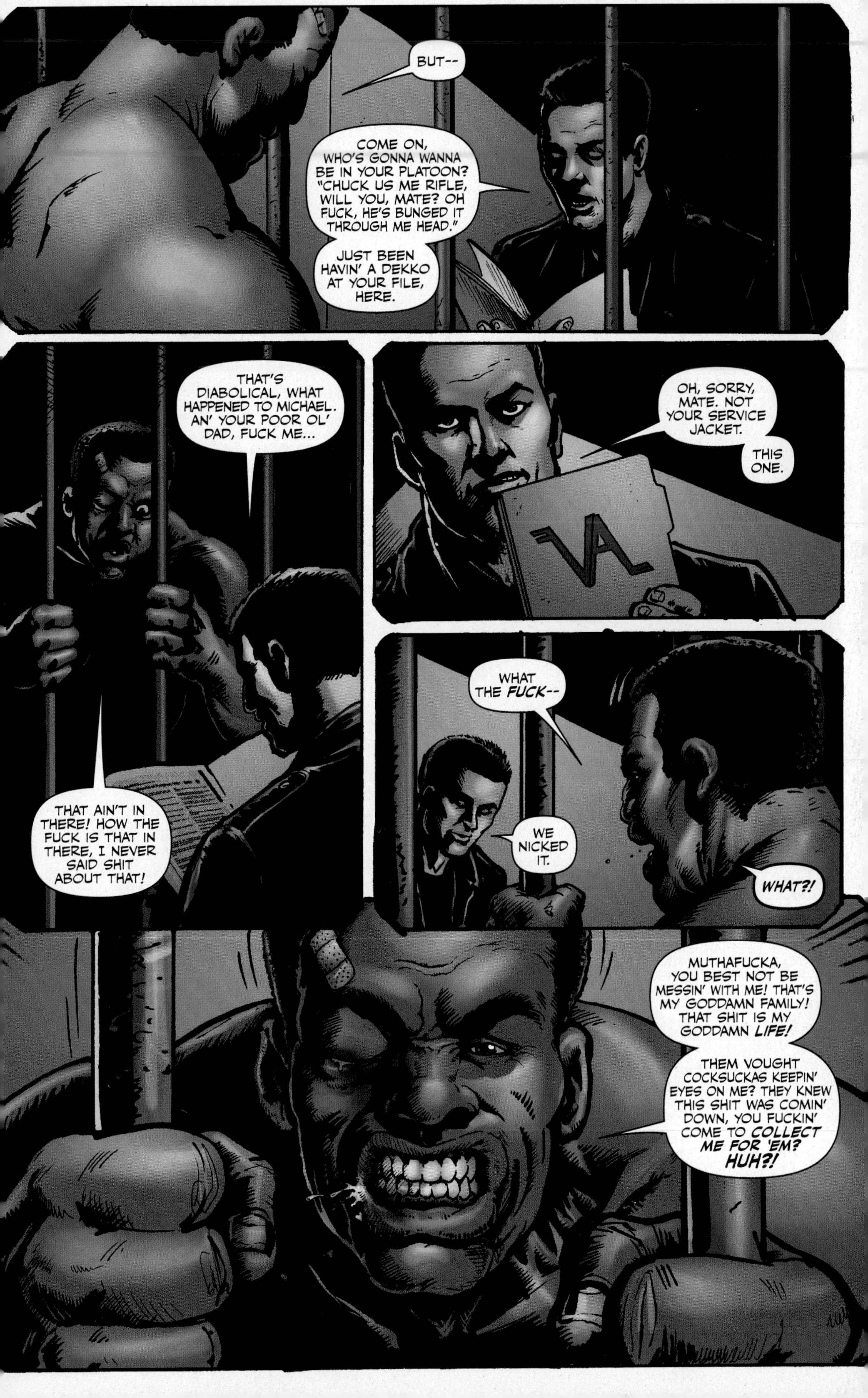
BUT--
COME ON, WHO'S GONNA WANNA BE IN YOUR PLATOON? "CHUCK US ME RIFLE, WILL YOU, MATE? OH FUCK, HE'S BUNGED IT THROUGH ME HEAD."
JUST BEEN HAVIN' A DEKKO AT YOUR FILE, HERE.
THAT'S DIABOLICAL, WHAT HAPPENED TO MICHAEL. AN' YOUR POOR OL' DAD, FUCK ME...
THAT AIN'T IN THERE! HOW THE FUCK IS THAT IN THERE, I NEVER SAID SHIT ABOUT THAT!
OH, SORRY, MATE. NOT YOUR SERVICE JACKET.
THIS ONE.
VA
WHAT THE FUCK--
WE NICKED IT.
WHAT?!
MUTHAFUCKA, YOU BEST NOT BE MESSIN' WITH ME! THAT'S MY GODDAMN FAMILY! THAT SHIT IS MY GODDAMN LIFE!
THEM VOUGHT COCKSUCKAS KEEPIN' EYES ON ME? THEY KNEW THIS SHIT WAS COMIN' DOWN, YOU FUCKIN' COME TO COLLECT ME FOR 'EM? HUH?!

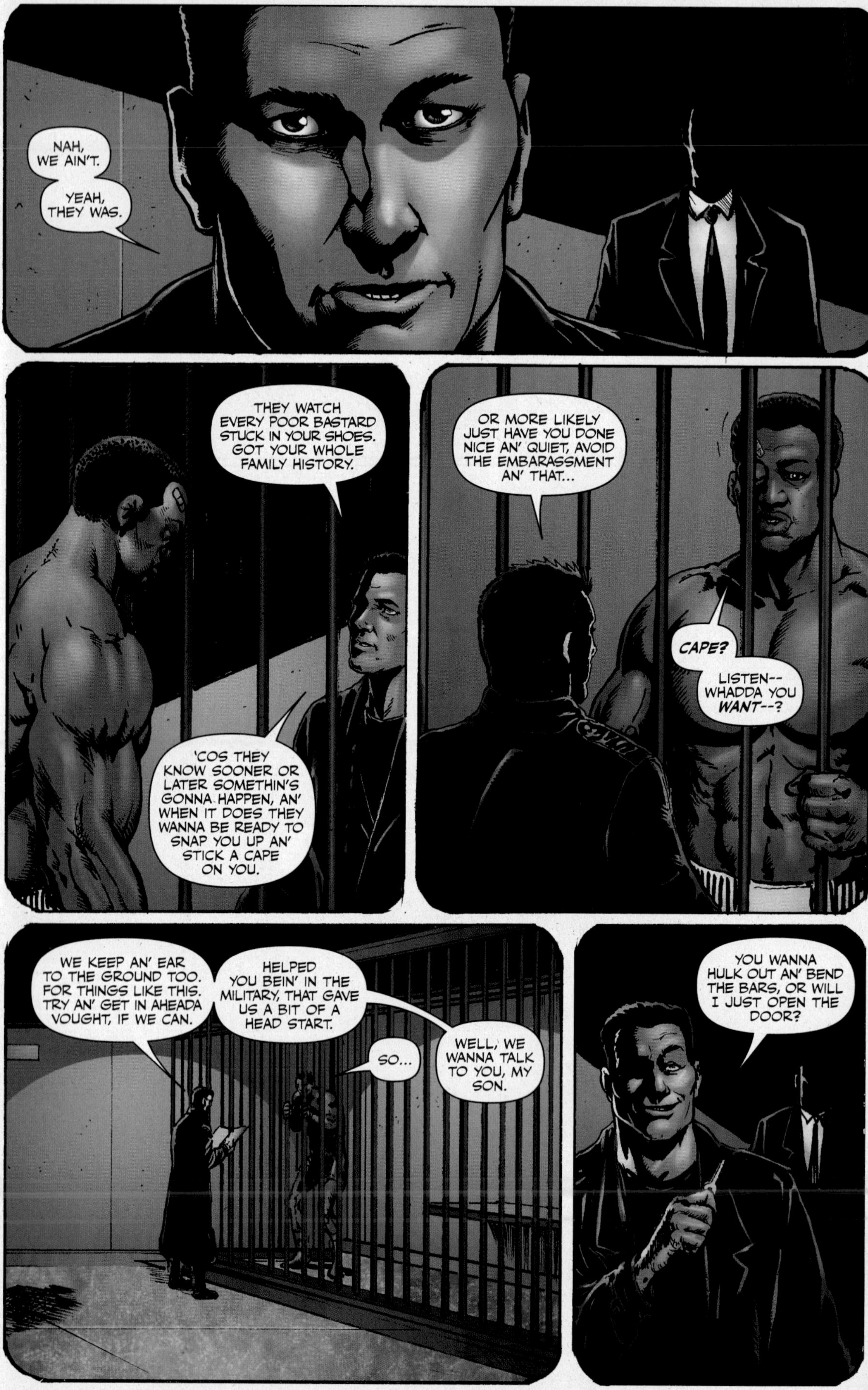
NAH, WE AIN'T.
YEAH, THEY WAS.
THEY WATCH EVERY POOR BASTARD STUCK IN YOUR SHOES. GOT YOUR WHOLE FAMILY HISTORY.
'COS THEY KNOW SOONER OR LATER SOMETHIN'S GONNA HAPPEN, AN' WHEN IT DOES THEY WANNA BE READY TO SNAP YOU UP AN' STICK A CAPE ON YOU.
OR MORE LIKELY JUST HAVE YOU DONE NICE AN' QUIET, AVOID THE EMBARASSMENT AN' THAT...
CAPE?
LISTEN-- WHADDA YOU WANT--?
WE KEEP AN' EAR TO THE GROUND TOO. FOR THINGS LIKE THIS. TRY AN' GET IN AHEADA VOUGHT, IF WE CAN.
HELPED YOU BEIN' IN THE MILITARY, THAT GAVE US A BIT OF A HEAD START.
SO...
WELL, WE WANNA TALK TO YOU, MY SON.
YOU WANNA HULK OUT AN' BEND THE BARS, OR WILL I JUST OPEN THE DOOR?

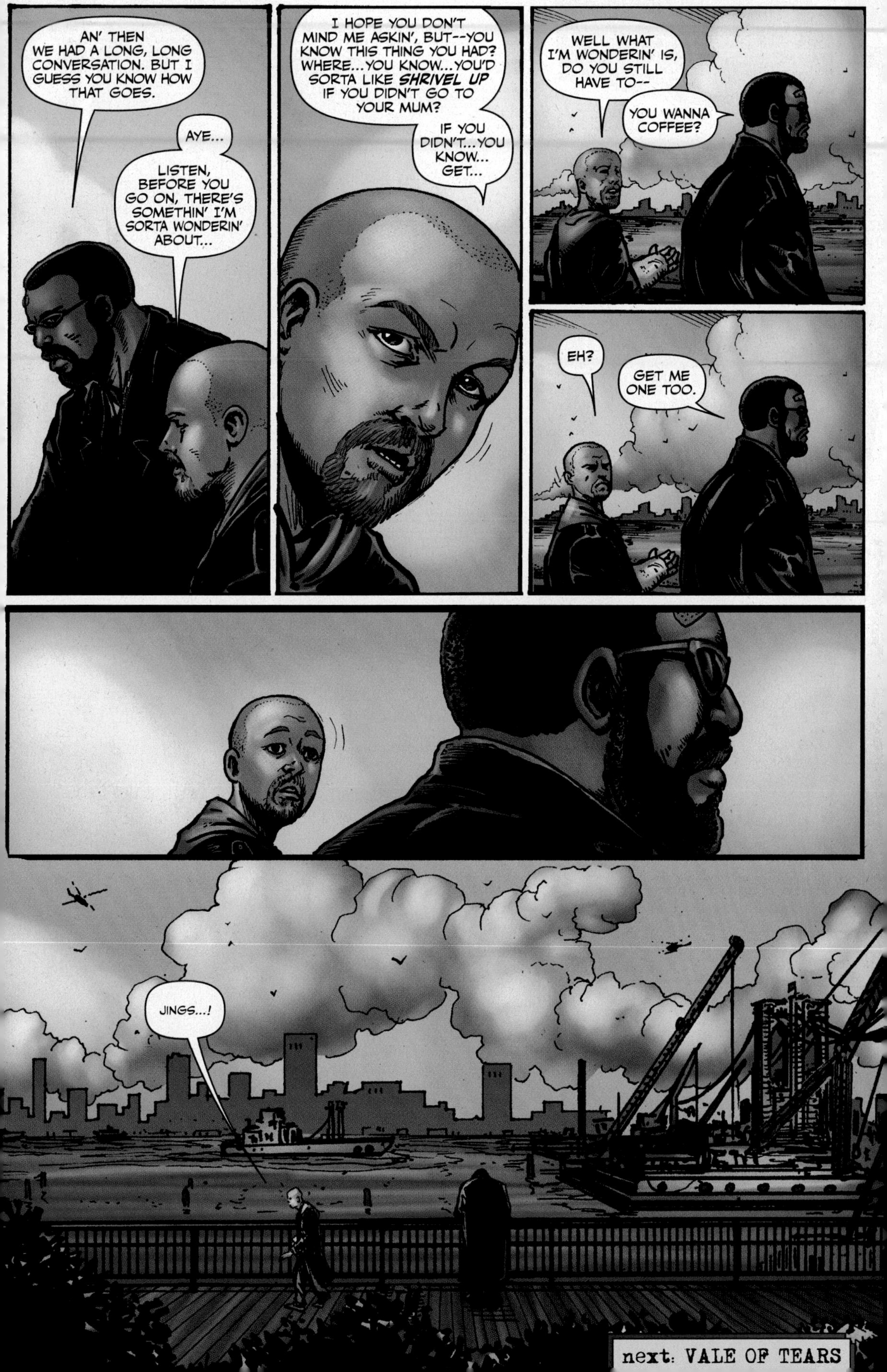
AN' THEN WE HAD A LONG, LONG CONVERSATION. BUT I GUESS YOU KNOW HOW THAT GOES.
AYE...
LISTEN, BEFORE YOU GO ON, THERE'S SOMETHIN' I'M SORTA WONDERIN' ABOUT...
I HOPE YOU DON'T MIND ME ASKIN', BUT--YOU KNOW THIS THING YOU HAD? WHERE...YOU KNOW...YOU'D SORTA LIKE SHRIVEL UP IF YOU DIDN'T GO TO YOUR MUM?
IF YOU DIDN'T...YOU KNOW... GET...
WELL WHAT I'M WONDERIN' IS, DO YOU STILL HAVE TO--
YOU WANNA COFFEE?
EH?
GET ME ONE TOO.
JINGS...!
next: VALE OF TEARS

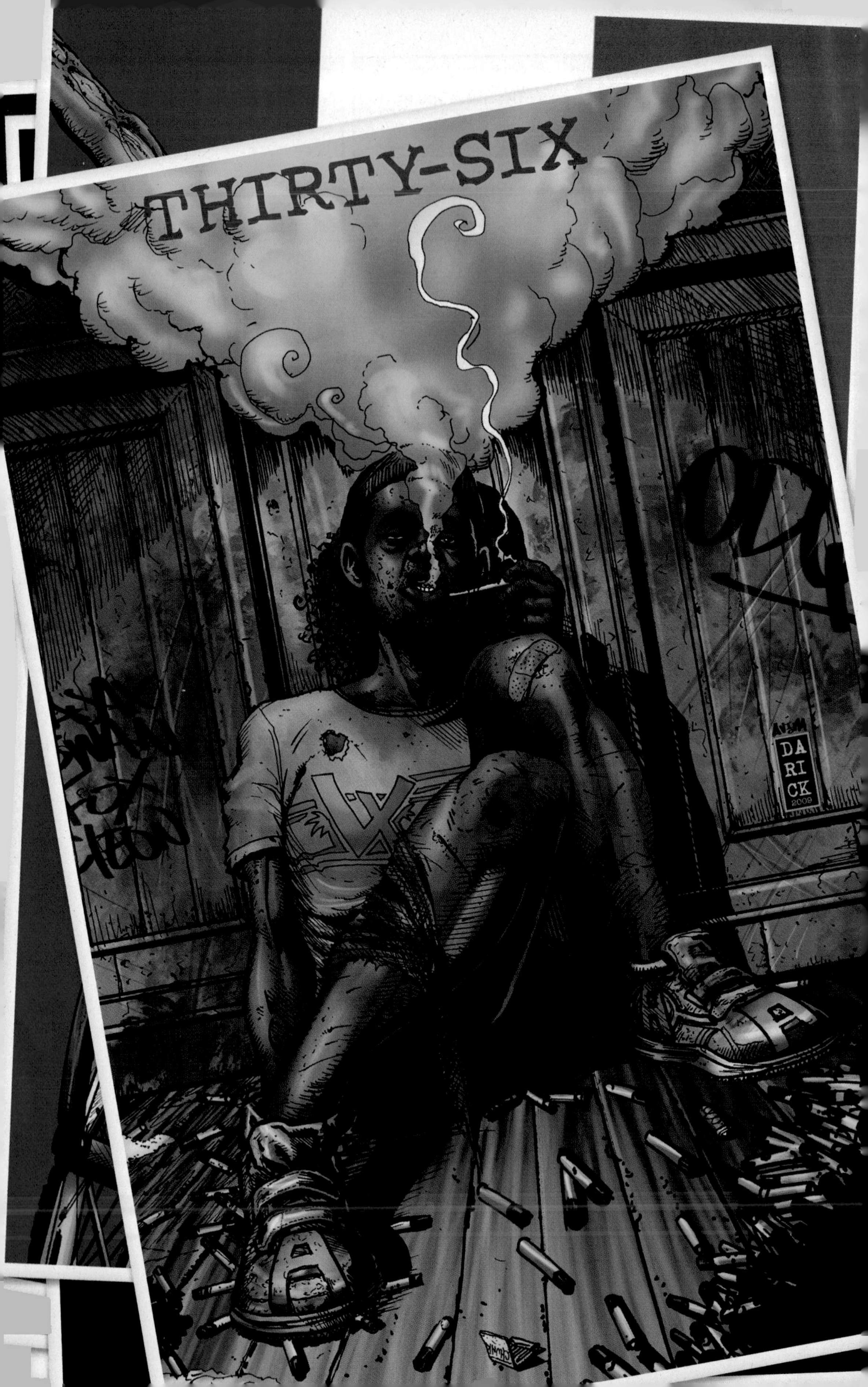
THIRTY-SIX
DA
RI
CK
2009

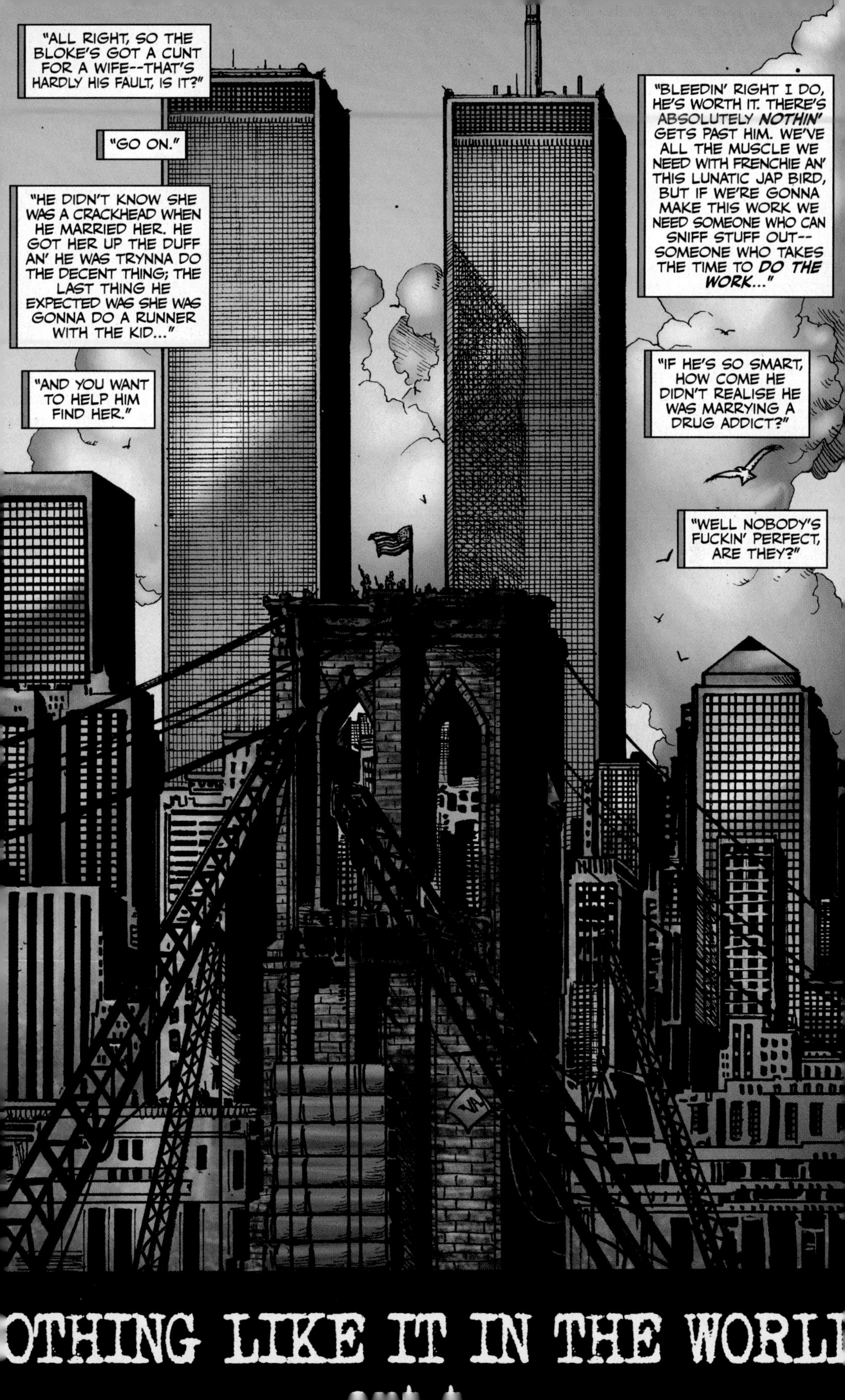
"ALL RIGHT, SO THE BLOKE'S GOT A CUNT FOR A WIFE--THAT'S HARDLY HIS FAULT, IS IT?"
"GO ON."
"HE DIDN'T KNOW SHE WAS A CRACKHEAD WHEN HE MARRIED HER. HE GOT HER UP THE DUFF AN' HE WAS TRYNNA DO THE DECENT THING; THE LAST THING HE EXPECTED WAS SHE WAS GONNA DO A RUNNER WITH THE KID..."
"AND YOU WANT TO HELP HIM FIND HER."
"BLEEDIN' RIGHT I DO, HE'S WORTH IT. THERE'S ABSOLUTELY NOTHIN' GETS PAST HIM. WE'VE ALL THE MUSCLE WE NEED WITH FRENCHIE AN' THIS LUNATIC JAP BIRD, BUT IF WE'RE GONNA MAKE THIS WORK WE NEED SOMEONE WHO CAN SNIFF STUFF OUT--SOMEONE WHO TAKES THE TIME TO DO THE WORK..."
"IF HE'S SO SMART, HOW COME HE DIDN'T REALISE HE WAS MARRYING A DRUG ADDICT?"
"WELL NOBODY'S FUCKIN' PERFECT, ARE THEY?"
OTHING LIKE IT IN THE WORLI

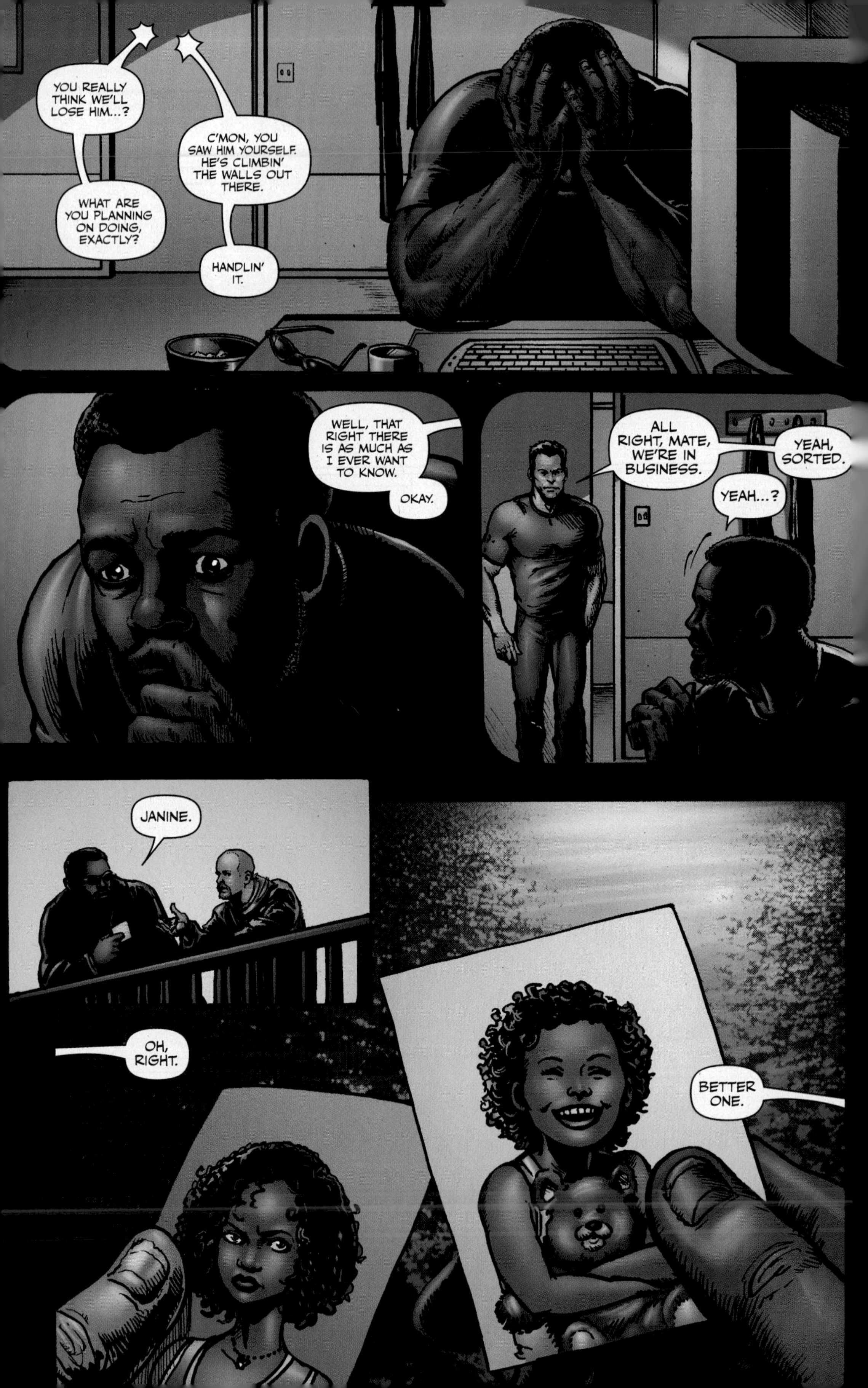
YOU REALLY THINK WE'LL LOSE HIM...?
C'MON, YOU SAW HIM YOURSELF. HE'S CLIMBIN' THE WALLS OUT THERE.
WHAT ARE YOU PLANNING ON DOING, EXACTLY?
HANDLIN' IT.
WELL, THAT RIGHT THERE IS AS MUCH AS I EVER WANT TO KNOW.
OKAY.
ALL RIGHT, MATE, WE'RE IN BUSINESS.
YEAH, SORTED.
YEAH...?
JANINE.
OH, RIGHT.
BETTER ONE.

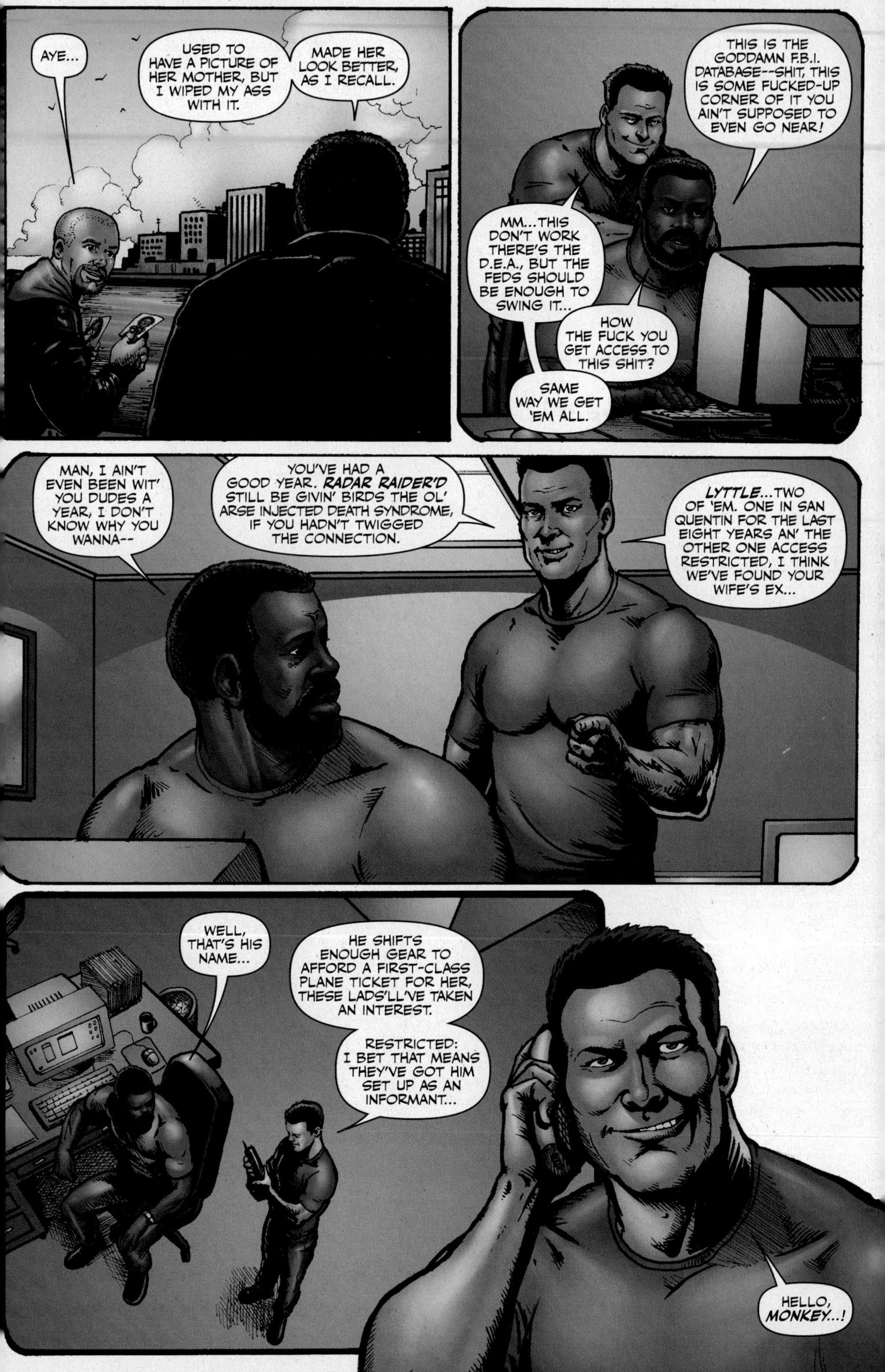
AYE...
USED TO HAVE A PICTURE OF HER MOTHER, BUT I WIPED MY ASS WITH IT.
MADE HER LOOK BETTER, AS I RECALL.
THIS IS THE GODDAMN F.B.I. DATABASE--SHIT, THIS IS SOME FUCKED-UP CORNER OF IT YOU AIN'T SUPPOSED TO EVEN GO NEAR!
MM...THIS DON'T WORK THERE'S THE D.E.A., BUT THE FEDS SHOULD BE ENOUGH TO SWING IT...
HOW THE FUCK YOU GET ACCESS TO THIS SHIT?
SAME WAY WE GET 'EM ALL.
MAN, I AIN'T EVEN BEEN WIT' YOU DUDES A YEAR, I DON'T KNOW WHY YOU WANNA--
YOU'VE HAD A GOOD YEAR. RADAR RAIDER'D STILL BE GIVIN' BIRDS THE OL' ARSE INJECTED DEATH SYNDROME, IF YOU HADN'T TWIGGED THE CONNECTION.
LYTTLE...TWO OF 'EM. ONE IN SAN QUENTIN FOR THE LAST EIGHT YEARS AN' THE OTHER ONE ACCESS RESTRICTED, I THINK WE'VE FOUND YOUR WIFE'S EX...
WELL, THAT'S HIS NAME...
HE SHIFTS ENOUGH GEAR TO AFFORD A FIRST-CLASS PLANE TICKET FOR HER, THESE LADS'LL'VE TAKEN AN INTEREST.
RESTRICTED: I BET THAT MEANS THEY'VE GOT HIM SET UP AS AN INFORMANT...
HELLO, MONKEY...!

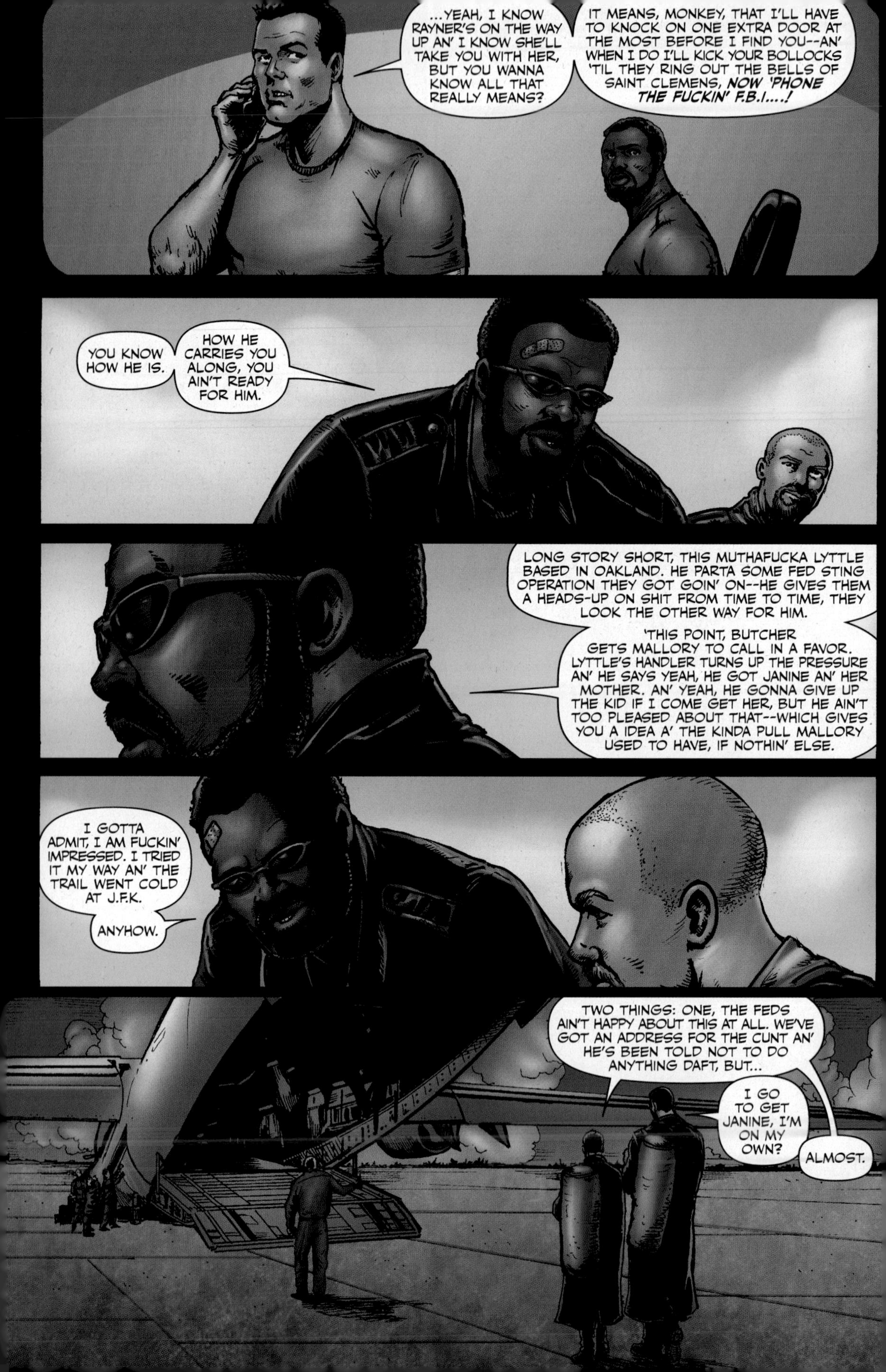
...YEAH, I KNOW RAYNER'S ON THE WAY UP AN' I KNOW SHE'LL TAKE YOU WITH HER, BUT YOU WANNA KNOW ALL THAT REALLY MEANS?
IT MEANS, MONKEY, THAT I'LL HAVE TO KNOCK ON ONE EXTRA DOOR AT THE MOST BEFORE I FIND YOU--AN' WHEN I DO I'LL KICK YOUR BOLLOCKS 'TIL THEY RING OUT THE BELLS OF SAINT CLEMENS, NOW 'PHONE THE FUCKIN' F.B.I....!
YOU KNOW HOW HE IS.
HOW HE CARRIES YOU ALONG, YOU AIN'T READY FOR HIM.
LONG STORY SHORT, THIS MUTHAFUCKA LYTTLE BASED IN OAKLAND. HE PARTA SOME FED STING OPERATION THEY GOT GOIN' ON--HE GIVES THEM A HEADS-UP ON SHIT FROM TIME TO TIME, THEY LOOK THE OTHER WAY FOR HIM.
'THIS POINT, BUTCHER GETS MALLORY TO CALL IN A FAVOR. LYTTLE'S HANDLER TURNS UP THE PRESSURE AN' HE SAYS YEAH, HE GOT JANINE AN' HER MOTHER. AN' YEAH, HE GONNA GIVE UP THE KID IF I COME GET HER, BUT HE AIN'T TOO PLEASED ABOUT THAT--WHICH GIVES YOU A IDEA A' THE KINDA PULL MALLORY USED TO HAVE, IF NOTHIN' ELSE.
I GOTTA ADMIT, I AM FUCKIN' IMPRESSED. I TRIED IT MY WAY AN' THE TRAIL WENT COLD AT J.F.K.
ANYHOW.
TWO THINGS: ONE, THE FEDS AIN'T HAPPY ABOUT THIS AT ALL. WE'VE GOT AN ADDRESS FOR THE CUNT AN' HE'S BEEN TOLD NOT TO DO ANYTHING DAFT, BUT...
I GO TO GET JANINE, I'M ON MY OWN?
ALMOST.

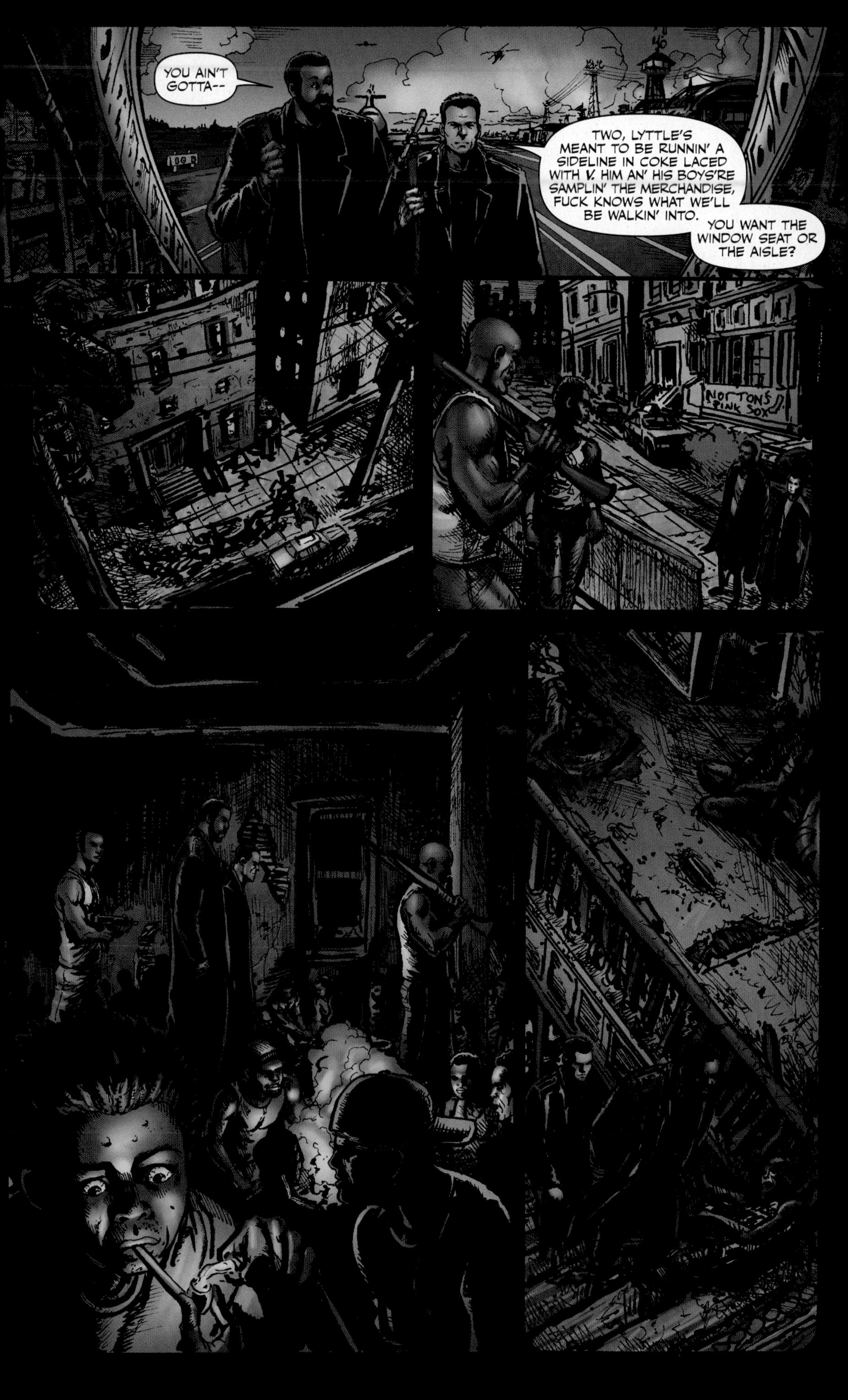
YOU AIN'T GOTTA--
TWO, LYTTLE'S MEANT TO BE RUNNIN' A SIDELINE IN COKE LACED WITH V. HIM AN' HIS BOYS'RE SAMPLIN' THE MERCHANDISE, FUCK KNOWS WHAT WE'LL BE WALKIN' INTO.
YOU WANT THE WINDOW SEAT OR THE AISLE?
NORTON'S PINK SOX

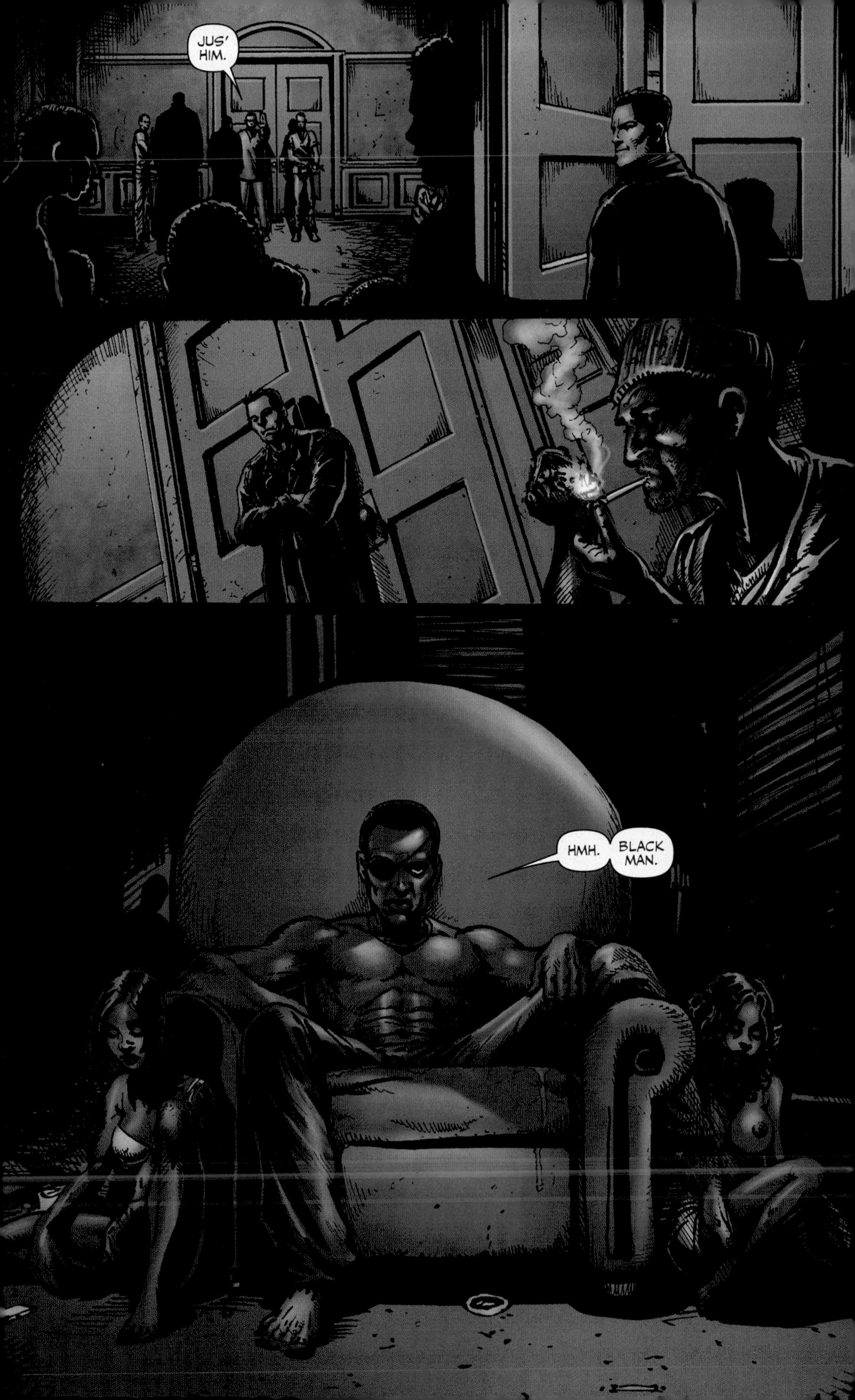
JUS' HIM.
HMH.
BLACK MAN.

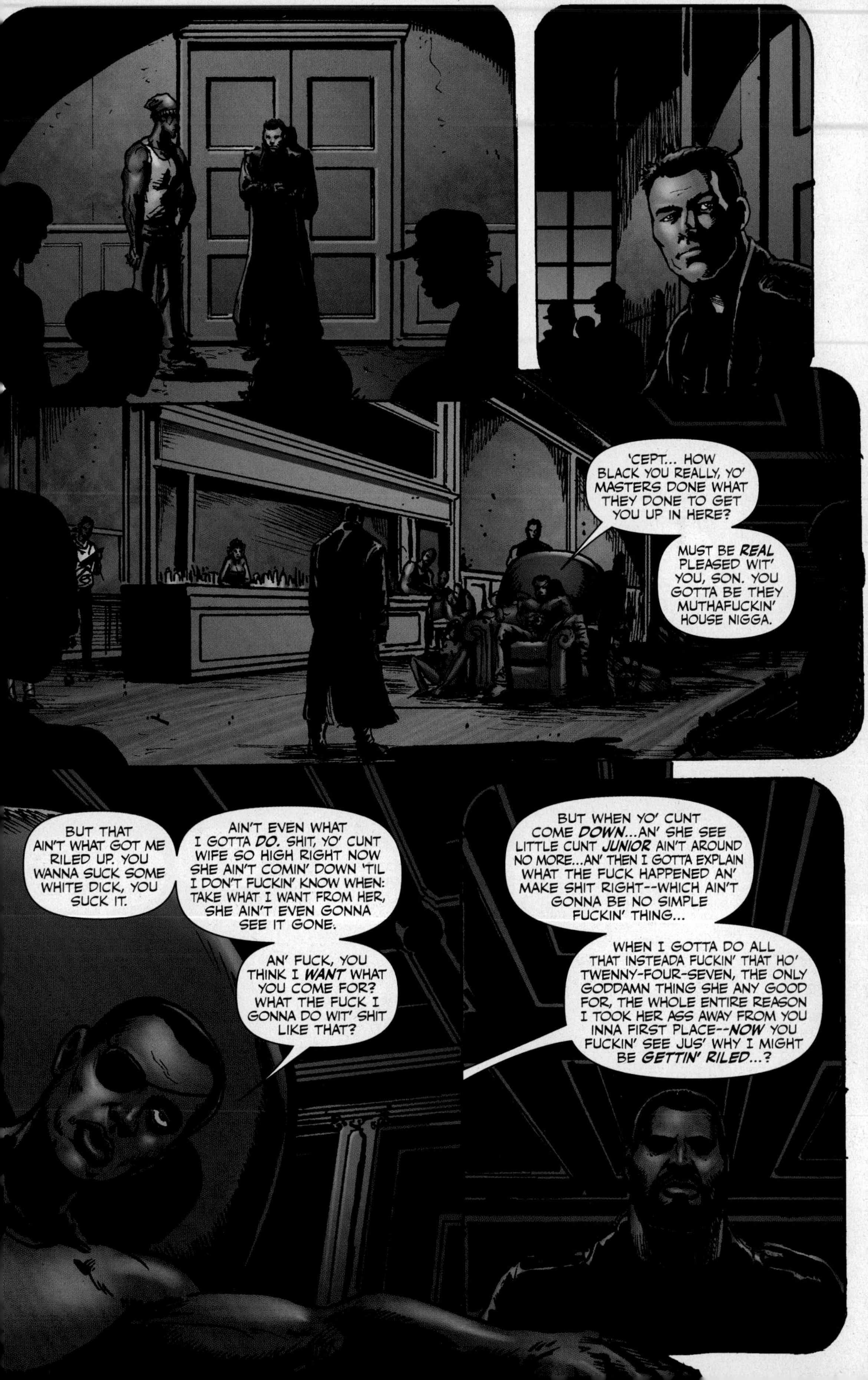
'CEPT... HOW BLACK YOU REALLY, YO' MASTERS DONE WHAT THEY DONE TO GET YOU UP IN HERE?
MUST BE REAL PLEASED WIT' YOU, SON. YOU GOTTA BE THEY MUTHAFUCKIN' HOUSE NIGGA.
BUT THAT AIN'T WHAT GOT ME RILED UP. YOU WANNA SUCK SOME WHITE DICK, YOU SUCK IT.
AIN'T EVEN WHAT I GOTTA DO. SHIT, YO' CUNT WIFE SO HIGH RIGHT NOW SHE AIN'T COMIN' DOWN 'TIL I DON'T FUCKIN' KNOW WHEN: TAKE WHAT I WANT FROM HER, SHE AIN'T EVEN GONNA SEE IT GONE.
AN' FUCK, YOU THINK I WANT WHAT YOU COME FOR? WHAT THE FUCK I GONNA DO WIT' SHIT LIKE THAT?
BUT WHEN YO' CUNT COME DOWN...AN' SHE SEE LITTLE CUNT JUNIOR AIN'T AROUND NO MORE...AN' THEN I GOTTA EXPLAIN WHAT THE FUCK HAPPENED AN' MAKE SHIT RIGHT--WHICH AIN'T GONNA BE NO SIMPLE FUCKIN' THING...
WHEN I GOTTA DO ALL THAT INSTEADA FUCKIN' THAT HO' TWENNY-FOUR-SEVEN, THE ONLY GODDAMN THING SHE ANY GOOD FOR, THE WHOLE ENTIRE REASON I TOOK HER ASS AWAY FROM YOU INNA FIRST PLACE--NOW YOU FUCKIN' SEE JUS' WHY I MIGHT BE GETTIN' RILED...?

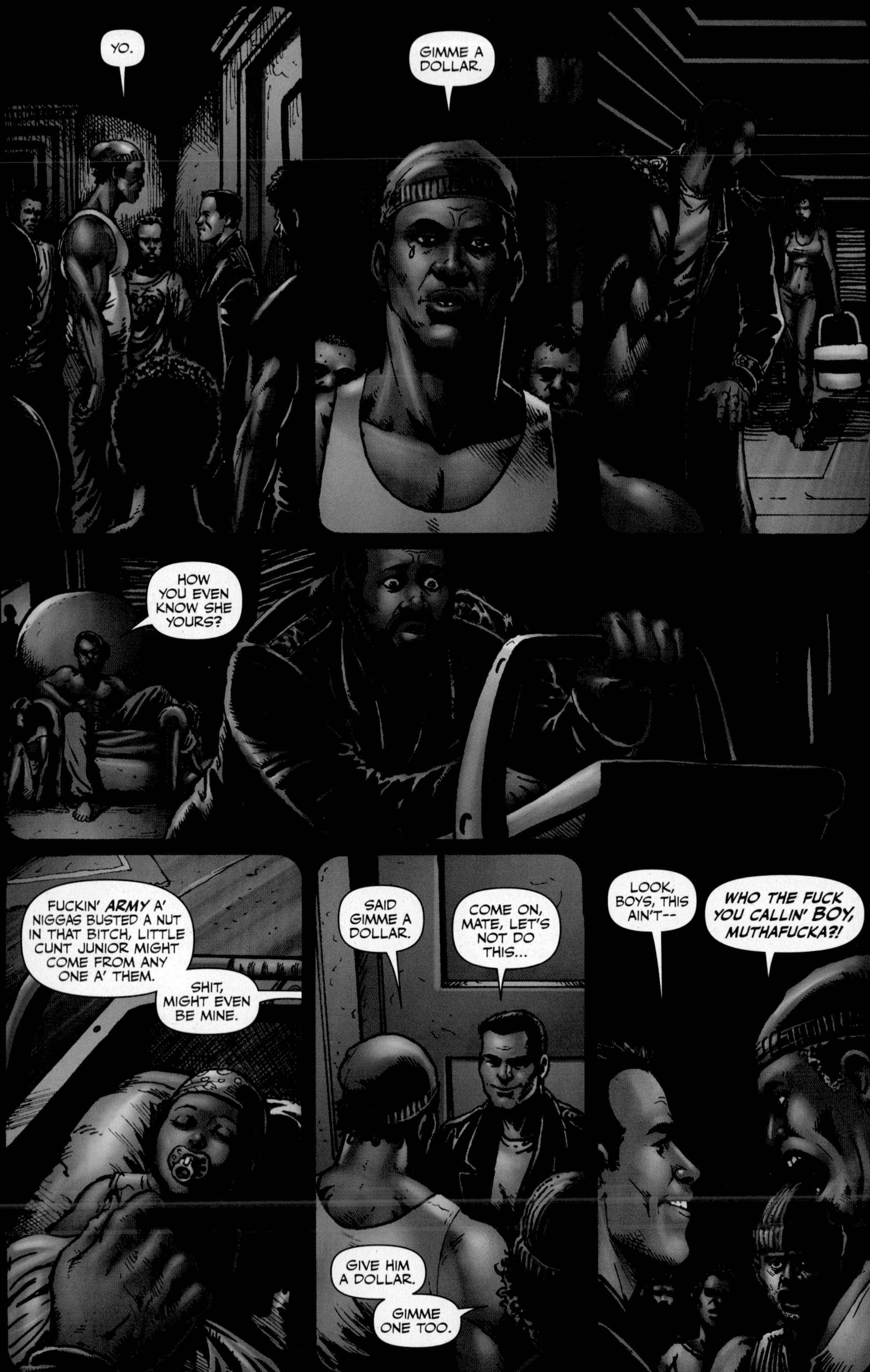
YO.
GIMME A DOLLAR.
HOW YOU EVEN KNOW SHE YOURS?
FUCKIN' *ARMY* A' NIGGAS BUSTED A NUT IN THAT BITCH, LITTLE CUNT JUNIOR MIGHT COME FROM ANY ONE A' THEM.
SHIT, MIGHT EVEN BE MINE.
SAID GIMME A DOLLAR.
COME ON, MATE, LET'S NOT DO THIS...
GIVE HIM A DOLLAR.
GIMME ONE TOO.
LOOK, BOYS, THIS AIN'T--
WHO THE FUCK YOU CALLIN' BOY, MUTHAFUCKA?!

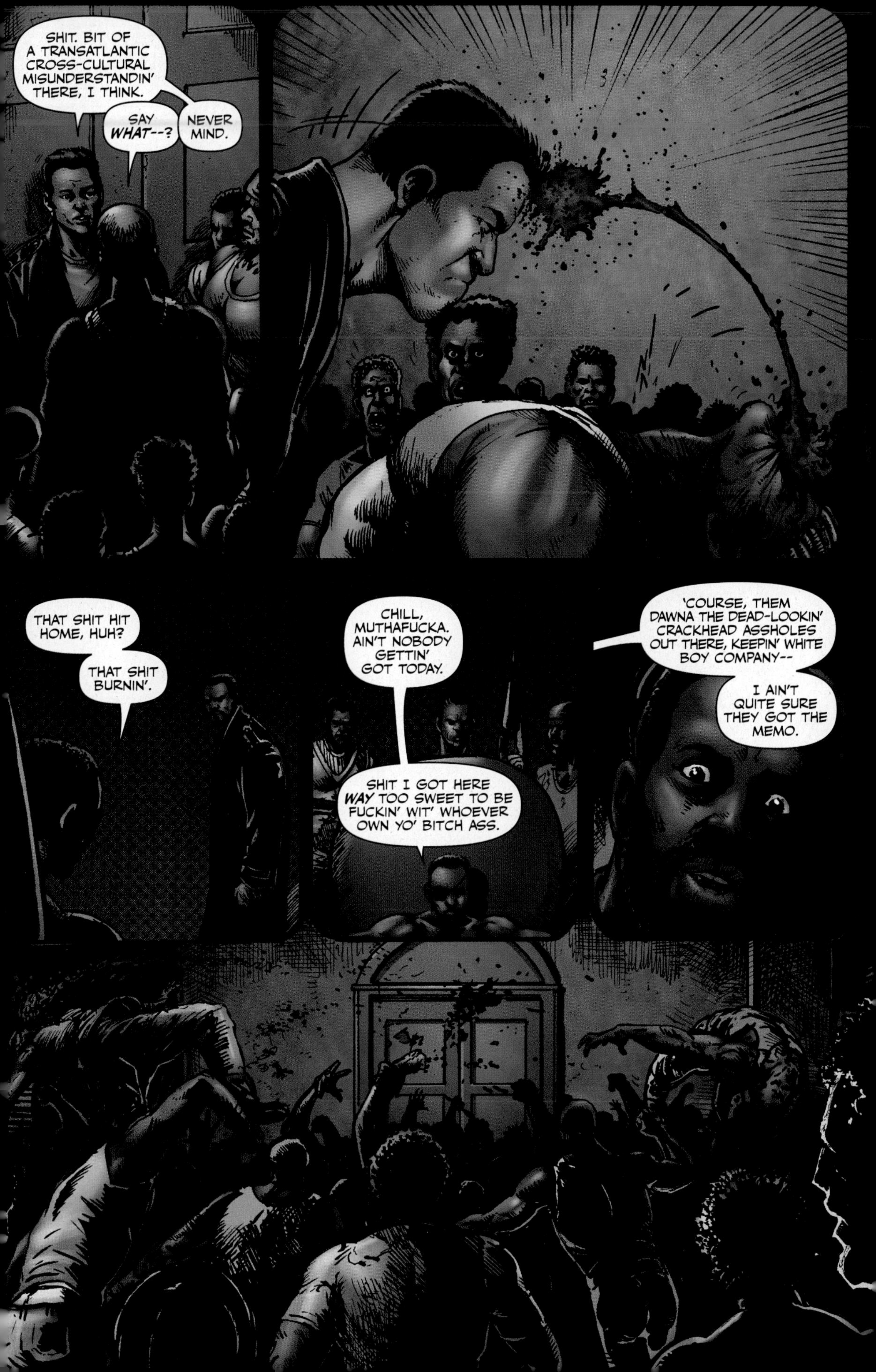
SHIT. BIT OF A TRANSATLANTIC CROSS-CULTURAL MISUNDERSTANDIN' THERE, I THINK.
SAY *WHAT*--?
NEVER MIND.
THAT SHIT HIT HOME, HUH?
THAT SHIT BURNIN'.
CHILL, MUTHAFUCKA. AIN'T NOBODY GETTIN' GOT TODAY.
SHIT I GOT HERE *WAY* TOO SWEET TO BE FUCKIN' WIT' WHOEVER OWN YO' BITCH ASS.
'COURSE, THEM DAWNA THE DEAD-LOOKIN' CRACKHEAD ASSHOLES OUT THERE, KEEPIN' WHITE BOY COMPANY--
I AIN'T QUITE SURE THEY GOT THE MEMO.

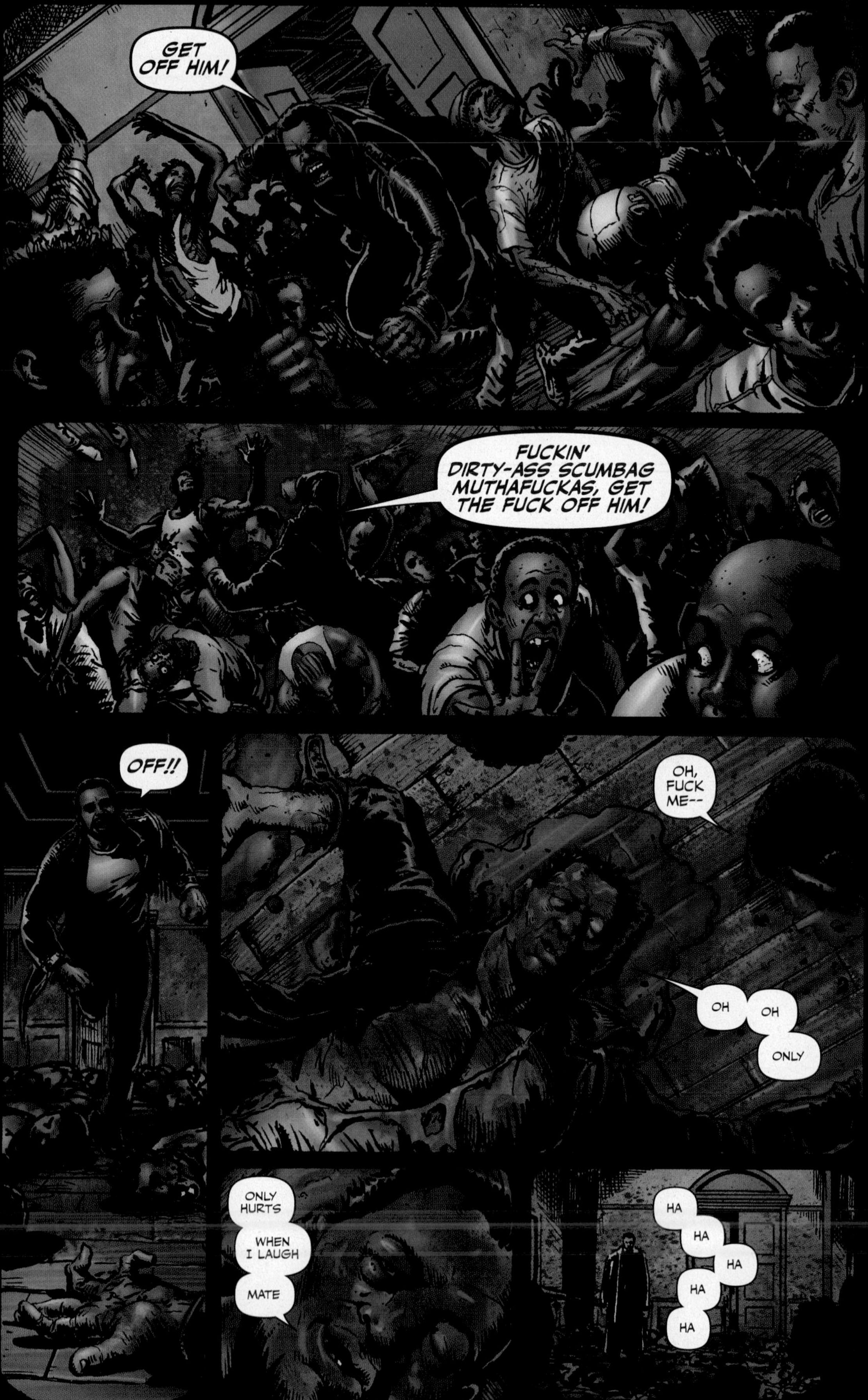
GET OFF HIM!
FUCKIN' DIRTY-ASS SCUMBAG MUTHAFUCKAS, GET THE FUCK OFF HIM!
OFF!!
OH, FUCK ME--
OH
OH
ONLY
ONLY HURTS
WHEN I LAUGH
MATE
HA
HA
HA
HA
HA

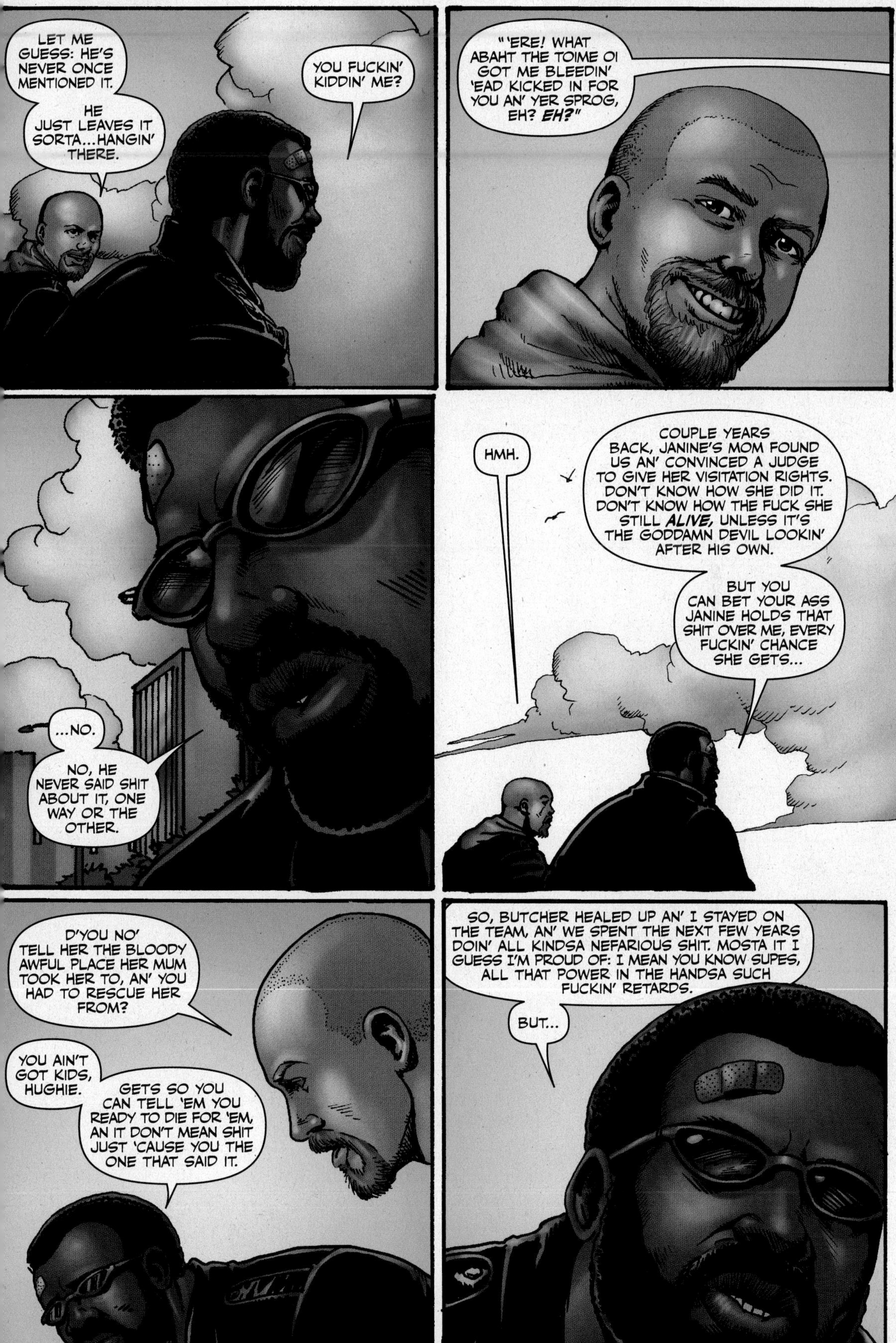
LET ME GUESS: HE'S NEVER ONCE MENTIONED IT.
HE JUST LEAVES IT SORTA...HANGIN' THERE.
YOU FUCKIN' KIDDIN' ME?
"'ERE! WHAT ABAHT THE TOIME OI GOT ME BLEEDIN' 'EAD KICKED IN FOR YOU AN' YER SPROG, EH? EH?"
...NO.
NO, HE NEVER SAID SHIT ABOUT IT, ONE WAY OR THE OTHER.
HMH.
COUPLE YEARS BACK, JANINE'S MOM FOUND US AN' CONVINCED A JUDGE TO GIVE HER VISITATION RIGHTS. DON'T KNOW HOW SHE DID IT. DON'T KNOW HOW THE FUCK SHE STILL ALIVE, UNLESS IT'S THE GODDAMN DEVIL LOOKIN' AFTER HIS OWN.
BUT YOU CAN BET YOUR ASS JANINE HOLDS THAT SHIT OVER ME, EVERY FUCKIN' CHANCE SHE GETS...
D'YOU NO' TELL HER THE BLOODY AWFUL PLACE HER MUM TOOK HER TO, AN' YOU HAD TO RESCUE HER FROM?
YOU AIN'T GOT KIDS, HUGHIE.
GETS SO YOU CAN TELL 'EM YOU READY TO DIE FOR 'EM, AN IT DON'T MEAN SHIT JUST 'CAUSE YOU THE ONE THAT SAID IT.
SO, BUTCHER HEALED UP AN' I STAYED ON THE TEAM, AN' WE SPENT THE NEXT FEW YEARS DOIN' ALL KINDSA NEFARIOUS SHIT. MOSTA IT I GUESS I'M PROUD OF: I MEAN YOU KNOW SUPES, ALL THAT POWER IN THE HANDSA SUCH FUCKIN' RETARDS.
BUT...

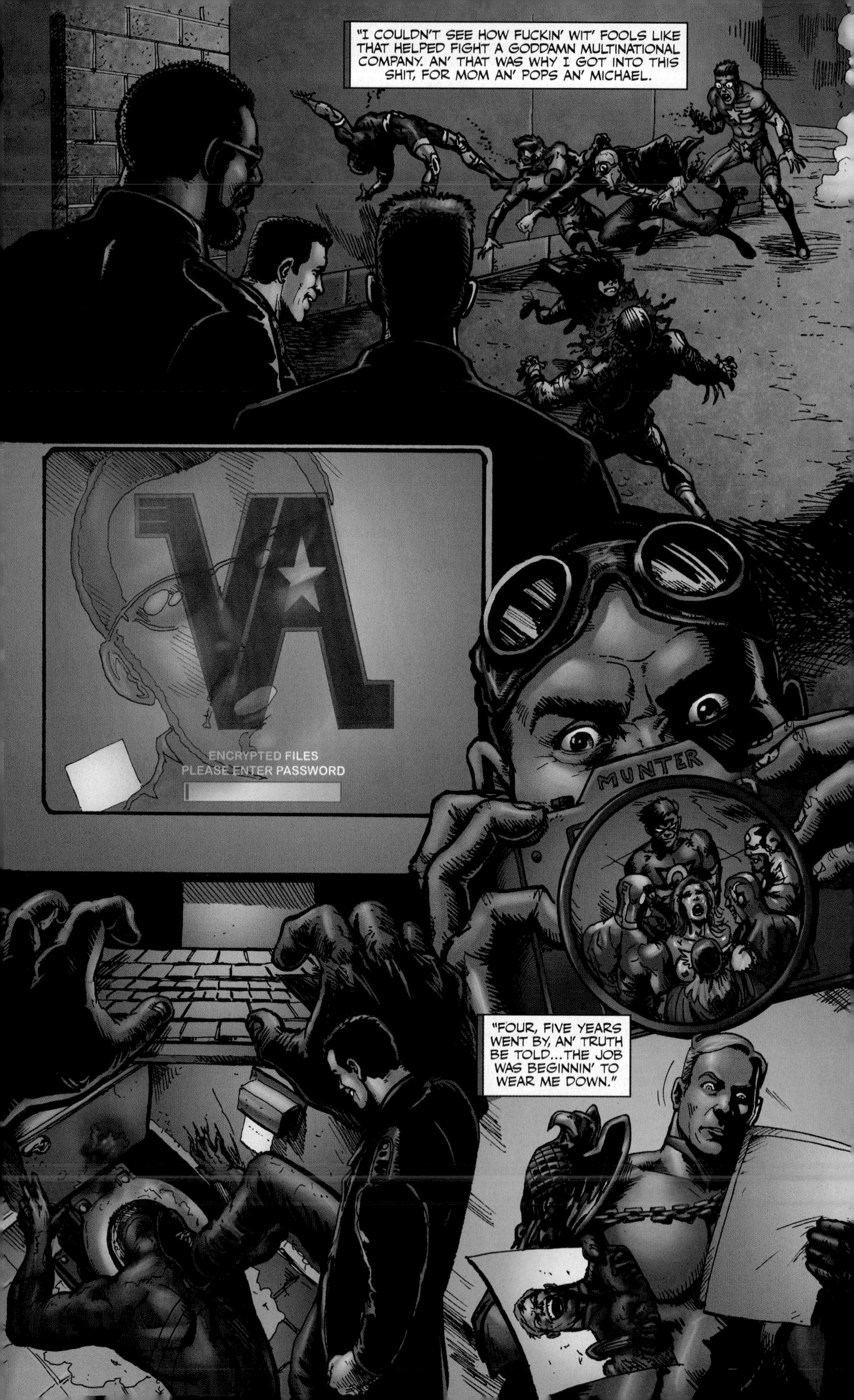
"I COULDN'T SEE HOW FUCKIN' WIT' FOOLS LIKE THAT HELPED FIGHT A GODDAMN MULTINATIONAL COMPANY. AN' THAT WAS WHY I GOT INTO THIS SHIT, FOR MOM AN' POPS AN' MICHAEL.
VA
ENCRYPTED FILES
PLEASE ENTER PASSWORD
MUNTER
"FOUR, FIVE YEARS WENT BY, AN' TRUTH BE TOLD...THE JOB WAS BEGINNIN' TO WEAR ME DOWN."

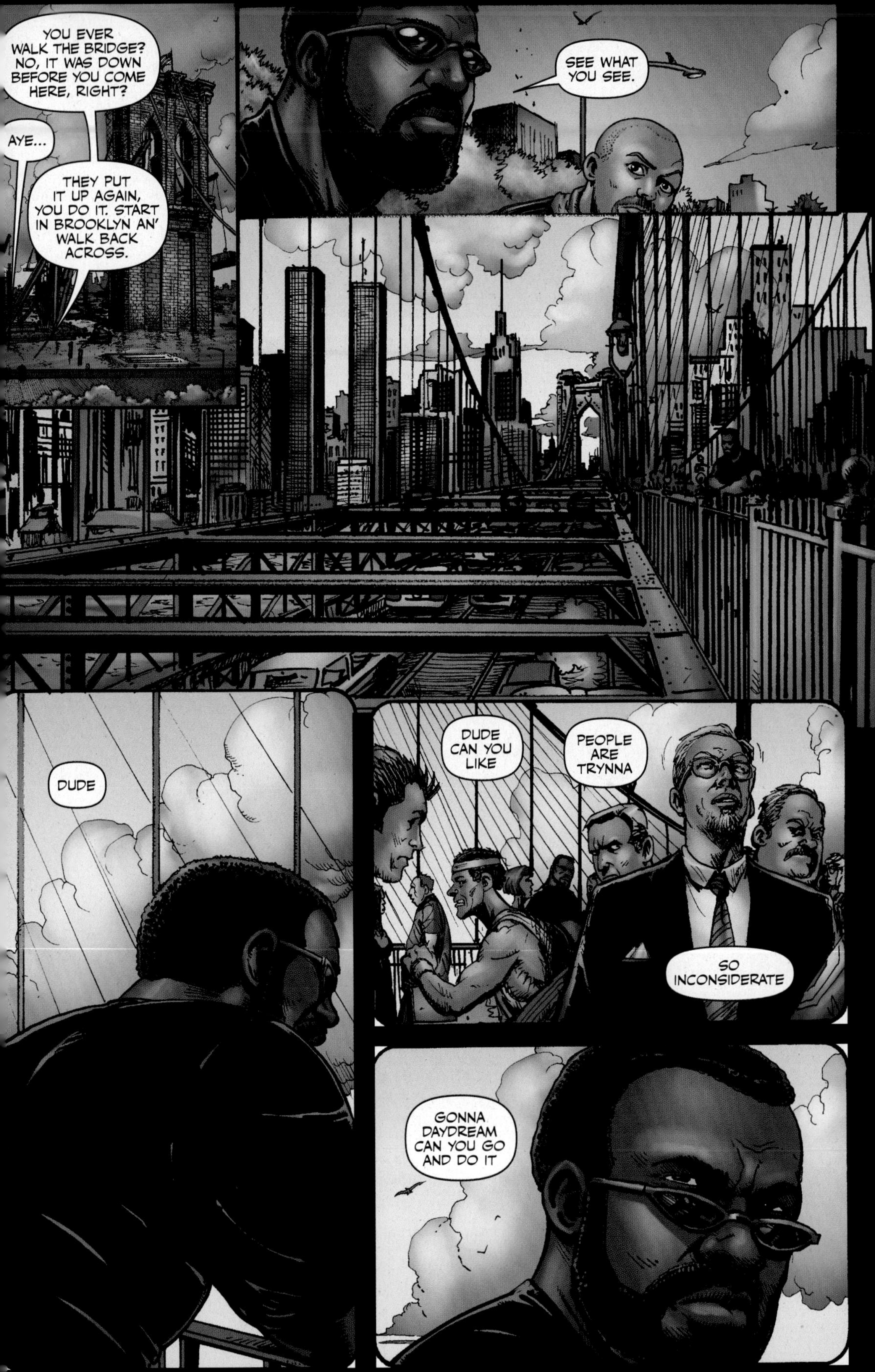
YOU EVER WALK THE BRIDGE? NO, IT WAS DOWN BEFORE YOU COME HERE, RIGHT?
AYE...
THEY PUT IT UP AGAIN, YOU DO IT. START IN BROOKLYN AN' WALK BACK ACROSS.
SEE WHAT YOU SEE.
DUDE
DUDE CAN YOU LIKE
PEOPLE ARE TRYNNA
SO INCONSIDERATE
GONNA DAYDREAM CAN YOU GO AND DO IT

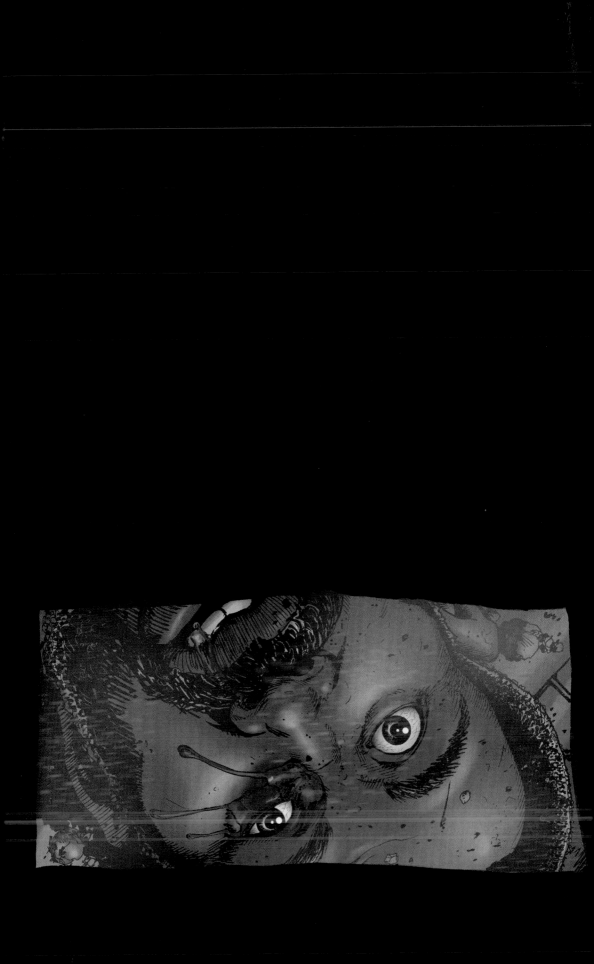

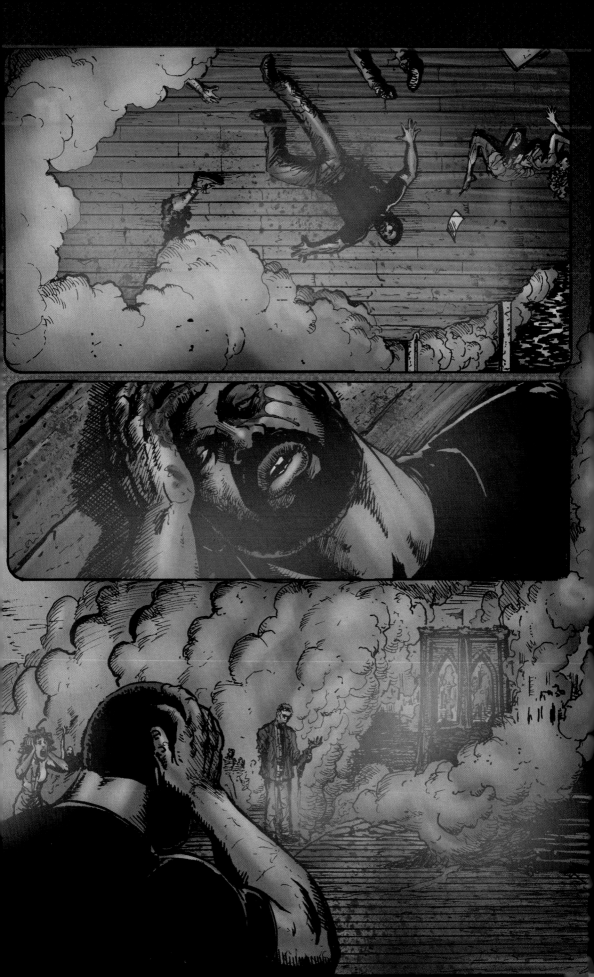

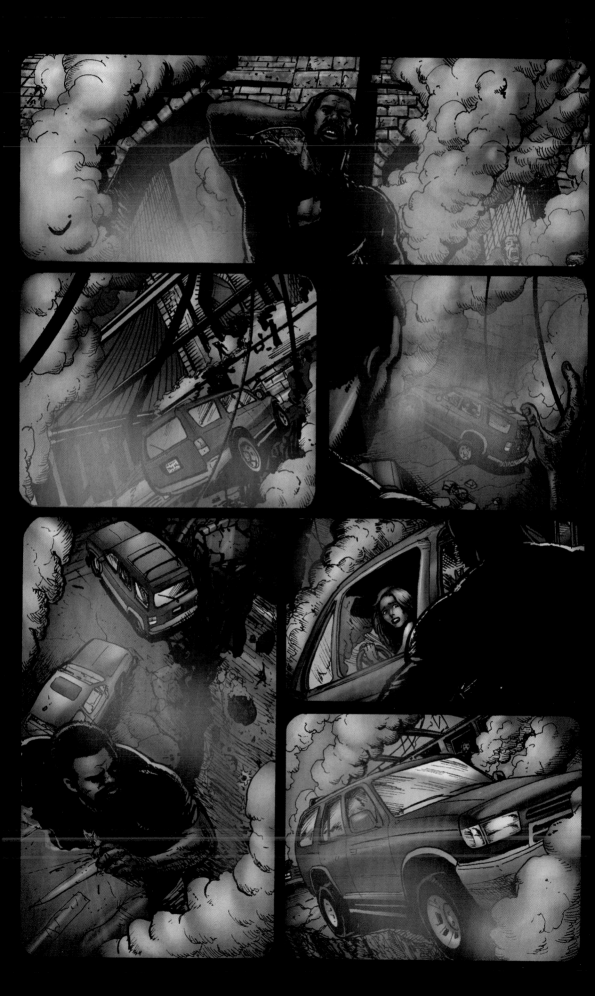

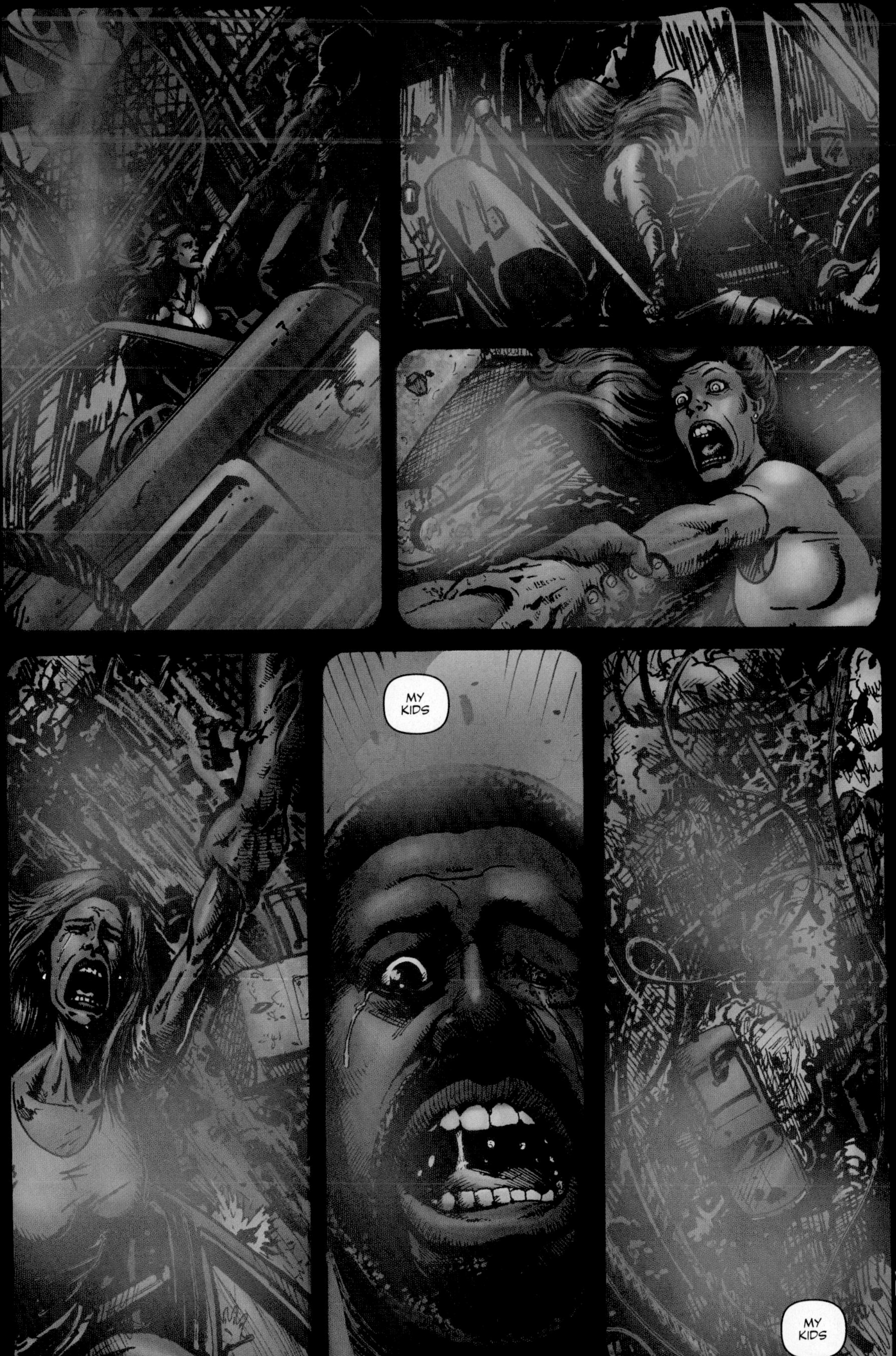
MY KIDS
MY KIDS

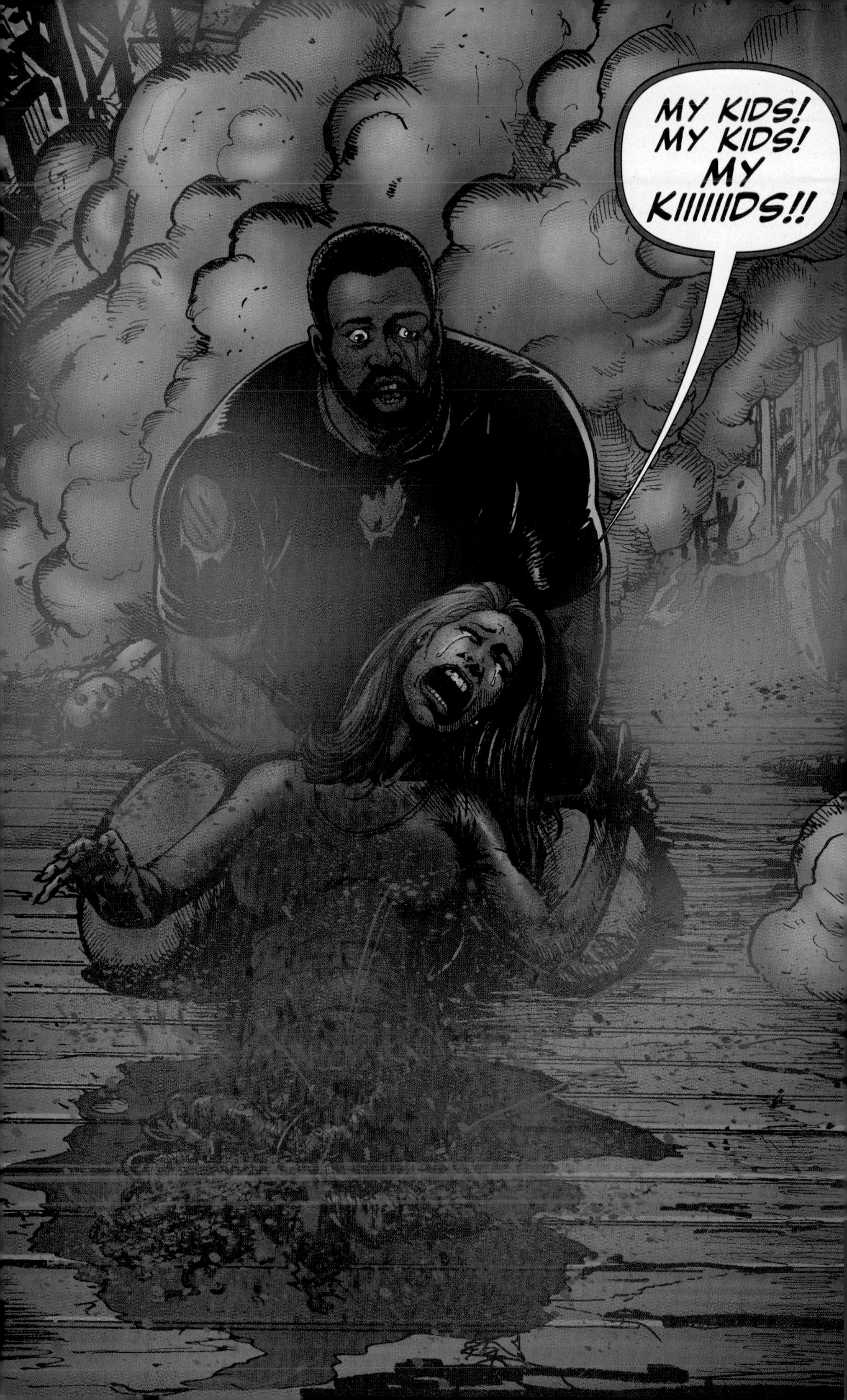
MY KIDS!
MY KIDS!
MY
KIIIIIIDS!!

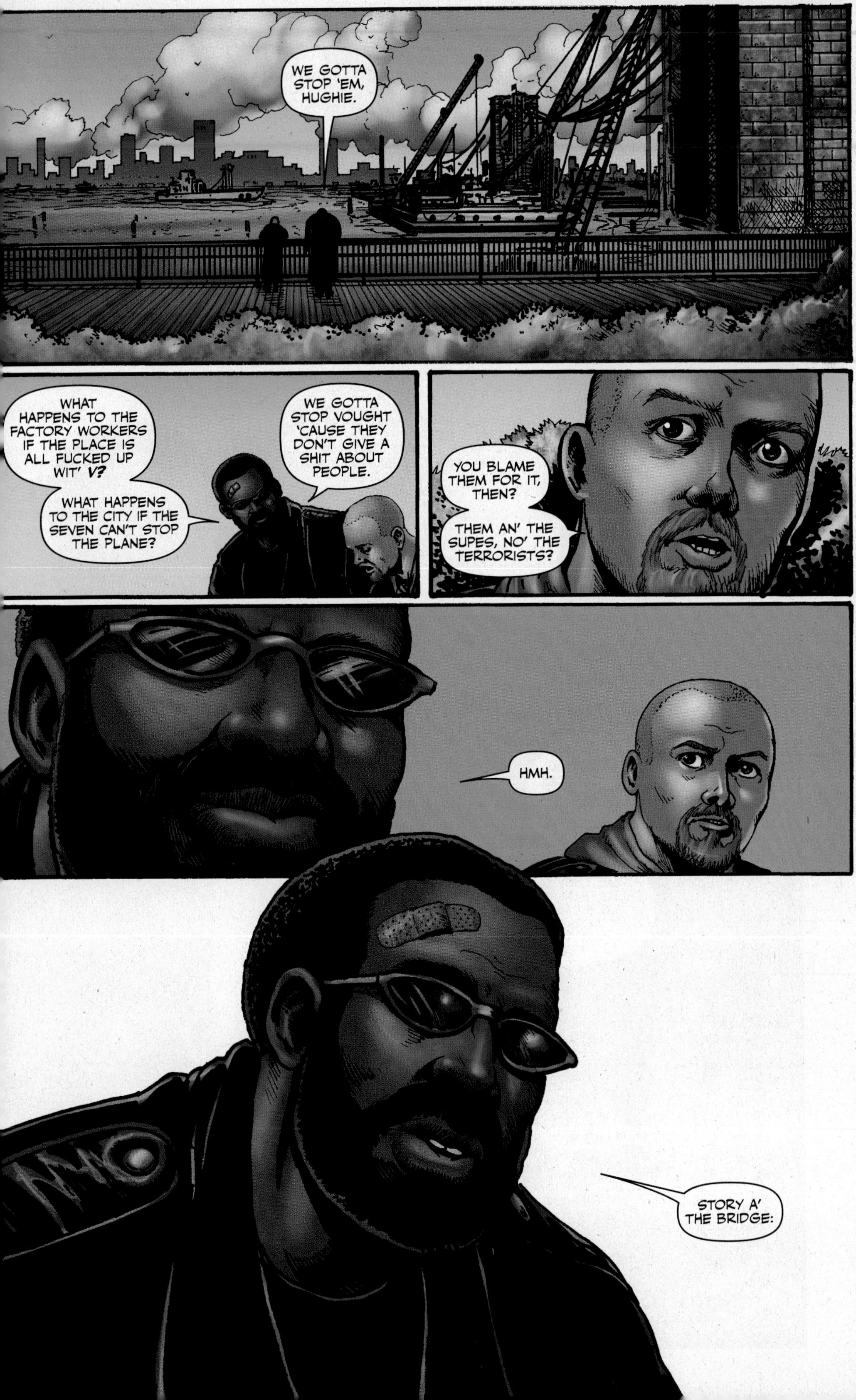

WE GOTTA STOP 'EM, HUGHIE.
WHAT HAPPENS TO THE FACTORY WORKERS IF THE PLACE IS ALL FUCKED UP WIT' *V?*
WHAT HAPPENS TO THE CITY IF THE SEVEN CAN'T STOP THE PLANE?
WE GOTTA STOP VOUGHT 'CAUSE THEY DON'T GIVE A SHIT ABOUT PEOPLE.
YOU BLAME THEM FOR IT, THEN?
THEM AN' THE SUPES, NO' THE TERRORISTS?
HMH.
STORY A' THE BRIDGE:

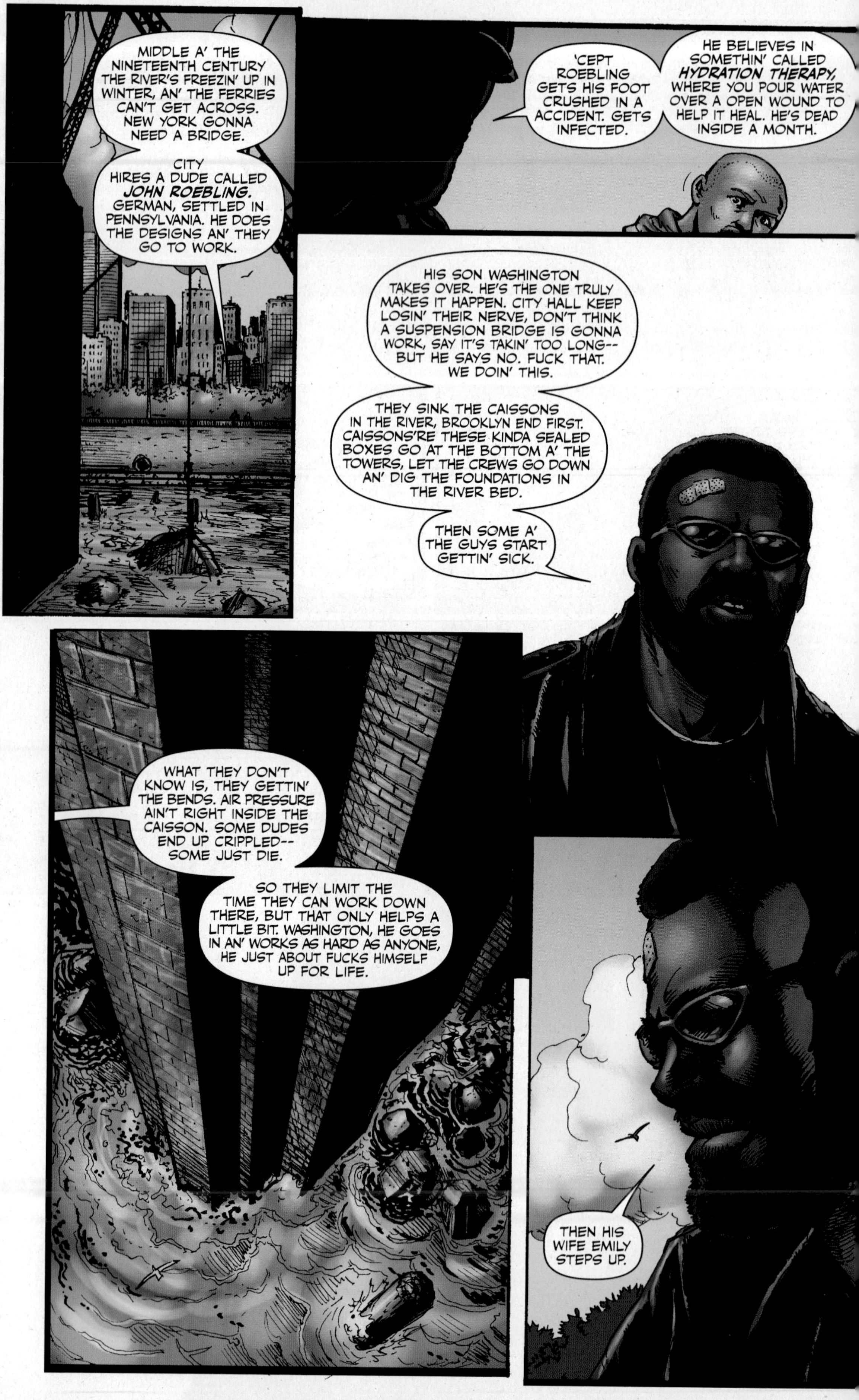
MIDDLE A' THE NINETEENTH CENTURY THE RIVER'S FREEZIN' UP IN WINTER, AN' THE FERRIES CAN'T GET ACROSS. NEW YORK GONNA NEED A BRIDGE.
CITY HIRES A DUDE CALLED JOHN ROEBLING. GERMAN, SETTLED IN PENNSYLVANIA. HE DOES THE DESIGNS AN' THEY GO TO WORK.
'CEPT ROEBLING GETS HIS FOOT CRUSHED IN A ACCIDENT. GETS INFECTED.
HE BELIEVES IN SOMETHIN' CALLED HYDRATION THERAPY, WHERE YOU POUR WATER OVER A OPEN WOUND TO HELP IT HEAL. HE'S DEAD INSIDE A MONTH.
HIS SON WASHINGTON TAKES OVER. HE'S THE ONE TRULY MAKES IT HAPPEN. CITY HALL KEEP LOSIN' THEIR NERVE, DON'T THINK A SUSPENSION BRIDGE IS GONNA WORK, SAY IT'S TAKIN' TOO LONG-- BUT HE SAYS NO. FUCK THAT. WE DOIN' THIS.
THEY SINK THE CAISSONS IN THE RIVER, BROOKLYN END FIRST. CAISSONS'RE THESE KINDA SEALED BOXES GO AT THE BOTTOM A' THE TOWERS, LET THE CREWS GO DOWN AN' DIG THE FOUNDATIONS IN THE RIVER BED.
THEN SOME A' THE GUYS START GETTIN' SICK.
WHAT THEY DON'T KNOW IS, THEY GETTIN' THE BENDS. AIR PRESSURE AIN'T RIGHT INSIDE THE CAISSON. SOME DUDES END UP CRIPPLED-- SOME JUST DIE.
SO THEY LIMIT THE TIME THEY CAN WORK DOWN THERE, BUT THAT ONLY HELPS A LITTLE BIT. WASHINGTON, HE GOES IN AN' WORKS AS HARD AS ANYONE, HE JUST ABOUT FUCKS HIMSELF UP FOR LIFE.
THEN HIS WIFE EMILY STEPS UP.

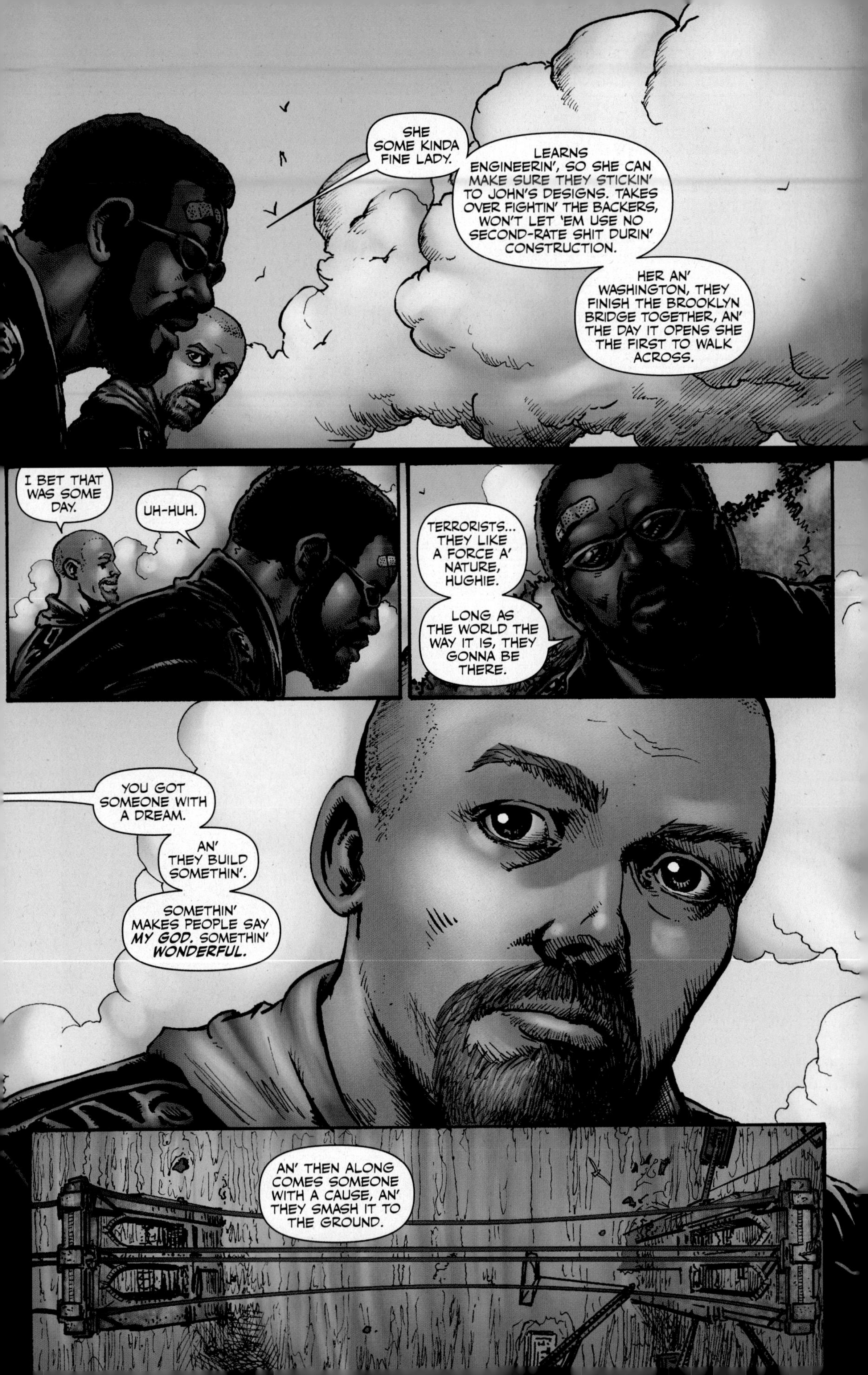
SHE SOME KINDA FINE LADY.
LEARNS ENGINEERIN', SO SHE CAN MAKE SURE THEY STICKIN' TO JOHN'S DESIGNS. TAKES OVER FIGHTIN' THE BACKERS, WON'T LET 'EM USE NO SECOND-RATE SHIT DURIN' CONSTRUCTION.
HER AN' WASHINGTON, THEY FINISH THE BROOKLYN BRIDGE TOGETHER, AN' THE DAY IT OPENS SHE THE FIRST TO WALK ACROSS.
I BET THAT WAS SOME DAY.
UH-HUH.
TERRORISTS... THEY LIKE A FORCE A' NATURE, HUGHIE.
LONG AS THE WORLD THE WAY IT IS, THEY GONNA BE THERE.
YOU GOT SOMEONE WITH A DREAM.
AN' THEY BUILD SOMETHIN'.
SOMETHIN' MAKES PEOPLE SAY *MY GOD*. SOMETHIN' ***WONDERFUL.***
AN' THEN ALONG COMES SOMEONE WITH A CAUSE, AN' THEY SMASH IT TO THE GROUND.

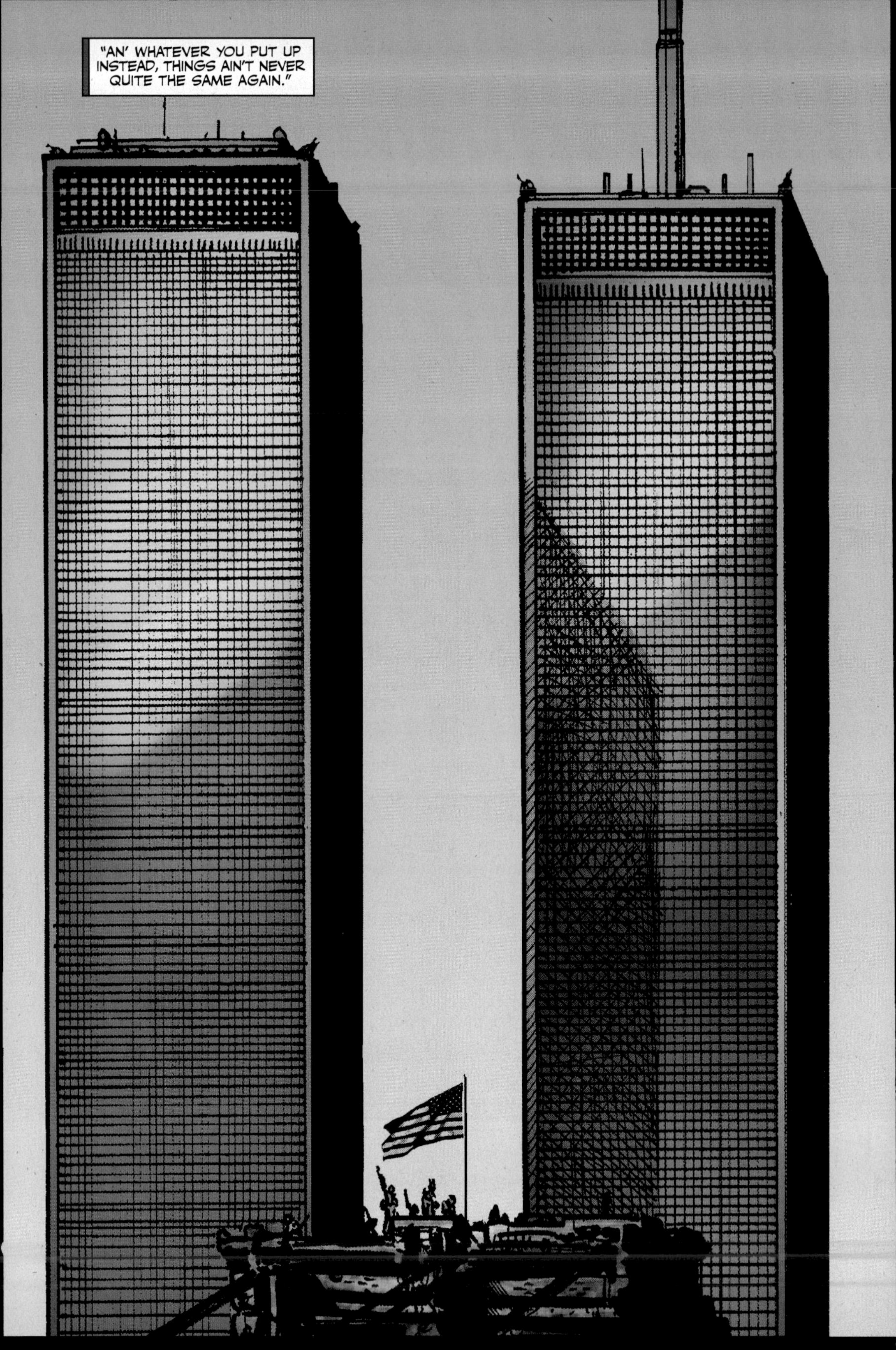
"AN' WHATEVER YOU PUT UP INSTEAD, THINGS AIN'T NEVER QUITE THE SAME AGAIN."

THE END

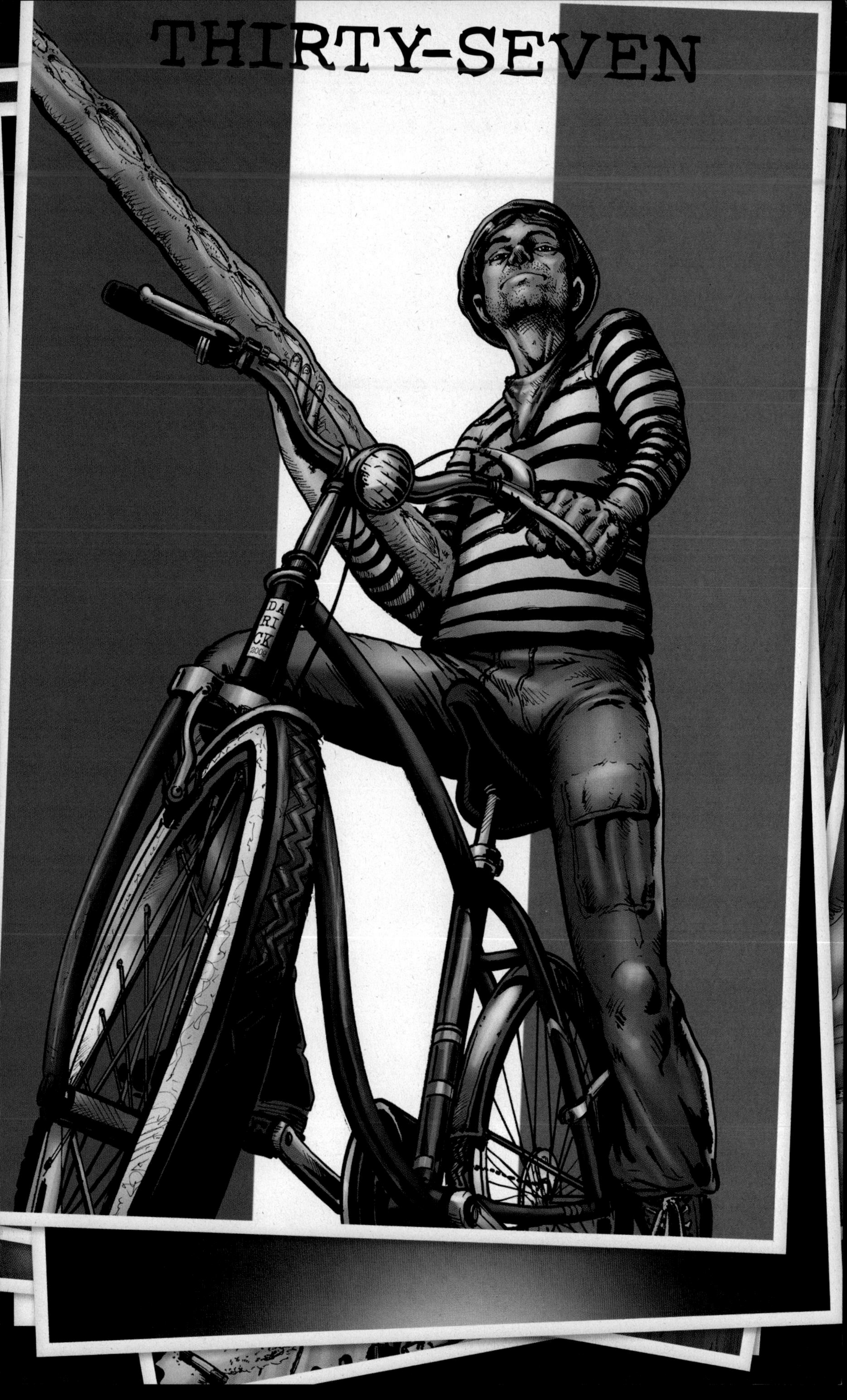
THIRTY-SEVEN

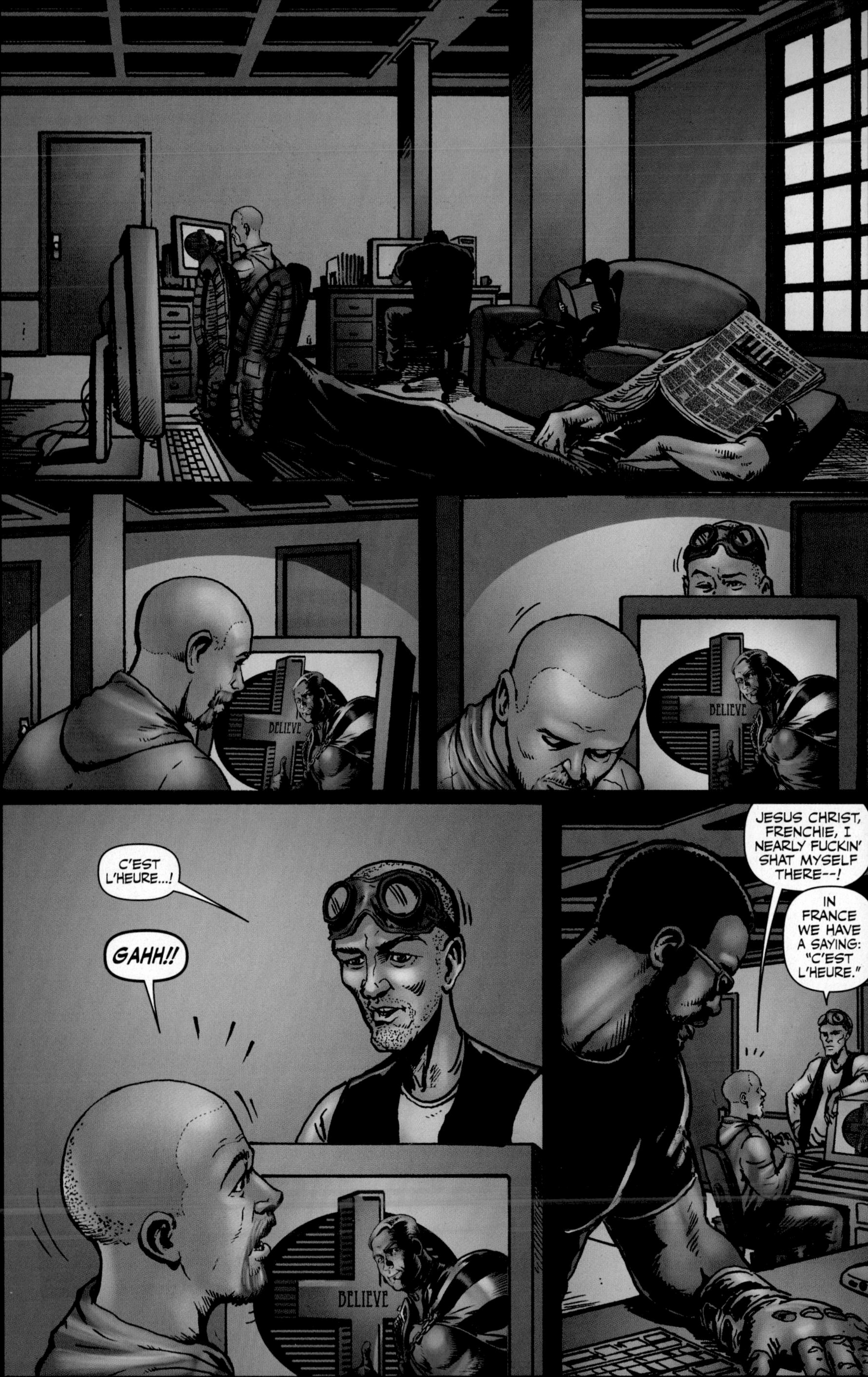
BELIEVE
BELIEVE
C'EST L'HEURE...!
GAHH!!
BELIEVE
JESUS CHRIST, FRENCHIE, I NEARLY FUCKIN' SHAT MYSELF THERE--!
IN FRANCE WE HAVE A SAYING: "C'EST L'HEURE."

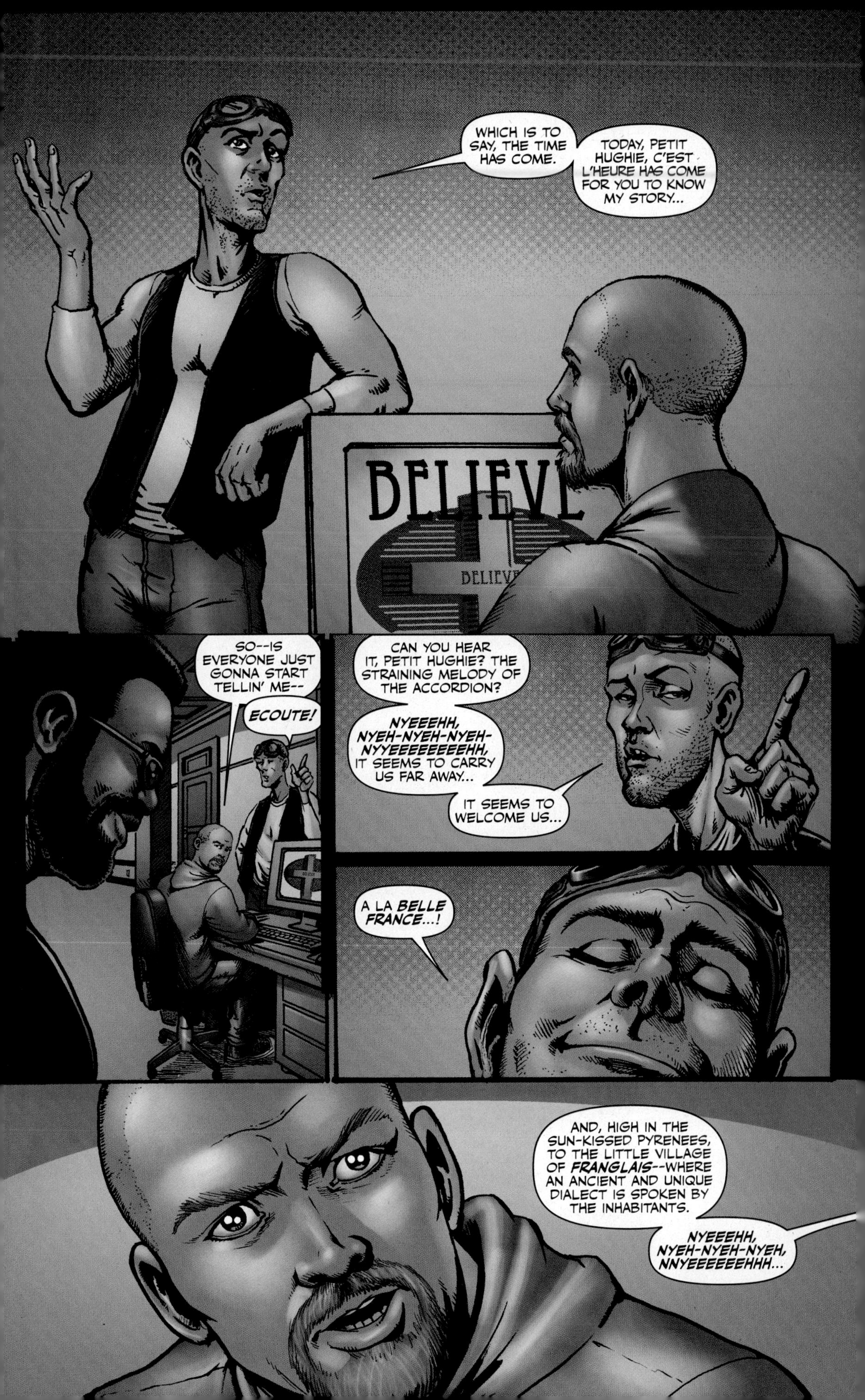
WHICH IS TO SAY, THE TIME HAS COME.
TODAY, PETIT HUGHIE, C'EST L'HEURE HAS COME FOR YOU TO KNOW MY STORY...
BELIEVE
BELIEVE
SO--IS EVERYONE JUST GONNA START TELLIN' ME--
ECOUTE!
CAN YOU HEAR IT, PETIT HUGHIE? THE STRAINING MELODY OF THE ACCORDION?
NYEEEHH, NYEH-NYEH-NYEH-NYYEEEEEEEEEHH, IT SEEMS TO CARRY US FAR AWAY...
IT SEEMS TO WELCOME US...
A LA BELLE FRANCE...!
AND, HIGH IN THE SUN-KISSED PYRENEES, TO THE LITTLE VILLAGE OF FRANGLAIS--WHERE AN ANCIENT AND UNIQUE DIALECT IS SPOKEN BY THE INHABITANTS.
NYEEEHH, NYEH-NYEH-NYEH, NNYEEEEEEEHHH...

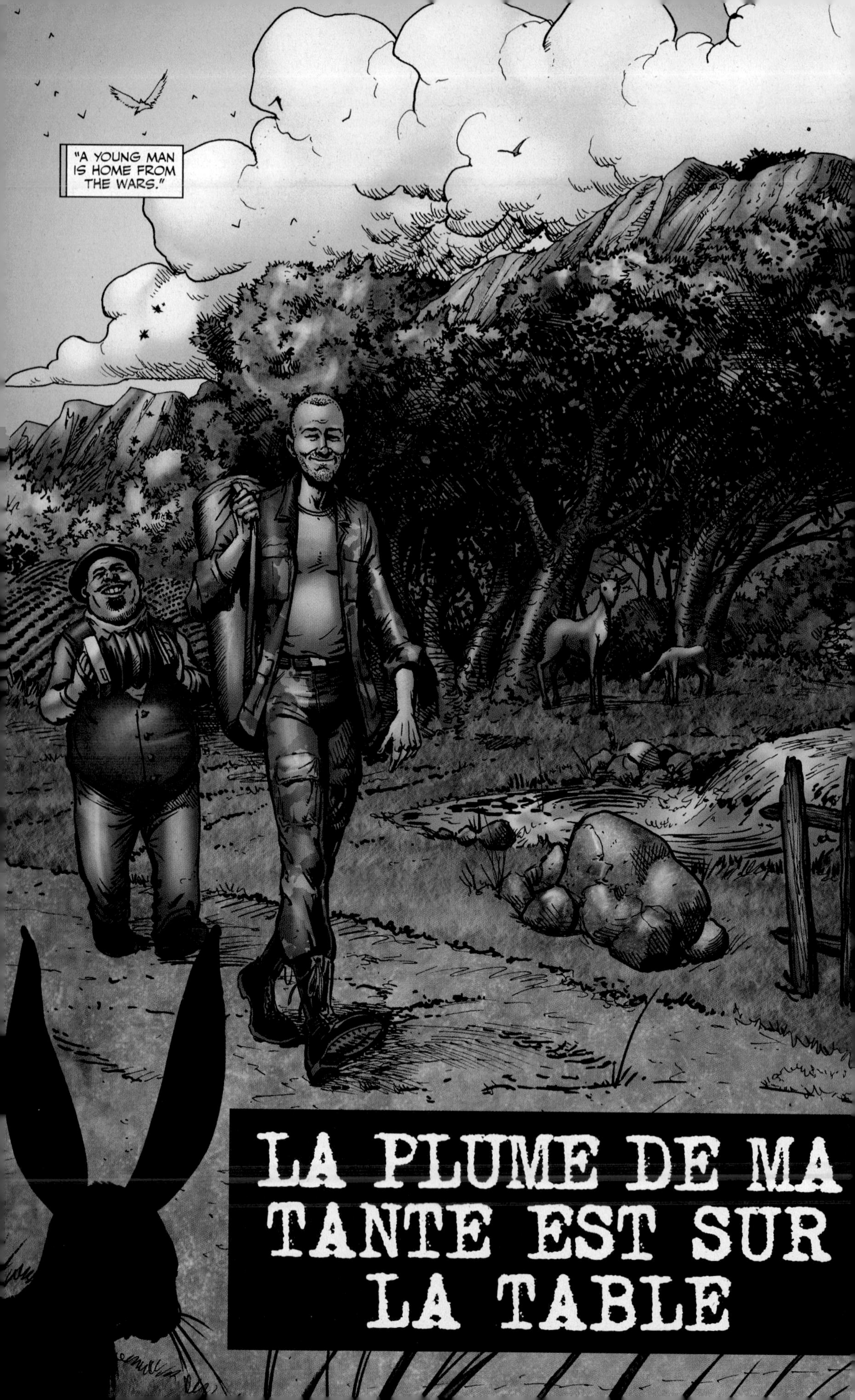
"A YOUNG MAN IS HOME FROM THE WARS."
LA PLUME DE MA TANTE EST SUR LA TABLE

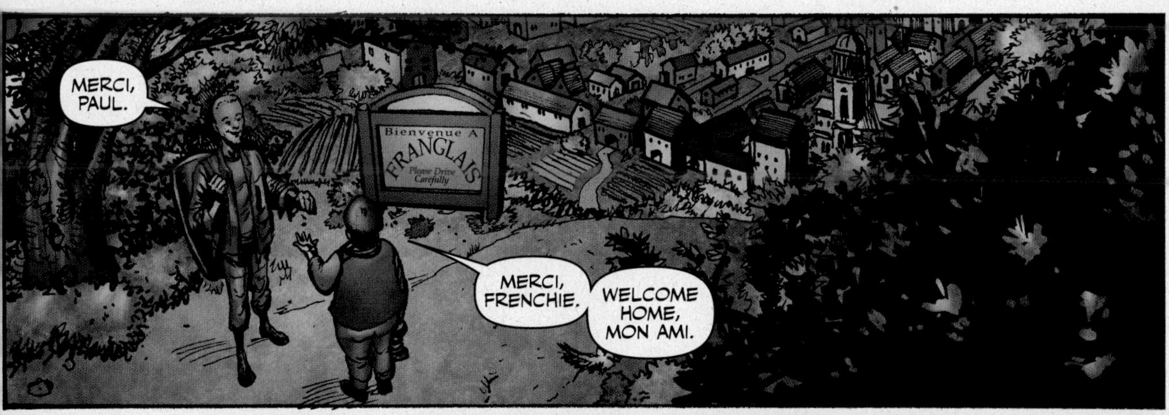
MERCI, PAUL.
Bienvenue A
FRANGLAIS
Please Drive Carefully
MERCI, FRENCHIE.
WELCOME HOME, MON AMI.

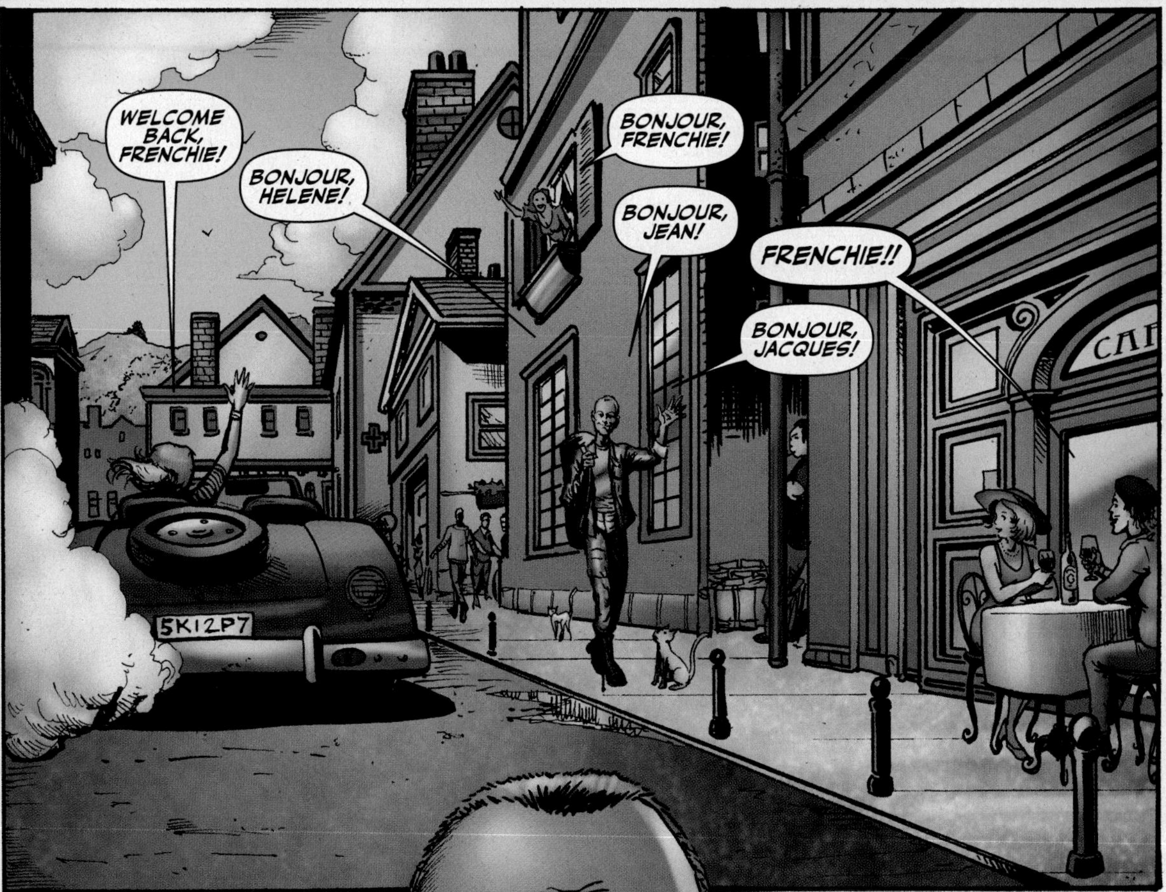
WELCOME BACK, FRENCHIE!
BONJOUR, HELENE!
BONJOUR, FRENCHIE!
BONJOUR, JEAN!
FRENCHIE!!
BONJOUR, JACQUES!
5K12P7

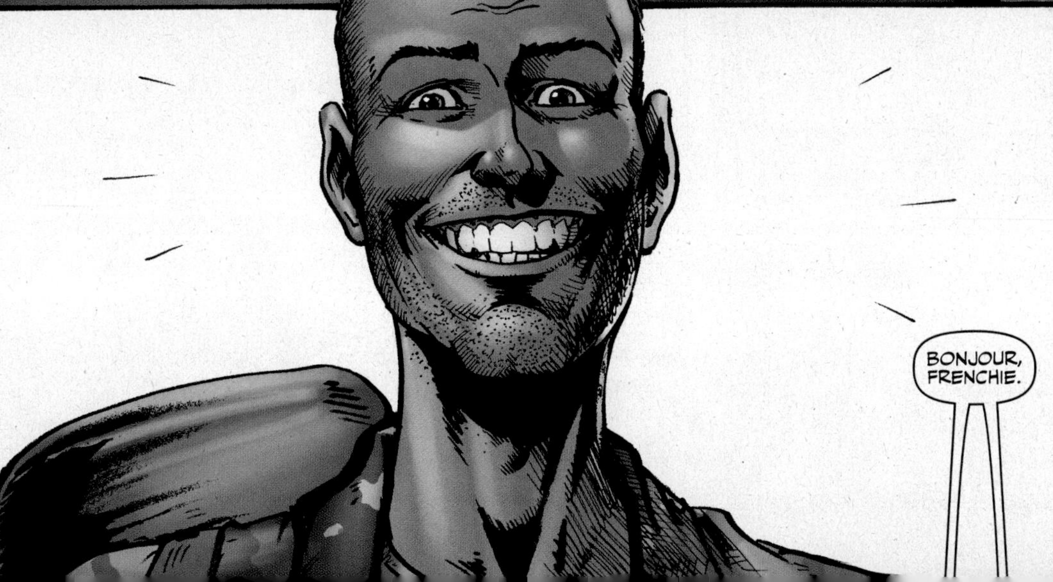
BONJOUR, FRENCHIE.

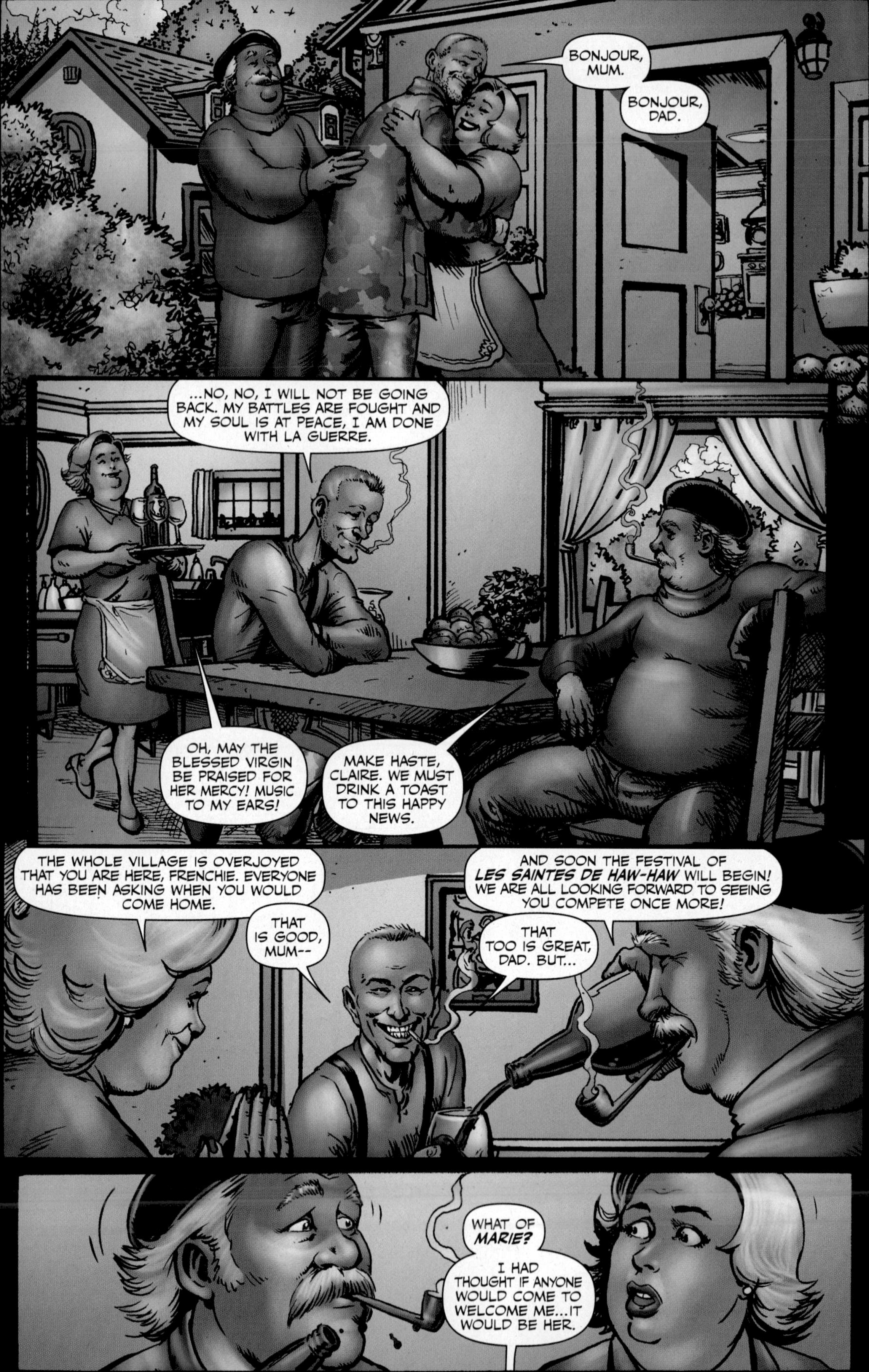
BONJOUR, MUM.
BONJOUR, DAD.
...NO, NO, I WILL NOT BE GOING BACK. MY BATTLES ARE FOUGHT AND MY SOUL IS AT PEACE, I AM DONE WITH LA GUERRE.
OH, MAY THE BLESSED VIRGIN BE PRAISED FOR HER MERCY! MUSIC TO MY EARS!
MAKE HASTE, CLAIRE. WE MUST DRINK A TOAST TO THIS HAPPY NEWS.
THE WHOLE VILLAGE IS OVERJOYED THAT YOU ARE HERE, FRENCHIE. EVERYONE HAS BEEN ASKING WHEN YOU WOULD COME HOME.
THAT IS GOOD, MUM--
AND SOON THE FESTIVAL OF *LES SAINTES DE HAW-HAW* WILL BEGIN! WE ARE ALL LOOKING FORWARD TO SEEING YOU COMPETE ONCE MORE!
THAT TOO IS GREAT, DAD. BUT...
WHAT OF ***MARIE?***
I HAD THOUGHT IF ANYONE WOULD COME TO WELCOME ME...IT WOULD BE HER.

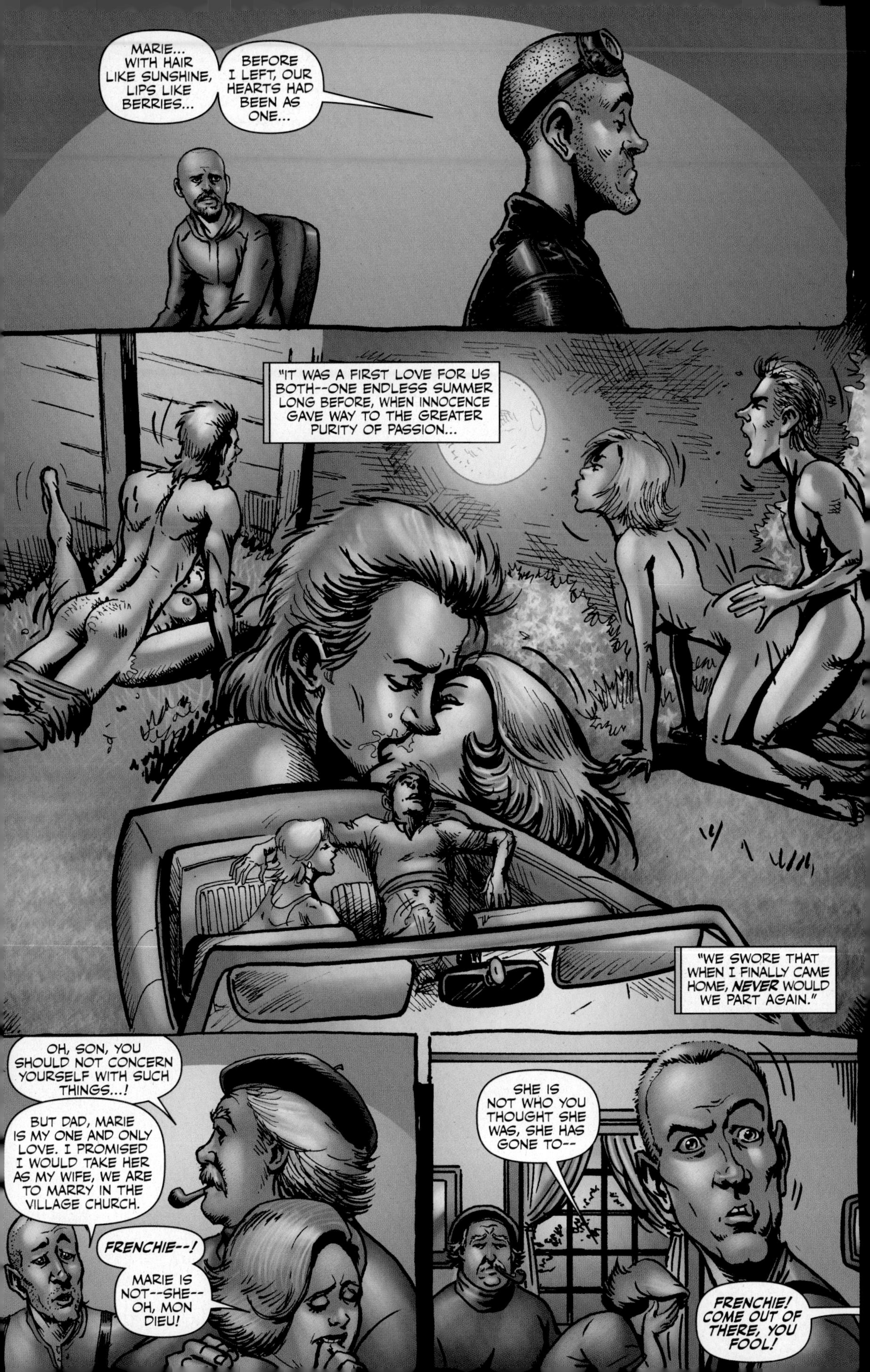

MARIE... WITH HAIR LIKE SUNSHINE, LIPS LIKE BERRIES...
BEFORE I LEFT, OUR HEARTS HAD BEEN AS ONE...
"IT WAS A FIRST LOVE FOR US BOTH--ONE ENDLESS SUMMER LONG BEFORE, WHEN INNOCENCE GAVE WAY TO THE GREATER PURITY OF PASSION...
"WE SWORE THAT WHEN I FINALLY CAME HOME, NEVER WOULD WE PART AGAIN."
OH, SON, YOU SHOULD NOT CONCERN YOURSELF WITH SUCH THINGS...!
BUT DAD, MARIE IS MY ONE AND ONLY LOVE. I PROMISED I WOULD TAKE HER AS MY WIFE, WE ARE TO MARRY IN THE VILLAGE CHURCH.
FRENCHIE--!
MARIE IS NOT--SHE--OH, MON DIEU!
SHE IS NOT WHO YOU THOUGHT SHE WAS, SHE HAS GONE TO--
FRENCHIE! COME OUT OF THERE, YOU FOOL!

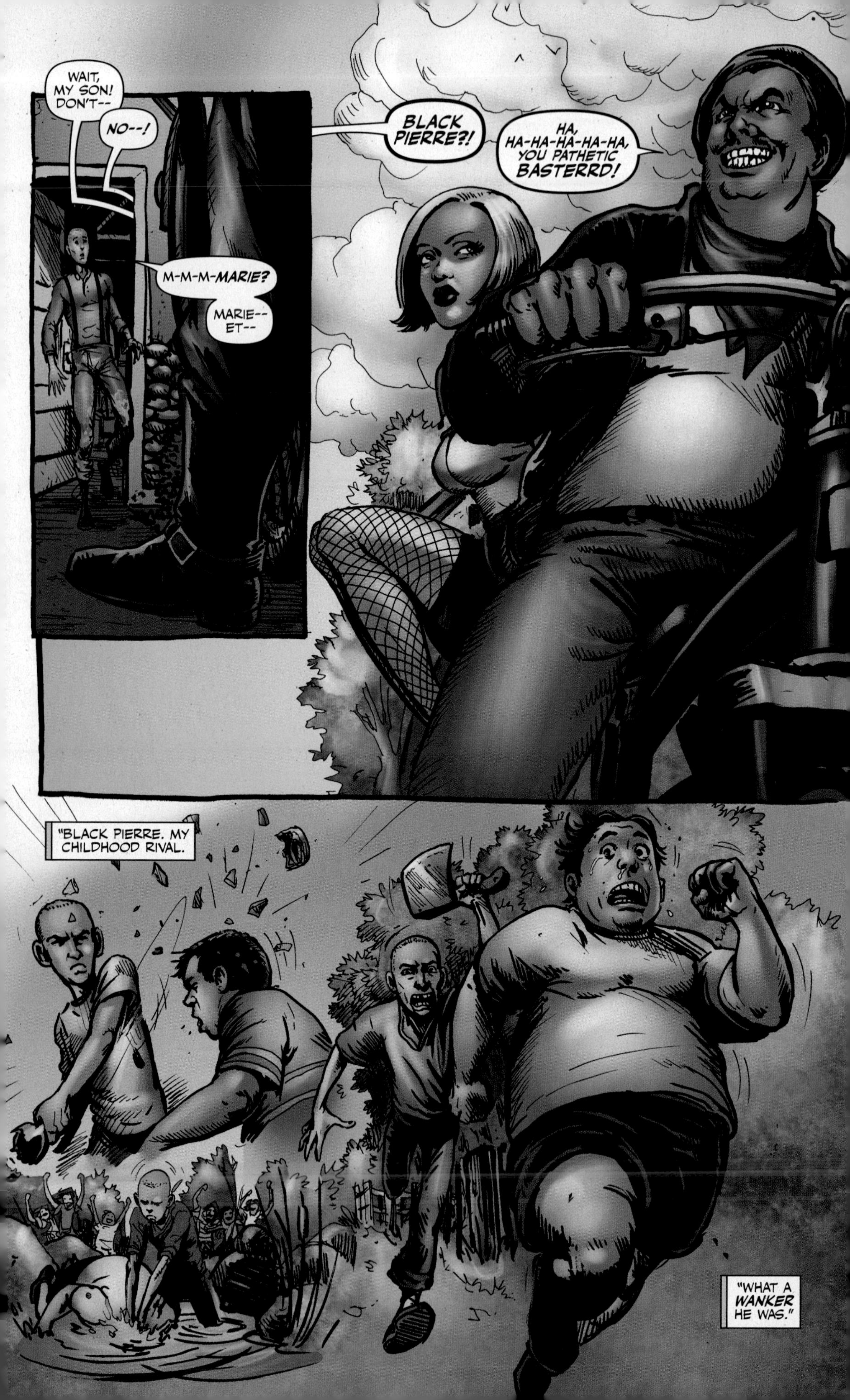

WAIT, MY SON! DON'T--
NO--!
BLACK PIERRE?!
HA, HA-HA-HA-HA-HA, YOU PATHETIC BASTERRD!
M-M-M-MARIE?
MARIE-- ET--
"BLACK PIERRE. MY CHILDHOOD RIVAL.
"WHAT A WANKER HE WAS."

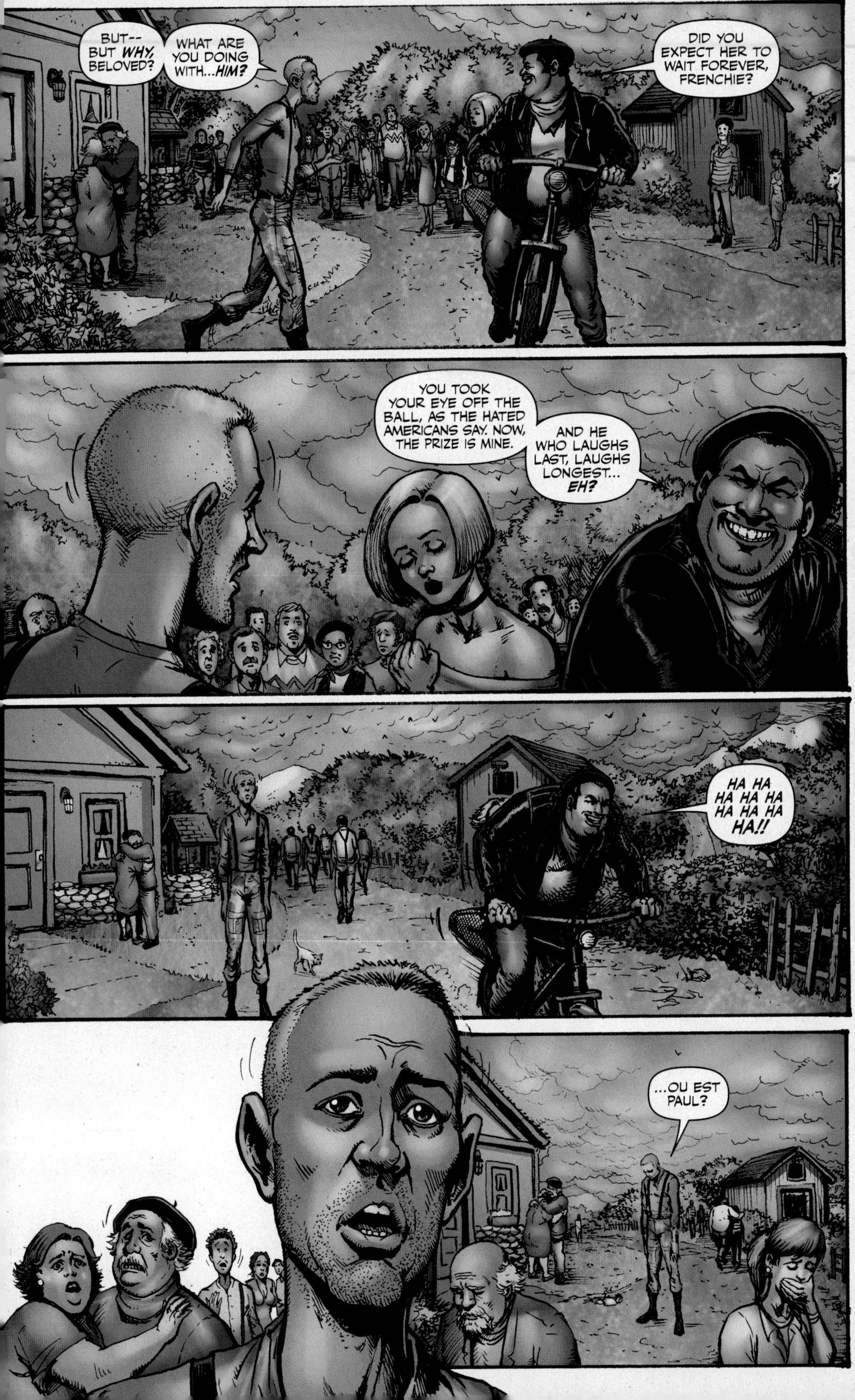
BUT-- BUT WHY, BELOVED?
WHAT ARE YOU DOING WITH...HIM?
DID YOU EXPECT HER TO WAIT FOREVER, FRENCHIE?
YOU TOOK YOUR EYE OFF THE BALL, AS THE HATED AMERICANS SAY. NOW, THE PRIZE IS MINE.
AND HE WHO LAUGHS LAST, LAUGHS LONGEST... EH?
HA HA HA HA HA HA HA HA HA!!
...OU EST PAUL?

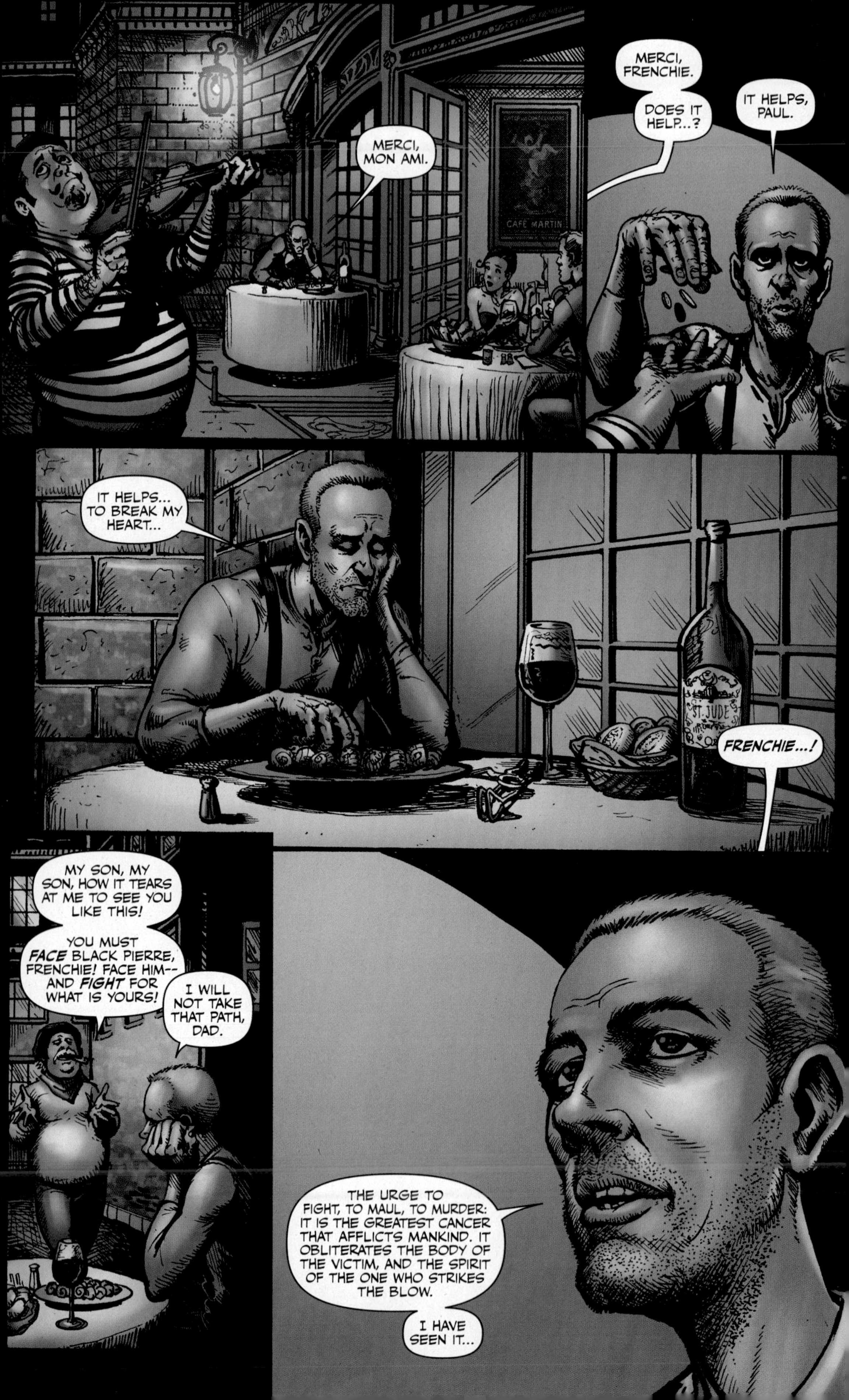
MERCI, MON AMI.
MERCI, FRENCHIE.
DOES IT HELP...?
IT HELPS, PAUL.
CAFÉ MARTIN
IT HELPS... TO BREAK MY HEART...
ST. JUDE
FRENCHIE...!
MY SON, MY SON, HOW IT TEARS AT ME TO SEE YOU LIKE THIS!
YOU MUST *FACE* BLACK PIERRE, FRENCHIE! FACE HIM-- AND *FIGHT* FOR WHAT IS YOURS!
I WILL NOT TAKE THAT PATH, DAD.
THE URGE TO FIGHT, TO MAUL, TO MURDER: IT IS THE GREATEST CANCER THAT AFFLICTS MANKIND. IT OBLITERATES THE BODY OF THE VICTIM, AND THE SPIRIT OF THE ONE WHO STRIKES THE BLOW.
I HAVE SEEN IT...

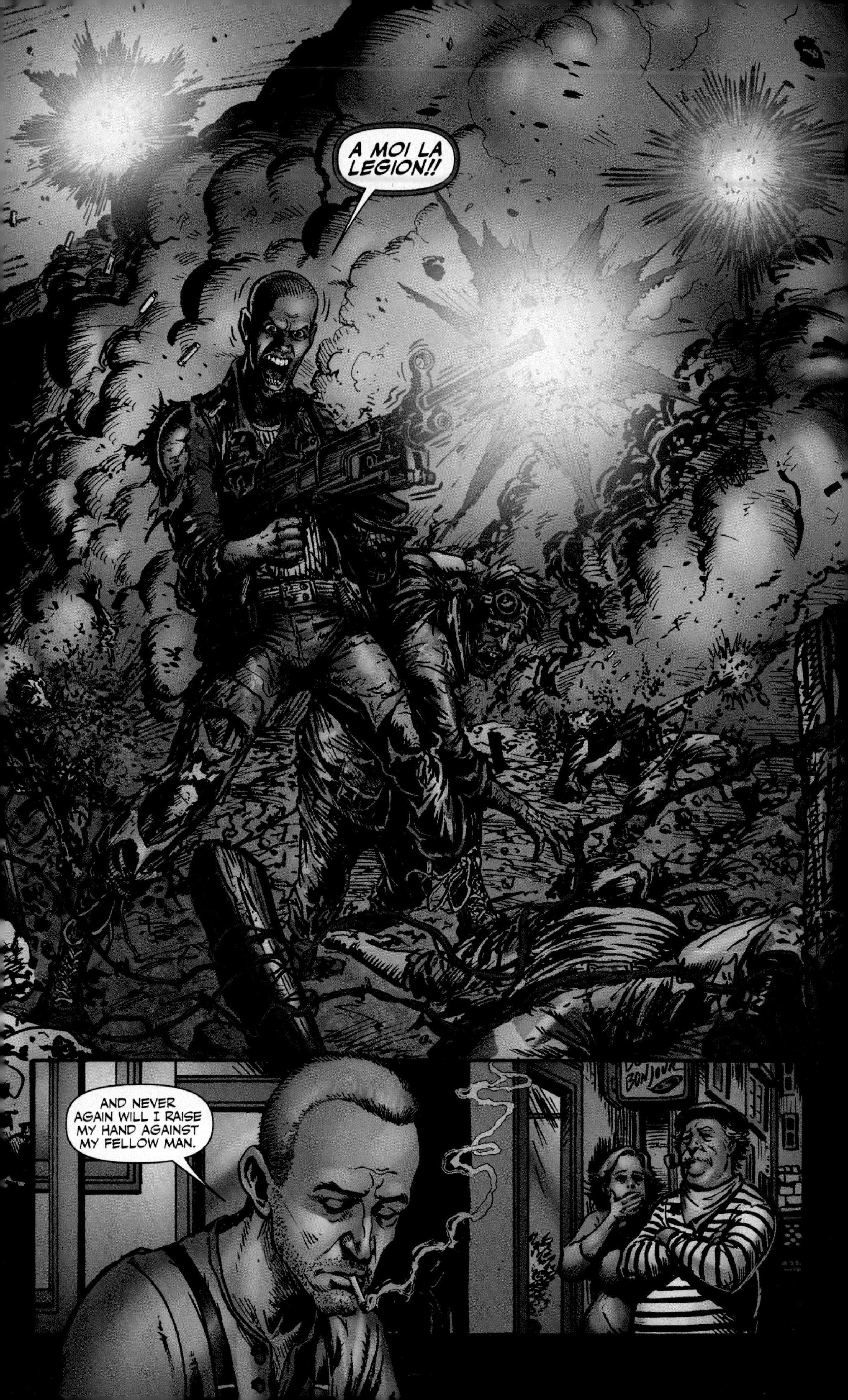
A MOI LA LEGION!!
AND NEVER AGAIN WILL I RAISE MY HAND AGAINST MY FELLOW MAN.
BONJOUR

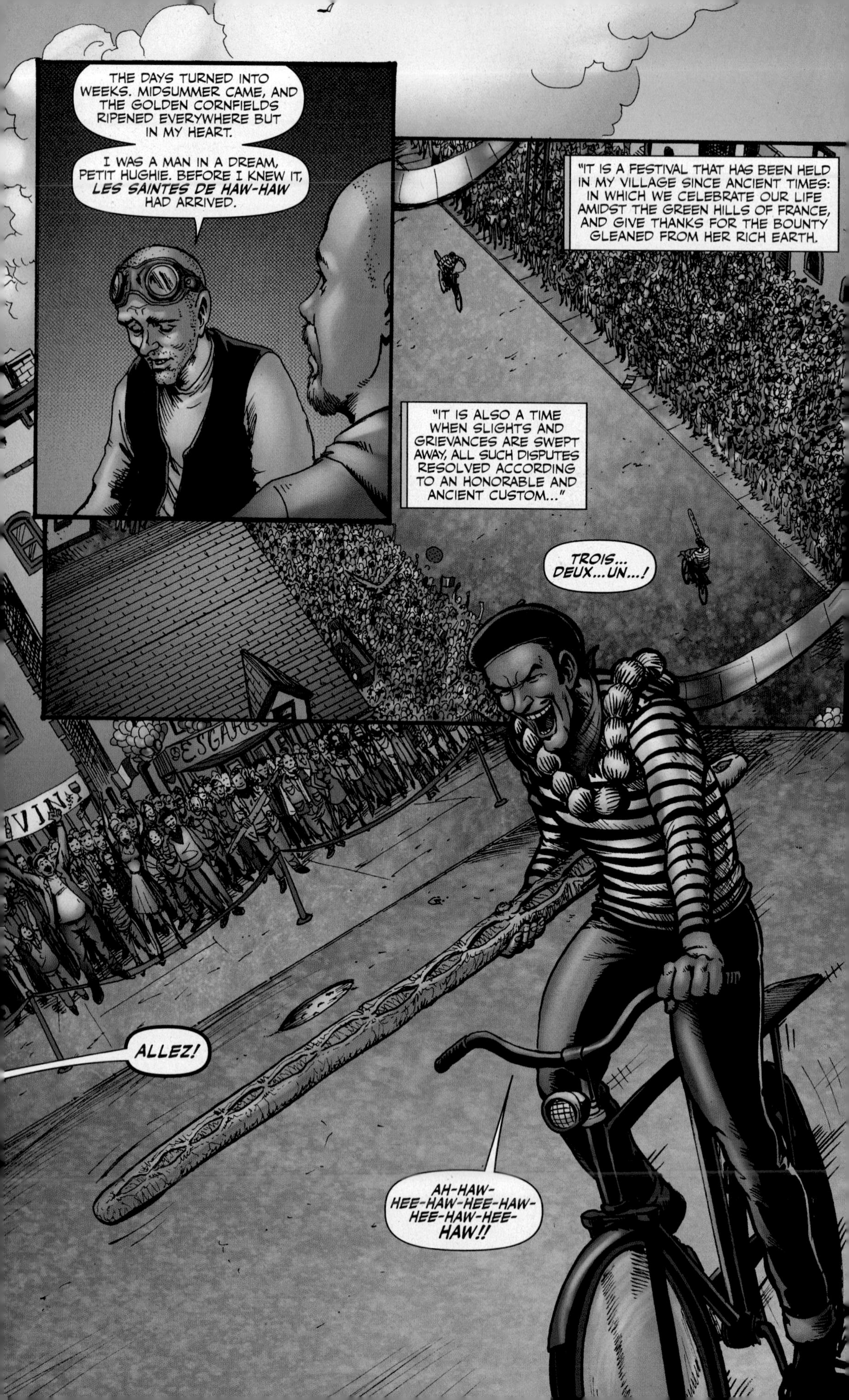
THE DAYS TURNED INTO WEEKS. MIDSUMMER CAME, AND THE GOLDEN CORNFIELDS RIPENED EVERYWHERE BUT IN MY HEART.
I WAS A MAN IN A DREAM, PETIT HUGHIE. BEFORE I KNEW IT, LES SAINTES DE HAW-HAW HAD ARRIVED.
"IT IS A FESTIVAL THAT HAS BEEN HELD IN MY VILLAGE SINCE ANCIENT TIMES: IN WHICH WE CELEBRATE OUR LIFE AMIDST THE GREEN HILLS OF FRANCE, AND GIVE THANKS FOR THE BOUNTY GLEANED FROM HER RICH EARTH.
"IT IS ALSO A TIME WHEN SLIGHTS AND GRIEVANCES ARE SWEPT AWAY, ALL SUCH DISPUTES RESOLVED ACCORDING TO AN HONORABLE AND ANCIENT CUSTOM..."
TROIS... DEUX...UN...!
VIN
ALLEZ!
AH-HAW-HEE-HAW-HEE-HAW-HEE-HAW-HEE-HAW!!

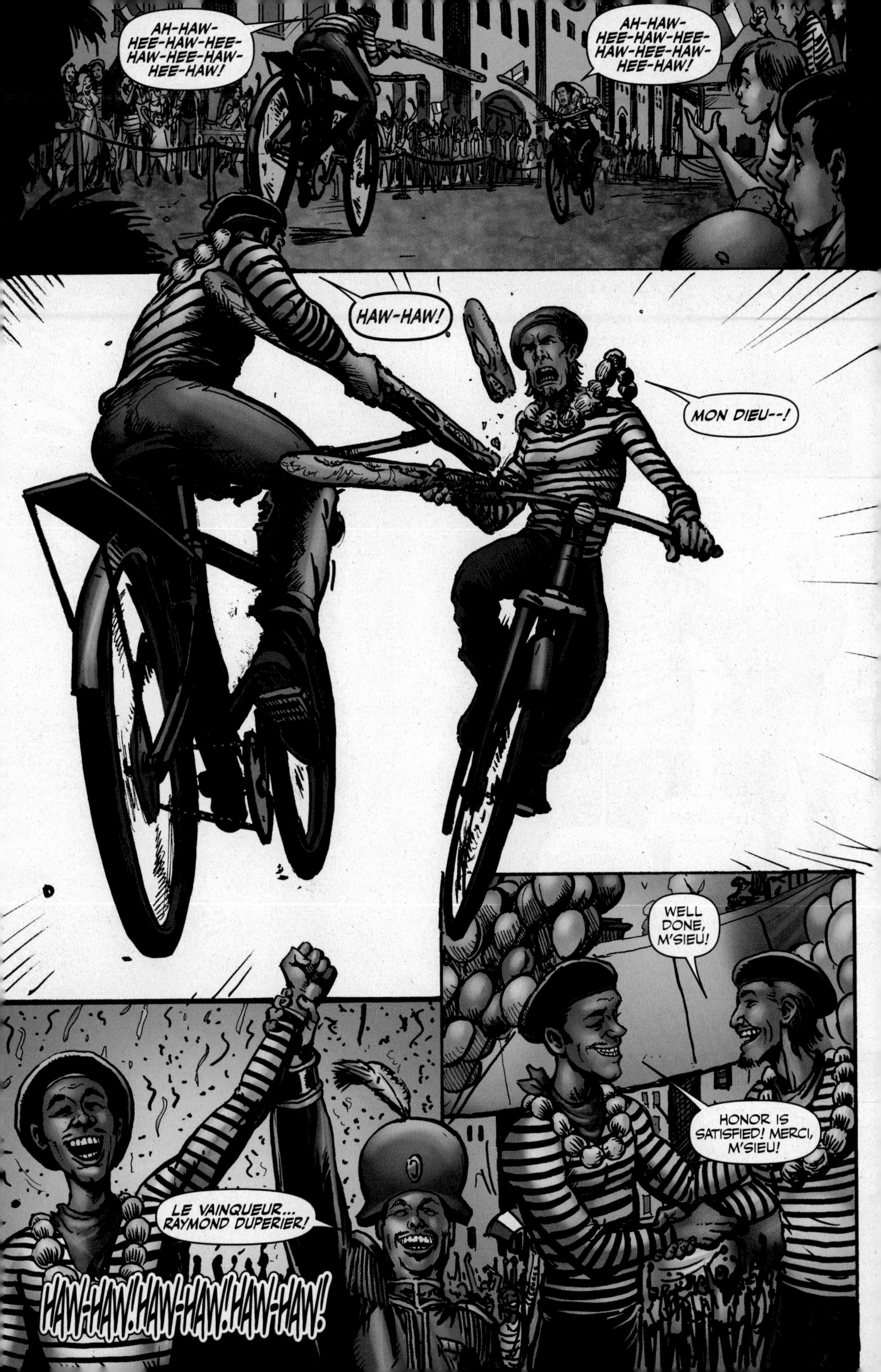
AH-HAW-
HEE-HAW-HEE-
HAW-HEE-HAW-
HEE-HAW!
AH-HAW-
HEE-HAW-HEE-
HAW-HEE-HAW-
HEE-HAW!
HAW-HAW!
MON DIEU--!
WELL DONE, M'SIEU!
HONOR IS SATISFIED! MERCI, M'SIEU!
LE VAINQUEUR... RAYMOND DUPERIER!
HAW-HAW! HAW-HAW! HAW-HAW!

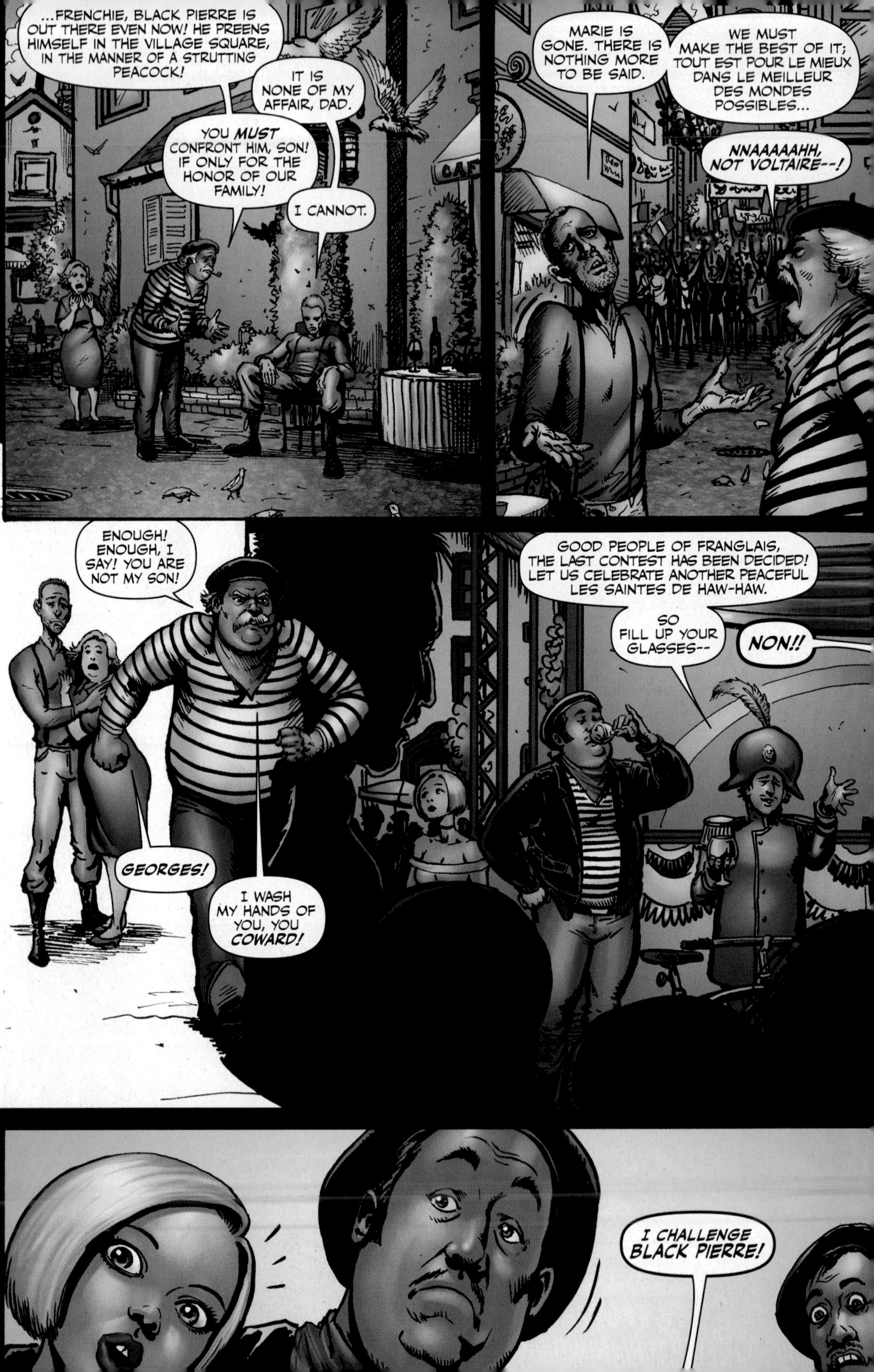
...FRENCHIE, BLACK PIERRE IS OUT THERE EVEN NOW! HE PREENS HIMSELF IN THE VILLAGE SQUARE, IN THE MANNER OF A STRUTTING PEACOCK!
IT IS NONE OF MY AFFAIR, DAD.
YOU MUST CONFRONT HIM, SON! IF ONLY FOR THE HONOR OF OUR FAMILY!
I CANNOT.
MARIE IS GONE. THERE IS NOTHING MORE TO BE SAID.
WE MUST MAKE THE BEST OF IT; TOUT EST POUR LE MIEUX DANS LE MEILLEUR DES MONDES POSSIBLES...
NNAAAAAHH, NOT VOLTAIRE--!
ENOUGH! ENOUGH, I SAY! YOU ARE NOT MY SON!
GEORGES!
I WASH MY HANDS OF YOU, YOU COWARD!
GOOD PEOPLE OF FRANGLAIS, THE LAST CONTEST HAS BEEN DECIDED! LET US CELEBRATE ANOTHER PEACEFUL LES SAINTES DE HAW-HAW.
SO FILL UP YOUR GLASSES--
NON!!
I CHALLENGE BLACK PIERRE!

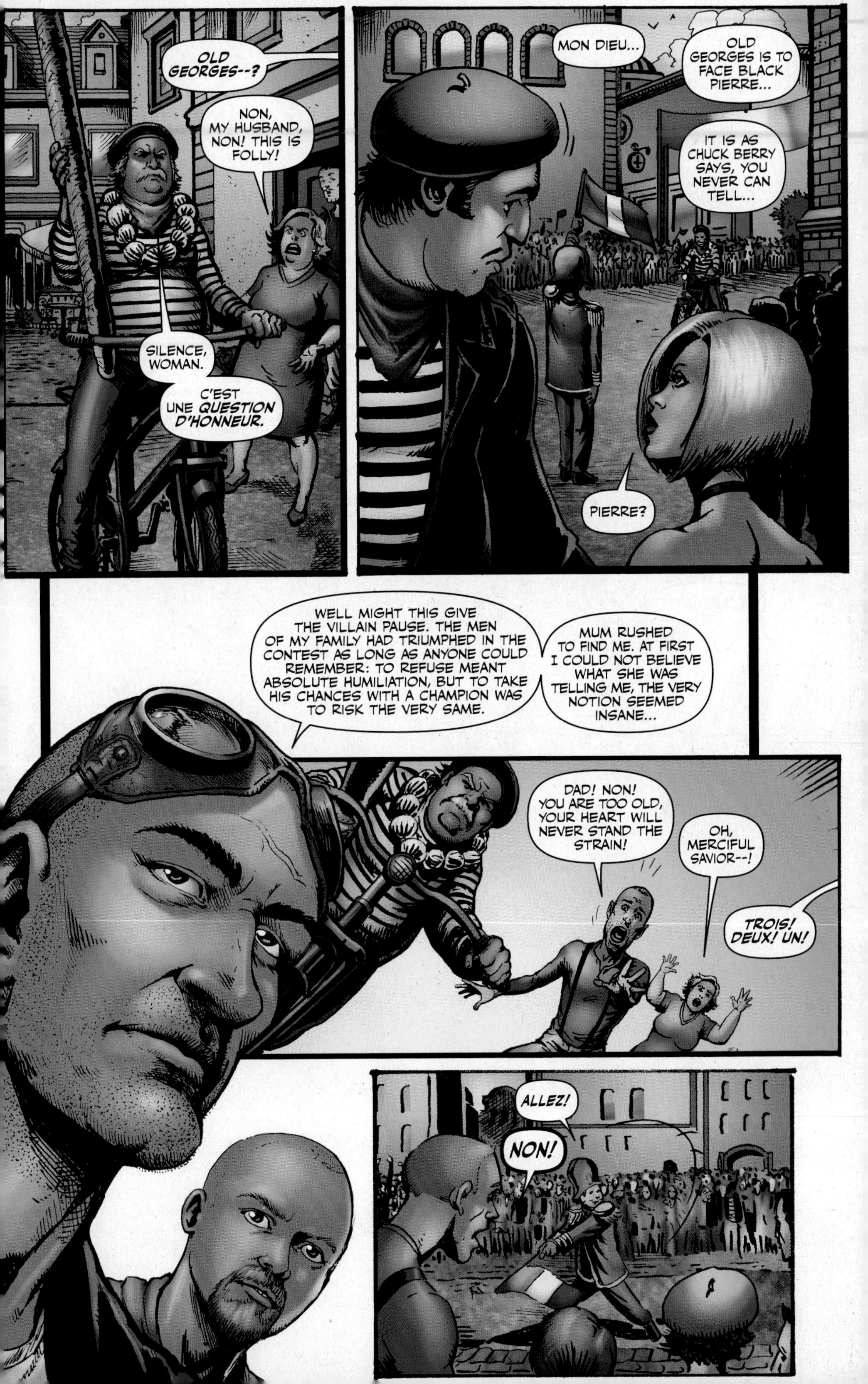
OLD GEORGES--?
NON, MY HUSBAND, NON! THIS IS FOLLY!
SILENCE, WOMAN.
C'EST UNE QUESTION D'HONNEUR.
MON DIEU...
OLD GEORGES IS TO FACE BLACK PIERRE...
IT IS AS CHUCK BERRY SAYS, YOU NEVER CAN TELL...
PIERRE?
WELL MIGHT THIS GIVE THE VILLAIN PAUSE. THE MEN OF MY FAMILY HAD TRIUMPHED IN THE CONTEST AS LONG AS ANYONE COULD REMEMBER: TO REFUSE MEANT ABSOLUTE HUMILIATION, BUT TO TAKE HIS CHANCES WITH A CHAMPION WAS TO RISK THE VERY SAME.
MUM RUSHED TO FIND ME. AT FIRST I COULD NOT BELIEVE WHAT SHE WAS TELLING ME, THE VERY NOTION SEEMED INSANE...
DAD! NON! YOU ARE TOO OLD, YOUR HEART WILL NEVER STAND THE STRAIN!
OH, MERCIFUL SAVIOR--!
TROIS! DEUX! UN!
ALLEZ!
NON!

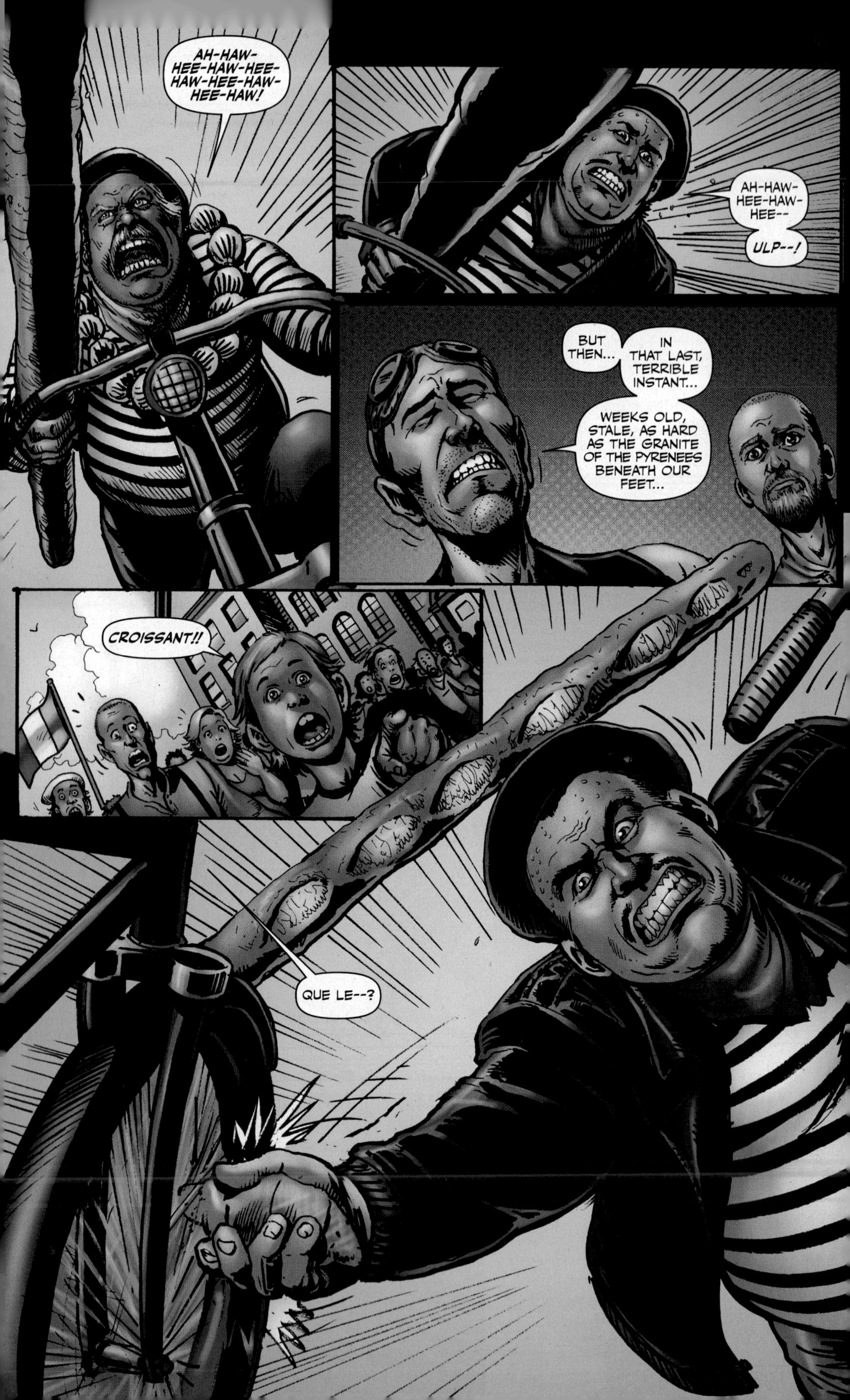
AH-HAW-
HEE-HAW-HEE-
HAW-HEE-HAW-
HEE-HAW!
AH-HAW-
HEE-HAW-
HEE--
ULP--!
BUT THEN...
IN THAT LAST, TERRIBLE INSTANT...
WEEKS OLD, STALE, AS HARD AS THE GRANITE OF THE PYRENEES BENEATH OUR FEET...
CROISSANT!!
QUE LE--?

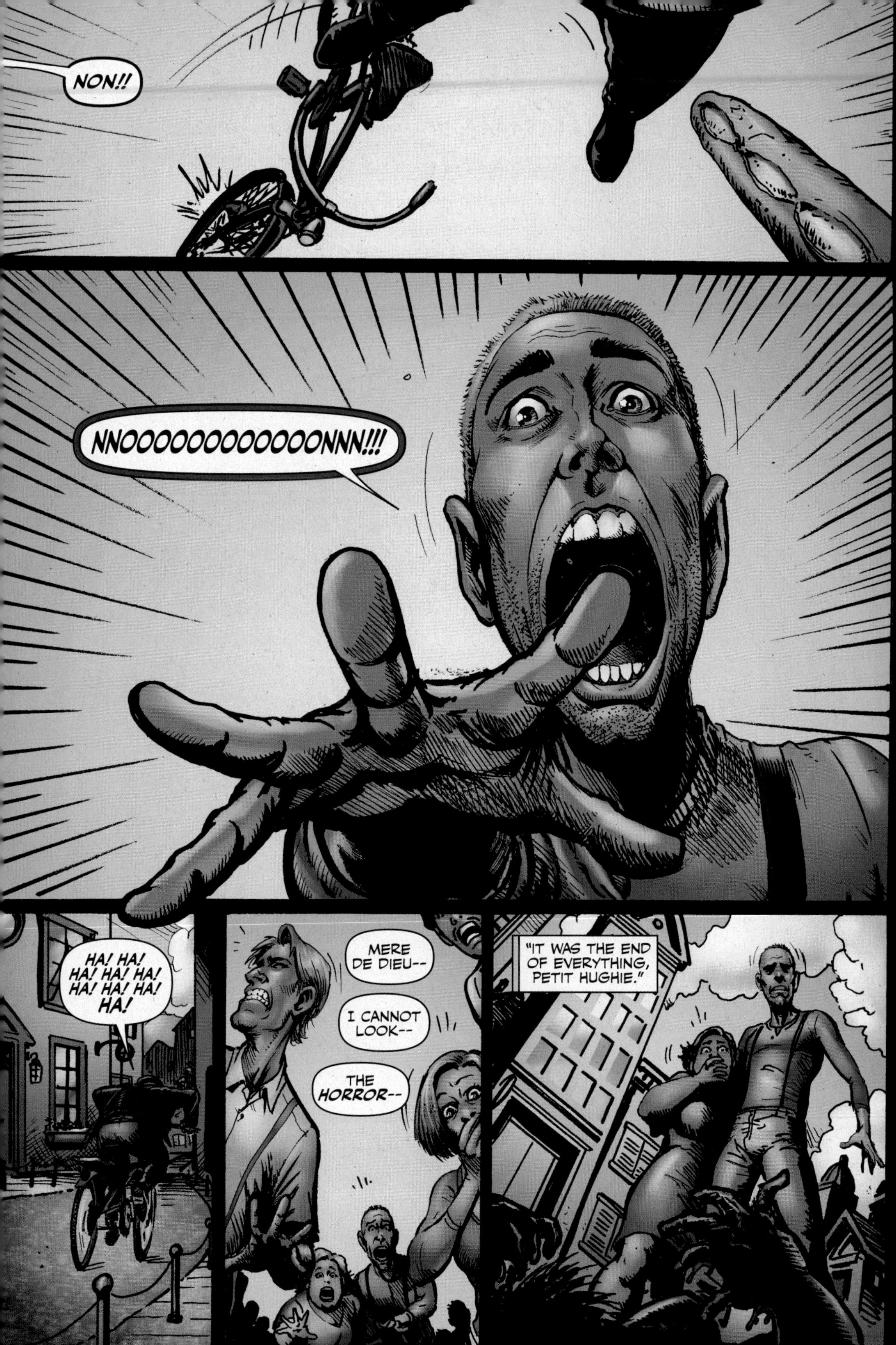
NON!!
NNOOOOOOOOOOOOONNN!!!
HA! HA! HA! HA! HA! HA! HA! HA! HA!
MERE DE DIEU--
I CANNOT LOOK--
THE HORROR--
"IT WAS THE END OF EVERYTHING, PETIT HUGHIE."

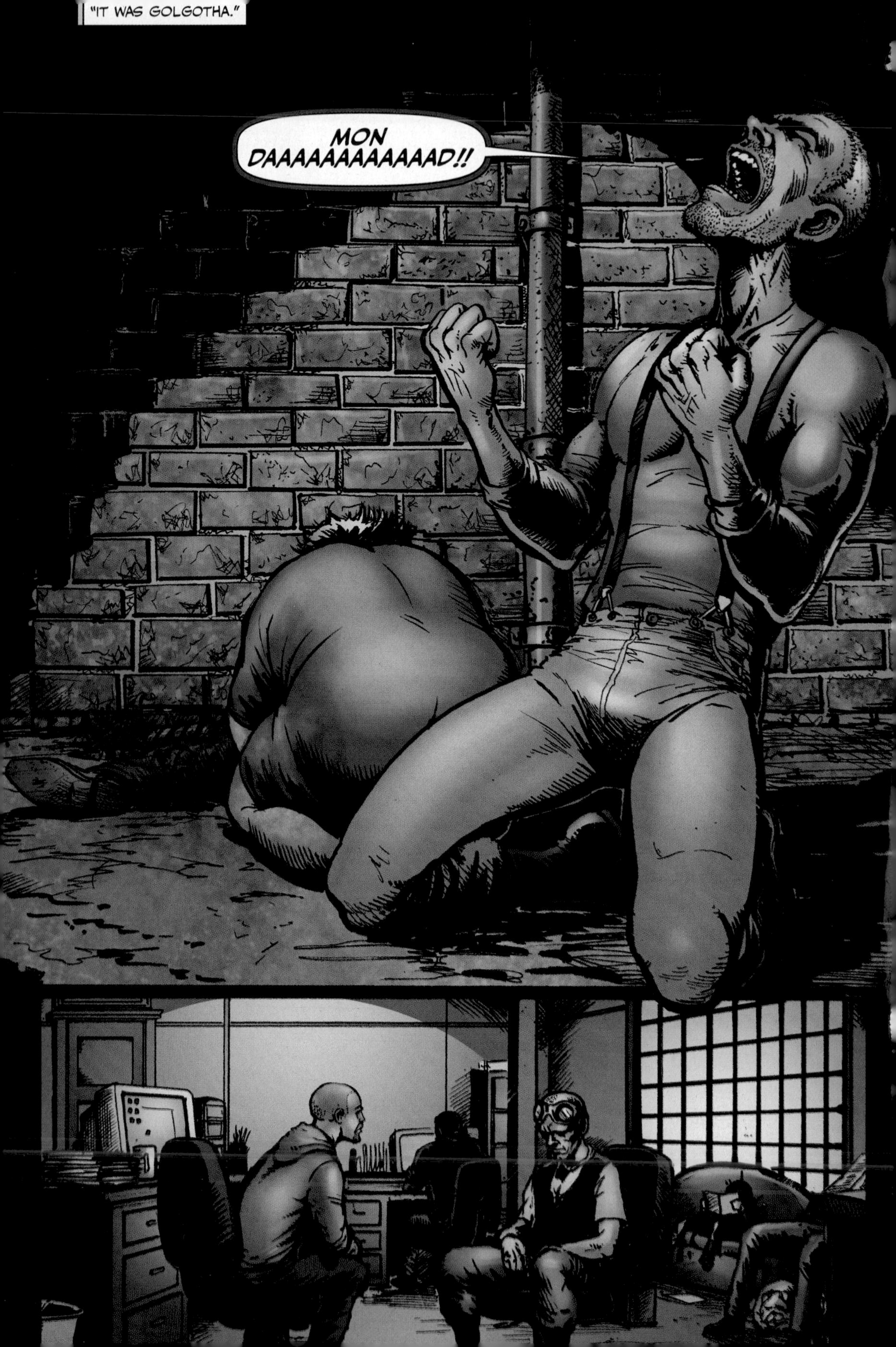
"IT WAS GOLGOTHA."
MON DAAAAAAAAAAAAD!!

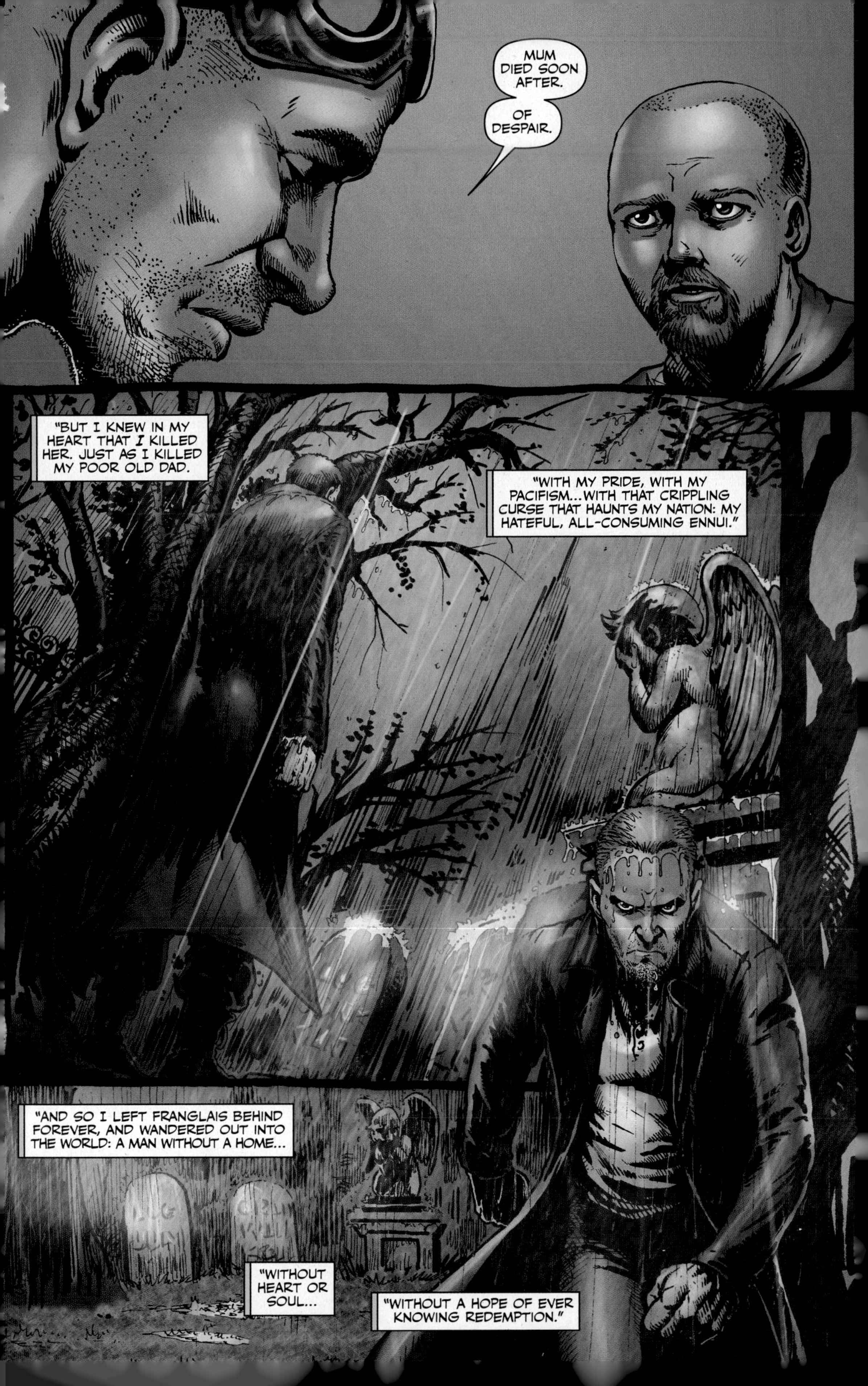
MUM DIED SOON AFTER.
OF DESPAIR.
"BUT I KNEW IN MY HEART THAT *I* KILLED HER. JUST AS I KILLED MY POOR OLD DAD.
"WITH MY PRIDE, WITH MY PACIFISM...WITH THAT CRIPPLING CURSE THAT HAUNTS MY NATION: MY HATEFUL, ALL-CONSUMING ENNUI."
"AND SO I LEFT FRANGLAIS BEHIND FOREVER, AND WANDERED OUT INTO THE WORLD: A MAN WITHOUT A HOME...
"WITHOUT HEART OR SOUL...
"WITHOUT A HOPE OF EVER KNOWING REDEMPTION."

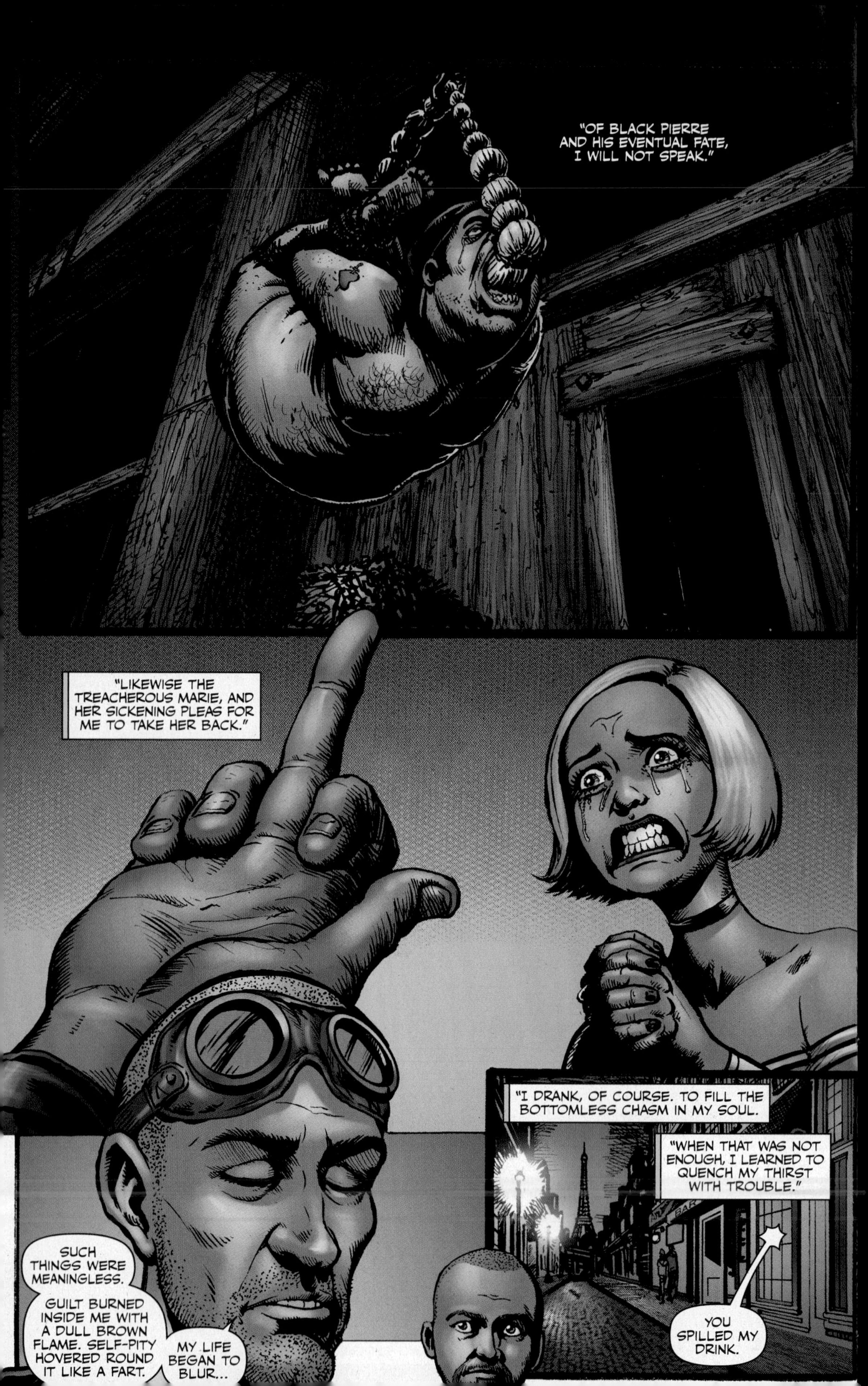
"OF BLACK PIERRE AND HIS EVENTUAL FATE, I WILL NOT SPEAK."
"LIKEWISE THE TREACHEROUS MARIE, AND HER SICKENING PLEAS FOR ME TO TAKE HER BACK."
SUCH THINGS WERE MEANINGLESS.
GUILT BURNED INSIDE ME WITH A DULL BROWN FLAME. SELF-PITY HOVERED ROUND IT LIKE A FART.
MY LIFE BEGAN TO BLUR...
"I DRANK, OF COURSE. TO FILL THE BOTTOMLESS CHASM IN MY SOUL.
"WHEN THAT WAS NOT ENOUGH, I LEARNED TO QUENCH MY THIRST WITH TROUBLE."
BAR
YOU SPILLED MY DRINK.

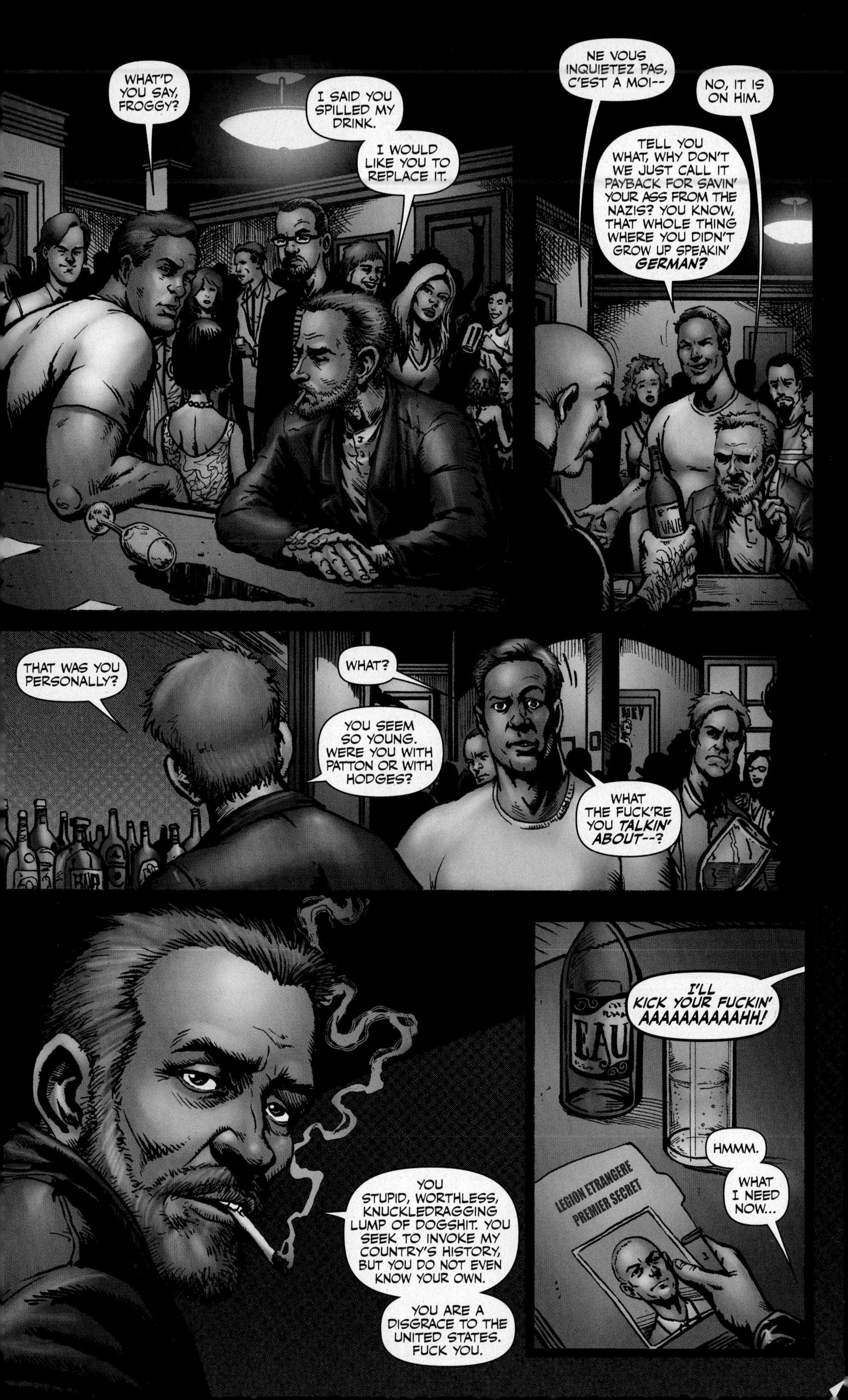
WHAT'D YOU SAY, FROGGY?
I SAID YOU SPILLED MY DRINK.
I WOULD LIKE YOU TO REPLACE IT.
NE VOUS INQUIETEZ PAS, C'EST A MOI--
NO, IT IS ON HIM.
TELL YOU WHAT, WHY DON'T WE JUST CALL IT PAYBACK FOR SAVIN' YOUR ASS FROM THE NAZIS? YOU KNOW, THAT WHOLE THING WHERE YOU DIDN'T GROW UP SPEAKIN' *GERMAN?*
THAT WAS YOU PERSONALLY?
WHAT?
YOU SEEM SO YOUNG. WERE YOU WITH PATTON OR WITH HODGES?
WHAT THE FUCK'RE YOU *TALKIN' ABOUT--?*
YOU STUPID, WORTHLESS, KNUCKLEDRAGGING LUMP OF DOGSHIT. YOU SEEK TO INVOKE MY COUNTRY'S HISTORY, BUT YOU DO NOT EVEN KNOW YOUR OWN.
YOU ARE A DISGRACE TO THE UNITED STATES. FUCK YOU.
EAU
I'LL KICK YOUR FUCKIN' AAAAAAAAAAHH!
HMMM.
WHAT I NEED NOW...
LEGION ETRANGERE
PREMIER SECRET

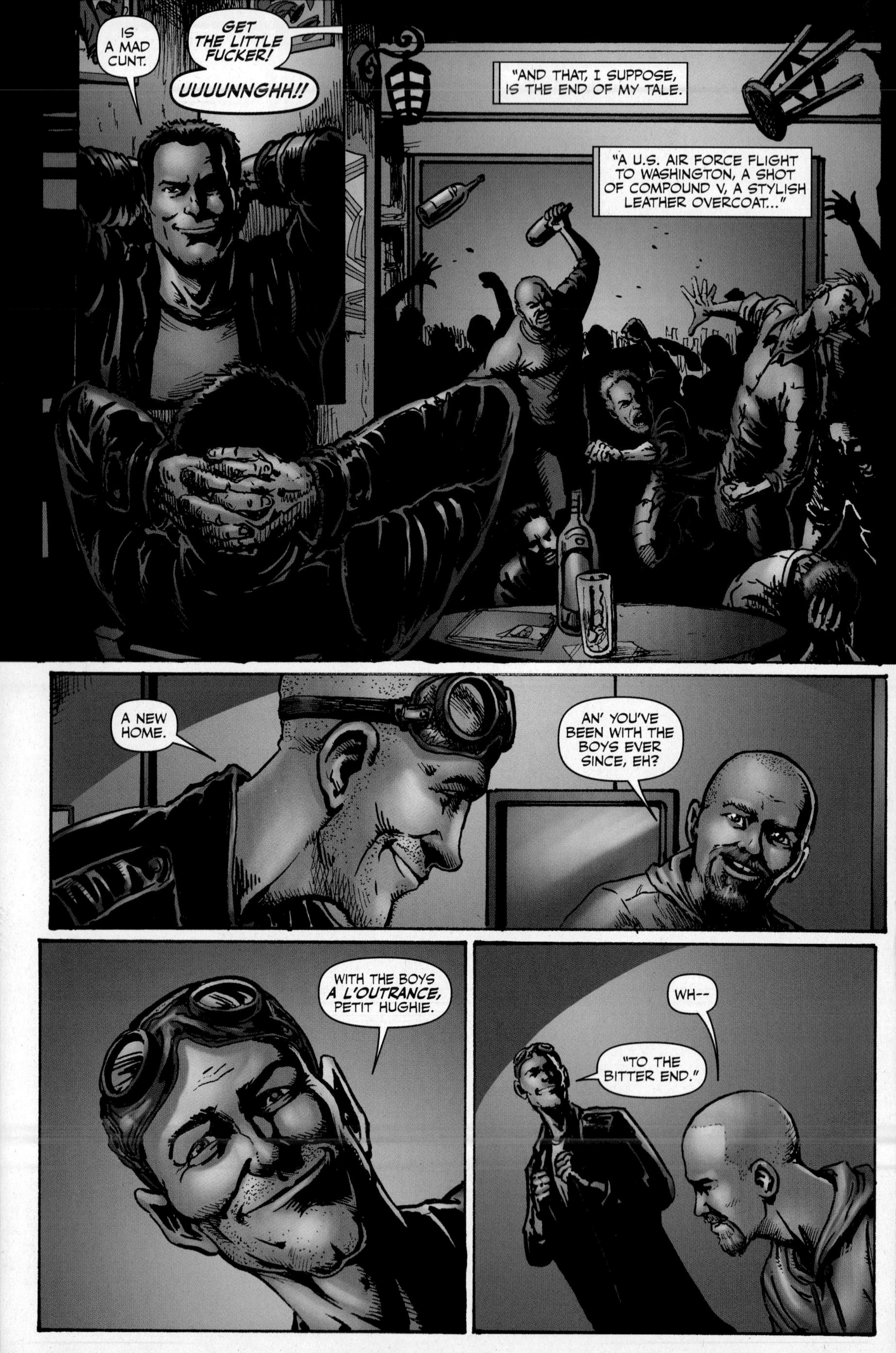
IS A MAD CUNT.
GET THE LITTLE FUCKER!
UUUUNNGHH!!
"AND THAT, I SUPPOSE, IS THE END OF MY TALE.
"A U.S. AIR FORCE FLIGHT TO WASHINGTON, A SHOT OF COMPOUND V, A STYLISH LEATHER OVERCOAT..."
A NEW HOME.
AN' YOU'VE BEEN WITH THE BOYS EVER SINCE, EH?
WITH THE BOYS *A L'OUTRANCE,* PETIT HUGHIE.
WH--
"TO THE BITTER END."

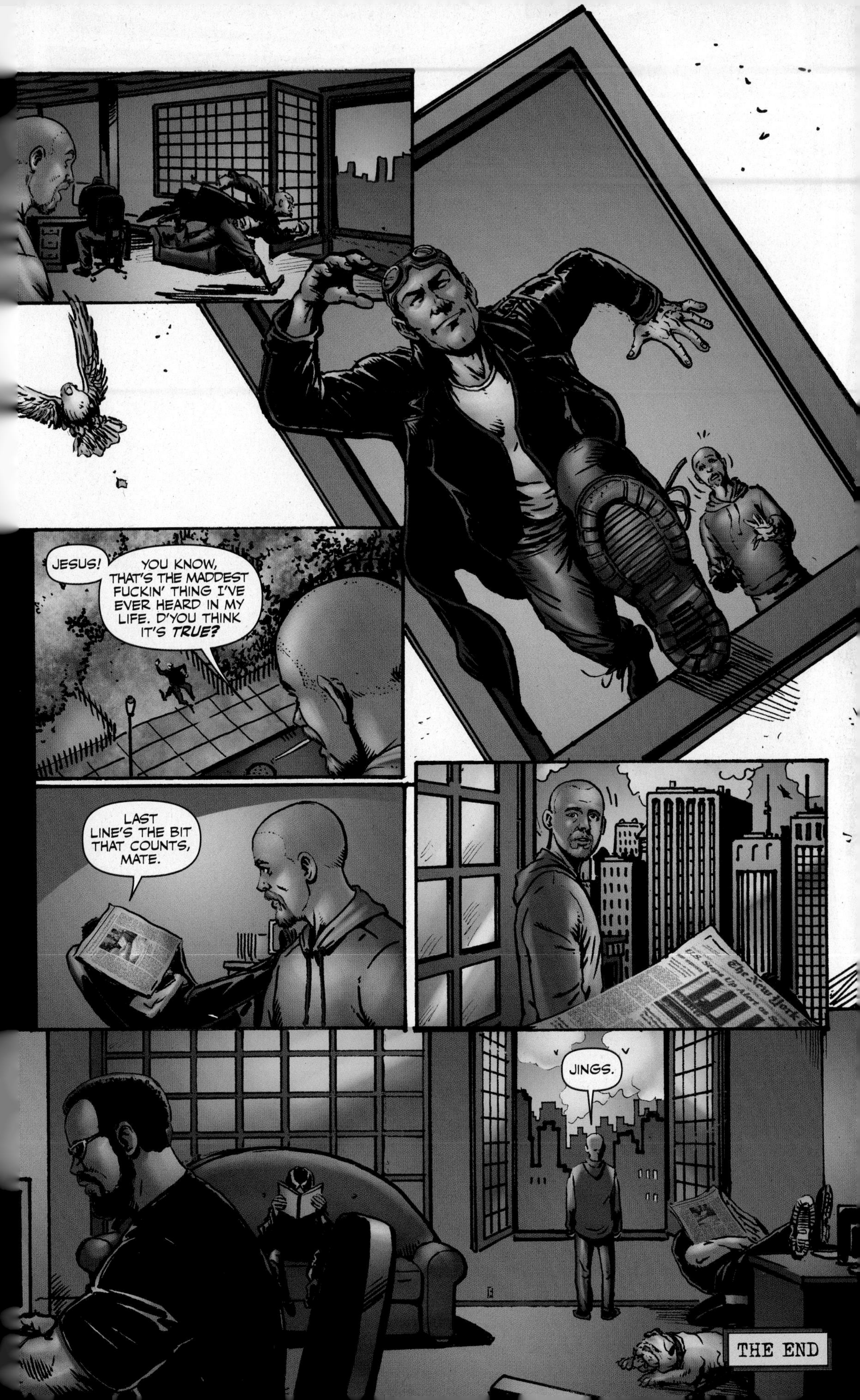
JESUS!
YOU KNOW, THAT'S THE MADDEST FUCKIN' THING I'VE EVER HEARD IN MY LIFE. D'YOU THINK IT'S TRUE?
LAST LINE'S THE BIT THAT COUNTS, MATE.
JINGS.
THE END

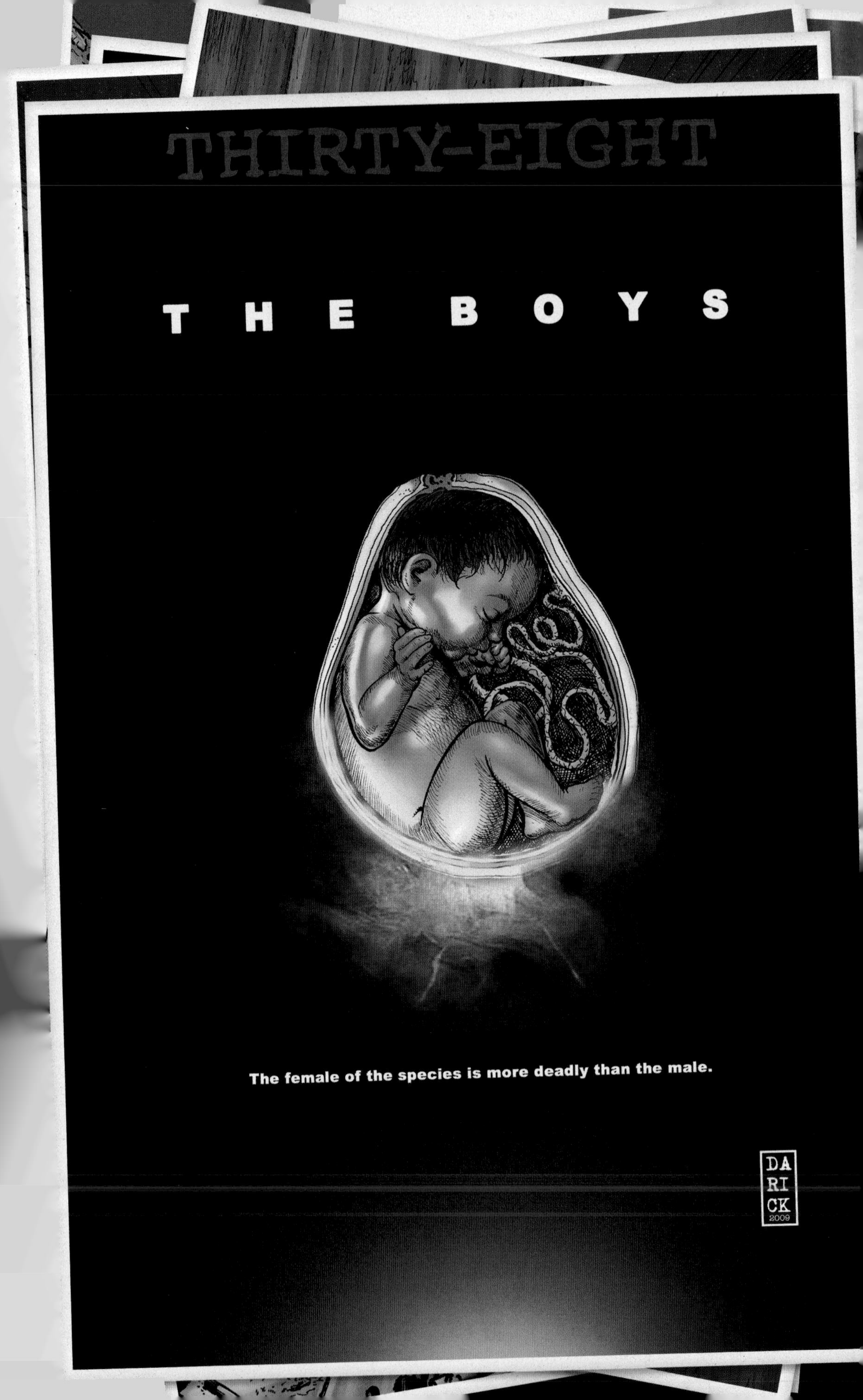
THIRTY-EIGHT
THE BOYS
The female of the species is more deadly than the male.
DA
RI
CK
2009

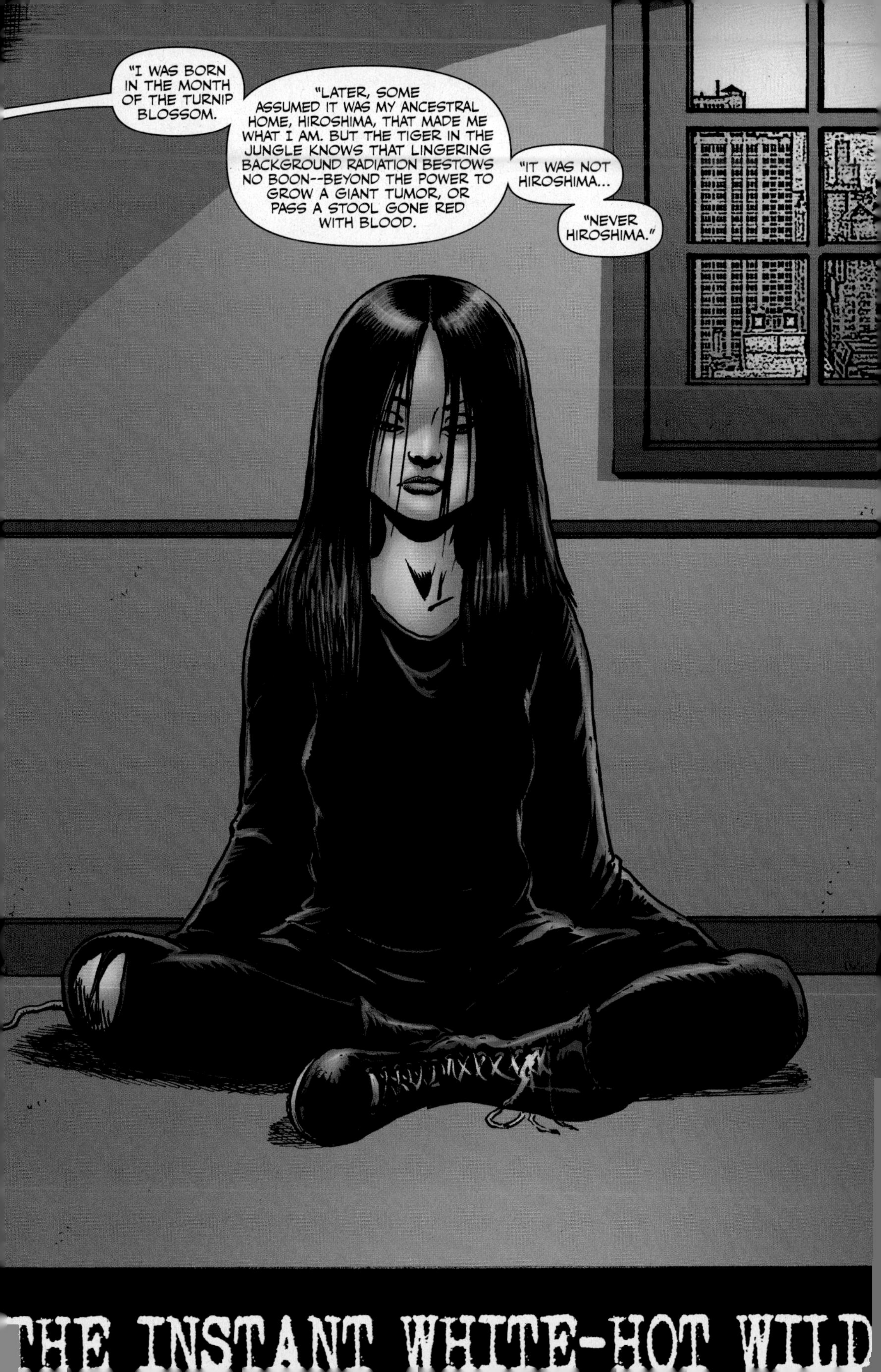
"I WAS BORN IN THE MONTH OF THE TURNIP BLOSSOM.
"LATER, SOME ASSUMED IT WAS MY ANCESTRAL HOME, HIROSHIMA, THAT MADE ME WHAT I AM. BUT THE TIGER IN THE JUNGLE KNOWS THAT LINGERING BACKGROUND RADIATION BESTOWS NO BOON--BEYOND THE POWER TO GROW A GIANT TUMOR, OR PASS A STOOL GONE RED WITH BLOOD.
"IT WAS NOT HIROSHIMA...
"NEVER HIROSHIMA."
THE INSTANT WHITE-HOT WILD

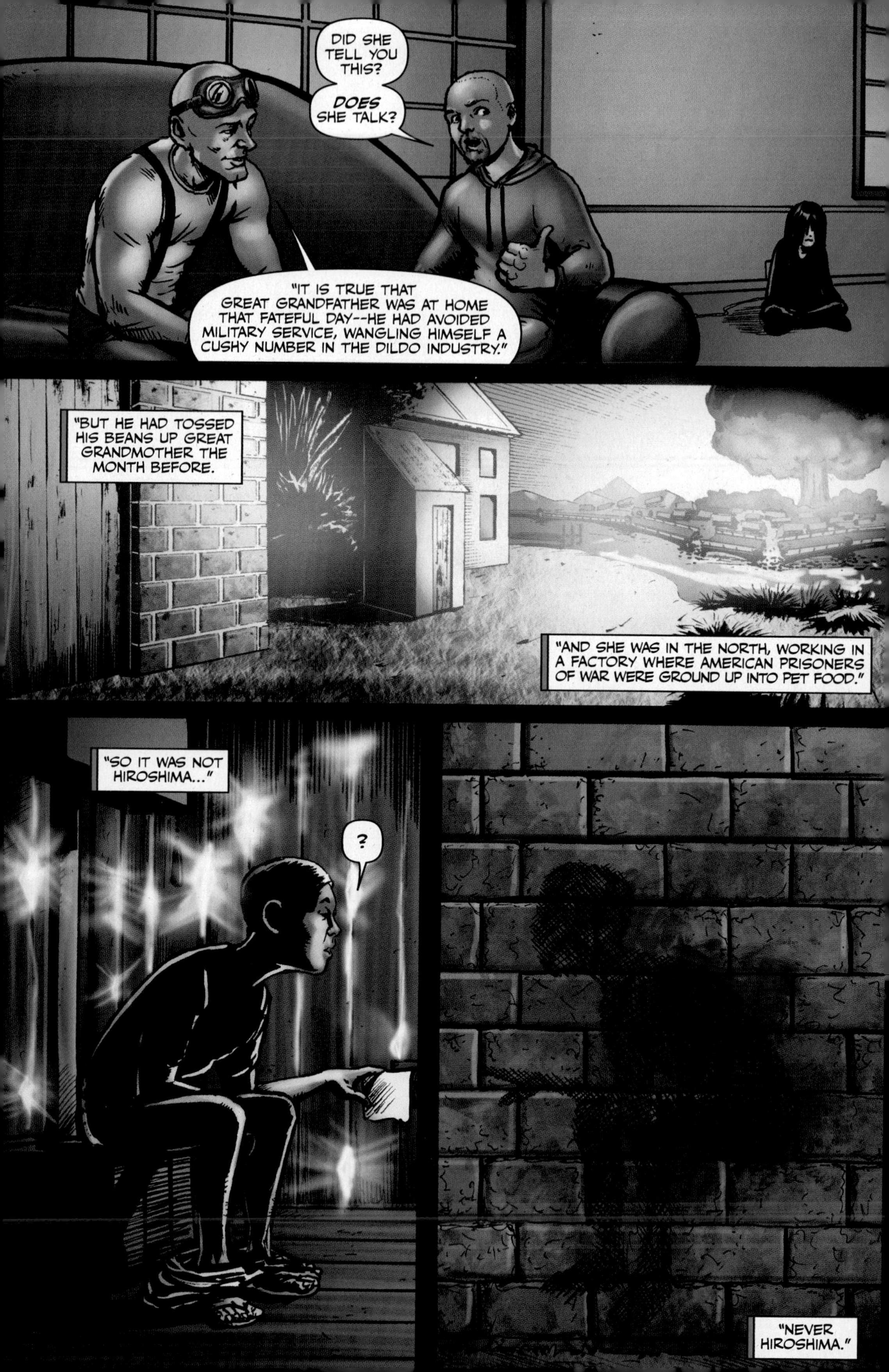
DID SHE TELL YOU THIS?
DOES SHE TALK?
"IT IS TRUE THAT GREAT GRANDFATHER WAS AT HOME THAT FATEFUL DAY--HE HAD AVOIDED MILITARY SERVICE, WANGLING HIMSELF A CUSHY NUMBER IN THE DILDO INDUSTRY."
"BUT HE HAD TOSSED HIS BEANS UP GREAT GRANDMOTHER THE MONTH BEFORE.
"AND SHE WAS IN THE NORTH, WORKING IN A FACTORY WHERE AMERICAN PRISONERS OF WAR WERE GROUND UP INTO PET FOOD."
"SO IT WAS NOT HIROSHIMA..."
?
"NEVER HIROSHIMA."

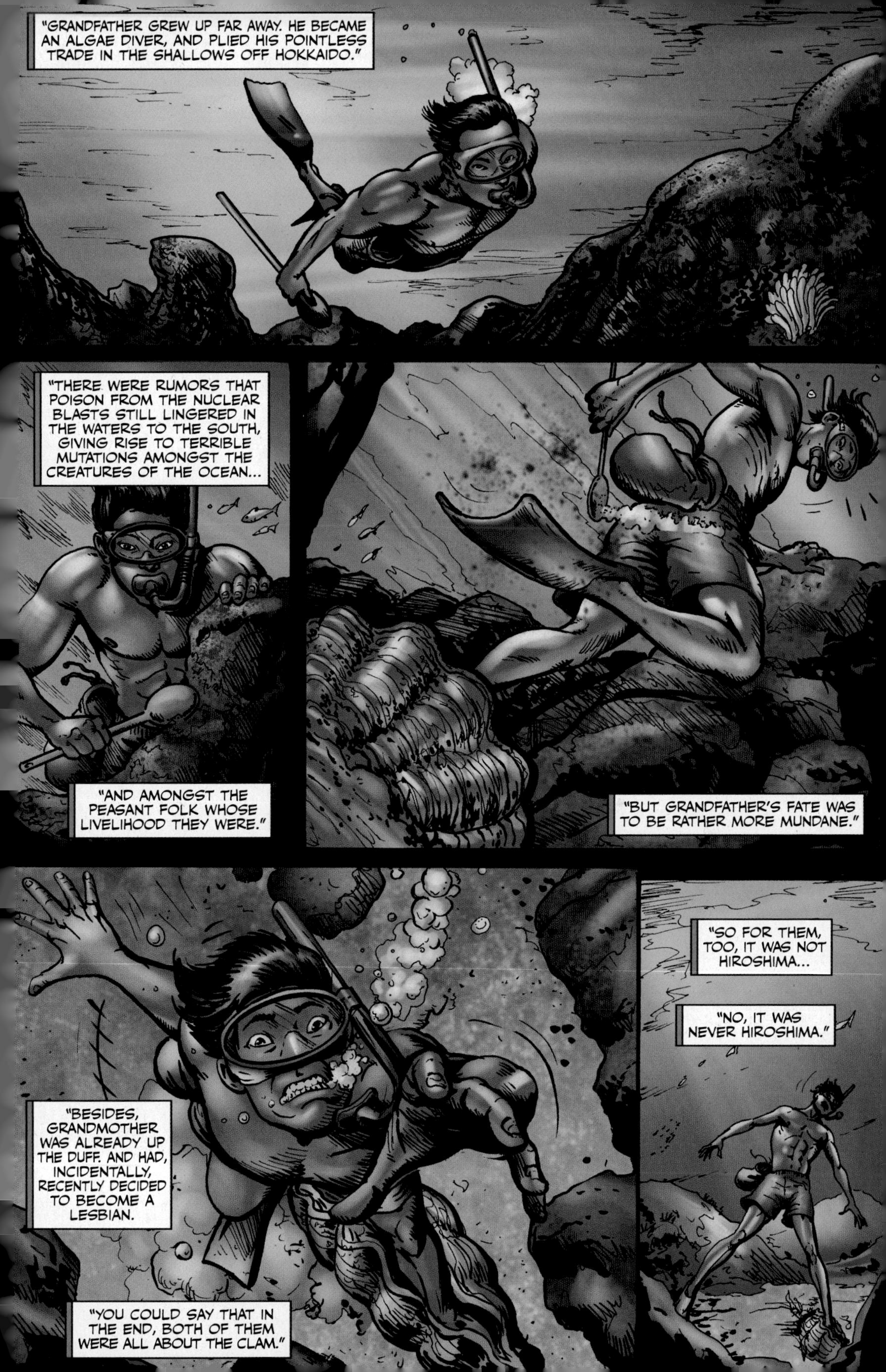
"GRANDFATHER GREW UP FAR AWAY. HE BECAME AN ALGAE DIVER, AND PLIED HIS POINTLESS TRADE IN THE SHALLOWS OFF HOKKAIDO."
"THERE WERE RUMORS THAT POISON FROM THE NUCLEAR BLASTS STILL LINGERED IN THE WATERS TO THE SOUTH, GIVING RISE TO TERRIBLE MUTATIONS AMONGST THE CREATURES OF THE OCEAN...
"AND AMONGST THE PEASANT FOLK WHOSE LIVELIHOOD THEY WERE."
"BUT GRANDFATHER'S FATE WAS TO BE RATHER MORE MUNDANE."
"BESIDES, GRANDMOTHER WAS ALREADY UP THE DUFF. AND HAD, INCIDENTALLY, RECENTLY DECIDED TO BECOME A LESBIAN.
"YOU COULD SAY THAT IN THE END, BOTH OF THEM WERE ALL ABOUT THE CLAM."
"SO FOR THEM, TOO, IT WAS NOT HIROSHIMA...
"NO, IT WAS NEVER HIROSHIMA."

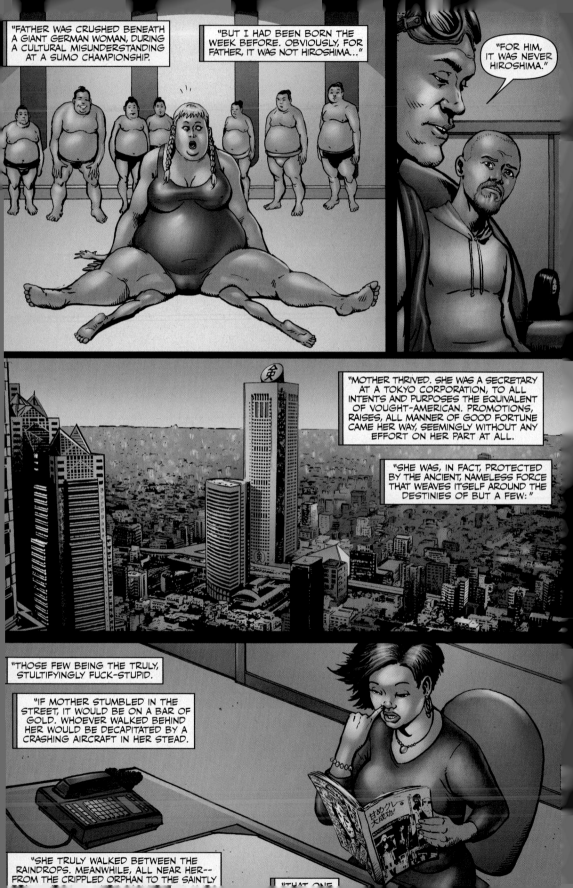

"FATHER WAS CRUSHED BENEATH A GIANT GERMAN WOMAN, DURING A CULTURAL MISUNDERSTANDING AT A SUMO CHAMPIONSHIP.

"BUT I HAD BEEN BORN THE WEEK BEFORE. OBVIOUSLY, FOR FATHER, IT WAS NOT HIROSHIMA..."

"FOR HIM, IT WAS NEVER HIROSHIMA."

"MOTHER THRIVED. SHE WAS A SECRETARY AT A TOKYO CORPORATION, TO ALL INTENTS AND PURPOSES THE EQUIVALENT OF VOUGHT-AMERICAN. PROMOTIONS, RAISES, ALL MANNER OF GOOD FORTUNE CAME HER WAY, SEEMINGLY WITHOUT ANY EFFORT ON HER PART AT ALL.

"SHE WAS, IN FACT, PROTECTED BY THE ANCIENT, NAMELESS FORCE THAT WEAVES ITSELF AROUND THE DESTINIES OF BUT A FEW:"

"THOSE FEW BEING THE TRULY, STULTIFYINGLY FUCK-STUPID.

"IF MOTHER STUMBLED IN THE STREET, IT WOULD BE ON A BAR OF GOLD. WHOEVER WALKED BEHIND HER WOULD BE DECAPITATED BY A CRASHING AIRCRAFT IN HER STEAD.

"SHE TRULY WALKED BETWEEN THE RAINDROPS. MEANWHILE, ALL NEAR HER-- FROM THE CRIPPLED ORPHAN TO THE SAINTLY

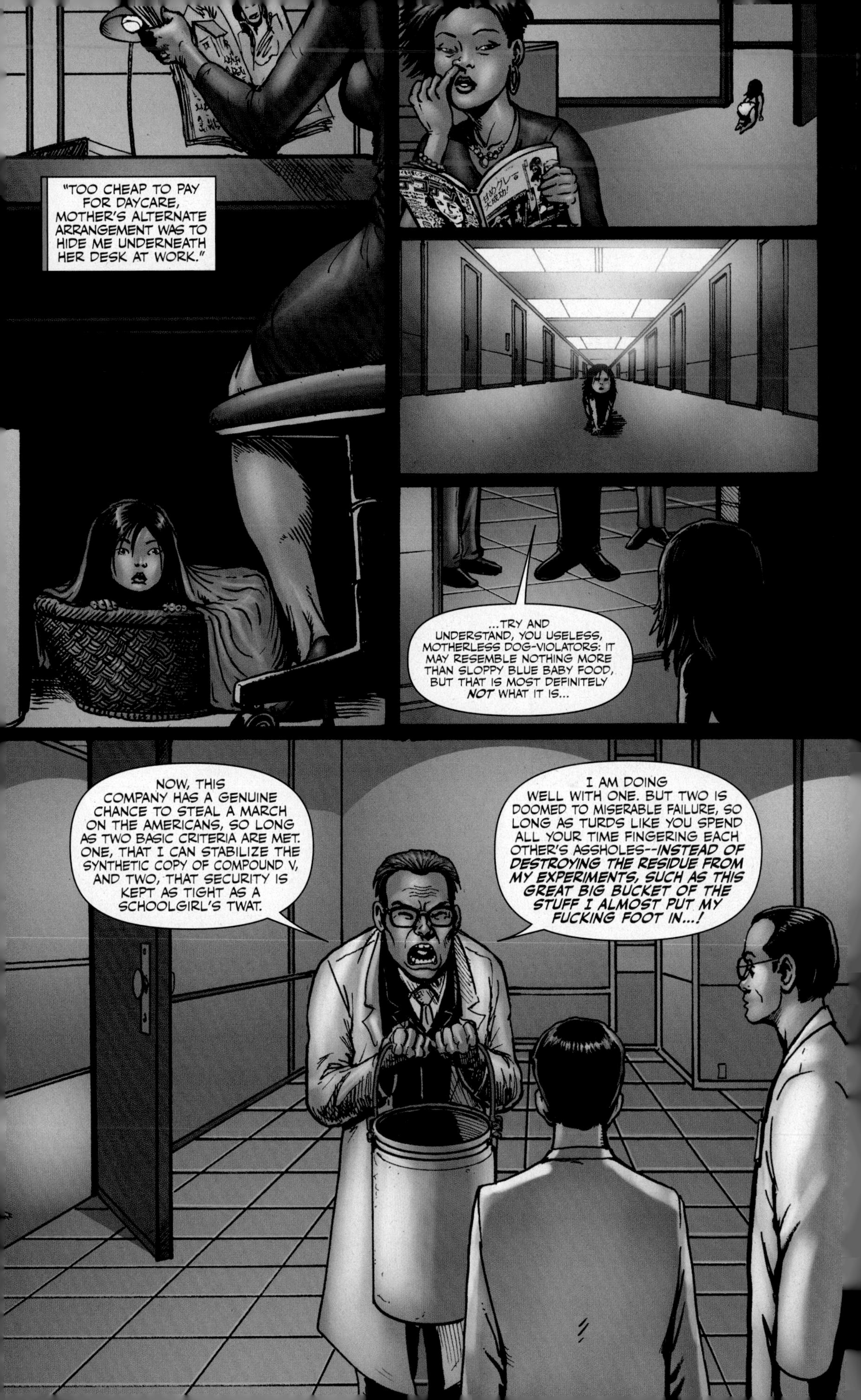
"TOO CHEAP TO PAY FOR DAYCARE, MOTHER'S ALTERNATE ARRANGEMENT WAS TO HIDE ME UNDERNEATH HER DESK AT WORK."
...TRY AND UNDERSTAND, YOU USELESS, MOTHERLESS DOG-VIOLATORS: IT MAY RESEMBLE NOTHING MORE THAN SLOPPY BLUE BABY FOOD, BUT THAT IS MOST DEFINITELY *NOT* WHAT IT IS...
NOW, THIS COMPANY HAS A GENUINE CHANCE TO STEAL A MARCH ON THE AMERICANS, SO LONG AS TWO BASIC CRITERIA ARE MET. ONE, THAT I CAN STABILIZE THE SYNTHETIC COPY OF COMPOUND V, AND TWO, THAT SECURITY IS KEPT AS TIGHT AS A SCHOOLGIRL'S TWAT.
I AM DOING WELL WITH ONE. BUT TWO IS DOOMED TO MISERABLE FAILURE, SO LONG AS TURDS LIKE YOU SPEND ALL YOUR TIME FINGERING EACH OTHER'S ASSHOLES--*INSTEAD OF DESTROYING THE RESIDUE FROM MY EXPERIMENTS, SUCH AS THIS GREAT BIG BUCKET OF THE STUFF I ALMOST PUT MY FUCKING FOOT IN...!*

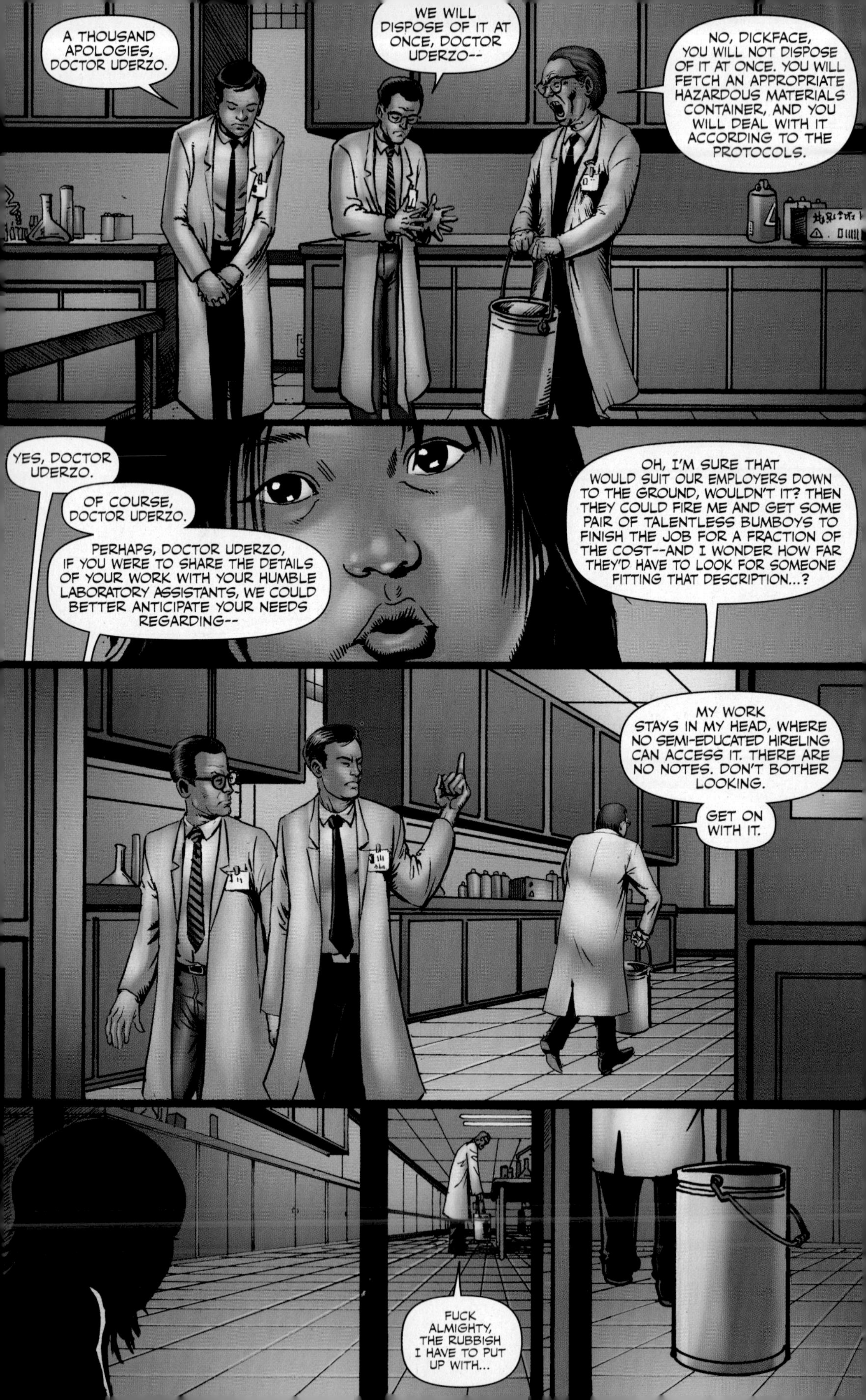
A THOUSAND APOLOGIES, DOCTOR UDERZO.
WE WILL DISPOSE OF IT AT ONCE, DOCTOR UDERZO--
NO, DICKFACE, YOU WILL NOT DISPOSE OF IT AT ONCE. YOU WILL FETCH AN APPROPRIATE HAZARDOUS MATERIALS CONTAINER, AND YOU WILL DEAL WITH IT ACCORDING TO THE PROTOCOLS.
YES, DOCTOR UDERZO.
OF COURSE, DOCTOR UDERZO.
PERHAPS, DOCTOR UDERZO, IF YOU WERE TO SHARE THE DETAILS OF YOUR WORK WITH YOUR HUMBLE LABORATORY ASSISTANTS, WE COULD BETTER ANTICIPATE YOUR NEEDS REGARDING--
OH, I'M SURE THAT WOULD SUIT OUR EMPLOYERS DOWN TO THE GROUND, WOULDN'T IT? THEN THEY COULD FIRE ME AND GET SOME PAIR OF TALENTLESS BUMBOYS TO FINISH THE JOB FOR A FRACTION OF THE COST--AND I WONDER HOW FAR THEY'D HAVE TO LOOK FOR SOMEONE FITTING THAT DESCRIPTION...?
MY WORK STAYS IN MY HEAD, WHERE NO SEMI-EDUCATED HIRELING CAN ACCESS IT. THERE ARE NO NOTES. DON'T BOTHER LOOKING.
GET ON WITH IT.
FUCK ALMIGHTY, THE RUBBISH I HAVE TO PUT UP WITH...

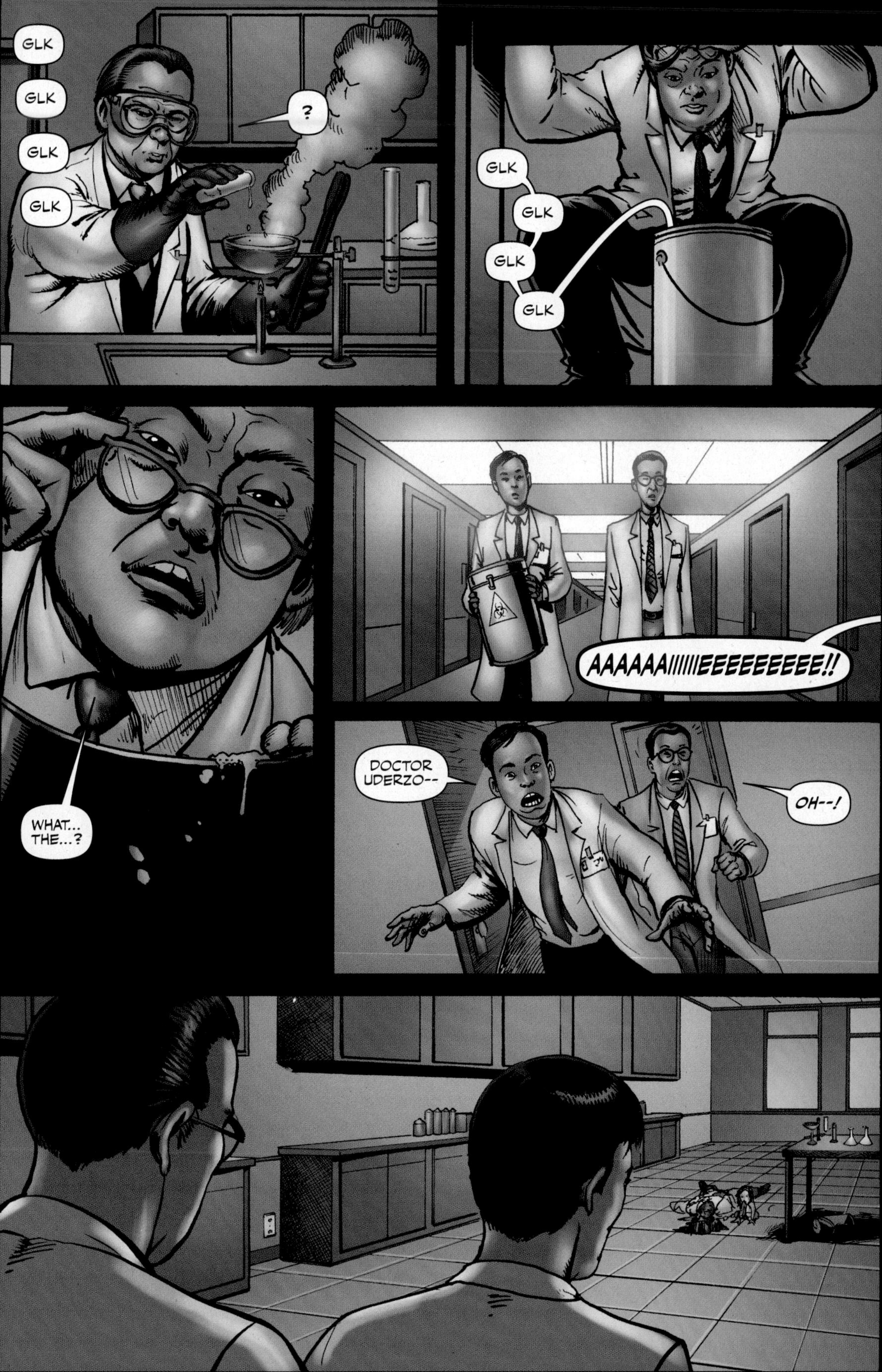
GLK
GLK
GLK
GLK
?
GLK
GLK
GLK
GLK
WHAT... THE...?
AAAAAAIIIIIIIEEEEEEEEEE!!
DOCTOR UDERZO--
OH--!

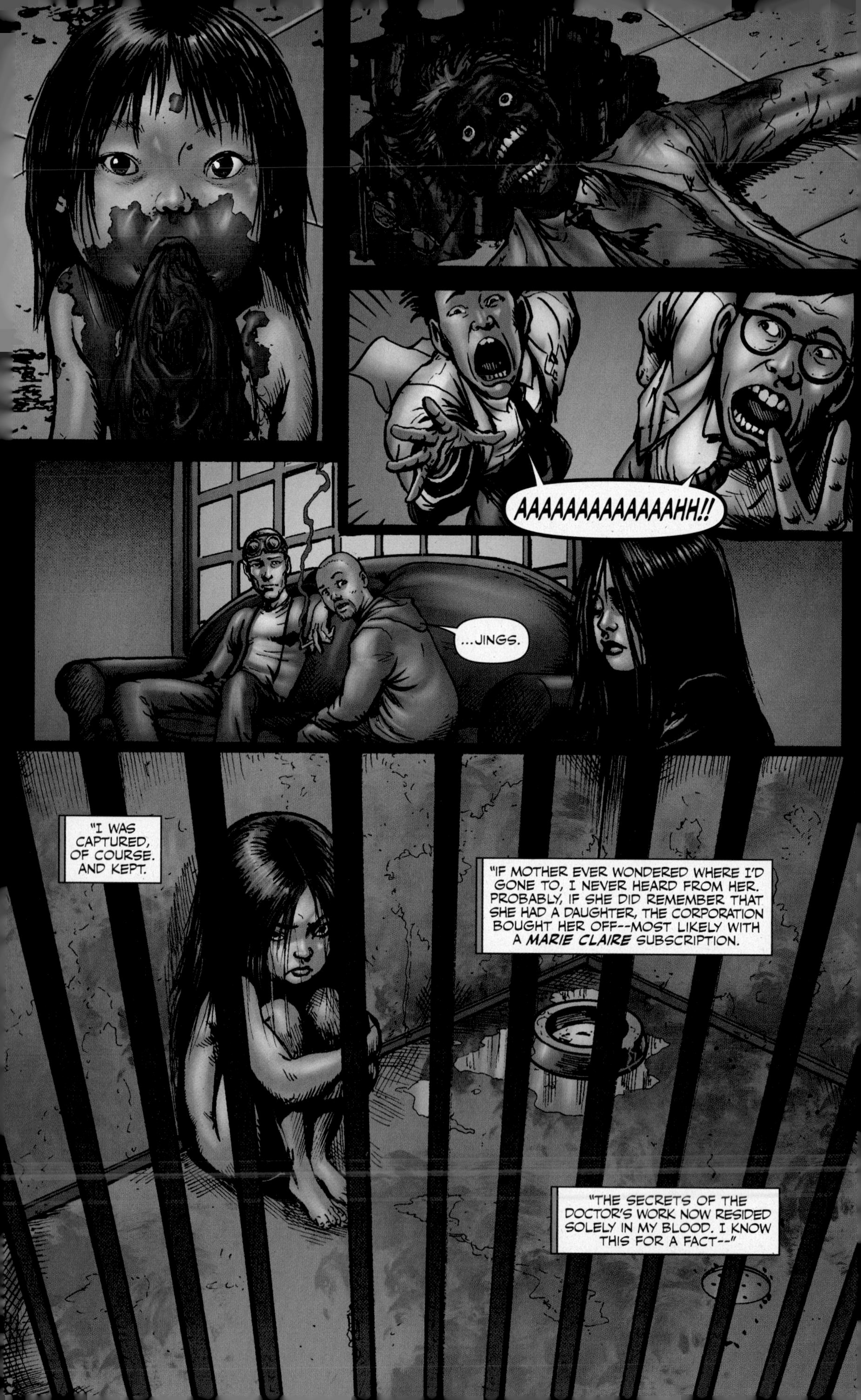
AAAAAAAAAAAAAAHH!!
...JINGS.
"I WAS CAPTURED, OF COURSE. AND KEPT.
"IF MOTHER EVER WONDERED WHERE I'D GONE TO, I NEVER HEARD FROM HER. PROBABLY, IF SHE DID REMEMBER THAT SHE HAD A DAUGHTER, THE CORPORATION BOUGHT HER OFF--MOST LIKELY WITH A MARIE CLAIRE SUBSCRIPTION.
"THE SECRETS OF THE DOCTOR'S WORK NOW RESIDED SOLELY IN MY BLOOD. I KNOW THIS FOR A FACT--"

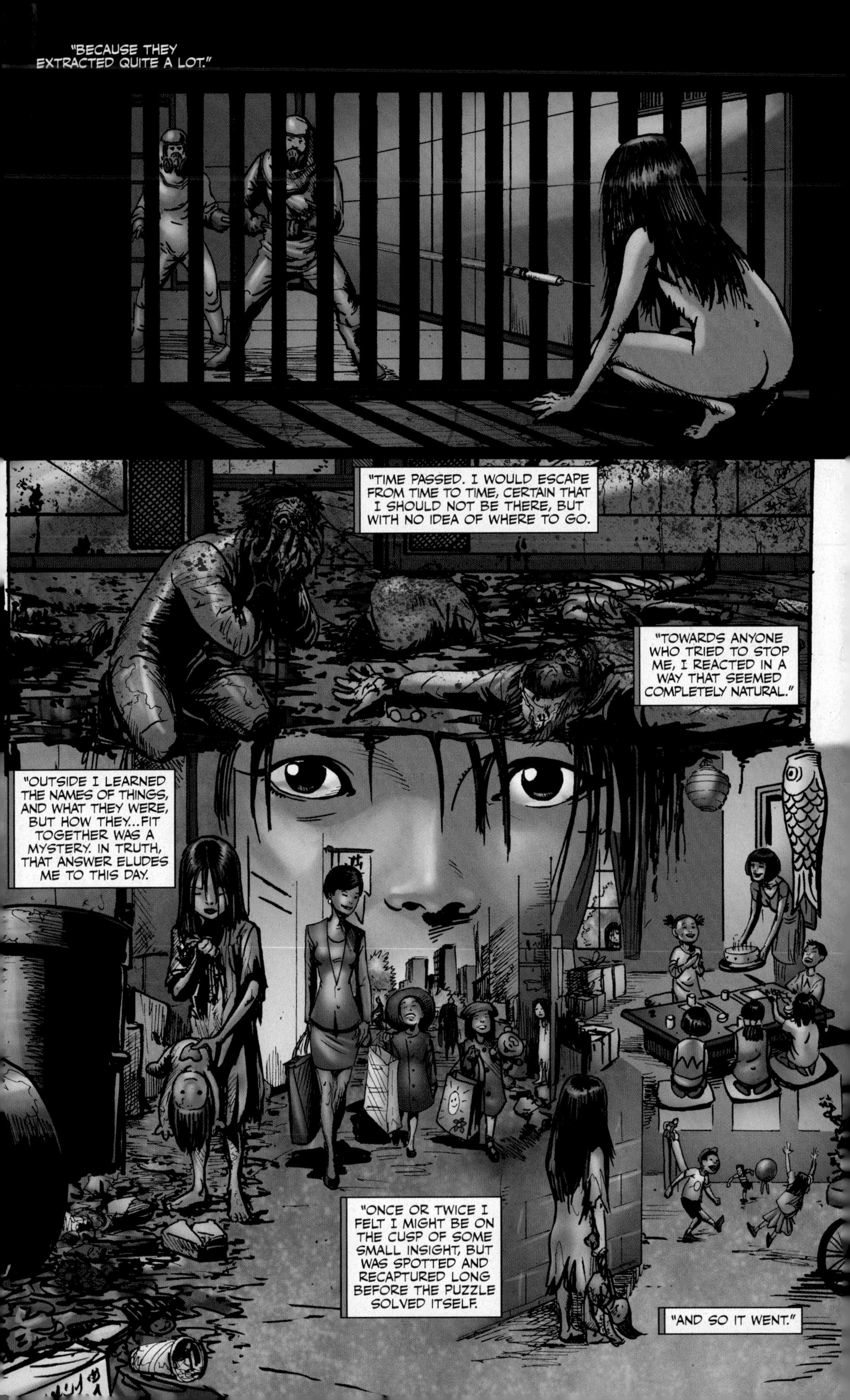
"BECAUSE THEY EXTRACTED QUITE A LOT."
"TIME PASSED. I WOULD ESCAPE FROM TIME TO TIME, CERTAIN THAT I SHOULD NOT BE THERE, BUT WITH NO IDEA OF WHERE TO GO.
"TOWARDS ANYONE WHO TRIED TO STOP ME, I REACTED IN A WAY THAT SEEMED COMPLETELY NATURAL."
"OUTSIDE I LEARNED THE NAMES OF THINGS, AND WHAT THEY WERE, BUT HOW THEY...FIT TOGETHER WAS A MYSTERY. IN TRUTH, THAT ANSWER ELUDES ME TO THIS DAY.
"ONCE OR TWICE I FELT I MIGHT BE ON THE CUSP OF SOME SMALL INSIGHT, BUT WAS SPOTTED AND RECAPTURED LONG BEFORE THE PUZZLE SOLVED ITSELF.
"AND SO IT WENT."

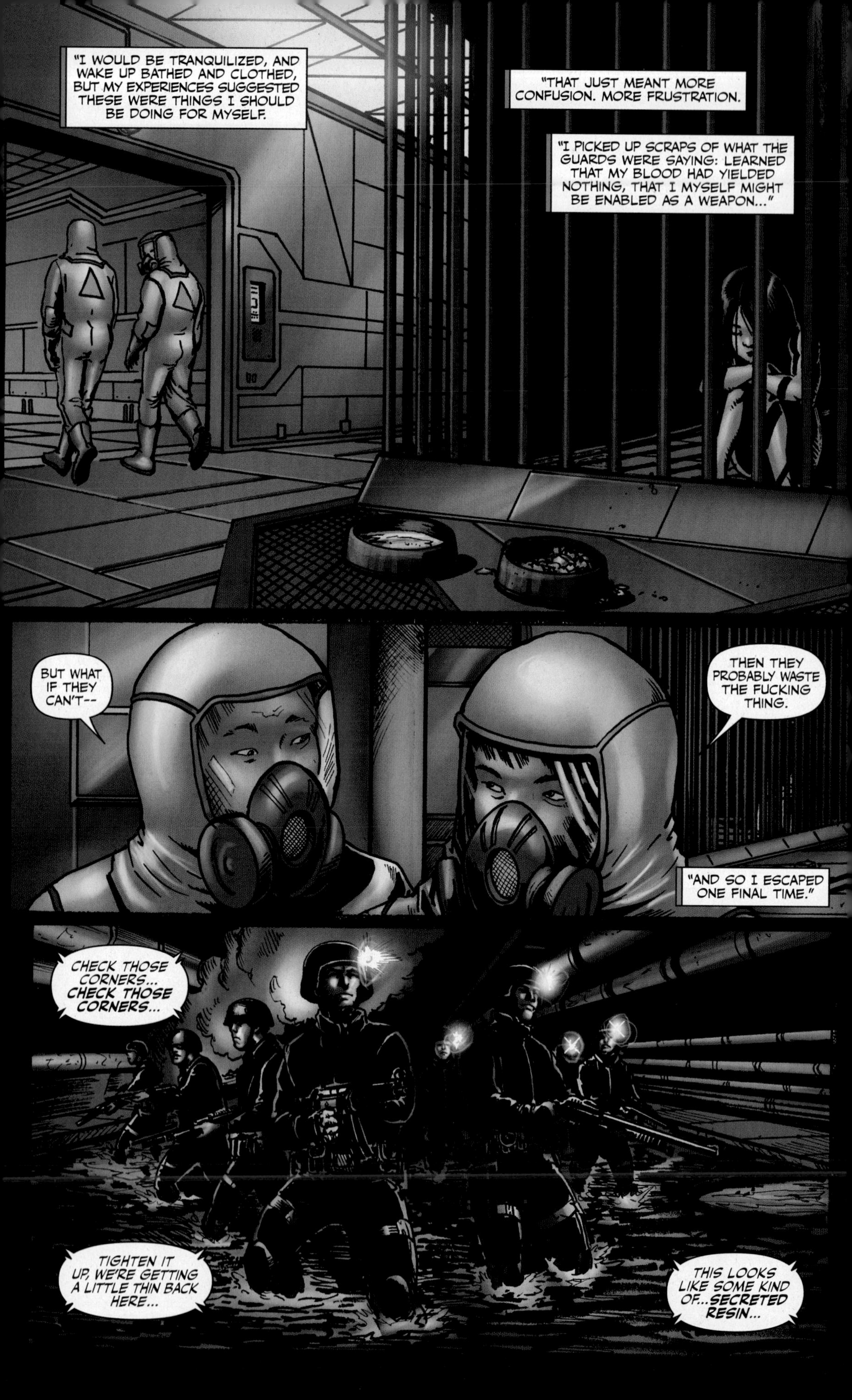
"I WOULD BE TRANQUILIZED, AND WAKE UP BATHED AND CLOTHED, BUT MY EXPERIENCES SUGGESTED THESE WERE THINGS I SHOULD BE DOING FOR MYSELF.
"THAT JUST MEANT MORE CONFUSION. MORE FRUSTRATION.
"I PICKED UP SCRAPS OF WHAT THE GUARDS WERE SAYING: LEARNED THAT MY BLOOD HAD YIELDED NOTHING, THAT I MYSELF MIGHT BE ENABLED AS A WEAPON..."
BUT WHAT IF THEY CAN'T--
THEN THEY PROBABLY WASTE THE FUCKING THING.
"AND SO I ESCAPED ONE FINAL TIME."
CHECK THOSE CORNERS... CHECK THOSE CORNERS...
TIGHTEN IT UP, WE'RE GETTING A LITTLE THIN BACK HERE...
THIS LOOKS LIKE SOME KIND OF...SECRETED RESIN...

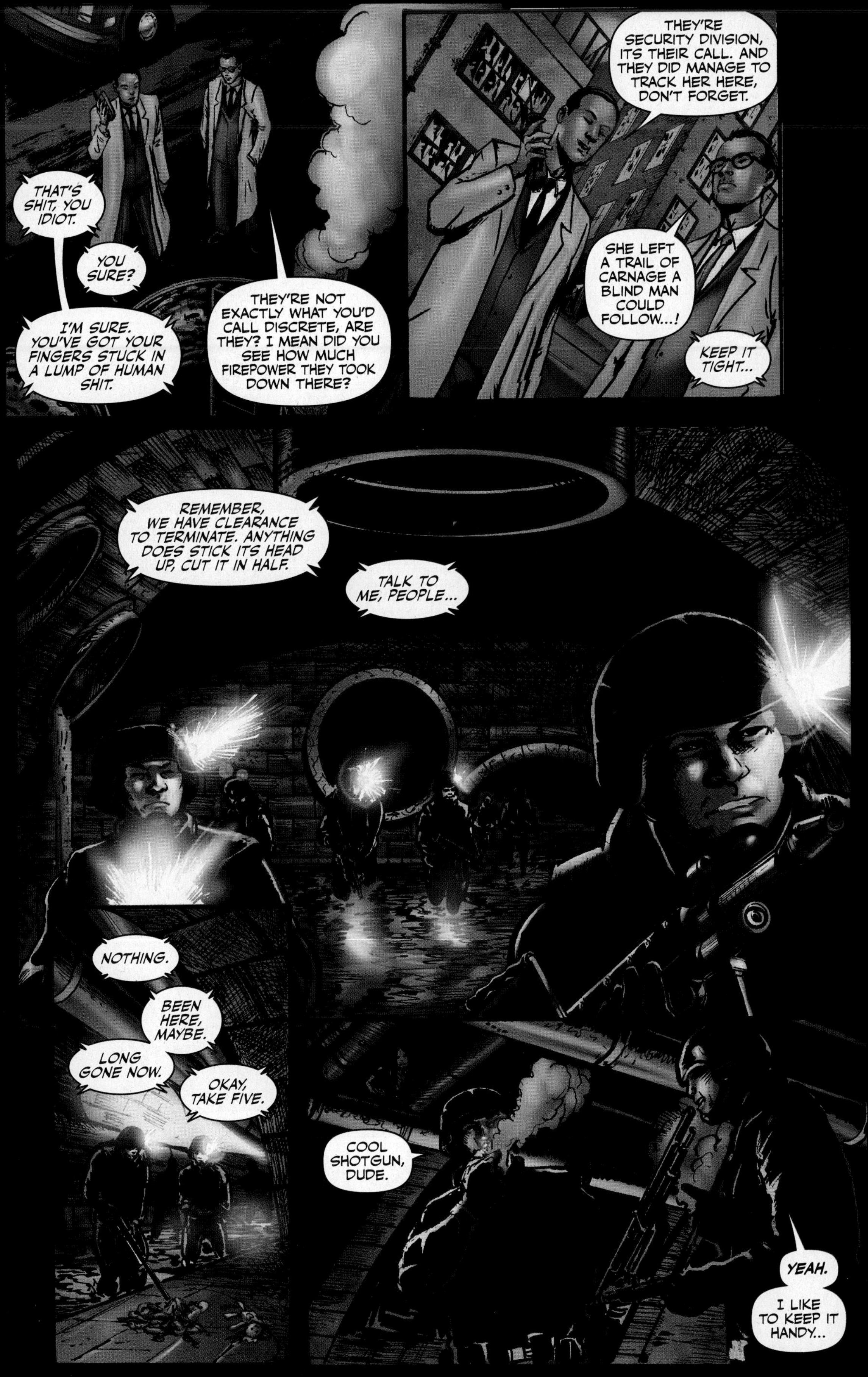
THAT'S SHIT, YOU IDIOT.
YOU SURE?
I'M SURE. YOU'VE GOT YOUR FINGERS STUCK IN A LUMP OF HUMAN SHIT.
THEY'RE NOT EXACTLY WHAT YOU'D CALL DISCRETE, ARE THEY? I MEAN DID YOU SEE HOW MUCH FIREPOWER THEY TOOK DOWN THERE?
THEY'RE SECURITY DIVISION, ITS THEIR CALL. AND THEY DID MANAGE TO TRACK HER HERE, DON'T FORGET.
SHE LEFT A TRAIL OF CARNAGE A BLIND MAN COULD FOLLOW...!
KEEP IT TIGHT...
REMEMBER, WE HAVE CLEARANCE TO TERMINATE. ANYTHING DOES STICK ITS HEAD UP, CUT IT IN HALF.
TALK TO ME, PEOPLE...
NOTHING.
BEEN HERE, MAYBE.
LONG GONE NOW.
OKAY, TAKE FIVE.
COOL SHOTGUN, DUDE.
YEAH.
I LIKE TO KEEP IT HANDY...

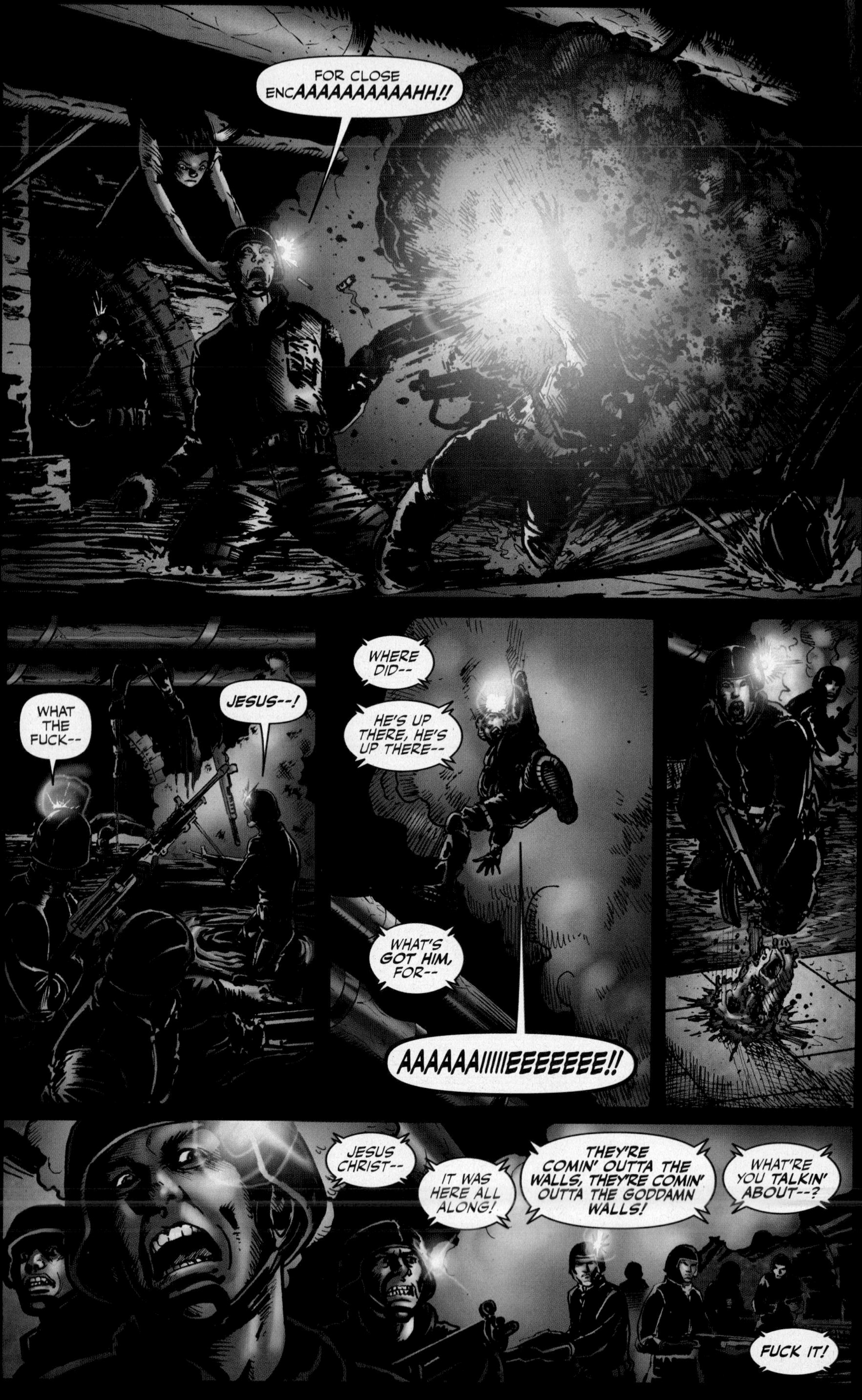
FOR CLOSE ENCAAAAAAAAAAAHH!!
WHAT THE FUCK--
JESUS--!
WHERE DID--
HE'S UP THERE, HE'S UP THERE--
WHAT'S GOT HIM, FOR--
AAAAAAIIIIIIEEEEEEE!!
JESUS CHRIST--
IT WAS HERE ALL ALONG!
THEY'RE COMIN' OUTTA THE WALLS, THEY'RE COMIN' OUTTA THE GODDAMN WALLS!
WHAT'RE YOU TALKIN' ABOUT--?
FUCK IT!

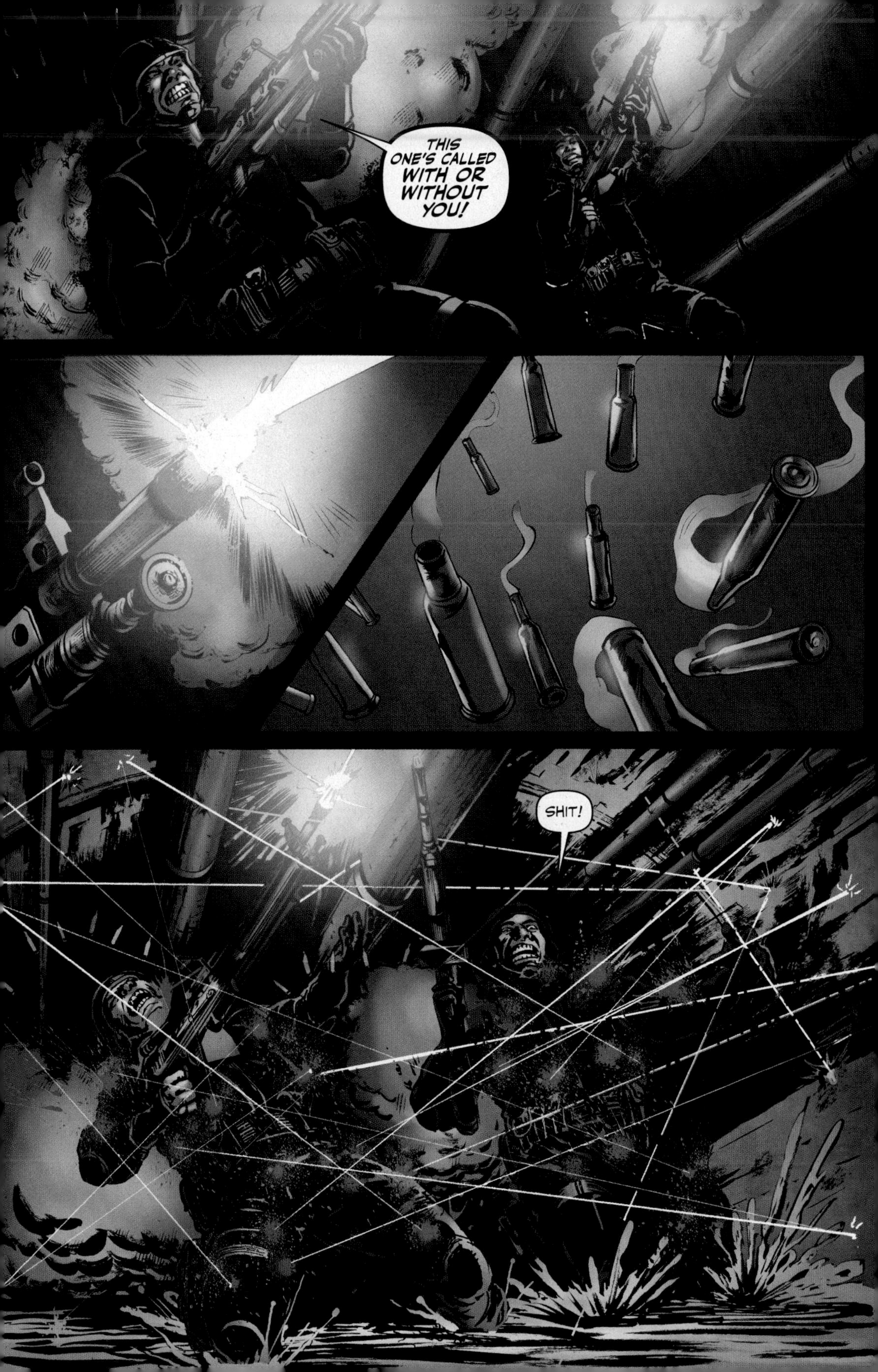
THIS ONE'S CALLED WITH OR WITHOUT YOU!
SHIT!

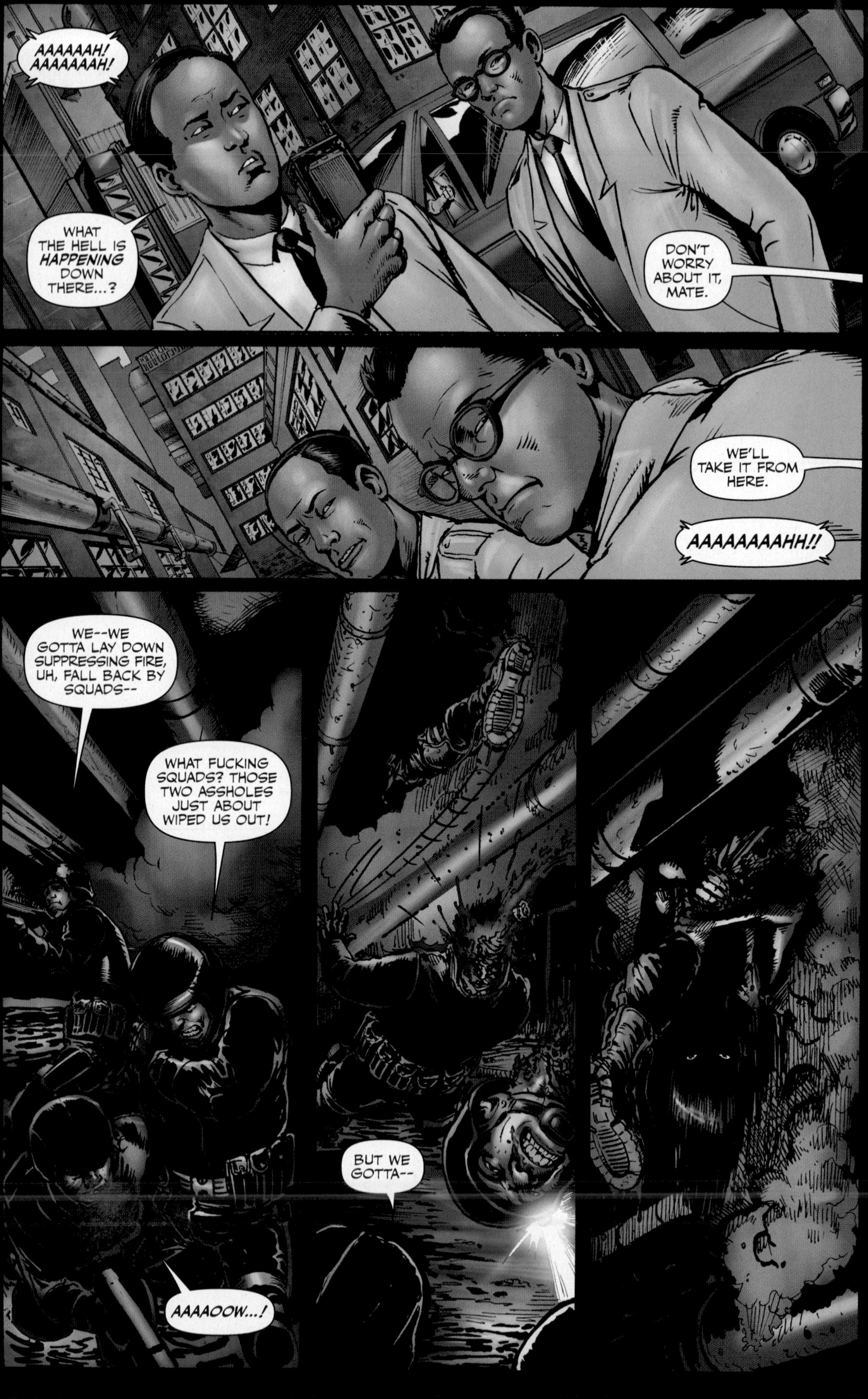
AAAAAAH! AAAAAAAH!
WHAT THE HELL IS *HAPPENING* DOWN THERE...?
DON'T WORRY ABOUT IT, MATE.
WE'LL TAKE IT FROM HERE.
AAAAAAAAHH!!
WE--WE GOTTA LAY DOWN SUPPRESSING FIRE, UH, FALL BACK BY SQUADS--
WHAT FUCKING SQUADS? THOSE TWO ASSHOLES JUST ABOUT WIPED US OUT!
AAAAOOW...!
BUT WE GOTTA--

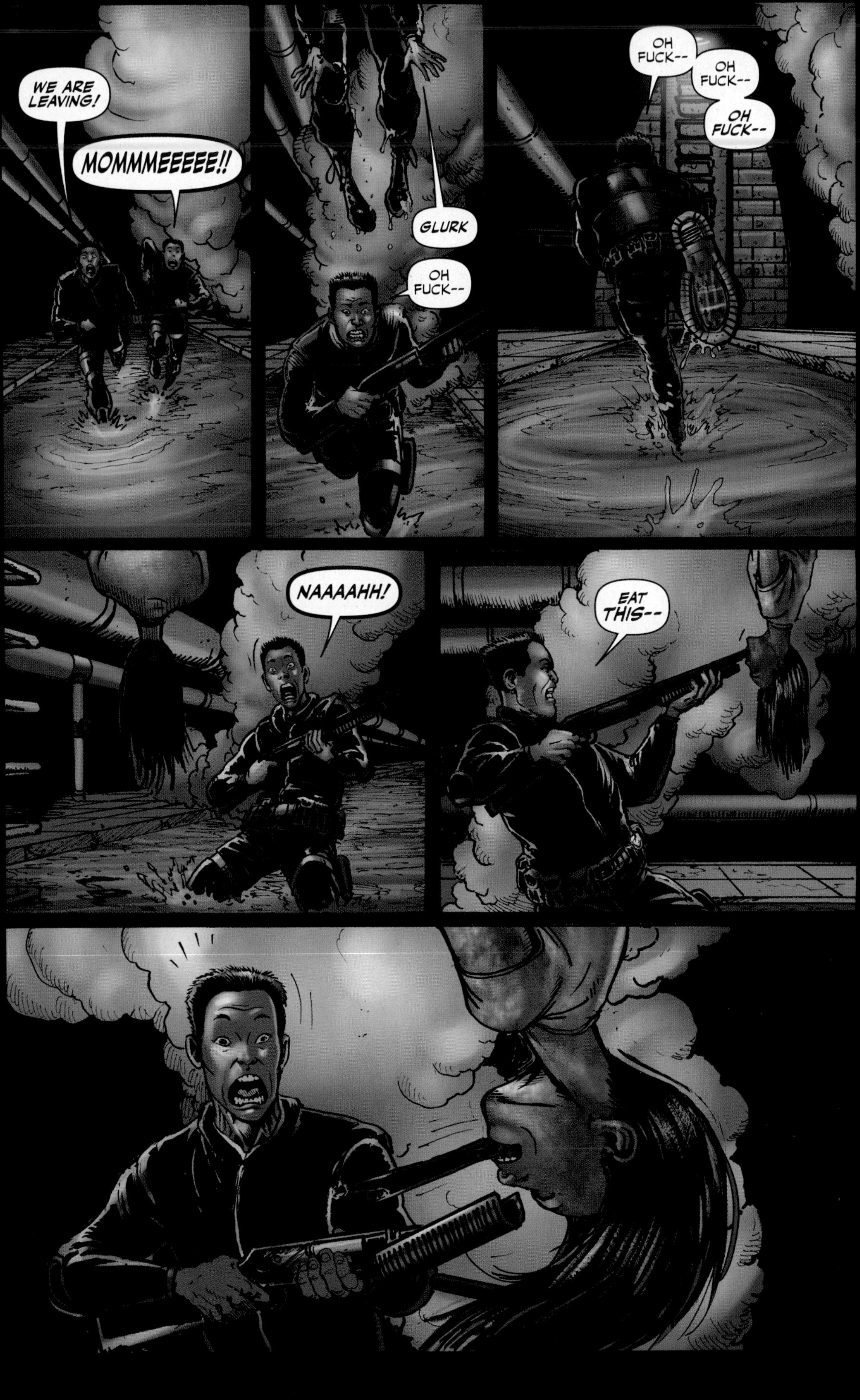
WE ARE LEAVING!
MOMMMEEEEE!!
GLURK
OH FUCK--
OH FUCK--
OH FUCK--
OH FUCK--
NAAAAHH!
EAT THIS--

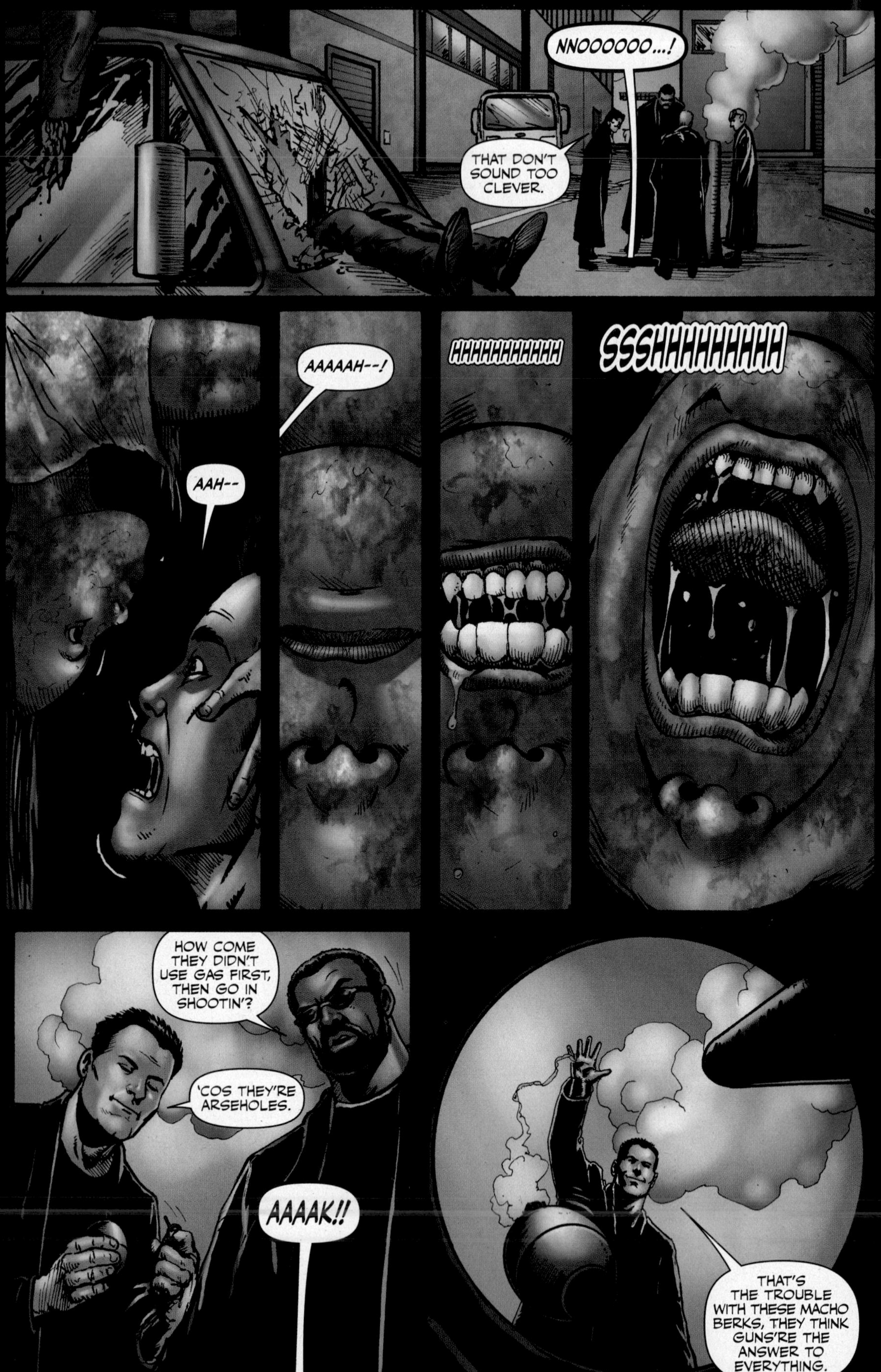
NNOOOOOO...!
THAT DON'T SOUND TOO CLEVER.
AAH--
AAAAAH--!
HHHHHHHHHHH
SSSHHHHHHHHH
HOW COME THEY DIDN'T USE GAS FIRST, THEN GO IN SHOOTIN'?
'COS THEY'RE ARSEHOLES.
AAAAK!!
THAT'S THE TROUBLE WITH THESE MACHO BERKS, THEY THINK GUNS'RE THE ANSWER TO EVERYTHING.

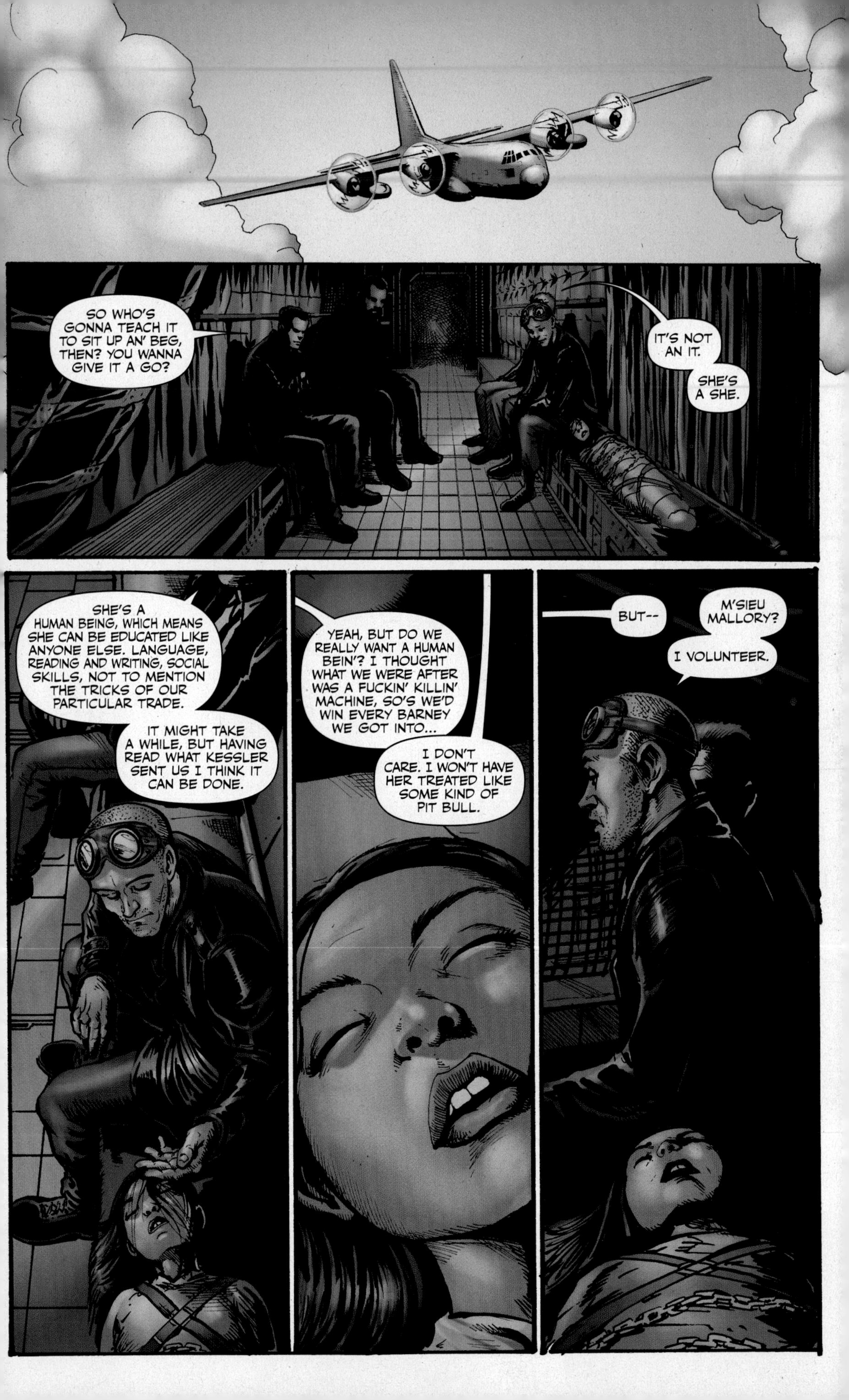
SO WHO'S GONNA TEACH IT TO SIT UP AN' BEG, THEN? YOU WANNA GIVE IT A GO?
IT'S NOT AN IT.
SHE'S A SHE.
SHE'S A HUMAN BEING, WHICH MEANS SHE CAN BE EDUCATED LIKE ANYONE ELSE. LANGUAGE, READING AND WRITING, SOCIAL SKILLS, NOT TO MENTION THE TRICKS OF OUR PARTICULAR TRADE.
IT MIGHT TAKE A WHILE, BUT HAVING READ WHAT KESSLER SENT US I THINK IT CAN BE DONE.
YEAH, BUT DO WE REALLY WANT A HUMAN BEIN'? I THOUGHT WHAT WE WERE AFTER WAS A FUCKIN' KILLIN' MACHINE, SO'S WE'D WIN EVERY BARNEY WE GOT INTO...
I DON'T CARE. I WON'T HAVE HER TREATED LIKE SOME KIND OF PIT BULL.
BUT--
M'SIEU MALLORY?
I VOLUNTEER.

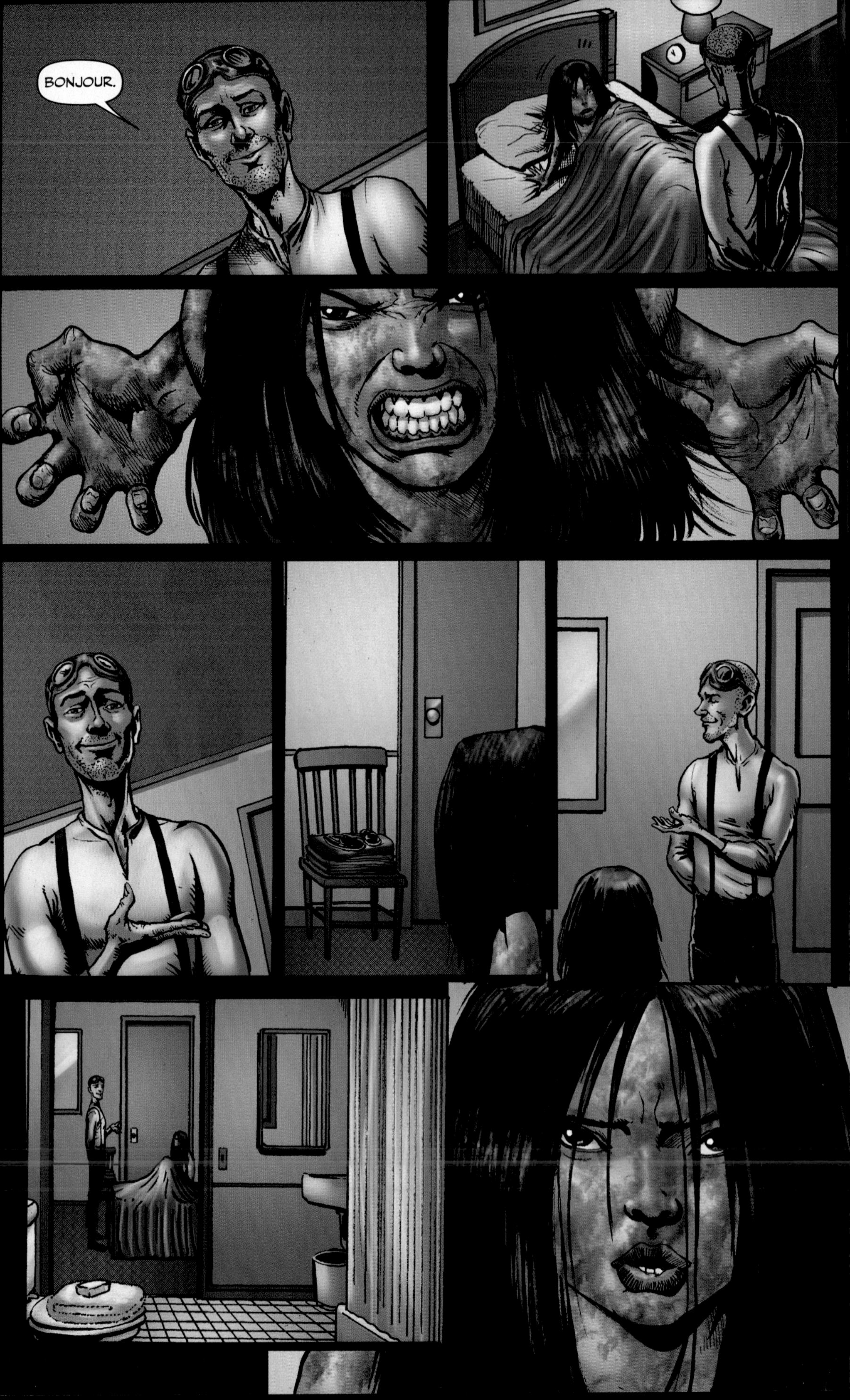
BONJOUR.

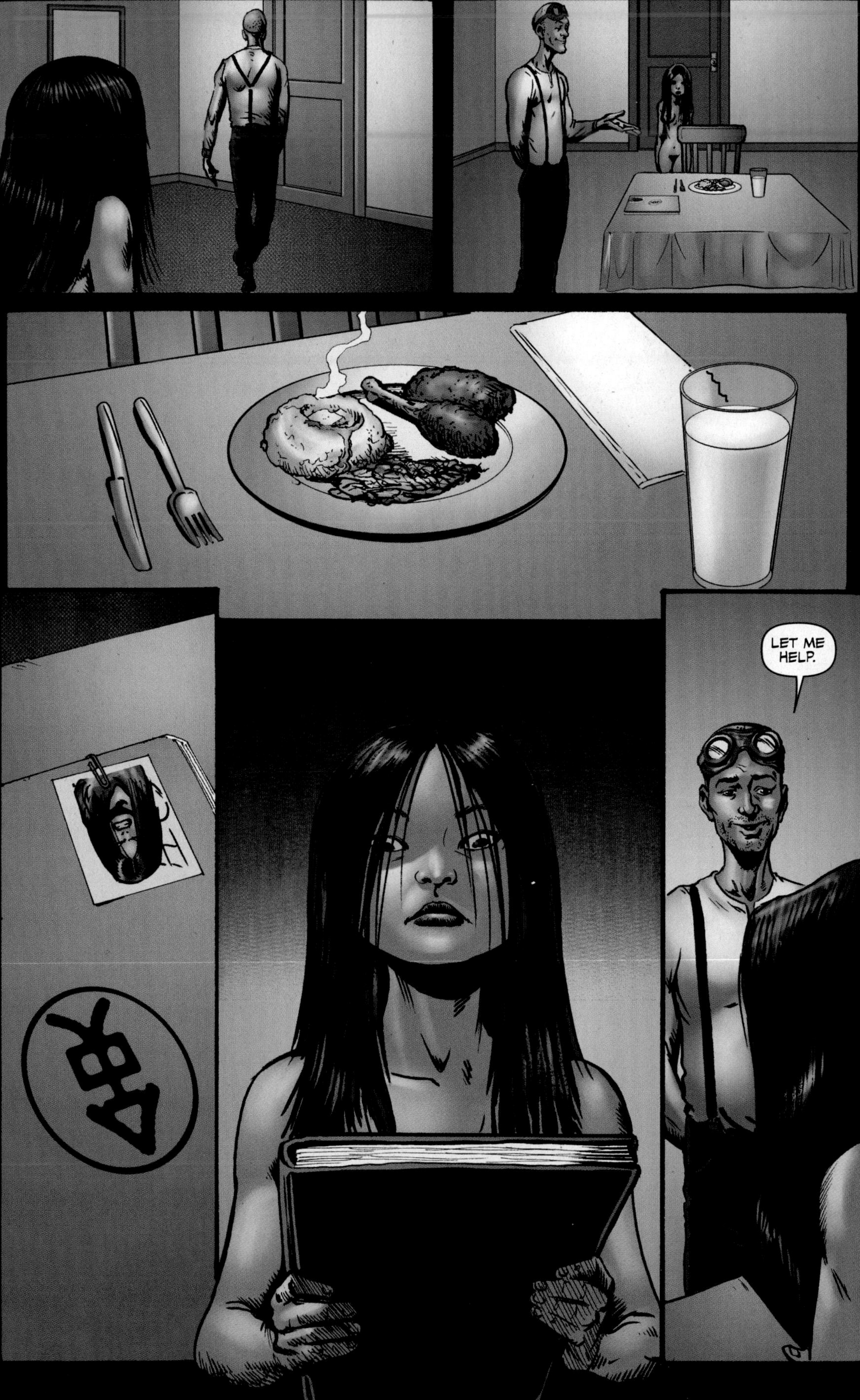
LET ME HELP.

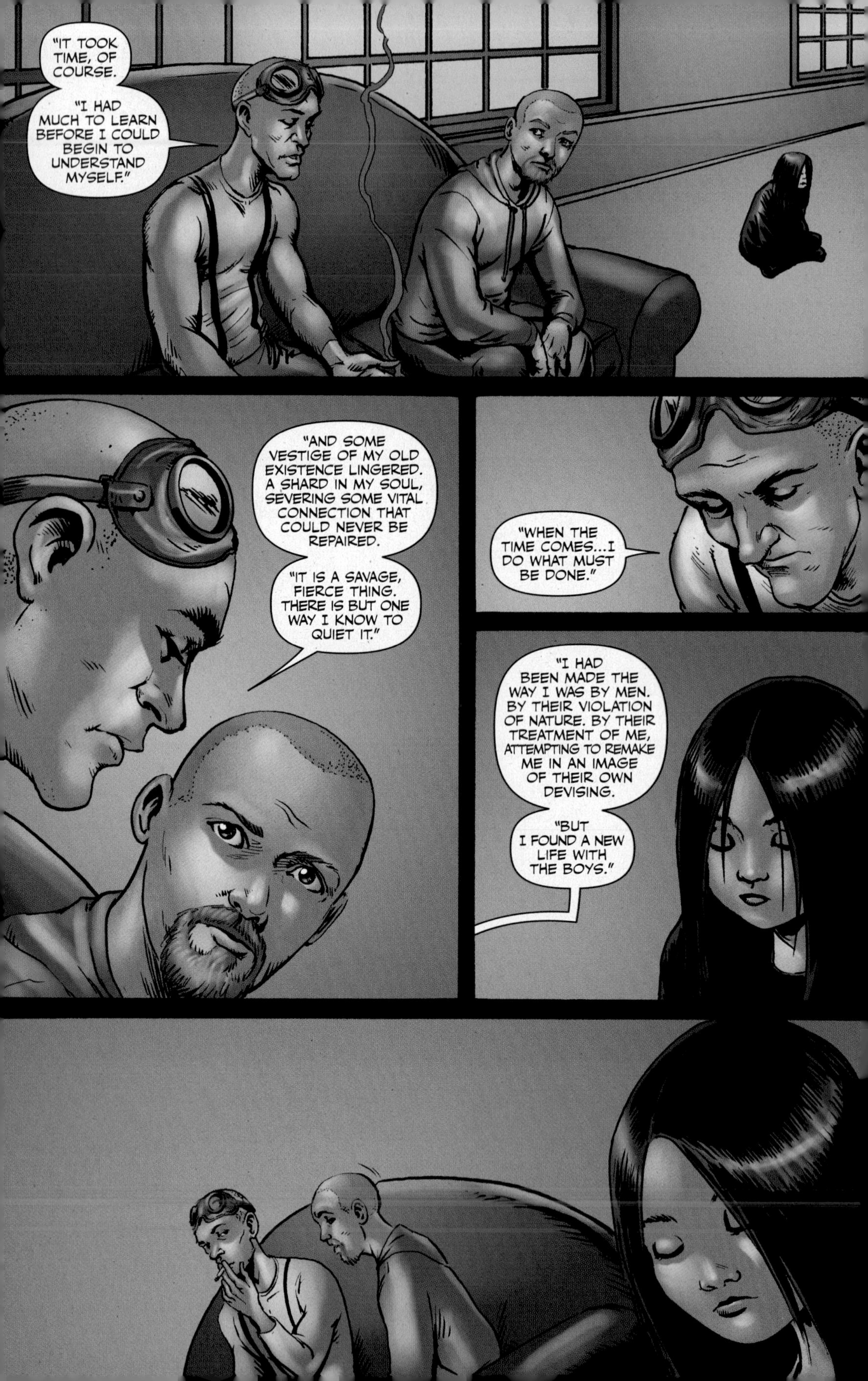
"IT TOOK TIME, OF COURSE.
"I HAD MUCH TO LEARN BEFORE I COULD BEGIN TO UNDERSTAND MYSELF."
"AND SOME VESTIGE OF MY OLD EXISTENCE LINGERED. A SHARD IN MY SOUL, SEVERING SOME VITAL CONNECTION THAT COULD NEVER BE REPAIRED.
"IT IS A SAVAGE, FIERCE THING. THERE IS BUT ONE WAY I KNOW TO QUIET IT."
"WHEN THE TIME COMES...I DO WHAT MUST BE DONE."
"I HAD BEEN MADE THE WAY I WAS BY MEN. BY THEIR VIOLATION OF NATURE. BY THEIR TREATMENT OF ME, ATTEMPTING TO REMAKE ME IN AN IMAGE OF THEIR OWN DEVISING.
"BUT I FOUND A NEW LIFE WITH THE BOYS."

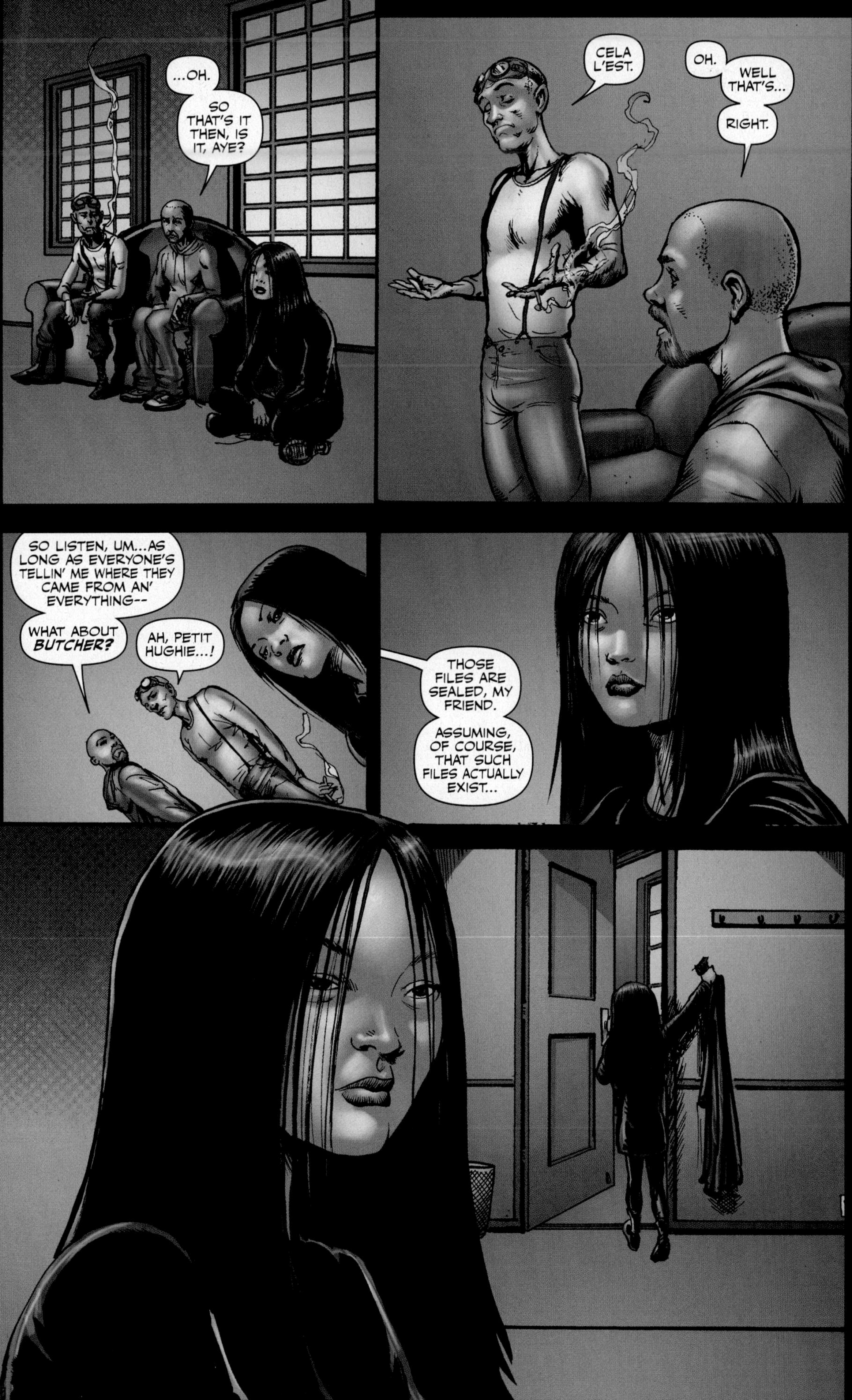
...OH.
SO THAT'S IT THEN, IS IT, AYE?
CELA L'EST.
OH.
WELL THAT'S...
RIGHT.
SO LISTEN, UM...AS LONG AS EVERYONE'S TELLIN' ME WHERE THEY CAME FROM AN' EVERYTHING--
WHAT ABOUT *BUTCHER?*
AH, PETIT HUGHIE...!
THOSE FILES ARE SEALED, MY FRIEND.
ASSUMING, OF COURSE, THAT SUCH FILES ACTUALLY EXIST...

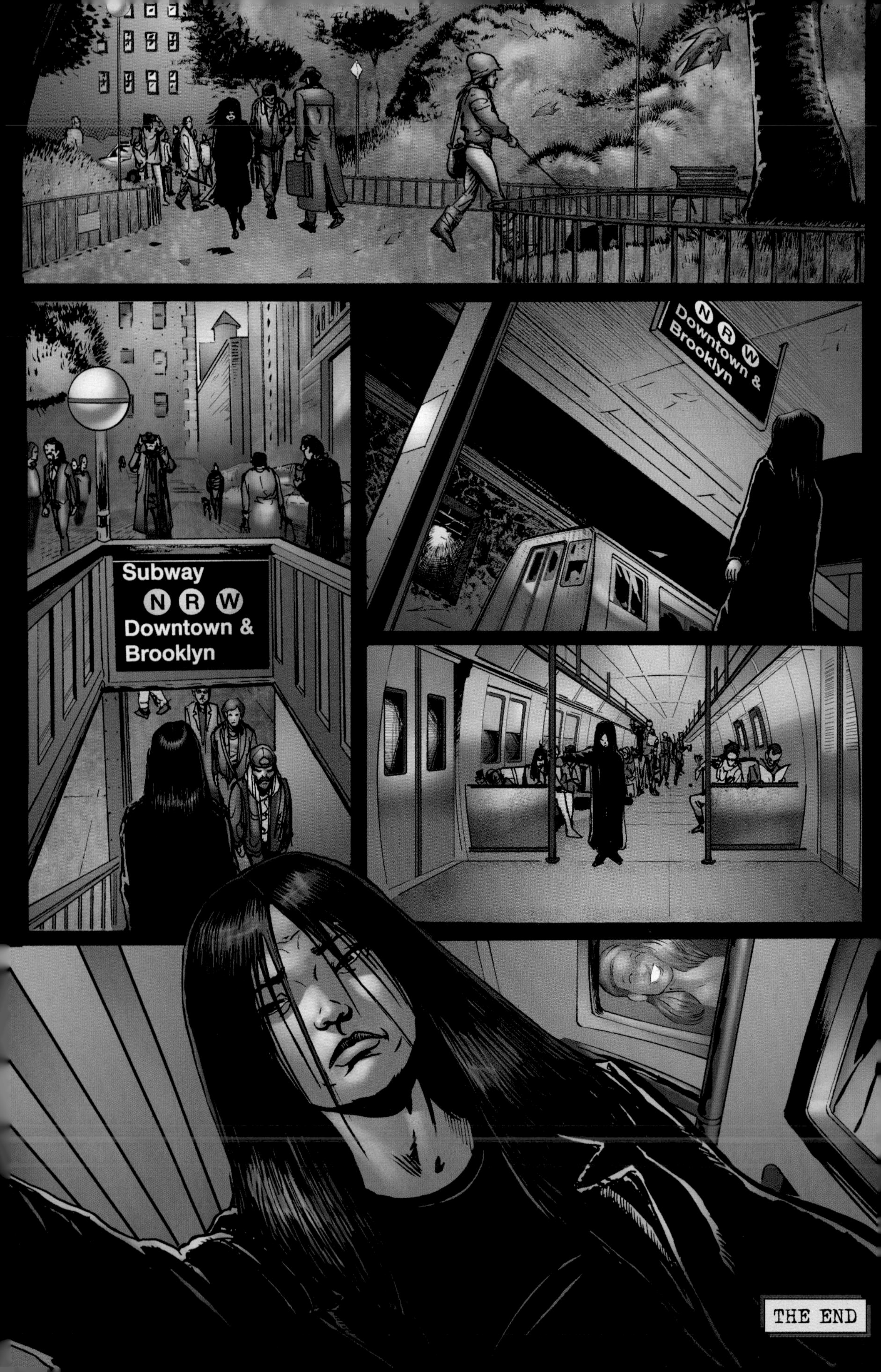
Subway
N R W
Downtown &
Brooklyn
N R W
Downtown &
Brooklyn
THE END